Studies in Economic Transition

General Editors: Jens Hölscher, Reader in Economics, University of Brighton; and Horst Tomann, Professor of Economics, Free University Berlin

This series has been established in response to a growing demand for a greater understanding of the transformation of economic systems. It brings together theoretical and empirical studies on economic transition and economic development. The post-communist transition from planned to market economies is one of the main areas of applied theory because in this field the most dramatic examples of change and economic dynamics can be found. The series aims to contribute to the understanding of specific major economic changes as well as to advance the theory of economic development. The implications of economic policy will be a major point of focus.

Titles include:

Lucian Cernat
EUROPEANIZATION, VARIETIES OF CAPITALISM AND ECONOMIC PERFORMANCE IN CENTRAL AND EASTERN EUROPE

Irwin Collier, Herwig Roggemann, Oliver Scholz and Horst Tomann (editors)
WELFARE STATES IN TRANSITION
East and West

Bruno Dallago and Ichiro Iwasaki (editors)
CORPORATE RESTRUCTURING AND GOVERNANCE IN TRANSITION ECONOMIES

Bruno Dallago (editor)
TRANSFORMATION AND EUROPEAN INTEGRATION
The Local Dimension

Hella Engerer
PRIVATIZATION AND ITS LIMITS IN CENTRAL AND EASTERN EUROPE
Property Rights in Transition

Saul Estrin, Grzegorz W. Kolodko and Milica Uvalic (editors)
TRANSITION AND BEYOND

Hubert Gabrisch and Rüdiger Pohl (editors)
EU ENLARGEMENT AND ITS MACROECONOMIC EFFECTS IN EASTERN EUROPE
Currencies, Prices, Investment and Competitiveness

Oleh Havrylyshyn
DIVERGENT PATHS IN POST-COMMUNIST TRANSFORMATION
Capitalism for All or Capitalism for the Few?

Jens Hölscher (editor)
FINANCIAL TURBULENCE AND CAPITAL MARKETS IN TRANSITION COUNTRIES

Jens Hölscher and Anja Hochberg (editors)
EAST GERMANY'S ECONOMIC DEVELOPMENT SINCE UNIFICATION
Domestic and Global Aspects

Iraj Hoshi, Paul J. J. Welfens and Anna Wziatek-Kubiak (editors)
INDUSTRIAL COMPETITIVENESS AND RESTRUCTURING IN ENLARGED EUROPE
How Accession Countries Catch Up and Integrate in the European Union

Mihaela Keleman and Monika Kostera (editors)
CRITICAL MANAGEMENT RESEARCH IN EASTERN EUROPE
Managing the Transition

Emil J. Kirchner (editor)
DECENTRALIZATION AND TRANSITION IN THE VISEGRAD
Poland, Hungary, the Czech Republic and Slovakia

David Lane (editor)
THE TRANSFORMATION OF STATE SOCIALISM
System Change, Capitalism, or Something Else?

David Lane and Martin Myant (editors)
VARIETIES OF CAPITALISM IN POST-COMMUNIST COUNTRIES

Jens Lowitzsch
FINANCIAL PARTICIPATION OF EMPLOYEES IN THE EU-27

Enrico Marelli and Marcello Signorelli (editors)
ECONOMIC GROWTH AND STRUCTURAL FEATURES OF TRANSITION

Tomasz Mickiewicz
ECONOMIC TRANSITION IN CENTRAL EUROPE AND THE COMMONWEALTH OF INDEPENDENT STATES

Milan Nikolić
MONETARY POLICY IN TRANSITION
Inflation Nexus Money Supply in Postcommunist Russia

Julie Pellegrin
THE POLITICAL ECONOMY OF COMPETITIVENESS IN AN ENLARGED EUROPE

Stanislav Poloucek (editor)
REFORMING THE FINANCIAL SECTOR IN CENTRAL EUROPEAN COUNTRIES

Gregg S. Robins
BANKING IN TRANSITION
East Germany after Unification

Johannes Stephan
ECONOMIC TRANSITION IN HUNGARY AND EAST GERMANY
Gradualism and Shock Therapy in Catch-up Development

Johannes Stephan (editor)
TECHNOLOGY TRANSFER VIA FOREIGN DIRECT INVESTMENT IN CENTRAL AND EASTERN EUROPE

Horst Tomann
MONETARY INTEGRATION IN EUROPE

Milica Uvalic
SERBIA'S TRANSITION
Towards a Better Future

Hans van Zon
THE POLITICAL ECONOMY OF INDEPENDENT UKRAINE

Hans van Zon
RUSSIA'S DEVELOPMENT PROBLEM
The Cult of Power

Adalbert Winkler (editor)
BANKING AND MONETARY POLICY IN EASTERN EUROPE
The First Ten Years

Studies in Economic Transition
Series Standing Order ISBN 978 0–333–73353–0
(outside North America only)

You can receive future titles in this series as they are published by placing a standing order. Please contact your bookseller or, in case of difficulty, write to us at the address below with your name and address, the title of the series and the ISBN quoted above.

Customer Services Department, Macmillan Distribution Ltd, Houndmills, Basingstoke, Hampshire RG21 6XS, England

---

Serbia's Transition

Towards a Better Future

Milica Uvalic

palgrave
macmillan

First published 2010 by
PALGRAVE MACMILLAN

Palgrave Macmillan in the UK is an imprint of Macmillan Publishers Limited, registered in England, company number 785998, of Houndmills, Basingstoke, Hampshire RG21 6XS.

Palgrave Macmillan in the US is a division of St Martin's Press LLC, 175 Fifth Avenue, New York, NY 10010.

Palgrave Macmillan is the global academic imprint of the above companies and has companies and representatives throughout the world.

Palgrave® and Macmillan® are registered trademarks in the United States, the United Kingdom, Europe and other countries.

ISBN 978–0–230–21160–5 hardback

This book is printed on paper suitable for recycling and made from fully managed and sustained forest sources. Logging, pulping and manufacturing processes are expected to conform to the environmental regulations of the country of origin.

A catalogue record for this book is available from the British Library.

Library of Congress Cataloging-in-Publication Data

Uvalic, Milica.
Serbia's transition: towards a better future/Milica Uvalic.
p. cm. — (Studies in economic transition)
ISBN 978–0–230–21160–5 (hardback)
1. Serbia—Economic conditions—1992– 2. Serbia—Economic policy.
3. Post-communism—Serbia. I. Title.
HC407.U93 2010
330.94971—dc22

2010012002

10 9 8 7 6 5 4 3 2 1
19 18 17 16 15 14 13 12 11 10

Printed and bound in Great Britain by
CPI Antony Rowe, Chippenham and Eastbourne

To Stefano, Matteo and Carlo, for their understanding, encouragement, and support

Contents

List of Figures

List of Tables

Preface

This book is the product of many years of research on Yugoslavia and, after its break-up in 1991, on its successor states, the region of Southeast Europe (SEE), and Serbia. It is a reflection on Serbia's transition to a market economy and multiparty democracy from someone who for many years has been both an insider and an outsider.

I have been an insider and remain one even today, despite having left Belgrade a long time ago. Belgrade, today the capital of Serbia, is the town where I was born and where I have spent much of my childhood, although I have also lived for many years outside the country due to my father, Radivoj's, diplomatic service in Norway, Austria, France, and India. Belgrade is the town where I got my first two university degrees, a BA and an MA at the Faculty of Economics of the University of Belgrade, where I got my first employment as researcher at the then prestigious Institute for International Politics and Economics, and where I have returned very frequently over the past three decades for private, professional, and political reasons.

Whereas my Belgrade origins explain why I feel like an insider, I also have to add that I have always felt very much like a 'Yugoslav'. At the last census in the Socialist Federal Republic (SFR) of Yugoslavia in 1991, I was among the 4 per cent of the population that declared themselves as 'Yugoslavs'. My Yugoslav background derives not only from the way my parents have brought me up but also from the origins of my parents and grandparents. Although they were all Serbs, they were from very different parts of the former Yugoslavia. On my mother's side, my grandmother was from an old Serbian family in Herceg Novi, today one of the most beautiful towns on the Montenegrin coast in Boka Kotorska, but at the time she was born it was still part of the Austro-Hungarian Empire. My grandfather was from Brcko in Bosnia and Herzegovina, the town on the banks of the Sava river on the very border with Croatia. Given that my mother was born in Bosnia and had spent much of her childhood there, her Bosnian origins played a prominent role in the upbringing of her three children and she has transmitted a lot of this to me personally. My father's parents were from Vojvodina, the northern part of Serbia which, like northern Bosnia, was also part of the Austro-Hungarian Empire. These origins explain why some of the 'secret' conversations in the family that we youngsters were not intended to overhear were in German, and why my grandmothers' recipes for the best cakes in the world are almost identical.

At the same time I am also an outsider, since I left Yugoslavia almost three decades ago. Since the early 1980s, I have lived and worked in Italy, where my research has frequently – though not exclusively – been dedicated to many topics regarding the Balkans, primarily the region of former Yugoslavia. As an external observer, I have not personally lived through the dramatic events that inflicted Serbia in the 1990s, though I have naturally been concerned about the tragic events in my country of origin. Milosevic's authoritarian policies, the slowness of changes on all fronts, the missed opportunities, and the transformation of what used to be a cosmopolitan country into one of the most isolated places in Europe, have been a continuous nightmare for me, like for many Serbs and Yugoslavs living abroad. This is why, whenever possible, I have tried to contribute to political changes in Serbia. In December 1990 I flew to Belgrade to vote in the very first multiparty elections in Serbia, as I did ten years later in September 2000 when Milosevic was to be overthrown. I have also been an active participant in some important political events in the 1990s and recently as well.

My first real encounter with politics in Serbia was in 1996, when I accepted the invitation of the Yugoslav National Bank's governor Dragoslav Avramovic to help prepare a new privatization programme for the Federal Republic (FR) of Yugoslavia. This assignment, which took me to Belgrade for over a month, turned out to be one of the most exciting, but also most distressing engagements in my whole professional career. The privatization programme we had prepared with great enthusiasm was not adopted, while Avramovic was forced to resign in May 1996. After the fall of the Milosevic regime in late 2000, I accepted the invitation of one of the most active and progressive non-governmental organizations (NGOs), the G17 Plus, to go to Belgrade and help implement radical economic reforms. As vice minister for foreign economic relations in the new federal government of FR Yugoslavia, I was in charge of two newly established departments – for the European Union (EU) and for international multilateral organizations – working closely with Miroljub Labus who at that time was the federal government's deputy prime minister and the federal minister for foreign economic relations (subsequently a presidential candidate).

This book is partly the outcome of my professional engagement in Belgrade. The experience accumulated in the Yugoslav federal government in 2000–1 has been valuable, though it was an extremely difficult period. After so many years abroad, living in Belgrade for nine months in 2001 was an excellent opportunity to reflect upon some of Serbia's most complex internal and external problems. If today I understand Serbian nationalism better, which I have always condemned as I consider it one of the main causes of the disintegration of my former country and all the misfortunes that have accompanied it, it is because I am more aware of the general climate that has produced such an ideology. If today I understand better the reasons why an average Serb still feels somewhat excluded from Europe and is frequently not particularly interested in European affairs, it is because I am more aware of the policies that have led to such negative attitudes.

The book is being concluded almost nine years since the political changes and my professional engagement in Serbia. In the summer of 2001 when I returned from Belgrade, it was much too early to write a book about the Serbian transition, since economic reforms in many areas were only starting. Today it is possible to give an assessment of Serbia's transition from a longer-term perspective, and not only of the post-2001 period. Given that the first radical economic reforms in Serbia started in 1989 while it was still part of SFR Yugoslavia, the year 2009 marks 20 years since the beginning of the country's transition to a market economy.

Acknowledgements

I need to thank many people for their comments, useful information, encouragement, and support while I was writing this book. With some friends and colleagues I have discussed at length the state of economic and political reforms in Serbia and the events I lived personally when I was part of the Yugoslav government in 2000–1. As prompted by many, they were significant enough to be recorded. With others I have discussed less substantial issues, yet their input has also been important. Susan Woodward was among the first to encourage me wholeheartedly to write about Serbia during our intensive talks on the island of Halki in September 2002; she helped me shape my initial thoughts and key messages, but has also supported me later by providing constructive critical comments. Mario Nuti was as generous with his time as ever, commenting on most parts of the manuscript, reminding me continuously of the importance of rigour in research which he taught all of us who were his students at the European University Institute, and positively influencing my own ideas on transition with his non-conventional reflections and judgements. Will Bartlett has provided extremely useful insights from the perspective of someone I consider the best expert today on Southeast Europe (SEE). Alberto Chilosi has critically commented on parts of the text and has more generally offered me lots of support throughout my research. With Saul Estrin I have discussed specific aspects and I am grateful for all his advice. Jan Svejnar was a source of inspiration, having contributed to changes in his own home country the Czech Republic, and his suggestions on various occasions have also been valuable. In Perugia I was fortunate to have friends like Mirella Damiani and Armando Pitassio with whom I have often discussed Serbia's complex problems, and collaborators such as Marcello Signorelli. Philippe Schmitter provided me with useful insights from the perspective of political science. A special thanks goes to Laza Kekic, who for many years has passed on his thoughtful writings on Serbia and found time to discuss the most difficult issues. Peter Sanfey has helped clarify both statistics and more substantial issues regarding Serbia.

The list of people I need to thank from Serbia is almost infinite and there is no way I can do justice to all of them. Some of my friends in Belgrade have been close in important moments of my life, like Ruza Nikolic, somebody who replaced my whole family in 2001 and will remain my lifetime friend. Many colleagues have commented on parts of the manuscript or provided very useful papers and documents. Bozidar Cerovic has passed on numerous publications, offered precious reflections from within Serbia, and always found time to answer my queries. Miladin Kovacevic was most generous in providing statistics, reports, and papers on all possible aspects of the Serbian economy. I would also like to thank Misa Arandarenko, Radovan Jelasic, Olja Labus, Pavle Petrovic, and Ivana Prica for their help on various occasions. Ljuba Zivkov was my frequent interlocutor on political issues. Edvard Jakopin from the Serbian Institute for Development, Branko Hinic, Milica Jovanovic, and Natalija Stevanovic from the National Bank of Serbia (NBS), Dragan Popovic from the Serbian Office of Statistics, and Dusan Belanovic from the Serbian Agency for Privatization have been extremely helpful in providing publications, statistics, or clarifications of important sources.

During my work for the Yugoslav government in 2000–1, Boris, Sanja and Dragica were my most faithful collaborators and I will never forget them. I also want to recall a few people who were actively engaged in the post-2000 Yugoslav/Serbian government (some still are), pushing forward the much-needed economic and political reforms with energy and determination, in an environment where radical changes were not always welcome. In particular I refer to Miroljub Labus, then vice prime minister and minister of foreign economic relations in the federal government, and to Mladjan Dinkic, then governor of the National Bank of Yugoslavia (NBY). They invited me to come to Belgrade in 2001, and their enthusiasm has to a large extent inspired my own political engagement in Serbia.

I owe special thanks to the Woodrow Wilson International Center for Scholars (WWICS) in Washington DC, where I spent four months as a Public Policy Scholar in Spring 2009, writing the last chapters of my book. The productive atmosphere at the WWICS, the many interesting seminars, the encounters and discussions with brilliant scholars, have all been intellectually very stimulating. In particular, I am grateful to Marty Sletzinger for having facilitated my invitation to the WWICS and for having contributed to the high-spirit atmosphere at the Center with his witticism and incredible sense of humour. I was also privileged to have met a well-known connoisseur of Yugoslavia, John Lampe, who offered me valuable comments on large parts of the manuscript. Veljko Vujacic also commented on parts of the text and helped me with the very complicated history of our country, but was also wonderful company throughout my stay. My intern Jill Pokorney was of immense help in her research of bibliographical sources, editorial advice, comments, and preparation of some of the complicated graphs.

During my stay in Washington DC, I was very lucky to have my niece Tea Trumbic, a young economist herself working at the World Bank, who has helped me very generously in both practical and professional issues, for which I thank her wholeheartedly. It is a coincidence that in Washington DC I rediscovered a group of very close friends from Belgrade, as well as other friends from my recent and more distant past – including Ivan and Jelica Vujacic, Branko Milanovic, Saska Posarac, Dusko Vujovic, Zoran Zic, Vlada Bilandzic, Milan Vodopivec, and Marta Muco. My discussions with them, many times in the past as in Washington DC about our former country or the Balkan region, have also contributed to the final messages of the book. Branko Milanovic has been the best possible interlocutor in discussing Serbia's transition, but he also offered me precious support during the difficult days of my work for the Yugoslav government in 2001.

I would also like to thank Manavalan BhuvanaRaj and his production team in Macmillan Publishing Solutions, Chennai, for their professionalism, efficiency and excellent cooperation during the last stage of preparing the book for print.

My 'boys' – Stefano, Matteo, and Carlo – have been close to me all along, understanding how important this whole project has been. My sister Stamenka has patiently listened to my daily complaints, encouraging me as she always has throughout our lives. My wise mother was never very happy about my involvement in Serbia since she feared that it could negatively influence my otherwise calm and settled life in Florence, but she helped me enormously by sending me daily clippings from Serbian newspapers and listening to me patiently whenever I needed her moral support.

Last but not the least, I would like to recall my father, Radivoj, who I lost much too early, to whom I dedicated my first book, *Investment and Property Rights in Yugoslavia* (Uvalic, 1992) that has just been reprinted in paperback form (by Cambridge University Press, just as the original version). What I wrote then in my book is still very much true: it is from my father that I learnt to love ideals but respect reality. It is the ideal of a better future for Serbia that made me go to Belgrade in late 2000, while it is the respect for reality that made me return to my family and home in Florence in August 2001.

1
Introduction

The present book is dedicated to a country that today is once more called Serbia. During most of its long history Serbia was part of larger imperial entities, namely the Byzantine, Ottoman, and Habsburg empires. Between the twelfth and fourteenth centuries, Serbia was a thriving medieval kingdom which survived until the Ottoman conquest in the late fourteenth and early fifteenth centuries. Subsequently, Serbia remained under the Ottoman Empire for almost five centuries, becoming an independent principality (1832) after two successive anti-Ottoman insurrections (1804, 1815). Serbia became an internationally recognized state in 1882, partially in the aftermath of the Congress of Berlin (1878) and partially as a result of decisions made by the great European powers. Between 1888 and 1918, Serbia was a constitutional monarchy with a parliament, political parties, and an independent press. On 1 December 1918, Serbia stood at the forefront of the foundation of the Kingdom of Serbs, Croats, and Slovenes which subsequently changed its name into the Kingdom of Yugoslavia (1929–41).[1] After World War II, Serbia and its two autonomous provinces (Vojvodina and Kosovo) became one of the six republics of the Socialist Federal Republic (SFR) of Yugoslavia.

Following the break-up of SFR Yugoslavia in June 1991, Serbia and Montenegro were the two republics that remained part of the 'rump' Yugoslavia constituted in April 1992 as the Federal Republic (FR) of Yugoslavia. More than a decade later, on 4 February 2003, FR Yugoslavia was transformed into the State Union of Serbia and Montenegro, in order to accommodate the diverging political interests of its constituent parts. At the referendum organized in Montenegro in May 2006, the majority of its citizens opted for independence which led to the split between the two republics. As of 4 June 2006, Montenegro and Serbia have become two independent states.

Since Serbia and Montenegro were for a long time part of the same country, they have shared in the most important political events over the whole 1992–2006 period. However, their paths in economic transition have been different, especially after 1997 when Montenegro decided to distance itself from Serbia by implementing its own economic policies. Considering their different economic histories, the book will focus primarily on Serbia and economic transition in Serbia, though part of the analysis and some statistics will refer to the country as it was defined at the time. Certain issues will necessarily have to be considered from the perspective of the whole country; thus after the political changes in late 2000, it was the Yugoslav federal government that was responsible for a number of issues, like relations with international financial organizations. It should also be borne in mind that Serbia represented by far the largest part of the post-1992 FR Yugoslavia in terms of territory, population, and economic weight.

Kosovo will not be explicitly included, but will only be considered within a wider context, with reference to issues directly relevant for Serbia and problems in Southeast Europe (SEE). Officially Kosovo remained a part of Serbia according to the 1999 UN Security Council Resolution 1244, but after the end of the 1999 military conflict this contested Serbian province has effectively been governed by the United Nations Mission in Kosovo (UNMIK). Moreover, on 17 February 2008 Kosovo unilaterally declared political independence and has been recognized by the United States of America and an increasing number of countries, though not all European Union (EU) member states.

This introduction briefly lays out the contents of the book. It explains the objectives, approach adopted, and the main messages of the book. It also gives a few basic definitions, the universe for comparisons, the time frame, and introduces the reader to the specific topics addressed in each of the chapters.

1.1 Why Serbia?

The book is an attempt to understand better why Serbia, which had a relatively good starting position in 1989, has encountered substantial delays in carrying forward the main objectives of the transition to a market economy and multiparty democracy. After the radical political changes in October 2000 good results have been achieved in many areas of economic reform, but progress has been slower than initially anticipated.

The choice of Serbia is motivated by the fact that many questions regarding Serbia's transition remain controversial. There is no consensus among experts on when the transition to a market economy actually started in Serbia. There is also disagreement about where Serbia stands today, how much it has progressed, what remains to be done, and what should be the main priorities for the future. The achievements in economic reforms after the end of Milosevic's rule have occasionally been evaluated as remarkable, but we also find much more critical views which stress that the failures have been just as important. The European Bank for Reconstruction and Development (EBRD), the World Bank, the International Monetary Fund (IMF), and the EU Commission have frequently praised Serbia for the progress achieved in transforming its economy over the last eight years, but this vision of economic progress is not shared by all experts, the Serbian population at large, and much of the Serbian mass media. Some of the principal aims of the economic transition have been realized remarkably quickly, but other important objectives have been neglected.

Moreover, political analysts of Serbian events have tended to be much more sceptical about progress with transition than economists, as indeed the country is still burdened with difficult political issues, including the status of parts of its territory and alleged insufficient collaboration with the International Criminal Tribunal for the Former Yugoslavia (ICTY) in The Hague. It is these political issues that are still hampering the integration of Serbia into the EU, as they have impeded, until 1 February 2010, the implementation of the long-awaited Stabilization and Association Agreement (SAA).[2] In addition, much of the recent political and international relations literature on the Balkans has also been rather sceptical about the credentials of most countries in the region, including Serbia, stressing the problem of weak or failed states, the need for international protectorates, and lack of fulfilment of some basic conditions necessary for EU membership.[3]

The divergent views about the effectiveness and completion of economic and political reforms in Serbia leave room for different interpretations. Will Serbia be able to comply with the main conditions required by the EU, become a candidate for membership in 2010, and be ready to join the EU by some future date, as frequently announced by the current Serbian government? Or is the 'Russian scenario' more likely, which entails further strengthening links with primarily Russia, which could take Serbia even further away from the EU?

Analysing some of these debated questions in an objective way is not an easy task, considering that the transition in Serbia has evolved under very specific political conditions, particularly in the 1990s. The present book will try to clarify why the transition from communism to capitalism in Serbia has proved to be more difficult than in many other countries of the former communist world, most of which in 1989 were institutionally lagging behind Serbia.

1.2 The main messages

Over the past two decades, the implementation of the transition to a market economy in Serbia has to a large extent been slowed down by events, factors, and policies that are essentially non-economic in nature. They derive not simply from the fact that the country has been involved in military conflicts during much of the 1990s and has neglected some important objectives of the transition. The features of the political system in Serbia in the 1990s has indeed played a crucial role in determining the highly unsatisfactory performance of the Serbian economy and delays in implementing more radical economic reforms, but the international aspects are also important. An analysis of both the internal and international constraints is necessary.

1.2.1 Internal constrains

The most important factor that has hampered the transition in FR Yugoslavia was the political regime in Serbia during the 1990s, which remained essentially anti-reformist and non-democratic, and which gave precedence to specific political aims over broadly defined economic objectives. Ten years of authoritarian rule in Serbia, with governments which have disregarded the longer-term consequences of continuous economic deterioration and dramatic erosion of living standards of its citizens, have left very deep scars on all aspects of Serbia's society. Some elements of the economic and political system laid down and further consolidated during the many years of Milosevic's rule are proving difficult to dismantle even today. The political objectives and ideology of the ruling political elite in Serbia were responsible not only for involvement in four military conflicts – in Slovenia (June 1991), in Croatia (1991–2), in Bosnia and Herzegovina (1992–5), and in Kosovo (1998–9) – but also for the dramatic economic decline.

During the 1990s, instead of carrying forward the most important reforms of the transition to a market economy, certain policies were reversals of progressive measures implemented earlier, even the return to practices long abandoned during socialist Yugoslavia. Moreover, the lack of willingness to implement radical reforms in other important areas, like police or the judiciary, have undermined the rule of law and led to rising corruption and criminality. Transition has also been slowed by the political and legal consequences of the break-up of former Yugoslavia since practically all laws had to be modified and adapted to the new state, but this was common to all successor states of SFR Yugoslavia.[4] The problems deriving from the complex relationship between Serbia and Montenegro are also responsible for delays in transition, as for example in the area of integration with the EU.

1.2.2 International responses

The external factors which have contributed to delays in the transition to a market economy in Serbia come under the broad heading of 'policies of the international community'. As a reaction to what was considered inappropriate policies in FR Yugoslavia, throughout the 1990s the measures of the most important international organizations and the most influential Western governments towards Serbia have been generally punitive. They have included various types of economic and political sanctions, culminating in the NATO bombing in 1999 after the unsuccessful talks over the Kosovo issue in Rambouillet.

The UN and EU sanctions against FR Yugoslavia imposed during much of the 1990s led to the almost complete isolation of the country and its citizens for a whole decade. Immediately after the disintegration of SFR Yugoslavia in late 1991, visas were introduced by all the Western and a majority of neighbouring countries, and in most cases have not been lifted for over 18 years.[5] The international sanctions interrupted not only normal trade flows and foreign direct investment, but also bank transfers, access to international financial markets, membership in international organizations, general inflow of information, and free travel abroad. During the early years of the most severe sanctions, Belgrade's airport was closed for almost three years. Owing to very complicated procedures for obtaining visas but also falling living standards, entire generations in Serbia have never travelled abroad.

The isolation of Serbia has had a profound impact on the mentality of its citizens, influencing broader political processes and attitudes towards the outside world. Given state control of most mass media throughout much of the 1990s, large segments of the Serbian population were continuously confronted with information orchestrated to promote exclusivist nationalism by the Milosevic regime. While in other former communist countries the 1989 revolutions finally brought freedom and opened the doors to the outside world, allowing them to travel abroad and see other realities, just the opposite happened in Serbia where after 1991 its citizens were to remain closed within national borders. The young generations in Serbia, in particular, were not able to travel or study abroad, but have spent their youth participating in demonstrations, living in poverty, hounded by the authorities to serve in the army, even arrested or beaten for their 'antistate' activities (Miljkovic and Hoare, 2005, p. 194).

The international isolation of Serbia has also very significantly hampered the internal processes of democratization, political transformation, and institution-building. As an expression of disapproval of Serbian/Yugoslav politics, FR Yugoslavia has been excluded from financial assistance programmes supporting the transition in former communist countries of the EU, the World Bank, the EBRD, and other international or regional multilateral organizations. From 1992 onwards, Serbia has not been able to benefit from major EU programmes which have fundamentally contributed to creating more efficient institutions in a large part of Eastern Europe in the 1990s, or from privileged access to EU markets and other benefits offered through Association Agreements, concluded at an early stage with the ten East European countries that today are EU member states.

While it is the combination of internal and external factors that has delayed the transformation of Serbia's political and economic system after 1991, the emphasis has more often been placed on the former. It has frequently been argued that the severe measures of the international community and of Western governments came as simply a reaction to internal politics of the Serbian government. As forcefully argued by others, however, many of these measures were quite ineffective and counterproductive, since the isolation of the country and other punitive measures actually reinforced Milosevic's position and his regime, contributing to even further delays in democratization and transition to a market economy. Alternative policies may have influenced democratic changes in Serbia much earlier and with peaceful means, thus substantially diminishing the overall costs of delayed transition. These costs have been incurred not only by Serbia, but also by the international community, considering the enormous amount of financial resources the UN, NATO, and EU have spent in policing the Balkan region.

All the political factors described had direct and irreversible effects on the Serbian/Yugoslav economy in the 1990s. Political choices imposed by the ideology and vested interests of the ruling elite in Serbia have crucially influenced poor macroeconomic performance and lack of systemic change, which has had direct negative repercussions for the country's international economic and political relations. What is not sufficiently recognized is that international policies towards FR Yugoslavia, today Serbia, have in turn contributed to even greater delays in implementing the transition, especially during the pre-2000 period.

1.3 Which transition?

Although the book focuses on *economic transition* in Serbia, the analysis is integrated with political and historical considerations. In reference to each of the periods, an effort is made to synthetically present the general political environment in FR Yugoslavia/Serbia. Such a snapshot of the country's political situation will inevitably not do justice to many important political events and complex political processes, but its inclusion is inevitable. The country's hyperinflation in 1992–3, or the deep recession in 1999, cannot be understood without reference to the political events of those times.

Though there is no universal definition of 'economic transition' in the literature, in this book it is understood to have a broader meaning. In the first place it implies the systemic transformation of economic institutions, particularly those that regulate enterprise property and exchange of goods, so as to enable the passage from a system based on non-market mechanisms of allocation of resources and dominance of non-private property in the economy, to a system relying prevalently on internal and external markets for the allocation of resources and on private ownership.

While this definition covers the two essential elements – the key role of the market mechanism and of private property rights – we must also consider that transition has led to very complex and fundamental transformations in societies, leading to socially desirable outcomes such as increased individual opportunity, as well as undesirable ones such as rising inequality. This is why the social aspects of transition cannot be disregarded, in line with the World Bank's (1996) clarification of what distinguishes the post-1989 transition in Eastern Europe:

> [T]he long-term goal of transition is the same as that of economic reforms elsewhere: to build a thriving market economy capable of delivering long-term growth in living standards. What distinguishes transition from reforms in other countries is the systemic change involved: reform must penetrate to the fundamental rules of the game, to the institutions that shape behavior and guide organizations. This makes it a profound social transition as well as an economic one.
>
> (p. 1)

This passage reveals another important aspect of transition which deals with its longer-term goal. Although the EBRD in 1995 has made a sharp distinction between the concepts of 'transition' and 'economic development' – transition being defined as the process of establishing open market economies through institutional change, while development referring to the enhancement of living standards – it is clear that transition to a market economy has been largely motivated by the pursuit of economic development (Kekic, 1996). In this sense, systemic changes implied by the transition to a market economy should also be a major instrument for attaining longer-term economic development.

1.4 Time frame

The book covers the whole period from 1989 to present. Even recent problems that present-day Serbia is facing cannot be fully understood without taking into account the highly unfavourable political conditions which prevailed during most of the 1990s. The legacy of the last decade of the twentieth century has had rather dramatic consequences for the country's political, economic, and social life. Surprisingly, many of these events have been almost forgotten, although some of their consequences are still being felt today. Without analysing the many problems accumulated during the 1990s, it would be almost impossible to understand the difficult tasks which lay in front of the Serbian/Yugoslav government in October 2000 when Milosevic was finally overthrown. In this sense, the book contrasts with the shorter-term perspective frequently found in many recent studies on Serbia. Much of the flourishing economic literature on Serbia has focused primarily on the post-2000 period, without taking into account the 1990s and the highly unfavourable conditions inherited immediately after the change of regime in late 2000.

Such an approach thus differs from the opinion of those experts who have considered 2000 as the year when transition actually began in Serbia. As will be argued here, Serbia's transition in late 2000 did not start from scratch, but with a heavy burden of the economic and political problems accumulated in the 1990s. Although there were substantial delays in implementing the most important transition-related economic reforms after 1991, Serbia did not avoid many negative effects of the transition. In the early 1990s, the Yugoslav economy also experienced a sharp decline in output, increasing inflation, social differentiation, and increasing poverty. In other words, in Serbia in late 2000, the situation was far more complex than in other transition countries when they embarked on transition in 1989.

Precisely because of the heavy legacy inherited from the 1990s, Serbia's task of catching up with the other transition countries has been extremely difficult. The numerous problems inherited from the 1990s have in many ways impeded quicker changes, yet this is sometimes overlooked. More than nine years after the end of the Milosevic era, there are too high expectations of what transition can deliver in Serbia. Citizens are expecting primarily a miraculous rise in living standards without much sacrifice, while many politicians are not aware of the unavoidable costs of the transition which have been borne by all post-communist countries.

A broader and longer-term approach to transition in Serbia should contribute to a better understanding of the general problems of Serbia's 20-year transition, but the book will not offer the reader a detailed analysis of all the relevant issues. Contrary to the situation in the 1990s when information on the Serbian economy was not readily available, when it was difficult for a non-native speaker to find statistics and fully up-to-date documents about Serbia's economy – the rare sources in English were the Economic Surveys of the UN Economic Commission for Europe and the London-based Economist Intelligence Unit publications – today we have abundant information produced on a systematic basis by the IMF, the World Bank, the EU Commission, the EBRD, and other institutions. Given that many national and international publications are available about Serbia's economy today, including extensive Internet sources, the book has no need to be fully comprehensive.

1.5 Which universe?

Since the analysis starts with 1989, the universe for the initial comparisons of Serbia will consist of all the post-communist countries at the beginning of the transition, namely the 27 EBRD countries (which today have become 29) in Central and Eastern Europe (CEE), the Baltics, SEE, and the Commonwealth of Independent States. In the early 1990s, the common objective of all post-communist states was the introduction of a market economy and multiparty democracy, though clearly the individual strategies pursued have varied.

Since some of these countries have in the meantime joined the EU and are considered to have completed their transition to a market economy, for the more recent period it will be more useful to compare Serbia with a smaller group of transition countries, primarily those in the region of SEE: Albania, Bosnia and Herzegovina, Croatia, Former

Yugoslav Republic (FYR) of Macedonia, Montenegro, and Kosovo (under UN Security Council Resolution 1244). All these countries except Albania share a common past, since before 1991 they were part of the same country, all have been negatively affected by the events in the Balkans of the 1990s, and all are presently aspiring to join the EU. For some issues, such as EU policies in the SEE region after the 1999 conflict in Kosovo, Bulgaria and Romania will also be considered as part of the SEE region, despite their 2007 entry into the EU.

1.6 Chapters and issues

The book follows a chronological order, covering the 20-year period of transition in Serbia. Chapter 2 looks at the situation in Serbia in 1989 while it was still part of SFR Yugoslavia, the initial conditions and economic position with respect to other republics within the Yugoslav federation. It also appraises the first radical economic reforms undertaken in SFR Yugoslavia by the last government of Prime Minister Ante Markovic in 1988–90, the main elements of the mounting political crisis, and the political and economic consequences of the break-up of the country in mid-1991.

The key economic developments in the new FR of Yugoslavia after it was constituted in 1992 are analysed in Chapter 3, moving from the unfavourable political environment, the military conflicts, and international sanctions against FR Yugoslavia, to concentrate on the economic policies which brought a severe recession and record hyperinflation in 1992–3. The chapter reviews the successful implementation of the 1994 stabilization programme proposed by the Yugoslav National Bank governor Dragoslav Avramovic which eliminated hyperinflation practically overnight, and explains why these results were short-lived.

Chapter 4 discusses the period after the Dayton Peace Accords signed in late 2005, which brought peace in Bosnia and Herzegovina and the lifting of the most severe international sanctions against FR Yugoslavia. Albeit the change in the political climate, due to the essentially unchanged political regime in FR Yugoslavia and unwillingness to implement fundamental changes in the economic system (despite some legislative changes, such as a new privatization law), there were no essential improvements in economic performance and the negative political pressures continued to dominate. The progressive worsening of the situation in Kosovo led to the NATO military intervention in 1999, which additionally contributed, and very substantially, to the worsening of all major economic indicators.

The second part of the book covers the period after the political changes in October 2000. Chapter 5 is dedicated to the crucial period prior and immediately after the elections of 24 September 2000 which brought victory to the Democratic Opposition of Serbia. The main factors that contributed to Milosevic's defeat as well as the immediate aftermath are discussed. The chapter also illustrates why the new Yugoslav government's tasks at that time were extremely complex. Parallel to the launch of the most important political and economic reforms, it was important to undertake measures for the return to good-standing in international organizations, raise donors' assistance, set up new institutions in support of transition, reorganize the public administration, and reach agreement that would accommodate both Serbian and Montenegrin interests.

A detailed account of the implementation of the transition to a market economy in Serbia from late 2000 onwards is given in Chapter 6. The chapter covers macroeconomic performance of the Serbian economy during 2001–8, including the effects of liberalization and macroeconomic stabilization on growth and inflation, public finance, external sector indicators, and inflows of foreign direct investment. The results achieved in various economic and institutional reforms are also discussed in some detail, including enterprise privatization and restructuring, the liberalization of foreign trade and prices, the reform of the banking and financial sectors, and reforms of infrastructure.

Chapter 7 draws attention to a few critical issues of Serbia's transition to a market economy related to the privatization strategy adopted in 2001 and delayed industrial restructuring. The principal reasons behind the slow microeconomic restructuring of the Serbian economy are analysed, as well as its main macroeconomic consequences, including the relatively slow growth of private sector output. The chapter concludes by addressing the principal shortcomings of the 2001 privatization model chosen in 2001.

Relations between the EU and Serbia are addressed in Chapter 8. This chapter outlines the main features of EU policies towards SEE region and FR Yugoslavia in the 1990s. It proceeds to discuss the new EU strategy towards SEE adopted in mid-1999, after the end of the Kosovo conflict, contained in the Stabilization and Association Process (SAP). Although this new phase of EU policies enabled Serbia to intensify its relations with the EU and also led to important steps towards closer integration, open questions remain to block further progress in Serbia's relations with the EU.

Chapter 9 concludes with attention drawn to the strong impact of the global financial and economic crisis of 2008–9 on the Serbian economy and remaining challenges. It evaluates the overall results of the transition model adopted in Serbia in 2001 and gives some possible blueprints for the future. Considering the country's legacies and various phases of economic and political transformation, it ends by drawing an account of some specific features of Serbia's 20-year transition.

The book draws extensively on papers written by the author during the last 20 years and her personal experience gained in the Yugoslav federal government in late 2000 and the first half of 2001 (but all the economic and statistical information used is also available in published sources). During this period the author was vice minister in the Yugoslav federal Ministry for foreign economic relations and was in charge of two departments, for relations with the EU, and with multilateral international organizations. She was also national coordinator of Working Table II of the Stability Pact for Southeast Europe devoted to economic reconstruction, cooperation, and development.

1.7 A note on statistical sources

The selected statistics are based on various national and international sources. Some of the information refers not only to Serbia but to the country that Serbia was part of until June 2006 – namely FR Yugoslavia during 1992–2003 and the State Union of Serbia and Montenegro during 2003–6. Given that before the split in 2006, the Serbian economy represented around 95 per cent of the country's Gross Domestic Product (GDP), the statistics for the whole country are also quite representative of Serbia. All statistics after 1999 do not include Kosovo.

There is still divergence in statistics for some of Serbia's macroeconomic indicators. Official national statistics compiled by the Serbian Office of Statistics and the National Bank of Serbia (NBS) are the most relevant source, but due to differences in methodologies they do not always coincide with data found in the IMF, the EBRD, or the EU Commission publications. It should be no surprise that statistical information on Serbia is still not uniform, despite all efforts of the Serbian Office of Statistics in reforming the system of collecting and reporting, introducing indicators in line with international standards, including the System of National Accounts. Certain problems were inherited from the 1990s, when statistics remained essentially unreformed. For example, the concept of Social Product (equivalent to Gross Material Product, which excludes certain 'non-productive' services such as education, health, defence, and banking) continued to be calculated up until 2005, despite the early introduction of the System of National Accounts – already in 1997.[6] During the 1990s statistics were also incomplete, as on private sector activities and on the government budget, or unreliable, as on inflation or public finance. The deficiencies in Serbian statistics are also related to the recent changes in borders. After 1999 most economic indicators for Kosovo are not included in official statistics for Serbia. Similarly, some statistics for Montenegro have, in the course of years, also become less reliable or unavailable, as for example on foreign trade.

Keeping in mind all these problems and the mushrooming of statistical sources, the choice has been made to rely primarily on official statistics whenever available, supplemented by statistics of the main international organizations. The choice has also been determined by the consistency of the data and the availability of key indicators covering the whole period considered (1989–2008). In assessing progress in transition-related reforms in Serbia, a variety of indicators are used that have been developed by the EBRD, the World Bank, and other international organizations.

2
Serbia on the Eve of Transition

When the transition to a market economy and multiparty democracy was starting in 1989 in CEE, Serbia was still a constituent part of SFR of Yugoslavia, a federation composed of six republics – Bosnia and Herzegovina, Croatia, Macedonia, Montenegro, Serbia with its two autonomous provinces Kosovo and Vojvodina, and Slovenia. At that time, the initial conditions in Serbia and the rest of SFR Yugoslavia were somewhat different than those in the CEE countries, primarily due to a longer tradition in market-oriented economic reforms and the country's specific international relations. Serbia also had an important role within the Yugoslav federation, as it was the largest republic according to several important indicators.

The present chapter evaluates the initial conditions in Serbia at the onset of transition. It recalls past economic reforms in SFR Yugoslavia and their main shortcomings, the progressive deterioration in economic performance, and the severe economic crisis of the 1980s. It also describes the first radical economic reforms implemented in SFR Yugoslavia in 1988–90. It is these reforms that marked the beginning of the transition from communism to capitalism. Though short-lived since the country disintegrated soon after, these initial reforms have influenced the future course of transition in all of its successor states, including Serbia. In order to understand better the initial conditions in Serbia in 1989, the main features which distinguished SFR Yugoslavia from the other socialist countries are reviewed, as well as the position of Serbia within the Yugoslav federation. The chapter concludes with the re-emergence of nationalism in the mid-1980s, the mounting political and social crisis, the first multiparty elections in the Yugoslav republics during 1990, and the break-up of the Yugoslav federation in June 1991 (though officially only some months later).

2.1 Main features of 'market socialism' in Yugoslavia

Economic reforms in SFR Yugoslavia aimed at introducing elements of a market economy had started already in 1950, soon after the Tito-Stalin conflict and the break with Cominform in 1948. Over the next decades, the desire of Yugoslav policy-makers to depart from the traditional Soviet model, but without abandoning some of the most essential features of communism – primarily a one-party political system and non-private ownership of the bulk of the economy – led to various experiments with 'market socialism'. Yugoslavia's unique economic system stimulated considerable academic interest from the 1950s to the 1980s, as an example of a potential 'third way' between capitalism and socialism (Estrin and Uvalic, 2008).

2.1.1 Continuous economic reforms

Starting from early 1952, centralized planning in SFR Yugoslavia was replaced by a more flexible system based on the planning of only global targets (Horvat, 1984, vol. 2, p. 10). Price controls were gradually relaxed, in order to introduce some elements of the market mechanism. Already in 1950, the first workers' councils were introduced, which marked the beginning of a unique system of workers' self-management that implied workers' participation in the process of enterprise decision making, both directly at the workers' general assembly and through representatives in the workers' councils. In 1950, 'social property' was introduced as 'property of the whole society', replacing the more traditional concept of state property. 'Social property' gave enterprises only the right to use socially owned assets and to appropriate the proceeds (*usus* and *usus fructus*), but not full property rights. Initially, enterprises paid a tax for the use of social capital, to be abolished in 1971. The state monopoly of foreign trade was replaced by a more decentralized system, giving more freedom to enterprises in their foreign trade operations. The economy was also gradually decentralized by transferring responsibilities from the federal level to those of the single republics (Uvalic, 1992).

The economic reforms implemented in the 1960s were meant to introduce an even greater reliance on the market, bringing important changes in the field of enterprise policies, investment, and banking. Especially after 1965, there were important measures towards the further liberalization of the economy and decentralized allocation based on free price formation and autonomous enterprise decision making. Prices of a substantial amount of goods were liberalized, while enterprises were given greater control over the distribution of their income, as the tax on social capital was reduced and finally abolished in 1971. Self-management was extended to all sectors and types of organizations. In the mid-1960s, the system of multiple exchange rates was replaced by a uniform exchange rate, the dinar was devalued, and import tariffs were lowered. The economy further opened up to foreign capital, with the adoption of joint ventures legislation in 1967.[1] The financial sector was also substantially reformed and decentralized. In 1963, the central investment funds were abolished and their resources transferred to a large number of local communal banks, though after 1965 the financial system was to rely on a network of less numerous and larger regional all-purpose commercial banks (Lampe, 2000, pp. 286–7).

There was another set of important institutional reforms in Yugoslavia in the 1970s, which aimed at further improving the system of self-management. Through the introduction of the 'contractual economy', markets were partly suppressed and replaced by new mechanisms of policy coordination, a complex system of 'social compacts' and 'self-management agreements', to be negotiated and concluded among enterprises and other interested parties.[2] This was paralleled at the enterprise level by the division of firms into smaller units, so-called 'basic organizations of associated labour', elaborated in the Associated Labour Law (Zakon o udruzenom radu, 1976). In the area of financial reforms, banks were transformed into 'service agencies' of enterprises and substantial innovation was implemented, including the diversification of financial instruments to include bonds, treasury bills, and promissory notes, but not enterprise shares.[3]

In addition to reforms of the system of self-management, the 1971 constitutional amendments and the 1974 federal constitution introduced far-reaching economic decentralization. The new constitution strengthened the rights and responsibilities of republics and autonomous provinces in virtually all economic areas, including prices, income distribution, taxation, employment, social security, foreign trade, and even borrowing abroad with the federation as the warrant. Many scholars have maintained that after 1974 there were no significant differences between the six republics and the two provinces, as both were directly represented in the SFR Yugoslav presidency and other federal bodies (Goati, 1995, p. 17). Political and economic decentralization was a response to the multiple diversities in the country – ethnic, religious, cultural and economic.

Following the deep economic crisis which started in 1980, further economic reforms were launched in 1982. Under the pressure of mounting financial problems and the inability of the government to fulfil its debt repayment obligations, several IMF-sponsored austerity programmes were implemented from 1981 onwards. A special 'Commission of the Federal Social Councils for the Problems of Economic Stabilization' was created in 1982, involving practically the whole economics profession of those times,[4] which prepared a very detailed, four-volume, programme of economic reforms (Komisija, 1982). In spite of long discussions and lengthy policy documents, the reform proposals were not very innovative. The resulting economic reforms were slow, inefficient, and did not bring any effective changes in the functioning of the Yugoslav economic system. As those in the past, the economic reforms of the 1980s were also aimed at a 'greater reliance on market forces', but without touching upon the most fundamental features of the Yugoslav economic system – social property and self-management.

It would only be in 1988–9 that genuinely radical institutional changes were proposed and adopted, consisting of a bold package of 19 new economic laws and amendments to the Yugoslav constitution.[5] It was these reforms that marked a departure from the existing socialist economic system. For the first time private property was officially allowed to expand throughout the economy, both through the privatization of socially owned enterprises and the entry of new private firms (as explained in detail below).

2.1.2 Privileged international relations

In addition to extensive economic reforms, another important advantage of SFR Yugoslavia was its specific position in international economic and political relations, from which all its republics had in one way or another benefited. Unlike the Soviet Union and the six satellite East European countries, SFR Yugoslavia was not a member of the Council for Mutual Economic Assistance (CMEA), but joined the Non-Alignment Movement in 1961. SFR Yugoslavia was one of the founding members of the IMF and of the International Bank for Reconstruction and Development (the World Bank) in Bretton Woods in 1944. After 1961, it took part in some of the work of the Organization for Economic Cooperation and Development (OECD) and it formally became a member of the General Agreement on Tariffs and Trade (GATT) in 1966.

SFR Yugoslavia also had a privileged relationship with the European Economic Community (EEC). After having established official relations in 1967, it concluded several trade agreements with the EEC. The initial non-preferential agreement, signed in 1970, covered a period of three years.[6] It was succeeded by a five-year agreement signed in 1973 which was in force until September 1978, when it was tacitly extended

(Commission of the EC, 1979). Under the terms of the agreement, the two parties accorded each other most-favoured-nation treatment. Yugoslavia was also included into EEC's General System of Preferences in July 1971. Cooperation was extended to financial matters in December 1976, when the European Investment Bank (EIB) was authorized to grant loans for the financing of projects of mutual interest to Yugoslavia and the Community.[7] There were also specific agreements on textile trade, one signed between the EEC and Yugoslavia covering the years 1976–7 and a second one which ran until the end of 1982, which also provided that Yugoslavia would exercise voluntary restraint in the export of a number of textile products of Yugoslav origin (cotton thread, pullovers, men's shirts, trousers, and so on). From 1971 Yugoslavia became an active participant of COST (European Cooperation in Science and Technology), participating in agreements in the fields of telecommunications, metallurgy, pollution of air and water, and other.

In 1980, SFR Yugoslavia signed the most important, broad-based, trade and economic cooperation agreement with the EEC, which entered into force after it was ratified by all 12 European Community (EC) member states and Yugoslavia on 1 April 1983. This agreement envisaged cooperation in various areas, as well as the setting up of a Council for Cooperation of EEC and Yugoslavia at the ministerial level; nine meetings of the Council were held during the 1980s, the last in mid-December 1990. In December 1987, an additional protocol was signed on trade, and the second financial protocol for the period 1987–91. Although a third financial protocol was also signed in June 1991, it never took effect. On 4 July 1990, SFR Yugoslavia was included into the programme of assistance luanched for the East European countries PHARE (Pologne, Hongrie: Assistance à la Restructuration Economique), though this was interrupted due to the mounting political crisis and Yugoslavia's break-up.

These agreements greatly contributed to intensifying economic and political relations between Yugoslavia and the EEC in the 1970s and the 1980s (Bartlett and Uvalic, 1986). They also facilitated – except possibly for the textiles agreements – a significant increase in Yugoslavia's trade with the EEC countries. During 1968–77, Yugoslavia's exports to the EEC tripled, while its imports rose by almost four and a half times. Yugoslavia rose from 12th position among EEC customers in 1968 to 11th in 1978. It occupied 25th place among EEC suppliers in 1968 and 1975 and 26th place in 1978. In 1977 more than 26.5 per cent of Yugoslav exports went to the Community and 39.5 per cent of its imports were of EEC origin (Commission of the EC, 1979).

2.1.3 Why did the model fail?

Despite Yugoslavia's privileged international position and continuous experiments with economic reforms, the model of 'market socialism' did not bring the desired results. Among the reasons is that some of the most fundamental systemic features of the Yugoslav economy had remained unchanged. The numerous economic reforms implemented during the 40 years of 'market socialism' were all partial. Markets were allowed to operate only for goods and services (though even here partially, restricted to some sectors), but not for factors of production, since a capital and a labour market were both rejected on ideological grounds (Uvalic, 1992, p. 206). Moreover, since the Yugoslav economy remained a *socialist* economy, it continued to be characterized by some systemic features (and problems) of the traditional socialist economy.[8] Although in SFR Yugoslavia some of the priorities of the centrally planned economy had been abandoned, such as full employment and price stability, other fundamental features were retained. As late as 1988–9, Yugoslavia had preserved one of the most important features of the socialist economy: the commitment to non-private property.

The rejection of private property on ideological grounds in SFR Yugoslavia meant that the private sector could not expand beyond certain limits, up until the reforms in 1988–9 (see below). As a result, the social sector remained dominant in the Yugoslav economy, in 1989 still contributing as much as 86.2 per cent of Gross Social Product (GSP).[9] There were minor variations across republics and provinces in this regard. The social sector's share in GSP was close to the Yugoslav average in most republics, ranging from 84.2 per cent in Bosnia and Herzegovina to 89.9 per cent in Slovenia; the only exception was Kosovo where it was exceptionally low, 76.9 per cent.[10] In Serbia with its two provinces, the social sector in 1989 contributed 85.1 per cent to its GSP (see Table 2.3).

The Yugoslav economy shared some additional features of the socialist economy which had been emphasized by the Hungarian economist Janos Kornai (1980) as typical of East European countries – including state paternalism, soft-budget constraints, and 'expansion drive' (Uvalic, 1992). State paternalism, or the paternalistic relationship between the state and the firm, was very much present also in SFR Yugoslavia, since external political interference into enterprise affairs was indeed frequent. Yugoslav firms also operated under soft-budget constraints; although there were more bankruptcies in Yugoslavia than in other socialist countries, the more frequent recourse was the socialization of losses. As other socialist countries, the Yugoslav economy was characterized by an 'expansion drive', namely very high investment rates, which were maintained until 1981 (as discussed further below).

These socialist features of the Yugoslav economy in combination with the ambiguous system of social property had a number of negative implications for incentives, both at the microeconomic and macroeconomic level. Under the system of social property, enterprises were given only the right to use socially owned resources but not full property rights, and there was no clear division of property rights between the state and the firm.[11] Although the firm formally had the right to income generated by socially owned capital, the state remained in charge of 'the rules of the game', by being able to impose regulations limiting enterprise autonomy, such as a minimum rate of savings, limits on wage increases, the obligation to maintain the value of social capital through prescribed rates of depreciation, and so forth (Uvalic, 1992, p. 61).

Similarly, at the macroeconomic level, in the absence of private property in the dominant part of the economy, it was the state that remained in charge of the most fundamental questions, including the coverage of losses through income redistribution from profitable to less profitable firms, and the entry and exit of enterprises. Since enterprises were frequently protected from bankruptcy rather than being closed down, there was no full risk borne by the individual firm, and therefore no efficient system of incentives, of rewards and penalties according to market performance, typical of a market economy.

Extensive economic reforms in SFR Yugoslavia had a limited impact on some features of the economy because of the unchanged nature of the political system (Uvalic, 1992). This is not to say that there were no changes in the political domain. Ample decentralization of power within the League of Communists to republican party authorities was gradually implemented – each republic and province had its own League of Communists – but the political system remained essentially a one-party system. This had direct implications for the economic system and the ideology behind it, where key socialist goals had to be retained, including non-private property, non-market mechanisms of economic coordination, and principles of solidarity and egalitarianism. Also in SFR Yugoslavia, socialist goals were pursued through the traditional instrument of the Soviet-type model of persistent state intervention in the economy.

2.2 Yugoslavia's deteriorating economic performance

The combination of elements from both the socialist and the capitalist economic system undoubtedly brought Yugoslavia and its citizens important advantages with respect to the other countries in Eastern Europe, including a higher standard of living, some form of economic democracy, and a more liberal political system, which assured greater personal freedom, including the right to travel freely abroad from 1965 onwards. In the long run, however, SFR Yugoslavia did not avoid the problems typical of either of the two economic systems, including unemployment, inflation, and a slowdown in economic growth.

Already starting from the mid-1960s, SFR Yugoslavia was confronted with the problem of unemployment, which increased particularly in the 1970s and the 1980s (Woodward, 1995a, pp. 194–208). From the early 1960s many Yugoslav workers found employment in Western Europe, particularly in Germany, but the prospects greatly deteriorated after the first, and especially after the second oil shock (in 1973–4 and 1979–80 respectively), forcing many workers to return home. The unemployment rate, measured as the number of job-seekers in total labour force, increased from 6 per cent in 1965, to 7.7 per cent in 1970, to 11.9 per cent in 1980, and further to 16.4 per cent in 1990.[12] There were, however, substantial differences in the unemployment rates across republics: Slovenia had practically full employment throughout the period, whereas unemployment was particularly high in Macedonia and Kosovo.

Starting from the mid-1960s when prices were further liberalized, Yugoslavia also experienced rising inflationary pressures. From an average of around 10 per cent in the 1960s, average annual inflation doubled to around 20 per cent in the 1970s, and it reached particularly high levels in the 1980s (see Tables 2.1 and 2.2). The inadequate instruments of monetary control of the National Bank of Yugoslavia (NBY), especially after the adoption of the 1974 constitution which secured greater monetary independence to its constituent parts, together with the maintenance of low nominal interest rates which remained negative in real terms, contributed to excessive credit expansion at all levels. In the 1980s, the attempts of the government to implement a tighter monetary policy were largely ineffective. A widespread new phenomenon was the uncontrolled growth in inter-enterprise credit, also through the issuing of promissory notes, as enterprises increasingly bypassed the banking system thus avoiding credit controls. Average annual inflation progressively increased, from 30 per cent in 1980 to three-digit figures in 1987–8, and became hyperinflation in 1989, when the average annual rate reached 1252 per cent.

Whereas during the first two decades the Yugoslav economy developed rapidly, registering very high rates of GSP growth and even higher rates of growth in industrial output, after the mid-1960s there was a slowdown. Still, GSP growth rates remained close to 6 per cent also during the 1966–1979 period. A sharp deterioration in growth performance

Table 2.1 SFR Yugoslavia: Main economic indicators, 1953–89 (average growth rates, %)

	1953–6	1957–60	1961–5	1966–70	1971–5	1976–80	1981–9
Gross social product	6.6	11.3	6.8	5.8	5.9	5.7	0.5*
Gross social product per head	5.2	10.2	5.7	5.9	5.1	4.3	–0.2*
Industrial output	12.9	14.1	10.6	6.1	8.1	6.7	2.0
Agricultural output	–3.6	16.7	3.6	4.6	3.8	7.5	–6.3
Employment	6.3	7.6	4.3	1.0	4.3	4.0	1.9
Retail prices	2.3	3.0	11.1	10.0	20.2	21.8	120.0
Real net wages per worker	1.1	9.1	5.4	7.3	1.5	0.9	–0.6
Exports	9.4	14.6	9.7	5.8	4.9	1.5	2.4
Imports	7.4	14.5	5.8	14.3	5.8	0.8	–1.0

*1981–8.
Source: Savezni zavod za statistiku (SZS), *Statisticki godisnjak Jugoslavije 1990*, Tables 102–9 and 102–10 (pp. 98–9) and Savezni zavod za statistiku (1982), p. 93.

would become apparent only after 1979, when a severe economic crisis started to develop. However, the origins of the economic crisis of the 1980s are to be sought in the internal and external imbalances accumulated much earlier, during the 1960s and the 1970s.

The development strategy in Yugoslavia, as in other socialist countries, was based on high investment spending. Until the early 1980s, the share of gross fixed investment in GSP continued increasing, from 27.7 per cent in 1952–60 to 31.8 per cent in 1961–70, and further to 32.3 per cent in 1971–80 (Savezni zavod za statistiku, 1986, p. 67). The trend of high investment spending was reversed only in the 1980s under the impact of the economic crisis. During 1981–5, average gross investment in fixed assets dropped to 24 per cent of GSP and by 1988 it reached a low 19 per cent of GSP. This was paralleled by a continuous fall in investment efficiency, measured as the increase in GSP obtained from 100 dinars of gross fixed investment. Investment efficiency gradually declined from 39 per cent in 1952–60 to 26.8 per cent in 1961–70; it dropped further to 21.1 per cent in 1971–80 and became negative (–3.5 per cent) in 1981–90 (Stamenkovic et al., 2004). The constant decline in investment returns was even more

Table 2.2 SFR Yugoslavia: Main economic indicators, 1980–9

Annual % change	**1980**	**1981**	**1982**	**1983**	**1984**	**1985**	**1986**	**1987**	**1988**	**1989**
Gross social product	2.2	1.5	0.5	–1.0	2.0	0.5	3.6	–1.1	–1.7	0.8
Gross fixed investment	–1.7	–9.8	–5.5	–9.7	–9.6	–4.0	3.5	–5.1	–5.8	0.5
Inflation*	30	41	32	41	53	74	89	120	195	1252
Real net wages (social sector)	–7.5	–5.0	–4.0	–11.0	–6.0	2.0	9.3	4.1	–5.8	–0.4
Employment	1.0	0.7	0.7	0.8	1.1	1.5	1.8	2.1	–1.2	–0.3
Exports	8.9	–0.4	–11.2	1.4	10.1	8.2	2.0	–0.6	5.7	7.2
Imports	–9.9	–12.3	–13.5	–5.5	–0.4	2.3	8.8	–5.8	1.1	12.7
In mln US$										
Trade balance	–6.1	–4.8	–3.1	–2.2	–1.7	–1.6	–2.0	–1.2	–0.6	–1.4
Current account balance	–2.3	–0.7	–0.5	0.3	0.5	0.8	–1.7	1.2	2.5	2.4
External debt (net of lending)	17.3	19.5	18.6	18.7	18.3	18.0	18.6	19.5	16.8	15.2

*Measured by the cost of living index (average change with respect to previous year).

Source: Uvalic, 1992, p. 12, based on official statistics of the Federal Institute of Statistics, OECD Economic Surveys on Yugoslavia, and the NBY *Bilten Narodne Banke Jugoslavije* (various issues).

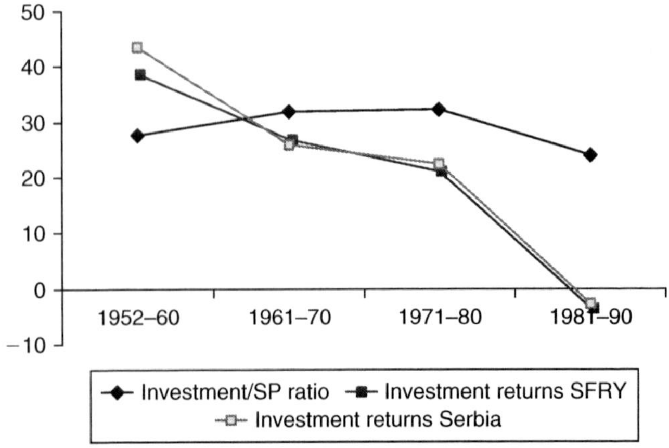

Figure 2.1 SFR Yugoslavia: Gross fixed investment (in % of GSP) and investment efficiency
Source: Savezni zavod za statistiku (1986) p. 67 and Stamenkovic et al. (2004), p. 1.

pronounced in Serbia than for Yugoslavia as a whole (see Figure 2.1). These problems were similar to those encountered in other East European countries, where an increasing share of investment expenditure also brought declining investment returns (World Bank, 1996, p. 3).

Yugoslavia was also confronted with increasing external imbalances. Already in the late 1960s there was a slowdown in the growth of exports, parallel with a substantial increase in imports, which led to a widening trade deficit and increasing balance of payment difficulties (Uvalic, 1992, pp. 10–11). Whereas the current account deficit was initially balanced by workers' remittances from abroad and by tourism, the situation deteriorated continuously during the 1970s. The Yugoslav government did not react to the 1973–4 oil shock by lowering domestic spending, but continued with an ambitious and unbalanced economic growth strategy and high investment rates, implying heavy reliance on imports and frequent recourse to external borrowing on international markets and World Bank loans.

Yugoslavia's external debt (net of lending) increased from less than US$2 billion in 1970 to US$14 billion in 1979 and, following the second oil shock, to US$ 18 billion in 1980. Structural imbalances started to emerge due to insufficient investment in crucial sectors (energy, raw materials) and rising dependence of the economy on imported inputs, while there was excess capacity in other sectors and the duplication of plants of suboptimal size across regions.

After a record trade and current account deficit in 1979, Yugoslavia was no longer able to service its external debt. The government was forced to implement restrictive economic policies, which after 1981 were supported by 'the Friends of Yugoslavia', loans orchestrated by the United States, several IMF stand-by arrangements (SBA), support of Western governments, and rescheduling of its foreign debt (Lampe, 2000, p. 327). Between 1980 and 1991, the IMF concluded seven SBAs with SFR Yugoslavia, totalling SDR 3.5 billion (of which 2.7 billion was disbursed) (www.nbs.rs).

By 1983, some objectives regarding the external sector of the austerity packages had been achieved. The current account deficit was transformed into a modest surplus in 1983–5, which increased further in 1987–9 (see Table 2.2). The price paid for these improvements, however, was a severe economic crisis in the later 1980s. Given that the initial reduction in the trade deficit was achieved primarily through restrictions on imports, rather than an increase in exports, reduced imports had a negative effect on many of the industrial sectors that were highly dependent on imported inputs.

After 1980, the Yugoslav economy was characterized by stagnating or declining GSP, negative rates of investment growth (except in 1986 and 1989), falling real net wages, modest growth of employment, rising unemployment, and inflation. Restrictive income policies in combination with rising inflation led to declining living standards: between 1980 and 1984 alone, there was a 34 per cent drop in real net wages. The various stabilization programmes implemented by the government during the 1981–9 period had proved largely unsuccessful. The economic crisis persisted throughout the 1980s, culminating in hyperinflation by the end of the decade.

2.3 Yugoslavia's last attempt at economic reforms

A decisive change in the general attitude of the Yugoslav authorities took place in 1988, in the direction of private ownership and a mixed market economy (Uvalic, 1992). Starting from November 1988, the government adopted important amendments to the federal constitution as well as a number of new laws which facilitated the development of the small-scale private sector, encouraged foreign direct investment, and called for privatization of the dominant social sector of the economy. In addition in December 1989, in response to hyperinflation – an annual average inflation rate of 1252 per cent – the last prime minister of the Yugoslav government, Ante Markovic, launched a macroeconomic stabilization programme, similar to the one implemented in Poland in early 1990.[13]

The new 1988 law on enterprises diversified both property types and legal forms of enterprise, while also limiting workers' self-management rights in an attempt to replace collective responsibility of workers by individual responsibility of managers and capital owners. A new law on foreign direct investment improved conditions for foreign investors by offering major protection of foreign ownership and management rights, and abolishing the limits on the share of foreign ownership. In agriculture, the limits on individual holdings were lifted. Changes in the banking system provided for the transformation of banks into joint stock and limited liability banks. A new law on securities introduced, for the first time, equity shares in the Yugoslav legal system.

Most importantly, the 'Law on the circulation and disposal of social capital', adopted in December 1989, called for the sale of social capital of enterprises to domestic and foreign buyers through auctions, therefore announcing privatization of the bulk of the economy. Given the insufficiently stimulating conditions of the law,[14] no sales took place and the law had to be amended in August 1990 in order to offer greater incentives. According to the new regulations, the privatization of social sector enterprises was to take place through sales of enterprise shares at a 30 per cent discount to present and former employees, other citizens and pension funds, on the basis of the book value of assets, but employees (both present and former) were given a further one per cent discount for each year of employment, up to a maximum of 70 per cent of the nominal value of the shares, to be paid within a 10-year period. Though several limits on share issues at a discount had to be respected, the law in practice offered extremely favourable conditions primarily to employed workers and managers ('insiders'). The part of social capital not subscribed at preferential terms was to be offered at public auctions to domestic and foreign buyers, but the destination of unsold social capital was not specified. This law effectively enabled the first ownership changes throughout Yugoslavia, the partial replacement of social by private property. Thus in Serbia, during August 1990–August 1991, over 33 per cent of all social sector enterprises started privatization under the provisions of the law (Zec et al., 1994, p. 228).

As a response to the deep economic crisis and hyperinflation, in December 1989 the Markovic government implemented a bold macroeconomic stabilization programme, the first of this kind. The 'shock therapy' was based on the pegging of the exchange rate to the German mark, introduction of resident convertibility, freezing of money wages, stricter monetary control, liberalization of 75 per cent of prices (except for public utilities, some metals and pharmaceuticals), and liberalization of 95 per cent of imports. The stabilization programme was initially very successful in halting inflation and maintaining convertibility, but by mid-1990 there was a deviation from the originally stipulated federal policies, resulting in the return of hyperinflation, to 588 per cent for the whole of 1990. All republics considered the programme contrary to their interests: the more developed republics, as major exporters, were adversely affected by the fixed exchange rate and were pressing for a devaluation, while the less developed republics were primarily hit by the monetary restrictions and limited loans for agriculture. Under the pressure of diverging interests, the federal government was forced to accept certain compromises which marked the beginning of progressive weakening of federal control (Uvalic, 1992).

Most republics failed to respect the limits on wage increases, the monetary regulations of the National Bank of Yugoslavia (NBY), and their obligations regarding the financing of the federal budget. In September 1990 Serbia failed to transfer sales tax revenues to the federal budget. In October 1990 there was the 'trade war', when Serbia imposed special taxes on Slovenian and Croatian products and blocked payments from the federal budget to these two republics. Slovenia and Croatia reacted by stopping the payment of customs duties and other federal taxes, while Slovenia also introduced taxes on livestock, meat and dairy products from Serbia (Dinkic, 1995, p. 30).

Soon after, there was the 'foreign currency war' among the republics. Due to increasing withdrawals of foreign currency from bank accounts, there was a general shortage of foreign exchange, a black market had re-emerged and resident convertibility had effectively been suspended. This led the commercial banks of each republic to compete in accumulating as much foreign currency as possible, both by offering the best possible conditions for the purchase of foreign currency and by buying foreign currency on the black market of neighbouring republics. Due to rising inflation and declining foreign exchange reserves, the exchange rate could no longer be sustained and the dinar was devalued twice, in January 1991 by 22 per cent and in April 1991 by a further 30 per cent (Uvalic, 1992).

In the second half of 1990, Croatia, Serbia and Slovenia started to undermine the federal monetary system by illegal monetary expansion. The NBY did not have full control over monetary emission, since the national banks of the single republics and provinces were also allowed to issue money through various channels of credit expansion.[15] In December 1990 Serbia staged a spectacular raid on the federal monetary system, illegally issuing a quantity of dinars equivalent to almost half of the planned primary issue in 1991 for the entire country (Dinkic, 1995, p. 30). The money was channelled towards workers' wages and pensions, to coincide with the first multiparty elections in Serbia (which did indeed bring victory to Slobodan Milosevic's Socialist Party of Serbia). The December 1990 raid on the monetary system by the NBS was the final blow to the Yugoslav federation, since it increased mistrust on the part of the other republics. Soon after, in February-March 1991, Croatia and Slovenia definitively stopped paying all federal taxes. By spring 1991, the federal institutions in Yugoslavia were already without any effective power.

The economic reforms implemented by the Markovic government were of short duration, given that in mid-1991 the Yugoslav federation effectively ceased to exist, thereafter imposing the need for new legislation to be elaborated and adopted in all of Yugoslavia's successor states. Notwithstanding its short period of implementation, the Markovic programme did have an important economic impact throughout the country, including Serbia. The liberalization of entry conditions allowed the creation of a large number of small firms, especially in services. The liberalization of imports and the incentives offered to small-scale private activity led to the flourishing of the private sector and increased competition on the domestic market, eliminating shortages and improving the supply of many high quality consumer goods. The 1989–90 privatization law led to the first property changes and commercialization of social sector firms, serving as an example to other enterprises which initially were hesitant to enter the process. A stock exchange was set up in four main cities – Belgrade, Ljubljana, Sarajevo, and Zagreb. During the first three quarters of 1990, the dinar was stable and convertible, and resident convertibility greatly increased citizens' confidence in the government and in transition-related reforms. Contrary to past economic reforms, the Markovic package laid down the foundations of an effective transition to a market economy, this time based not only on the increasing reliance on the market, but also on private property. These foundations of a market economy represented the starting point for all the successor states of SFR Yugoslavia in the early 1990s, including Serbia.

2.4 How different was Yugoslavia/Serbia?

What were the systemic features of the Yugoslav/Serbian economy at that time, on the eve of the transition? Despite having retained the most important features of the socialist economy, in comparison with other East European countries SFR Yugoslavia in 1989 also had a number of distinct features (Uvalic, 1991, 2007a). Some of these features were clear advantages, but others were disadvantages which risked slowing down the transition to a market economy. While a few of these advantages applied only to the country as a whole and thus were definitely lost after the 1991 split,[16] other features were equally applicable to its single republics.

The most important factor in 1989 that seemed to facilitate the transition to a market economy in SFR Yugoslavia was a shorter reform agenda, due to the long tradition in market-oriented economic reforms, which had introduced many institutional changes that elsewhere in CEE would be implemented only after 1989. Past reforms had also enabled major economic and political decentralization through various channels – the transfer of power from federal to lower-level political authorities, self-management mechanisms of policy coordination, and forms of direct democracy within enterprises through the system of workers' self-management. Greater openness towards the West (and independence from the East) brought many benefits at both the enterprise and macroeconomic level, including permanent contacts with international partners and a higher degree of economic integration of the Yugoslav economy into world markets, as described earlier.

On the eve of transition, SFR Yugoslavia also faced certain disadvantages which threatened transition-related economic reforms (Uvalic, 1991). Among the most important disadvantages were the ongoing political crisis within the Yugoslav federation, ambiguous property rights, and general resistance to change. Of the three, the most serious was undoubtedly the severe political crisis, the continuous and increasing disputes among the republics over both economic and political issues, which effectively would lead to the violent break-up of the Yugoslav federation.

Another disadvantage of the Yugoslav economy was the ambiguous system of property rights associated with 'social property', in combination with workers' self-management. These features raised specific problems regarding privatization. Although Yugoslav enterprises were never given full property rights, the system of self-management ensured workers ample decision-making rights, to the extent that many workers felt they were the real owners of their firm. This was in line with the frequently held view that with the passing of time, 'group property', namely property of the employed workers, had unofficially replaced social property (Bajt, 1988).

These specific features of the Yugoslav economic system rendered privatization in SFR Yugoslavia, and later in its successor states, more complicated than in the other former socialist countries. Since enterprises were owned 'by everyone and no-one', who was authorized to sell them – the state, the enterprise, or the employed workers? And to whom would the proceeds from privatization go? These questions crucially influenced the course of privatization in Yugoslavia's successor states, and were tackled differently in the privatization laws of each of them (Uvalic, 1997a).

A further disadvantage in 1989 was the greater resistance to radical systemic changes in SFR Yugoslavia than in other CEE countries, due to a higher degree of popular support in Yugoslavia for the existing political and economic system. The support of the regime derived not only from the discussed specific features of the Yugoslav model, which effectively assured a higher standard of living and more personal freedoms to Yugoslavs in comparison with citizens in other East European countries. Yugoslavia's ideological distance from the Soviet bloc and cultural openness to the West was one of the main informal sources of Yugoslav national pride as well as of the legitimacy and stability of Tito's communist regime (Vujacic, 2004, p. 10). Popular support of the regime also derived from the much deeper roots of communist ideology in Yugoslavia, since communism was not imposed from the outside as in CEE, but through the grass-roots revolution during World War II.

After the break-up of the Yugoslav federation in mid-1991, these systemic features inherited by its successor states have been preserved, transformed, or eliminated in the different national contexts, thereafter leading to substantial divergence in the transition paths of the newly created states (Estrin and Uvalic, 2008).

At the time of disintegration of SFR Yugoslavia, Serbia had a relatively favourable position with respect to many other countries embarking on transition to a market economy. Kekic (1996) has calculated an overall index of initial conditions in the late 1980s in 26 post-socialist economies (also for those that were thereafter to become independent states due to the disintegration of federal states). The index was based on a number of indicators: dependence on CMEA trade, GDP per head, external debt, share of industry and services in GDP, energy intensity, and general government expenditure. The index of initial conditions for Serbia and Montenegro was one of the highest (19), the same as for the Czech Republic and higher than for most other countries, except for Slovenia (24), Croatia (22), Hungary (21), and Macedonia (20).

What has remained of the relatively favourable initial conditions that Serbia had in 1989? A number of negative developments have fundamentally affected Serbia's economic and political situation in the meantime, which have practically dissolved most, if not all, of the advantages it had in 1989, while some disadvantages, such as 'social property', have been preserved up to the present days. These issues will again be recalled when analysing the more recent systemic features of the Serbian economy in Chapter 9.

2.5 Serbia's position within the Yugoslav federation

Another important aspect to be considered is the position of Serbia within the Yugoslav federation at the outset of the transition. There were important regional differences among the Yugoslav republics and provinces regarding economic structure, level of development, trade orientation, foreign direct investment, and other features. Serbia was the biggest and the most populous republic of SFR Yugoslavia, and carried a major weight regarding a number of economic indicators.

In 1989–90, Serbia represented the largest part of the Yugoslav territory (34.5 per cent) and population (41.5 per cent), contributed the highest share of GSP (38 per cent) and investment (38 per cent), and accounted for the majority of both employed workers (38.1 per cent) and those seeking employment (46.9 per cent). Almost half of agricultural output was produced in Serbia (48.6 per cent of the total), as well as over a third of industrial output (37.8 per cent of total). In 1989, productivity in Serbia, measured by GSP of the social sector per worker, was at the Yugoslav average (see Table 2.3 and Figure 2.2. below).

A specific feature of Serbia was that it was the only Yugoslav republic to have two 'autonomous provinces' within its territory – Vojvodina in the north and Kosovo in the south – motivated by the necessity of incorporating the sizeable national minorities of Hungarians and Albanians into the new state.[17] According to the 1991 census, around 66 per cent of Serbia's inhabitants were Serbs, 17 per cent were Albanians, 3.5 per cent were Hungarians, 3.2 per cent were Yugoslavs, and the remaining were Muslims, Montenegrins, and Croats. There were also many Serbs living outside Serbia: out of the total of 8.5 million people who declared themselves as Serbs in 1991, only 6.4 million lived in Serbia, while 1.4 million lived in Bosnia and Herzegovina, 580,000 in Croatia, 57,000 in Montenegro, and 44,000 in Macedonia (Crnobrnja, 1994, p. 30).

Serbia had an important role in Yugoslavia's foreign economic relations. Although Slovenia and Croatia were the more export-oriented republics, directing a larger percentage of their respective GSP to foreign markets, Serbia in 1990 accounted for the largest share, among all republics, of Yugoslavia's total exports (30.2 per cent) and imports (33.4 per cent). Still, Serbia was a relatively closed economy, its exports accounting only for 18 per cent of its GSP in 1987. In general, all Yugoslav republics traded more among themselves than with the outside world: in 1987, Serbia

Table 2.3 SFR Yugoslavia: Main economic indicators of republics/provinces, 1989–90 (in %)

	Bosnia & Herzegovina	Croatia	Macedonia	Montenegro	Slovenia	Serbia total	Serbia without K&V	Kosovo	Vojvodina
Territory (1990)	20.1	22.1	10.1	3.4	7.9	34.5	21.9	4.2	8.4
Population (1990)	19	19.7	8.9	2.7	8.2	41.5	24.6	8.3	8.6
Employment (1990)	15.8	23.5	7.8	2.5	12.3	38.1	25.5	3.2	9.4
Job-seekers (1990)	21.7	12.3	11.9	3.7	3.4	46.9	25.9	11.3	9.8
Fixed assets (1989)	15.2	25.8	5.8	3.2	17	33	20.6	2.8	9.6
Investment (1989)	14.2	22.2	4.9	2.3	18.4	38	27	2.1	8.9
GSP (1989)	12.9	25	5.8	2	16.5	38	25.6	2.1	10.3
Industry GSP (1989)	14.5	21.6	6.7	1.7	17.7	37.8	25.7	2.1	10
Agriculture GSP (1989)	12	22.5	6.6	1.8	8.7	48.4	26.2	4	18.2
Exports (1990)	14.4	20.4	4	1.6	28.8	30.2	20.7	1.2	8.3
Imports (1990)	10	23.5	5.6	1	25	33.4	21	1	11.4
GSP per head (1989), SFRY average = 100	65	124	65	71	200	88	100	24	118
Productivity (1989) SFRY average = 6.2	4.8	6.6	4.6	5.3	8.6	6.2	6.3	3.7	6.7
Contribution of social sector to GSP (%), SFRY average = 86.2%	84.2	86.5	86.2	88.4	89.9	85.1	85.9	76.9	84.7

Note: All indicators give the share, in per cent, of each republic in SFR Yugoslavia (SFRY = 100), except the last three indicators. The indicators on GSP per head, and on productivity, show the position of each republic with respect to the Yugoslav average. The contribution of the social sector to GSP is its share in the respective republic's or province's GSP.
Source: Savezni zavod za statistiku, *Statisticki Godisnjak Jugoslavije 1991*, Tables 201–1, 201–2, and 205–1 (pp. 410–11, 475).

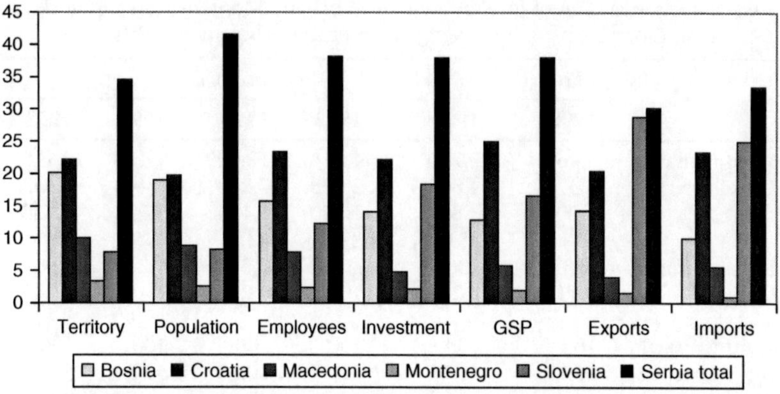

Figure 2.2 SFR Yugoslavia: Relative shares of the republics in main indicators, 1989–90 (in % of total)
Source: Data reported in Table 2.3.

(with its provinces) delivered approximately 40 per cent of its GSP to the other republics, and only 18 per cent to external markets (Uvalic, 1993).

In the late 1980s, around 60 per cent of Serbia's exports went to the OECD countries, whereas Serbian exports to the CMEA, though relatively low (8 per cent of Serbia's GSP), were double that of Slovenia (only 4 per cent of its GSP). In 1990, foreign trade of Serbia and Montenegro (the future FR Yugoslavia) was predominantly with the European Community – 44 per cent of exports and 43 per cent of imports (see Table 2.4).

Serbia was also the republic with the greatest concentration of international contracts with foreign partners. In 1989, Serbia had concluded the highest number of contracts with foreign partners (33 per cent of the total), though the value of capital invested in joint ventures in Serbia (21 per cent of the total) was one third of Slovenia (65 per cent) (see Table 2.5).

Following the 1988–9 Markovic reforms which substantially eased the conditions for foreign investors, Serbia attracted more than 45 per cent of total foreign direct investment in SFR Yugoslavia during the next three years, from January 1989 until December 1991 (see Table 2.6). Sustained by substantial reforms and opening up of the Yugoslav economy, Serbia at that time was clearly attractive for foreign investors.

Regarding the level of development, in 1989 the joint GDP per head at Purchasing Power Parity (PPP) of Serbia and Montenegro (that would soon become the FR Yugoslavia) was estimated at around US$ 4731, which was around half of the GDP per head of Slovenia (Kekic, 1996, p. 15).

Table 2.4 Destination of foreign trade of Serbia and Montenegro/FR Yugoslavia, 1990–2 (in dinars at current exchange rates and in per cent of total)

	Exports			Imports		
	1990	1991	1992	1990	1991	1992
Total (dinars)	9,462	7,780	4,014	12,109	9,136	6,119
Developed	5,373	4,804	2,098	7,290	5,440	3,353
-EC	4,205	3,807	1,620	5,184	3,992	2,350
-EFTA	587	451	217	937	645	460
Developing	973	738	455	1,583	1,240	524
Other	3,116	2,238	1,461	3,236	2,456	2,242
Total (in %)	100	100	100	100	100	100
Developed	56.79	61.75	52.27	60.20	59.54	54.80
-EC	44.44	48.93	40.36	42.81	43.70	38.41
-EFTA	6.20	5.80	5.41	7.74	7.06	7.52
Developing	10.28	9.49	11.34	13.07	13.57	8.56
Other	32.93	28.77	36.40	26.72	26.88	36.64

Source: Savezni zavod za statistiku, *Statisticki Godisnjak Jugoslavije 1995 (Statistical Yearbook of Yugoslavia 1995)*, Table 19.3, p. 276.

With respect to the other Yugoslav republics, Serbia in 1989 had a GSP per capita which was 88 per cent of the Yugoslav average. There were large discrepancies within its territory, however. Whereas Serbia proper, the central part of Serbia without the two provinces, had a GSP per capita at the same level as the Yugoslav average, Vojvodina's GSP per capita was 18 per cent above, and Kosovo's 24 per cent below, the Yugoslav average (see Table 2.3). Within the context of regional policies which provided financial assistance through the Federal Development Fund to the less developed republics and provinces, Serbia proper (without the two provinces) and Vojvodina were considered among the more developed and were both net contributors to the Fund; while Montenegro and the province of Kosovo were among the net recipients.[18]

There were also wide differences in the unemployment rates across republics and provinces. In 1973, the average unemployment rate (measured as registered job-seekers in percentage of total domestic labour force) in SFR Yugoslavia was 8.1 per cent, but Slovenia effectively had full employment with a 1.8 per cent unemployment rate, while Kosovo had an unemployment rate of over 20 per cent (Woodward, 1995a, p. 23). By 1990, the unemployment rate in SFR Yugoslavia doubled, increasing to over 16 per cent, but the regional differences widened further. In 1990 the registered unemployment rate in Slovenia was still a low 5.2 per cent, in Serbia with its two provinces it was

Table 2.5 Yugoslavia's international cooperation agreements, by type and by republic and province, 1989

Number of international cooperation agreements	**SFRY**	**Bosnia & Herzegovina**	**Croatia**	**Macedonia**	**Monte-negro**	**Slovenia**	**Serbia total**	**Serbia without K&V**	**Kosovo**	**Vojvo-dina**
Long-term production cooperation	1095	66	178	65	7	465	323	226	0	97
Investment of capital by foreign partner	148	13	28	3	2	37	65	54	0	11
Investment works by foreign partner	14	4	3	1	0	1	5	2	0	3
Acquisition of technology by foreign partner	22	2	5	0	0	8	7	0	0	7
Domestic acquisition of foreign technology	131	6	34	21	0	25	45	29	0	16
Business and technical cooperation	90	5	25	3	1	37	19	17	0	2
National firms abroad	218	15	49	12	0	54	88	85	0	3
Mixed property firms abroad	139	14	17	1	0	77	30	30	0	0
Investment by domestic firms abroad	990	86	319	21	12	203	349	329	0	20
Total number of agreements	2847	211	658	127	22	898	931	772	0	159
Share in % (total = 100)	100	7.4	23.1	4.5	0.7	31.5	32.7	27.1	0	5.6
Foreign investment in joint ventures										
Value of foreign capital, in 000 of dinars	651,974	82	90,570	2,400	198	421,987	136,737	136,229	0	508
Share in % (total = 100)	100	0.01	13.89	0.37	0.03	64.72	20.97	20.89	0	0.07

Source: Savezni zavod za statistiku, *Statisticki Godisnjak Jugoslavije 1991*, Tables 218-6 and 218–7, pp. 565–7.

Table 2.6 Foreign direct investment in SFR Yugoslavia, by republics and provinces, January 1989–December 1991

Republic/ Autonomous province	Number of firms	In % of total	Value of foreign share (in DM)	In % of total
Bosnia & Herzegovina	382	6.7	280,291	6.9
Croatia	1,470	25.7	515,733	12.6
Macedonia	450	7.8	224,925	5.5
Montenegro	106	1.8	119,906	3.0
Serbia without provinces	1,862	32.5	1,655,033	40.7
Kosovo	22	0.4	36,294	0.9
Vojvodina	312	5.4	178,448	4.4
Slovenia	1,114	19.8	1,053,791	25.5
Unknown	8	0.1	3,234	0.1
SFR Yugoslavia	5,726	100.0	4,068,000	100,0

Source: Vidas Bubanja (1994), p. 146, based on data of the Federal Secretariat for international economic relations.

19.5 per cent, while in Kosovo it was as high as 40.8 per cent (Bartlett and Uvalic, 1992, p. 9).

The regional policies implemented in SRF Yugoslavia aimed at bridging the gap between the more and the less developed parts of the country had not been very successful. Despite all the transfers aimed to help the less developed regions, the gap between the per capita GSP of the most developed Slovenia and the least developed Kosovo actually widened, from 5:1 in 1955 to 8:1 in 1989 (Uvalic, 1993). The main mechanism for transfers was the Federal Development Fund, to which all republics and provinces had to contribute a certain percentage (less than 2 per cent) of their respective GSP, while the sole recipients were the less developed republics and Kosovo. Financial assistance through the Fund initially consisted of grants, but after 1971 it took the form of loans at highly preferential terms. In order to introduce a more decentralized and market-based mechanism of investment, in line with the changes introduced by the Associated Labour Law, after 1975 some 20 per cent of the republican quota in the Fund could be invested directly in enterprises located in the less developed regions through various forms of 'association of labour and resources', which was further increased to 50 per cent in 1981 (Uvalic, 1993).

In addition to the Federal Development Fund, there were other mechanisms of redistribution of income in SFR Yugoslavia. Among the most important were budgetary transfers through the fiscal system; loans of the National Bank of Yugoslavia extended at highly preferential terms to specific administrative entities or special recipients (exporters, farmers); and the clearing system of payments in foreign trade with the CMEA countries, which favoured exporters and penalized importers.

These mechanisms of redistribution provoked a long-lasting controversy over who was 'exploiting' whom (Uvalic, 1993). The more developed republics – Slovenia and Croatia – felt exploited because of the obligatory transfer of resources to the Federal Development Fund, which usually remained outside their direct control, or other policies to their disadvantage, like the retention of foreign currency earnings from exports and tourism. The less developed republics felt exploited because of the unfavourable terms of trade deriving from the structure of their economies, namely a large share of basic industries, primarily agriculture, characterized by low efficiency and/or high capital-output ratios, in combination with distortions in relative prices, due to more widespread price controls on basic than on manufacturing products, which in general implied lower prices for the former.

The debate lasted for decades, without offering clear evidence which republics were actually more advantaged or disadvantaged. After the adoption of the 1974 federal constitution, when significant discretionary powers were transferred to the republics and autonomous provinces, economic nationalism was reinforced within republican borders. This led to uncoordinated investment strategies, unnecessary duplication of plants in many sectors, rising fragmentation of the Yugoslav market, and impediments to the mobility of capital and labour across the country (Uvalic, 1993).

There was a sharp revival of the debate in the second half of the 1980s, when the topic of economic exploitation of Serbia was highlighted in a document prepared in 1986 by a group of intellectuals of the Serbian Academy of Sciences and Arts – the 'Memorandum on the position of Serbia in Yugoslavia'. The authors of the Memorandum lamented, without providing sufficiently convincing arguments, that Serbia was constantly discriminated against within Yugoslavia, both economically and politically. Supposedly, the type of economic policies implemented in Yugoslavia had 'intentionally plunged Serbia into economic backwardness'.[19] Furthermore, as argued in the Memorandum, existing constitutional arrangements which created autonomous provinces within Serbia, had made it the only republic unable to exercise full sovereignty over its whole territory.[20] This document, initially kept secret, greatly contributed to the new wave of nationalism in Serbia in the second half of the 1980s (see below).

2.6 The mounting political crisis

Throughout the 1980s, SFR Yugoslavia was also facing growing social and political unrest. After President Tito's death in May 1980, he was replaced by the 'rotating presidency' that was to ensure that Yugoslavia would have a new president every two years, each time from a different republic. This mechanism proved ineffective in maintaining political stability in Yugoslavia, as it could in no way substitute Tito's authority. The political crisis accelerated in the second half of the 1980s, since there was rising tension within the Yugoslav federation. Tension was intensified particularly by the resurgence of nationalism, initially in Serbia where the Serbian national question came to the centre of public debates, and soon after also in Slovenia and Croatia.[21]

It was primarily the issue of Kosovo that triggered a new wave of Serbian nationalism. Following the Albanian students' demonstrations in Kosovo in 1981, there were growing demands for a change in Kosovo's status within the Yugoslav federation, from a province (within Serbia), to a republic (independent of Serbia). Given the continuous exodus of Serbs from Kosovo, by that time 83 per cent of the population in Kosovo was already Albanian. As a result, the Serbs in Kosovo felt uneasy and started to write petitions to the Serbian authorities, advancing complaints about Serbian discrimination within Kosovo. The inability of the party and government structures to halt the continued exodus of Serbs from the region 'raised the spectre of the final loss of this symbolic heartland of the nation' (Vujacic, 2004, p. 26).

The tensions over Kosovo intensified in the second half of the 1980s. Although the 1974 Yugoslav constitution had given ample rights to Kosovo and Vojvodina, a part of the Serbian leadership wanted the return of Kosovo to its 'maternal' republic. There was a clash between the different positions in Serbia in September 1987 when Slobodan Milosevic, at that time President of the Central Committee of the LCS, eliminated his political opponents and pushed through changes in the Serbian constitution (Goati, 1995, p. 18). In March 1989, Serbia officially reinforced its rights over Kosovo and Vojvodina by adopting amendments to the Serbian constitution, which limited the autonomy of the two provinces (Trbovic, 2008, p. 232).

In the meantime, there was a Serbian 'national revival', which took a variety of forms, 'from historical tracts attacking Titoism from both democratic and nationalist points of view, the rehabilitation of the Chetnik record in World War II, calls for the recentralization of the federation on a new democratic foundation, and repeated attacks on party policies in

Kosovo' (Vujacic, 2004, p. 26). Additionally, there was a revival of various aspects of the national past through works of Serbian writers; books deemed reactionary only a few years earlier could suddenly be published.

New forms of mass political action became increasingly popular after 1987, alternatively called mass rallies, protest marches, popular movements, or demonstrations, which were organized throughout the country primarily by supporters of the Milosevic regime. Some rallies were called the 'meetings of truth', as they were supposedly inspired by fears for the human rights of Serbs and Montenegrins in Kosovo and were used to inform the population about the predicament of the Serbian minority in Kosovo (Crnobrnja, 1994, pp. 142, 101–2). These rallies were also used as a populist campaign for Serbian unity, given that there were indeed many Serbs living outside Serbia. Under the pressure of these meetings, the leadership of Vojvodina and Montenegro 'voluntarily' resigned in order to be replaced by people loyal to Milosevic. Between July 1988 and the spring of 1989, 100 such meetings took place across Serbia, involving an estimated 3.5 to 5 million people (Goati, 1995, p. 18; Thomas, 1999, p. 45). These rallies of solidarity with the Serbs in Kosovo reveal the complexity of Milosevic's appeal, where extreme nationalism, populist adoration for the leader, frustrated aspirations for social justice and reform, and nostalgia for the glorious days of Yugoslavia were mixed together (Vujacic, 2004, p. 29).

The biggest of these 'meetings of truth' was organised in Kosovo on 28 June 1989 to mark the 600th anniversary of the Battle of Kosovo.[22] Milosevic delivered a historical speech, invoking traditions, myths, and symbols of Serbian nationalism. This event marked the peak of his charismatic appeal, as he admonished Serbs to remember the main values bequeathed to them by the legacy of the Kosovo battle, such as unity, courage, and heroism (Vujacic, 2004, p. 31). Why were these elite appeals to Serbian nationalism credible to the masses? The ambivalence, complexity, and populist character of Milosevic's wide popularity are well described by Vujacic (2004, p. 30):

> Milosevic's simultaneous appeal to very different constituencies (not just 'nationalism') was key to his political success: Yugoslavia, unity, and Titoism for the party orthodox and army officers; Serbia for the nationalists and state support for the Kosovo Serbs; reform and rehabilitation for the intellectuals; social justice and protection for state-dependent workers and pensioners. ... Milosevic appears as the conciliator of the 'greater Serbian' aspirations of Serbian nationalists and the Yugoslav orientations of army officers, party officials, and

> others; of technocratic aspirations for economic reform and workers' aspirations of social justice; and, finally, as an orthodox communist who violated traditional norms of party behavior by giving free rein to mass activity and thereby satisfied the aspirations for political participation of an audience disgusted with the ineffectiveness of institutions without giving it true representation.

By the end of the 1980s, the economic crisis had been transformed into a more general crisis of a political, social, and moral character. The latent nationalist problem, which President Tito had successfully handled for over three decades,[23] had emerged again, this time in its most extreme form. Whereas Serbian nationalism was disruptive to the delicate Yugoslav balance because of its centralizing assertiveness, Croatian and Slovenian nationalism contributed to the dissolution of Yugoslavia in just the opposite direction, by asking for further decentralization and reduction of federal authority (Crnobrnja, 1994, p. 107).

2.7 From the first multiparty elections to Yugoslavia's break-up

A major problem at the end of the 1980s was the lack of consensus on the future organization of the Yugoslav federation. While Croatia and Slovenia were in favour of transforming Yugoslavia into a loose confederation, Serbia supported by Montenegro wanted a more efficient and more centralized federal state. With the passing of time, it became clear that these two positions could not be reconciled. Within the Communist party, Milosevic insisted on the principle of 'democratic centralism' which meant maintaining his own power, whereas the Slovenes insisted on a looser arrangement in which the League of Communists of Yugoslavia (LCY) would be an alliance of national parties (Crnobrnja, 1994, p. 144). The lack of willingness to find a compromise between these diverging views contributed to the effective dissolution of the LCY on 20–2 January 1990, when the Slovenian delegation walked out of the 14th Extraordinary Congress of the LCY.

The dissolution of the LCY opened the door to political pluralism, to the official acceptance of new political parties, and to the first free multiparty elections. At the end of 1989, the last Yugoslav federal government sought to hold multiparty elections for the Yugoslav parliament, but these elections were, unfortunately, never held. Without free elections at the federal level, the opportunity was lost to form a Yugoslav democratic alternative (Goati, 1995, p. 21). The first multiparty elections in SFR Yugoslavia were held exclusively at the level of the single republics, all of which were organized during 1990 – first in Slovenia in April 1990, followed by Croatia in April–May 1990, in most of the other republics in autumn 1990, and last in Serbia in December 1990. The republican elites often found support among the emerging nationalist opposition, so it is not surprising that in most republics the elections resulted in victory for the nationalistic parties.

In Slovenia, the new government adopted a parliamentary declaration in December 1990 which stated that if a solution on the future of Yugoslavia was not reached in the next six months, Slovenia would proclaim political independence. A plebiscite on independence was organized on 23 December 1990, when 88 per cent of Slovenia's population voted for independence. Since the relations in the federation further deteriorated in the meantime, Slovenia indeed declared its independence on 25 June 1991. The Yugoslav National Army intervened immediately in order to uphold the territorial integrity of SFR Yugoslavia. This was the shortest of the Yugoslav wars: it lasted only 10 days.

The two rounds of elections in Croatia in April–May 1990 brought victory to the right-wing nationalistic Croatian Democratic Alliance (HDZ) led by Franjo Tudjman, who became the first president of Croatia. In the new Croatian constitution, the status of Serbs was reduced from a nation to a national minority, and symbols of traditional Croatian nationalism were adopted, thus provoking increasing fears of the Serb population in Croatia.[24] This provoked the first tensions in the summer of 1990, when the Serbs in the Kninska Krajina proclaimed self-rule and threw log barricades on the main railway line. Thereafter conflicts intensified. In March 1991, a violent confrontation between Croats and Serbs occurred in western Slavonia and the Yugoslav army stepped in to prevent bloodshed. By the time Croatia proclaimed political independence in June 1991, there was a full-fledged Serb-Croat war under way and the Yugoslav National Army sided openly with the Serbs. A cease-fire agreement would be reached only at the end of 1991 (Crnobrnja, 1994, pp. 166, 157).

In Serbia, in the meantime, Slobodan Milosevic arranged the fusion of the League of Communists of Serbia (LCS) with the Socialist Alliance of the Working People of Serbia in July 1990, which led to the creation of the Socialist Party of Serbia (SPS). The Milosevic-led SPS marked its transition from communism to socialism symbolically by abandoning the five-pointed red star in favour of the red rose of European socialism, but beneath the superficial changes there remained a fundamental ideological continuity between the SPS and the LCS, as reflected in the SPS programme prepared in October 1990 (Thomas, 1999, p. 64).

At the December 1990 presidential elections in Serbia, among the candidates for president of Serbia were Slobodan Milosevic (SPS), Vuk Draskovic (Serbian Renewal Movement or SPO), and Ivan Djuric (Alliance of Reform Forces). Slobodan Milosevic was the only candidate that offered continuity of previous policies, thus the status quo, and for many citizens his programme was reassuring; the election slogan of the SPS was 'With us there is no uncertainty'. Vuk Draskovic was a fierce anti-communist, a monarchist and a nationalist, and his right-wing programme that promised cuts in government spending (which also implied lower social transfers), had frightened people. The third candidate Ivan Djuric was the only real reformist, but he entered the campaign too late to gather many votes. Given that the old regime had relatively broad popular support and that the SPS enjoyed a number of institutional advantages, including almost total control over the electronic media, the outcome was not a big surprise. Slobodan Milosevic won the elections with the large majority of votes, 65.34 per cent of the votes cast, Draskovic gained 16.4 per cent, while Ivan Djuric received only 5.52 per cent (Thomas, 1999, p. 74).

The first multiparty elections in Serbia, unlike those in the CEE countries, were not a 'referendum against communism', since the majority of voters supported the SPS as a party of continuity (Goati, 1995, p. 16). In the elections to the parliament, the SPS also scored a convincing victory, garnering 46.1 per cent of the votes. Due to the majority electoral system this assured the SPS 78 per cent of all parliamentary seats, the SPO received 7.6 per cent, while the Democratic Party got only 2.8 per cent (Thomas, 1999, p. 74). In simultaneous elections in Montenegro, the League of Communists won 64 per cent of the votes, and Momir Bulatovic was elected president.

The authoritarian side of the Milosevic regime would come to the surface just a few months after the first multiparty elections. On 9 March 1991, the principal opposition parties – the Serbian Renewal Movement (SPO) and the Democratic Party (DS) – called for the liberalization of the Serbian media, but the meeting was banned by the authorities. Some 40,000 opposition supporters gathered in the centre of Belgrade. The authorities sent tanks against them, which led to the killing of an 18-year old student and a policeman. Vuk Draskovic was arrested, while the independent Studio B TV station and the student radio station B-92 were closed. The SPS organized a counter-meeting attended by a smaller number of pensioners and war veterans, increasing political tensions further.

While in 1987–90 Milosevic's strategy had been formulated within the framework of a federal Yugoslavia, in which Serbia under his control would play the leading role, from March 1991 onwards Milosevic became the enthusiastic advocate and executor of 'Greater Serbia' ideas (Thomas, 1999, p. 86). Franjo Tudjman and Slobodan Milosevic met secretly on a number of occasions during March and April 1991 to discuss a territorial division of Bosnia (Woodward, 1995b, p. 172), thus even before the country split apart.

SFR Yugoslavia effectively disintegrated on 25 June 1991, when Slovenia and Croatia declared political independence. The day after the Yugoslav army intervened in Slovenia, and Prime Minister Markovic called on Slovenia and Croatia to suspend their moves towards independence for three months. The Brioni Agreement on July 7 on ceasefire in Slovenia, between the EC troika and representatives of the Yugoslav federal government and the republics, effectively cleared the way for their eventual recognition (Woodward, 1995b, 168). The EC and the team from the Conference on Security and Cooperation in Europe (CSCE) viewed the problem primarily from the perspective of European security, as a border dispute between Slovenia and the federation, ignoring the origins of the conflict and accepting the solutions proposed by radical nationalist governments in Slovenia, Croatia, and Serbia (Woodward, 1995b, pp. 168–9).

On 16 December 1991, the EC invited all Yugoslav republics to formally apply for recognition of independence within existing borders by December 23, according to criteria established by the Badinter Commission. Slovenia, Croatia, Bosnia and Herzegovina, and Macedonia responded by the set deadline, while Serbia and Montenegro did not. Without waiting for the decision of the Badinter Commission, however, Germany recognized Slovenia and Croatia on December 23, ignoring the EC's joint approach (Woodward, 1995b, p. 184). The EU recognized Croatia and Slovenia on 15 January 1992, and Bosnia and Herzegovina and Macedonia in April 1992. Official recognition of most successor states of SFR Yugoslavia by the United Nations came in May 1992.

The new Yugoslav federation, now consisting of Serbia and Montenegro, became the Federal Republic of Yugoslavia on 27 April 1992, when it also adopted a new constitution. However, it did not get official international recognition for a long time. Milosevic rejected the framework offered, since he insisted on the continuity of former Yugoslavia, hoping that this would assure Serbia and Montenegro a privileged position as the natural successor to the previous Yugoslavia in international relations and international institutions. The insistence on the principle of continuity of FR Yugoslavia blocked its membership in international organizations for almost a whole decade. Only when the United Nations General Assembly adopted Resolution 55/12 on 1 November 2000, did FR Yugoslavia finally become a full-fledged member of the United Nations (Svilanovic, 2000, p. 14).

The transition to a market economy in Serbia was thus interrupted by the break-up of the Yugoslav federation. Thereafter, a number of essentially political events have had very negative implications for most of its successor states, but Serbia was among the most affected. The countries born from the dissolution of SFR Yugoslavia started transition under essentially similar institutional conditions, but thereafter each followed its own transition path, applying different policies, guided by diverse objectives. At present, 20 years later, the gap among the successor states of former Yugoslavia is enormous. This book will pursue the question why Serbia still lags behind some of the other countries.

It could be argued that transition to a market economy in Serbia/SFR Yugoslavia started much earlier, due to the long tradition in market-oriented economic reforms. However, two fundamental events in SFR Yugoslavia in 1989–90 marked a radical break with the past: in the economic sphere, the intention to privatize the bulk of the economy; and in the political sphere, the first free multiparty elections. These two events effectively meant a radical departure from the previous economic and political system, as they announced the intentions to abandon the two main systemic features of communist Yugoslavia – dominance of non-private ownership in the economy and a one-party political system. This is why 1989–90 should be considered the period when transition started in Serbia. The fact that the ruling ideology after 1992 slowed down its implementation and introduced serious reversals does not alter this conclusion.

3
The Early 1990s: Political and Economic Instability

The years after the constitution of FR Yugoslavia came into force on 27 April 1992, now consisting of Serbia and Montenegro, were years of extreme political and economic instability. During this period the Yugoslav economy was negatively affected by a number of external shocks, including the direct effects of the break-up of the Yugoslav federation, several armed conflicts and severe sanctions of the international community. Though these shocks were by their nature 'external', they were the direct outcome or indirect consequence of the political choices of the Serbian/Yugoslav government. The government frequently blamed these external shocks for the progressive worsening of the country's overall situation, not willing to recognize its own responsibility for dragging the country into a very deep political, economic, social, and moral crisis.

The present chapter describes these early days in the new FR Yugoslavia. After giving a brief account of the political situation, it discusses the dramatic consequences for the Yugoslav economy of disintegration, wars, and sanctions, which were further aggravated by highly inadequate economic policies of the government. The macroeconomic stabilization programme implemented in early 1994 by the Yugoslav National Bank governor Dragoslav Avramovic succeeded in halting hyperinflation and reviving production, but the effects were of short duration. Owing to lack of systemic changes and many policy reversals away from transition-related economic reforms, there were no permanent improvements in economic performance. Some of the social consequences of the deep economic crisis are also discussed, including the effects of various financial pyramid schemes.

3.1 Political background

In the new FR Yugoslavia constituted in April 1992, the distribution of political power remained similar to the one created after the first multi-party elections of Serbia in December 1990, which had brought victory to Slobodan Milosevic and his SPS. Despite parliamentary democracy with a number of parties represented in the Serbian parliament,[1] during the 1992–5 period the political system in Serbia was effectively dominated by one party, Milosevic's SPS (Antonic, 1995, p. 32).

During 1992–5, the elections in Serbia for the Yugoslav and the Serbian parliament brought a series of victories to the SPS, either a comfortable parliamentary majority or enough votes to enable it to form a coalition in which it clearly dominated. In addition to Milosevic's popularity, the ruling SPS enjoyed a number of institutional advantages, including ample financial resources and full control of the electronic media, the local government organizations, and the police. The opposition did not formulate a long-term strategy, but remained fragmented and unable to form coalitions, and frequently boycotted the work of the parliament in protest of breaches of procedural rules, where it had to employ all forms of parliamentary obstruction (Antonic, 1995, p. 34). The SPS's convincing dominance in all the elections led to extremely arrogant behaviour in legislative practice; only in July 1994 did the parliamentary majority for the first time vote in favour of a law proposed by the opposition.

Though the facade of democracy was there, the political system had many features of an authoritarian regime. Milosevic did not hesitate to use force and send tanks and special police forces against citizens in mass demonstrations, which after March 1991 became a favourite way of popular protest against the government. There were a number of cases of imprisonment and beating up of demonstrators and key opposition leaders, harassment of the opposition mass media, censorship, arbitrary arrests, and threats. The authoritarian nature of the Milosevic regime can partly explain why it survived for so long, but the inability of the opposition to find common ground and offer a united political platform also bears part of the responsibility.

In an attempt to make his position even stronger, Milosevic tried to involve well-known personalities – such as the respected writer and dissident Dobrica Cosic, who was the first president of FR Yugoslavia; and Milan Panic, an American businessman of Serbian origin, who was its first federal prime minister. But whoever was not willing to fully obey Milosevic was forced to leave. Panic was in favour of peace and the return of FR Yugoslavia to the international community, profoundly disagreeing with Milosevic's policies which, as he put it, had 'built a Chinese wall around Serbia' (Thomas, 1999, pp. 123, 130). Panic was forced out of the government before the expiration of his term, while Cosic was similarly dismissed some time later.

The delay in the effective democratization of Serbia has had its direct implications for the slow pace of economic reforms. There are several distinct features of the process of consolidation of democracy in Serbia in comparison with other CEE countries (Goati, 1995, pp. 9–15).

The first and most important feature was the *continuity* of the League of Communists of Serbia which, after having changed its name into SPS, managed to win all three elections held after the introduction of multiparty democracy (1990, 1992, 1993). Thus the same party which had ruled under the communist regime managed to retain power, and this explains why thereafter there were relatively few changes in the ruling political elite in Serbia. The opposition parties have managed to get only fragments of power in some local councils where they won a majority.

The second distinctive feature is the *deep division* between the ruling SPS and the opposition parties, which resulted primarily from the exclusion of the opposition from participation in crucial decisions in the formative phase of the new system (Goati, 1995, p. 11). The ruling party completely ignored the opposition during the process of establishing the new state, since the Serbian constitution was adopted in September 1990 by the one-party Serbian parliament, therefore before the first multiparty elections held three months later. Given that Serbia's ruling political elite had secured legitimacy as a champion of national interests in 1988–9 and thus enjoyed the support of the majority of Serbian citizens, it did not have to make any concessions to other political forces during the transition to a democratic form of government, but projected the new institutions on its own (Antonic, 1995, p. 27). Thus the 1990 Serbian constitution sharply limited the political power of the parliament, while giving very wide powers to the president, more than in any other East European country (Antonic, 1995, pp. 28–30). In addition, the Yugoslav federal constitution adopted in April 1992 ensured that despite a federal president and prime minister, the essential power was to remain firmly in the hands of the presidents of the two republics, in particular with Slobodan Milosevic as head of Serbia.

The third peculiarity is that Yugoslavia's dissolution and intervention by the Milosevic regime to support Serbs outside Serbia led to *civil war* in 1991. Though the war did not spread to Serbian territory, Serbia's involvement in the wars in Croatia and later in Bosnia and Herzegovina 'threw a dark shadow over Serbia's political life' (Goati, 1995, p. 12).

These military conflicts generated extreme nationalist options on Serbia's political scene, including the ultra-nationalist Radical Party of Serbia (SRS) which was in an informal coalition with the SPS from December 1992 onwards (its leader, Vojislav Seselj, is currently being prosecuted by the ICTY).[2] The war also contributed to an even greater polarization of the political scene in Serbia, particularly after mid-1994 when Milosevic changed his position and decided to support the Vance-Owen Peace Plan (VOPP) for Bosnia. Since the VOPP would have cut off the Serbian held territories in Bosnia from Serbia, this created a new division between those parties that accepted the peace plan and those who regarded it as a betrayal of Serbian national interests (Thomas, 1999).

Another important feature of the Serbian political scene, though not specific to Serbia, was that there was no clear dividing line between *political and economic interests,* since the Serbian political leadership had important business affairs. Large-scale smuggling and the busting of international sanctions had created an entire class of wealthy individuals, some also engaged in criminal activities, with close ties to the political, military, and economic leadership (Pavlakovic, 2005, p. 22).

These are the most essential elements which explain how after 1991 Milosevic successfully consolidated his power within Serbia and FR Yugoslavia. He had strong political power both because of broad popular support and the far-reaching powers assured by the constitution. Milosevic effectively remained the president of Serbia from December 1990 until 1997, when he would be re-elected as president of FR Yugoslavia, retaining this position until October 2000. During this whole period the SPS was to remain dominant in both the federal and the Serbian parliament. These characteristics of the political system in Serbia also help understand the meagre results achieved in the area of transition-related economic reforms.

3.2 External shocks of the early 1990s

The political events of the early 1990s are directly responsible for the highly unsatisfactory economic performance of the Yugoslav economy during that period. Several groups of external shocks have very severely affected the Yugoslav economy – the break-up of the federation, military conflicts, and the UN sanctions (Uvalic, 2001a).

The first external shock on the economies of Serbia and Montenegro was the disintegration of the Yugoslav federation in mid-1991. To these two republics, which would soon become the new FR Yugoslavia, the break-up brought a number of costs and practically no benefits, especially in the longer run. The end of SFR Yugoslavia caused the disintegration of its economic and monetary union, which had a number of negative consequences particularly for Serbia (Uvalic, 1993). The immediate effect included the strong inflationary impact of monetary independence of the other republics, which unloaded their dinar holdings in the Serbian market, in this way contributing to even higher inflation. The end of the economic union also implied the segmentation of monetary channels, provoking serious payment problems immediately before and following the break-up of the country, as well as negative effects of the reduced currency area and lower revenues for the federal government due to the break-up of the customs union. Among the consequences which had a more long-lasting effect was the halt in supplies of inputs at low prices from the other republics, the loss of a large protected market in other parts of the country for Serbian goods, disruptions caused by the termination of long-established traditional links between partners, the substantial drop in trade caused by the introduction of trade barriers by the newly created neighbouring states, lack of interest of foreign investors due to the reduced size of the market, and very high political risk. The disintegration of the Yugoslav economic and monetary union therefore had a number of very negative effects on Serbia's economy, directly contributing to the very deep recession of the early 1990s. Most estimates consider that the disruption of links with other Yugoslav republics has contributed to a drop in GDP of FR Yugoslavia of about 20–25 per cent (Teokarevic, 1998, p. 330).

The second group of external shocks were the military conflicts of the early 1990s, in which FR Yugoslavia was directly or indirectly involved. As already described in Chapter 2, the Yugoslav National Army intervened shortly in June 1991 in Slovenia, immediately after the declaration of its independence; from mid-1991, Serb paramilitary forces and the Yugoslav National Army were involved in the Serb-Croat civil war in Croatia; and during the war in Bosnia and Herzegovina, from May 1992 to November 1995, FR Yugoslavia was supporting the Republika Srpska with military, economic, and humanitarian aid. These wars were extremely costly for FR Yugoslavia, not only in terms of loss of many human lives. The military conflicts have heavily burdened the government budget through war-related expenditure, including the need to maintain some 600,000 refugees and displaced persons. Though the exact level of war-related expenditure has never been determined, some estimates suggest that during 1992–5 20 to 40 per cent of GSP[3] was spent for economic and humanitarian aid to Bosnia and Herzegovina (Teokarevic, 1998, p. 330). The rapid increase in government expenditure has substantially contributed to rising public deficits and the resulting hyperinflation in FR Yugoslavia in 1992–3 (see below).

The third external shock for the Yugoslav economy was the sanctions of the international community. Because of its involvement in armed conflicts during the 1990s, FR Yugoslavia has been subject to various types of sanctions of the United Nations and the EU. Before SFR Yugoslavia officially disintegrated, in late 1991, the UN Security Council prohibited exports of arms to all Yugoslav republics in an attempt to stop the conflict under way. In November 1991, the European Community suspended all trade preferences that were granted under various agreements concluded with SFR Yugoslavia. When the war started in Bosnia and Herzegovina, the UN Security Council passed UN Resolutions 752 and 757 in May 1992 introducing trade and financial sanctions against FR Yugoslavia because of its involvement in the war. These sanctions were broadened and intensified by Resolution 777 of September 1992, Resolution 787 of November 1992, and particularly by Resolution 820 of April 1993.[4]

The May 1992 sanctions called on all UN members and international organizations to block exports and imports, as well as the flow of financial resources into FR Yugoslavia; to deny permission to any aircraft to land on its territory; to reduce the level of staff at diplomatic missions in Belgrade; to prevent the participation of Yugoslavs in sporting events; to suspend scientific and technical cooperation and cultural exchanges with FR Yugoslavia. The only items excluded from the embargo were medicine and foodstuff and other basic items of humanitarian aid. In November 1992 the transshipment through the Yugoslav territory of major commodities was prohibited, including crude oil, oil products, coal, iron, steel, chemicals, rubber, vehicles, metals, aircraft, and motors of all types.

In April 1993, the sanctions were further strengthened: the transport of all kinds of goods across the borders of FR Yugoslavia was prohibited, as well as entry of its ports, while the transshipment of goods along the Danube was subject to prior permission of the Sanctions Committee. In addition, the financial assets of FR Yugoslavia in banks or enterprises abroad were frozen; financial transfers were restricted to the point even of impeding the payment of foreign pensions to Yugoslav beneficiaries; and the provision of financial and non-financial services for doing business with FR Yugoslavia was prohibited (the only exemptions were telecommunications and legal and postal services). The use of Yugoslav freight vehicles and aircrafts abroad were also prohibited, as well as all commercial maritime traffic from entering Yugoslav territorial waters. The coverage of sanctions was extended to include Serb-held areas of Bosnia and Herzegovina and Croatia.

FR Yugoslavia also refused to join, was expelled, or its membership was frozen, in all international organizations, including UN bodies and agencies – IMF, the World Bank, CSCE, and GATT (as of 16 June 1993). On 8 November 1991, the EC Council suspended the broad trade and cooperation agreement concluded with SFR Yugoslavia in 1980, as well as the trade, financial, and textile protocols. SFR Yugoslavia was also excluded from all EC programmes, including COST, supporting cooperation among scientists and researchers, and PHARE, supporting transition to a market economy throughout Eastern Europe. In November 1992, the OECD decided to suspend the cooperation agreement with SFR Yugoslavia, which implied the end of relations with all its successor states.

As of 14 December 1993, FR Yugoslavia had an unregulated legal status in the IMF. On that date the IMF decided to divide SFR Yugoslavia's quota of 613 million special drawing rights (SDR) among its five successor states according to specific criteria, treating all countries as new states (which later would become 918 million SDR). FR Yugoslavia got 36.5 per cent, Croatia 28.5 per cent, Slovenia 16.4 per cent, Bosnia and Herzegovina 13.2 per cent, and Macedonia 5.4 per cent of assets and liabilities of the former federal state. The IMF also fixed a deadline of one month, starting from 15 December 1992, for the Yugoslav successor states to decide whether they wanted to continue membership in the IMF on the basis of the proposed succession, and they had six months to respond to their obligations regarding the repayment of debt (though these deadlines were later prolonged) (Jovovic, 1994, p. 130). FR Yugoslavia was to get 335 million SDR (almost US$ 500 million), somewhat less than what it expected, but by June 1993 it should have paid its financial obligations towards the IMF and the World Bank of about US$ 300 million, approximately US$ 100 million to the IMF and US$ 200 to the World Bank (Jovovic, 1994, pp. 132–3).

In February 1993, FR Yugoslavia and the other Yugoslav republics were admitted to the World Bank as successor states of the former Yugoslavia under the set conditions, but FR Yugoslavia was not invited to the annual meeting of the IMF and to that of the World Bank held in Washington in October 1993, presumably due to the insistence of the US government (Jovovic, 1994, pp. 132–3).

The UN sanctions were therefore very widely based, to include not only a trade embargo and very severe economic sanctions, impeding all business transactions with Yugoslav firms, bank and other financial transfers, foreign direct investment, transport of goods through its territory, access to credits on international financial markets and to programmes of major international organizations, but also cultural, scientific, and sports contacts of FR Yugoslavia with the outside world. Belgrade's airport remained closed for almost three years. The possibilities of travelling abroad were further limited by the general introduction of visas, even by neighbouring countries. During a period of four years, the country was effectively isolated.

On 22 November 1995, immediately after the signing of the Dayton Accords (the General Framework Agreement on Peace) ending the war in Bosnia and Herzegovina, the UN Security Council passed Resolution 1022, suspending the economic sanctions against FR Yugoslavia, their lifting being conditional on the respect of the Dayton Peace Agreement and the first free elections in Bosnia and Herzegovina. After the elections had taken place, the UN Security Council Resolution 1047 of 1 October 1996 called for the definite lifting of all economic sanctions against FR Yugoslavia, which had lasted for four years, four months, and one day (from 30 May 1992 to 1 October 1996).

What remained thereafter, however, was the so-called 'outer' wall of sanctions as some states, primarily the US, were reluctant to fully normalize relations with FR Yugoslavia. The 'outer' wall of sanctions implied that FR Yugoslavia could not normalize its relations with major international organizations and was to remain excluded from the international financial community. In addition, foreign assets that Yugoslav banks and businesses had abroad remained blocked, since the issue of succession regarding the distribution of rights and obligations of SFR Yugoslavia had not been agreed upon. The lifting of the 'outer' wall of sanctions was conditional on FR Yugoslavia's cooperation with the ICTY in The Hague, respect of the Dayton Peace Accords and the agreement on succession with the other successor states of SFR Yugoslavia.[5] Only with the political changes in October 2000 would these sanctions be definitely lifted (though in the meantime, as described in Chapter 4, new sanctions would be introduced in 1998–9 following the crisis in Kosovo).

Several studies have tried to quantify the various effects for the Yugoslav economy of the break-up, wars, and sanctions, giving a wide range of estimates. There are several reasons why the actual costs of these external shocks are very difficult to calculate (Teokarevic, 1998, pp. 329–33). First, there are no reliable figures on the importance of the grey economy and illegal trade during those years, which would indicate the extent to which international sanctions were not respected. Second, it is virtually impossible to establish the relative weight of each of these groups of interconnected shocks – loss of markets, military conflicts, and UN sanctions – in determining the sharp fall in GDP. A number of studies in FR Yugoslavia, in an attempt to attribute all the negative effects solely to UN sanctions, have grossly overestimated the effects of sanctions, thus underestimating the role of other factors, even totally neglecting the role of the flawed economic policies of the Yugoslav government. Some of these estimates have also tried to include 'lost GDP' within the overall costs of the external shocks, based on highly unrealistic hypotheses on GDP growth of the Yugoslav economy in the 1990s. These various estimates therefore remain controversial.

Notwithstanding the difficulties of quantifying the various effects, there is no doubt that both the economic and political costs of UN sanctions against FR Yugoslavia have been enormous. Though the trade embargo was not respected in full, it still caused a very sharp drop in foreign trade, severely affecting not only exports but also a large part of the Yugoslav industry which was traditionally dependent on imported raw materials or semi-finished products. The lack of possibilities to import spare parts or modernize existing industrial capacity have pushed entire sectors into technological backwardness. The sharp reduction in cooperation with foreign universities and scientific contacts has left profound consequences for research, education, and the state of universities and libraries (Uvalic, 2005a).

3.3 Economic performance: 'Hyper-stagflation'

Following the disintegration of SFR Yugoslavia, the joint effect of the collapse of inter-regional trade, loss of markets in neighbouring republics, military conflicts, international sanctions, and highly inappropriate economic policies led the Yugoslav economy in 1992–3 into a state of 'hyper-stagflation'. FR Yugoslavia experienced one of the deepest recessions among all transition countries, parallel with what at that time was the second highest and second longest hyperinflation ever recorded in economic history (Petrovic et al., 1999).

Already in 1990 and 1991, the joint real GSP of Serbia and Montenegro, the two republics which would soon form the FR Yugoslavia, registered a sharp fall of 7.9 per cent and 11.6 per cent respectively (see Table 3.1). Following the break-up of the Yugoslav federation in mid-1991, the economy of the new FR Yugoslavia virtually collapsed, as its GSP in 1992 dropped by 27.9 per cent, and in 1993 by a further 30.8 per cent.

Thus from 1990 to 1993, in only four years, real GSP of Serbia and Montenegro/FR Yugoslavia registered a cumulative fall of approximately 80 percentage points (see Table 3.1).

Industrial production over the same period (1990–3) fell even more sharply – by 12 per cent in 1990, 18 per cent in 1991, 22 per cent in 1992, and 37 per cent in 1993 – reaching the lowest point immediately before and after the monetary reconstruction programme on 24 January 1994 (Avramovic, 1995a). At the end of 1993 industry functioned at less than a fourth of its capacity. GSP per capita of Serbia and

Table 3.1 Serbia and Montenegro/FR Yugoslavia: Main macroeconomic indicators, 1989–95

	1989	1990	1991	1992	1993	1994	1995
Inflation (% change in annual retail prices)	1,269	593	121	9,237	116.5 trillion	3.3	78.6
Real GDP growth (%)	1.3	–7.9	–11.6	–27.9	–30.8	2.5	6.1
Industrial production (%)	1	–12	–18	–22	–37	1	4
Public deficit (% of GDP)	NA	–3	–13	–21	–34	NA	–4.3
Employed (in thousands)	2,790	2,707	2,625	2,536	2,464	2,413	2,379
Unemployed (in thousands)	607	663	714	748	739	726	775
Unemployment (% of labour force)	NA	NA	NA	NA	23.1	23.1	24.6
Exports* (million US$)	5,348	5,815	4,704	2,479	NA	NA	NA
Imports* (million US$)	6,195	7,460	5,548	3,638	NA	NA	NA
Current account (% of GDP)	NA	–1.8	–2.1	–5.0	NA	NA	NA

*No official figures for exports, imports and the current account are available for 1992–5, while the country was under the UN trade embargo.

Sources: EBRD (2001), *Transition Report Update;* Republicki zavod za statistiku Srbije (various publications); Economist Intelligence Unit (1995); general government balances 1989–94 are unofficial estimates, based on data reported in Petrovic (1996), Petrovic et al. (1999), Institut ekonomskih nauka, *Mesecne Analize i Prognoze*, April 1995 and CES MECON (1993).

Montenegro had fallen from US$ 2200 in 1990 to US$ 950 in 1993 (Petrovic, 1996, p. 174).

The economic policies of the Yugoslav and Serbian governments during 1991–3 were guided primarily by political priorities. The policy measures implemented in order to stop the further deterioration of the economic situation were inadequate and counterproductive. Yugoslav hyperinflation was driven by an excess money supply that monetized the various deficits that emerged after the disintegration of SFR Yugoslavia. Money growth fuelled currency depreciation and increasing inflation, so at a certain point the central bank lost control over the money supply (Petrovic et al., 1999).

During 1991–3, there was a dramatic increase in public expenditure, used for military and other forms of aid in the ongoing war in Bosnia and Herzegovina, maintaining refugees and displaced persons, enterprise subsidies, and social transfers. FR Yugoslavia was left with much of the huge bureaucracy, including the sizable military and police, which previously served a much larger country (Petrovic et al., 1999, p. 338).

After the introduction of the UN sanctions, the government's deliberate policy of maintaining social peace led to the reinforcement of the principle of employment security and toleration of losses, which additionally burdened the government budget. At the same time, public revenues were drastically reduced under the impact of the strong recession and sharp drop in production, declining transfers from the republics to the federal budget, loss of customs revenues after the break up of the Yugoslav federation, the effects of the UN trade embargo, and decreasing real value of revenues which accompanied the acceleration of inflation.

Though there are no fully reliable statistics on public expenditure and revenues of Serbia and Montenegro in those years, some estimates indicate that public expenditure increased from 49 per cent in 1990 to 63 per cent in 1991, and to 70–5 per cent of GSP in 1992; at the same time, public revenues declined continuously, from 46 per cent of GSP in 1990 to a low 11 per cent in 1993 (Popovic and Stamenkovic, 1994; Petrovic, 1996). There was a total collapse of the tax system. The resulting estimated public deficit, in per cent of GSP, increased from 3 per cent in 1990 to 13 per cent in 1991, further to 21 per cent in 1992, and to 34 per cent in 1993 (see Table 3.1).

The monetization of the fiscal deficit started already in 1991. The seigniorage[6] was high throughout the 1991–3 period, at approximately 10 per cent of GDP, similar to that in Bolivia in the 1980s (Petrovic et al., 1999). The Yugoslav government budget financed all public expenditure irrespective of revenues. The escalation of the war in Croatia and later in Bosnia and Herzegovina were associated with transfers to the Serb-controlled parts of the two successor states, which led the government to postpone fiscal adjustments. The public deficits at various levels were covered either directly through the unrestrained issuing of money, or indirectly, by tolerating soft-budget constraints thus prolonging the life of loss-making enterprises, issuing of cheques without effective backing, and the deliberate postponements of various payments (Popovic and Stamenkovic, 1994). New emission was also used to directly finance enterprises which were severely affected by the UN embargo. The coverage of public deficits through the printing of money directly contributed to inflation, while inflation continuously decreased the real value of public revenues (the Olivera-Tanzi effect),[7] thus contributing to an increasing public deficit which in turn required the additional monetary emission.

War-driven expansionary fiscal and monetary policies quickly led the economy into hyperinflation. The inflation rate in Serbia and Montenegro, as elsewhere in SFR Yugoslavia, had already in 1989 become hyperinflation. Although the stabilization programme implemented in 1990–1 resulted in some improvements (see Table 3.1), after the break up of the country and the severe fall in production in 1991–2, inflation rapidly accelerated. During 1991 inflation was still at a monthly rate of 10 per cent, but in February 1992 it exceeded 50 per cent, thus becoming hyperinflation (according to established conventions), and in 1993 it exploded into extreme hyperinflation. Monthly rates went from 200 per cent at the beginning of 1993 to 400 per cent in June–July, 2000 per cent in August and October, 20,000 per cent in November, 180,000 per cent in December, and finally 313,000,000 per cent in January 1994 (Petrovic, 1996, p. 174).

On an annual basis, the average retail price inflation in FR Yugoslavia increased from 9237 per cent in 1992 to 116.5 trillion (or 116.5×10^{12}) per cent in 1993, corresponding to a 15-digit inflation rate of 116,545,906,563,330 per cent (see Figure 3.1). The peak was reached in January 1994, when prices rose by 60 per cent per day, or an estimated monthly rate of 313 million per cent, thus becoming, at that time, the second highest recorded rate of inflation after the Hungarian hyperinflation of 1945–6 (today third, since Zimbabwe's hyperinflation in 2008 has become second).[8] In addition, the hyperinflation in FR Yugoslavia lasted 24 months, making it the second longest recorded in world history, after the Russian hyperinflation in the 1920s which lasted 26 months (Petrovic et al., 1999, p. 336).

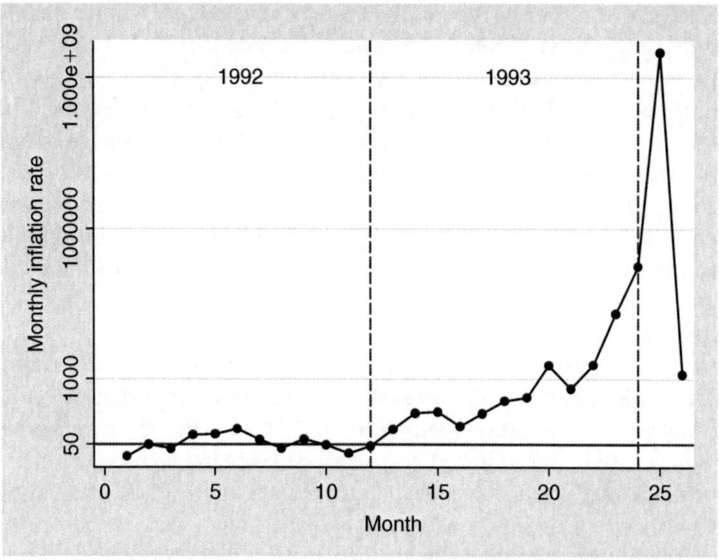

Figure 3.1 Monthly rate of inflation in Serbia and Montenegro/FR Yugoslavia (January 1992–February 1994)
Note: The scale is logarithmic.
Source: Based on data in Kedzic (2005), p. 51.

The money supply in FR Yugoslavia during this period of hyperinflation grew unpredictably (Petrovic et al., 1999, p. 351). The NBY lost control over money creation also because currency was being issued illegally by the four regional central banks in Serbia, Montenegro, Vojvodina, and Kosovo, as well as the Social Auditing Office. Households were also issuing checks extensively without backing. Only a fraction of the total increase in money supply was used to cover the fiscal deficit of the federal government, which accounted for one-fifth to one-sixth of the total public deficit. The remaining budget deficit was due largely to the deficit of the Serbian government, and to a much lesser extent to that of Montenegro. The bulk of the money supply went to cover regional deficits, but was also distributed in the form of soft loans to support production of large socially owned firms that were severely hit by the UN economic embargo (Petrovic et al., 1999, p. 341).

Hyperinflation and sharply declining production were accompanied by shortages of many products. In early 1992 there were shortages of washing powder, cooking oil, and sugar, while the government introduced restrictions on the sale of basic foodstuff including wheat, maize, flour, sugar, and cooking oil, creating an artificial monopoly over products which Serbia normally had in abundance. While ordinary citizens raced around shops looking for goods, the political elite and well-connected businessmen grew rich by selling these commodities at monopoly prices (Dinkic, 1995, p. 33). After the introduction of the UN sanctions in May 1992, the government adopted a package of emergency measures which were to protect the fall in the standard of living, including the freezing of wages and prices of about half of all goods (including basic food items, energy, and infrastructure services), and coupons for petrol. Despite abundant food production in Serbia, these measures only contributed to further shortages, and by the end of 1993 shops were almost completely empty.

While excessive money supply was the driving force of Yugoslav hyperinflation, currency depreciation also played an important role in the dynamics of hyperinflation (Petrovic et al., 1999, p. 336). The strong growth of money supply was followed by a sharp decrease in real money holdings. Hyperinflation led to the practical disappearance of the dinar (the Yugoslav national currency) as a means of payment and a unit of account. In order to protect themselves from inflationary losses, citizens and enterprises increasingly exchanged their dinar holdings into foreign currency on the black foreign exchange market, which led to the replacement of domestic with foreign currency and the almost complete 'DMarkization', namely the prevalent use of the German mark in transactions.

Owing to the general shortage of foreign currency, resident convertibility was officially suspended already in December 1991. A new Yugoslav dinar was also introduced which was devalued in January and April 1992, but with inflation rising at a monthly rate of over 80 per cent in May 1992 the margin between the black market exchange rate and the official rate rapidly increased. In June 1992, the official exchange rate was still held at YD 200 = DM1, while the black market rate was already six times higher, YD 1200 = DM 1 (see Figure 3.2). In only two and a half years, from the Markovic stabilization programme in SFR Yugoslavia in December 1989 to June 1992, the exchange rate moved from DM1 = YD 7 to DM1 = YD 1200, corresponding to a depreciation of 99.42 per cent. In June 1992, therefore, the dinar was worth a bit more than half per cent of its value in 1989 (Uvalic, 1993).

Several other currency reforms were implemented from mid-1992 onwards, which proved equally unsuccessful. On 1 July 1992 the Yugoslav dinar was converted into a new dinar at a rate of 10:1 (one zero was eliminated in all accounting) and was pegged to the US dollar at the exchange rate of YD 200 = US$1. For a short period, the withdrawal of foreign exchange from bank accounts was possible, but only in dinars

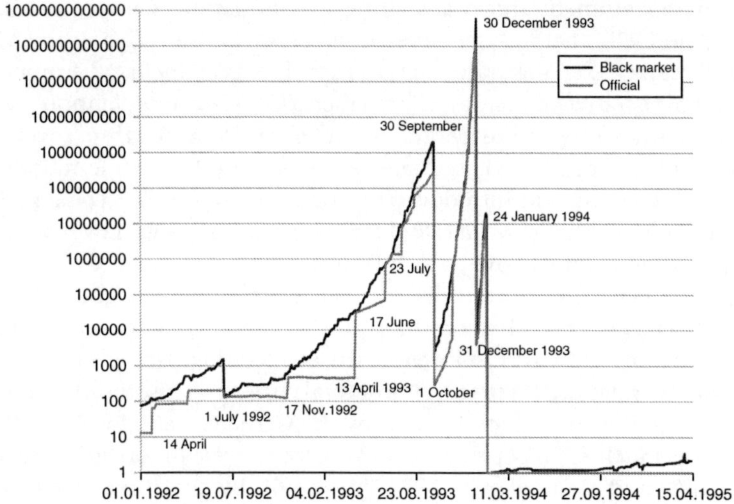

Figure 3.2 FR Yugoslavia: Official and black market exchange rate of the dinar, 1992–5
Note: The scale is logarithmic.
Source: Data of the National Bank of Yugoslavia.

at the official exchange rate, and up to the equivalent of DM 150 per month. These measures initially somewhat reduced inflation – the monthly rate of retail prices in August was down to 42 per cent – but thereafter inflation accelerated and the black market exchange rate again increased well above the official rate.

On 17 November 1992, the dinar was again officially devalued and the new exchange rate was fixed at YD 750 = US$1. Thereafter, up until mid-April 1993, thus for a period of five months, there were no further changes in the official exchange rate, despite the acceleration of inflation. This was the longest period that the NBY kept the official exchange rate constant, which along with galloping inflation resulted in a precipitous increase in the black market exchange rate and a widening gap between the official and black market rate. After 13 April 1993, the adjustments of the official exchange rate became more frequent, as the NBY adjusted the official exchange rate continuously, but not even daily adjustments kept pace with the increasing black market rate. On 17 June and again on 23 July 1993 there were two further major adjustments of the official exchange rate, with equally unsuccessful results (see Figure 3.2).

Given the continuous deterioration of the economic situation, in August 1993 a new package of economic measures was implemented by the government aimed at halting hyperinflation, reviving production, and eliminating the differential between the official and the black market exchange rate. The package, however, included a number of administrative measures which increased state intervention even further. The price freeze became even more widespread, to cover all items in the consumer basket and all public utilities, while rationing through coupons was introduced for some basic foodstuff (cooking oil, sugar, flour, washing powder) and for energy and strategic raw materials (Popovic and Stamenkovic, 1994; Dinkic, 1995).

As in the past, price controls only aggravated the shortages and contributed to a further fall in production. The minor reduction in inflation in September 1993 was followed by its acceleration. Under pressure of galloping inflation, there was almost total currency substitution and the replacement of the Yugoslav dinar by the German mark. By the end of 1993, as much as 98 per cent of banking assets were in foreign currency (Popovic and Stamenkovic, 1994, pp. 20–6). By that time, there was such a sharp acceleration in the rate of change of the official exchange rate that the currency regime practically lost all attributes of a fixed regime.

Owing to galloping hyperinflation, on 30 September 1993 the dinar was again redenominated by eliminating six zeros, but the effects were of very short duration since inflation was increasing even more rapidly and the black market exchange rate precipitated again. The last attempt to stabilize the economy through an even more drastic adjustment of the exchange rate was undertaken on 31 December 1993, when the dinar was redenominated by dropping another nine zeros. Since all these attempts were highly unsuccessful, something more radical had to be devised to stabilize the Yugoslav economy. This was done in the Avramovic stabilization programme that was implemented on 24 January 1994 (see below).

Econometric evidence testing the direct pass-through of the exchange rate into the price level in FR Yugoslavia confirms these conclusions (Mladenovic and Petrovic, 2009). During the years of hyperinflation, in 1991–3, the pass-through from the exchange rate to prices was complete (equal to 1) and instant, taking place within a month. During this period of hyperinflation in FR Yugoslavia, the exchange rate therefore was the immediate driver of increasing inflation (though this is also true for the post-hyperinflation period, see Chapter 4).

Economic policies of the FR Yugoslav government during 1992–4 were therefore not only ineffective, but highly inconsistent and counterproductive. Most policies were characterized by stop-go measures – in the area of prices, exchange rate, interest rates – and thus produced just the opposite effects of what they were aimed to achieve. Periods of general price freezes were followed by price liberalization, resulting in the acceleration of inflation. The official exchange rate was initially adjusted to the black market exchange rate only sporadically and with substantial delays, without any consistent policy in this area. After April 1993, the exchange rate began being adjusted more frequently, even on a daily basis, but with galloping inflation the economy was only dragged into even higher monetary instability. Interest rates did not follow inflationary trends and continued to be negative in real terms. The government was unwilling or unable to undertake the necessary fiscal adjustments in response to the severe decline in output and external trade flows, which resulted in an increasing fiscal deficit, hyperinflation, and currency replacement.

3.4 The Avramovic stabilization programme

Hyperinflation was finally stopped through a macroeconomic stabilization programme implemented on 24 January 1994 by the newly appointed governor of the NBY, Dragoslav Avramovic. The programme consisted of stopping the printing of the old dinars completely on 24 January 1994 with the aim of freezing prices in old dinars, and introducing a currency board. Although FR Yugoslavia had remained with very limited foreign exchanges reserves, which were mostly blocked abroad and the IMF could not help due to membership being suspended because of sanctions,[9] a currency board was introduced using the reserves of around DM 350 million as backing for the issue of the new convertible dinar (the 'super dinar'), which was pegged to the German mark at a one-to-one basis (YD1 = DM1). For six months in 1993, there were two domestic currencies in circulation linked by the fixed exchange rate (DM 1 = new YD 1 = old YD 12 million) (Avramovic, 1995a). The old dinars remained in circulation since there was not enough foreign exchange to back up its entire replacement; they could be used for all payments domestically, but could not be converted into foreign exchange. In support of the programme, a policy of positive real interest rates was implemented, measures were undertaken to accelerate the collection of unpaid taxes, and some new taxes were introduced.

The macroeconomic stabilization programme was initially successful in halting hyperinflation, introducing resident convertibility of the new national currency, and reversing the trend of declining output. Though prices were still high in February, they started declining from

March onwards and annual inflation for the whole of 1994 was only 3.3 per cent. Production started increasing in February 1994 and GSP for the whole year registered a positive 2.5 per cent growth rate (see Table 3.1 and Avramovic, 1995a, p. 9). The fixed exchange rate was initially maintained and in only three months foreign currency reserves had almost doubled, reaching DM 600 million. Though the programme started with a high public deficit, with the abrupt halt in inflation there was the inverse Olivera-Tanzi effect and fiscal revenues started increasing, thus substantially reducing the budget deficit.

The positive effects of the stabilization programme, however, lasted for only around five months. The reasons can be traced to 9 June 1994, when monetary emission stopped being backed by foreign exchange reserves (Labus, 1995). Official reserves were increasing, but not fast enough to provide for the rising demand for money. Although the official exchange rate remained fixed at DM1 = YD1 (this parity was maintained up until 26 November 1995), the currency board regime was abandoned. The hyper-fixed exchange rate, through the presumed irrevocable currency board parity, could no longer be backed by foreign currency.

The stabilization programme was undermined by the policies of the same institution that had introduced it – the NBY. After July 1994, there was a marked change in credit policy, as the NBY decided to stimulate industrial growth through easing of money supply. Excessive monetary expansion took place during summer to autumn 1994, which led to an excessive expansion of effective demand (Avramovic, 1995a). The revival of production and rising money supply was coupled with increasing demand for foreign exchange, since importers of raw materials were granted additional quotas of import licences (Labus, 1995). From September 1994 onward prices started increasing again – by 1.4 per cent in October, 7 per cent in November, and 2.5 per cent in December. By December 1994, the gap between the official and the black market exchange rate again widened and resident convertibility was suspended (Avramovic, 1995a).

Macroeconomic stabilization could not be sustained since the basic premise for the success of the stabilization programme, the hyper-fixed exchange rate backed by foreign currency, was abandoned. This is because there were no radical and permanent fiscal reforms, nor fundamental changes in the economic system (Petrovic, 1996). The halt in inflation was erroneously considered sufficient for fiscal stabilization, while the NBY did not make any commitments about the timing or ending of budgetary deficit financing (Labus, 1995). A huge hidden fiscal deficit remained, deriving from subsidies to loss-making state enterprises in the electricity sector, funds needed for buying out agricultural surpluses, and the coverage of losses of a large number of social sector enterprises. The postponement of the repayment of loans which had been extended at the beginning of the programme was also frequent (Petrovic, 1996). Restrictive monetary and fiscal policies had effectively been relaxed.

Although in January 1995 the NBY tightened monetary policy sharply to restore stability, together with the freezing of wages at their November 1994 level and tighter control over banks, the incomes policy was not successful since the limits set were not respected. By the end of March 1995, there were many signs of serious imbalances, suggesting that inflationary pressures were still deeply rooted in the economic system. After a low 3 per cent average inflation rate in 1994, inflation again jumped to over 78 per cent in 1995 (see Table 3.1 above). The parity introduced by the Avramovic stabilization programme, fixed at DM1 = YD1, would be abandoned only on 26 November 2005 (when it passed to DM 1 = YD3.3).

3.5 Delayed transition

Owing to extreme political and economic instability after 1992 in FR Yugoslavia, reforms of the economic system were also substantially delayed. While part of the slowdown was caused by the exceptional political and economic circumstances which brought other priorities to the government agenda, the transition was also blocked by the unwillingness of the government to implement any more radical economic reforms.

Although transition to a market economy in Serbia started before the break-up of SFR Yugoslavia in 1988–9 (see Chapter 2), the difficult conditions that emerged after mid-1992 effectively led to its suspension. Instead of the liberalization of markets and trade, the adoption of various emergency packages introduced a series of administrative measures – general and selective price freezes, frequent wage limits and controls, and rationing of the most essential products. The international trade embargo, by prohibiting foreign trade with FR Yugoslavia, effectively reversed the trade liberalization measures implemented in 1990–1. The foreign exchange system was characterized by serious distortions, including the official non-convertibility of the dinar, a high black market premium, and rationing of foreign exchange. Instead of policies aimed at increasing competition and industrial restructuring, enterprise bankruptcy was suspended during the international sanctions, while those firms most affected by the embargo were directly subsidized through new emissions. These measures clearly implied just the opposite of what was required by the transition to a market economy.

The restructuring of the labour market was also greatly delayed by the emergency measures aimed at easing the effects of sanctions. The government promised the population there that would be no layoffs during the period of international sanctions, and in April 1993 the Serbian parliament transformed this promise into a law, by officially prohibiting the firing of employees for the duration of the embargo (Babic, 2000). This regulation practically froze employment in a large part of the economy, creating the parallel existence of over-employment and effective under-employment. Since many factories were working at limited capacity, workers frequently had to go on 'forced vacation' during which they had the right to a wage of 50–100 per cent of the minimum net wage (Popovic and Stamenkovic, 1994, p. 34). The protection of workers' right to employment had been maintained, where jobs were an in-kind benefit and a key element of social welfare, as was the practice in SFR Yugoslavia (Bartlett and Uvalic, 1992).

One area where some new legislation was adopted during this period was privatization, though the changes introduced actually slowed down its implementation and reconfirmed the non-critical attitude of the Serbian government towards 'social property'. Although privatization in Serbia and Montenegro started on the basis of the 1989–90 Law on social capital (see Chapter 2), with disintegrating tendencies gaining ground all Yugoslav republics decided to adopt their own privatization legislation. Serbia adopted a new privatization law in August 1991 and Montenegro in January 1992.

The 1991 Serbian privatization law was also based on sales to employed workers and managers at privileged terms, but the conditions were more restrictive in comparison to the previous law. Insiders had the right to a basic discount of 20 per cent and an additional 1 per cent for each year of employment (up to a maximum of 60 per cent) and a 5-year repayment period, but there were limits on the maximum that could be subscribed (the dinar equivalent of DM 20,000 per worker and DM 30,000 per manager/director). Unlike all the other successor states of former Yugoslavia as well as the republic of Montenegro, however, Serbia decided to retain 'social property' as one of the main property forms, implying that privatization was in no way imposed on enterprises as obligatory. Such an attitude towards social property was sanctioned already in the Serbian constitution adopted in 1990, which guaranteed the equal treatment of all property forms; Article 56 stated that 'Social, state, private and cooperative property … shall be guaranteed' and that 'All forms of ownership enjoy equal protection of law.'

In comparison with the first wave of privatizations in Serbia implemented in 1990–91, the Serbian law brought far worse results. During the first year of application of the federal law of SFR Yugoslavia, from mid-1990 to mid-1991, some 1220 social sector enterprises in Serbia (or 33 per cent of the total) had started privatization (Zec et al., 1994). By contrast, during almost three years of application of the Serbian law (August 1991 – April 1994), privatization was commenced by only 688 enterprises, thus a bit more than half of the number that had done so before August 1991 (see Table 3.2).

If we consider the overall results of privatization in Serbia from 1990 to April 1994, around 61 per cent of all socially owned enterprises had entered the process of property transformation. Most of these firms were privatized through share issues to employees at privileged terms, transforming their status into shareholding or other types of companies typically in mixed ownership, though a few firms have also been completely privatized. Some 80 per cent of workers in privatizing firms decided to participate in privatization, leading to the creation of some 525,000 workers-shareholders who had subscribed shares of their enterprise. The capital structure in these enterprises after transformation, on average, was 80 per cent private and 20 per cent social capital (Zec et al. 1994, p. 241).

These results were to a great extent invalidated through amendments of the privatization law adopted in August 1994. Since the 1991 Serbian privatization law envisaged the revaluation of the unpaid portion of shares only once a year, under hyperinflationary conditions such as those in 1992–3 many individuals were able to pay off subscribed shares with extremely small amounts of money. Stressing the unfair outcome of privatization, some opposition parties pushed for amendments which introduced the obligatory *ex post* revaluation of capital in all privatizing or fully privatized enterprises.

These 1994 amendments on capital revaluation were inappropriate, untimely, and unfair to the new shareholders, and also had very negative longer-term consequences. They introduced wrong revaluation coefficients which grossly overvalued social capital and consequently reduced the relative share of privatized capital (Vujacic, 1996, pp. 398–9). After the process was terminated, enterprises were to be left with 1–40 per cent of private capital, depending on when privatization had started; those firms that started privatization in 1993 under hyperinflation had

Table 3.2 Privatization results in Serbia, 1990–4

Laws	Federal	Law	Serbian	Law			TOTAL
	Aug.–Dec. 1990	**Jan.–Aug. 1991**	**Aug.–Dec. 1991**	**Jan.–Dec. 1992**	**Jan.–Dec. 1993**	**Jan.–April 1994**	**Aug. 1990–April 1994**
Transformed enterprises – Total	169	1051	34	139	469	46	1904
– Central Serbia	63	617	19	76	255	21	1051
– Vojvodina	106	431	15	59	200	23	834
– Kosovo	0	3	0	4	10	2	19
In % of all firms*		33.17				27.8	60.97

*Refers to enterprises in the social sector.

Source: Uvalic (1997a), pp. 285–9, based on Zec et al. (1994).

remained with no more than 1–2 per cent of capital in private ownership. Many workers also had to renounce subscribed shares, since the new price was too high (Uvalic, 1994). These amendments have also blocked the further implementation of privatization, by obliging all firms to undergo the burdensome process of capital revaluation which led to many controversial cases that have been in the courts for years (Cerovic, 2000).

Parallel with the slowdown in privatization, a state sector was also created in 1992–3 through the tacit re-nationalization of parts of the Yugoslav economy. Some strategically important enterprises in the social sector, mainly public utilities – in railways, highways, air transport, water supply, post and telegraph, radio and television, forestry, and energy – were transformed into public and state-owned firms. Already in 1992, these firms represented 42 per cent of fixed capital and 23 per cent of total employment of the Yugoslav economy (Zec et al., 1994, p. 289). Their number increased over the next few years, as by the end of 1994, there were 604 public enterprises in FR Yugoslavia, of which 530 were in Serbia (Savezni zavod za statistiku, 1995, p. 45). These nationalizations of social property to the benefit of the state were legally regulated through a law adopted in 1995, amended in 1996 and 1997.[10] Many Serbian economists have evaluated this transfer of enterprises from the social to the state sector as a step backwards, as a loss of some advantages that Yugoslavia had with respect to other communist countries (Cerovic, 2000).

Proposals for more radical systemic changes were advanced in November 1995 by the central bank governor Dragoslav Avramovic in his 'Programme II', which was aimed at increasing competitiveness of the Yugoslav economy once the international sanctions had been lifted in late 1995 (Avramovic, 1995b). Avramovic stressed the need to liberalize markets, both internal and external, and to restore the value of the national currency through the return of convertibility. The liberalization of foreign trade required the reduction or elimination of trade barriers, while the inadequate industrial structure required the breaking up of existing monopolies and increasing competition. What was also urgent was large-scale privatization which Avramovic called 'the democratization of property relations', along with encouraging foreign direct investment and the re-establishment of relations with the IMF. None of the measures proposed in 'Programme II' were implemented, however. Avramovic would face increasingly fierce opposition from within the Yugoslav government, and in May 1996 would be forced to resign (Chapter 4).

3.6 Social consequences of the economic crisis

The economic crisis which hit FR Yugoslavia in the early 1990s brought dramatic social consequences. If we consider the situation on the labour market, the number of employed persons in Serbia and Montenegro declined by almost 20 per cent over the 1989–95 period, although the process was somewhat slowed down after 1992 (see Table 3.1). There were minor labour adjustments after 1992 because of rigid labour legislation guaranteeing employment security and populist policies which prohibited the firing of workers while international sanctions were in force. Since workers could not be laid off, enterprises would send them on 'forced vacation'.

For the same reasons the upward trend in registered unemployment was discontinued after 1992. In addition, many jobseekers were discouraged by the reduced demand for labour, thus no longer registering with the employment agencies. Consequently, after an increase in registered unemployment from over 600,000 in 1989 to 750,000 in 1992, during 1993–4 there was a slight reduction. Nevertheless, the official unemployment rate in 1993–4 was already at 23 per cent and would rise further to 25 per cent in 1995 (see Table 3.1). By 1994, in addition to some 1,412,000 pensioners, 600,000 refugees and almost 750,000 registered unemployed persons, there were also 800,000 to 1 million workers who were effectively without work on 'forced vacation' (Posarac, 1996).

There were also increasing signs of impoverishment of the Serbian society, as real incomes declined dramatically from 1991 onwards. Total earnings of households in 1994 were by some 55–60 per cent lower than in 1989 (Posarac, 1996). Monthly real wages of social sector employees had fallen dramatically, from around DM 800 in 1991 to barely DM 26 in January 1994. In 1990 only 6.23 per cent of the population in Serbia were living below the poverty line, but the proportion had risen to 35.6 per cent by mid-1994 (Posarac, 1996). In 1990 the rural population was relatively poorer than the urban population, but by 1994 the situation had been reversed. Many citizens had to rely on agricultural products provided by relatives living in the countryside or free meals offered by the state as part of social assistance to the poor. The inequality in the distribution of income in Serbia also increased, as the Gini coefficient during 1990–4 increased by 12.2 per cent (Posarac, 1996, p. 188).[11]

The difficult economic situation in Serbia under international sanctions, falling production, and widespread shortages created ideal conditions for the flourishing of the grey economy. The sanctions had made smuggling and breaking the embargo a very profitable business.

While the most important illegal activities were in the hands of a small group of businessmen close to the political authorities, the government generally tolerated the underground economy since it provided an alternative income to many citizens who had effectively remained unemployed. Estimates indicate that the share of the grey economy went up from 24 per cent of total economic activity (including both registered GSP and the grey economy) in 1991, to around 29 per cent in 1992, while the share of wages in the total income of the population declined from 51 per cent in 1991 to 37 per cent in 1992 (Bozovic, 1994, pp. 106–9). The violations of the rule of law, corruption, and the criminalization of society became widespread, greatly hindering the development of true democratic institutions (Pavlakovic, 2005, p. 22).

3.7 Hyperinflation and income redistribution

During the 1991–3 period the impoverishment of large parts of the Serbian society took place through a number of channels which brought massive income redistribution from the population at large in favour of the state and the economic and political elite. Hyperinflation in 1992–3, through the inflation tax, was the main instrument for the redistribution of income in favour of the state, but there were also other channels which, given the abnormal conditions as those in 1992–3, effectively deprived many Yugoslav citizens of their life-time savings. These events left behind extremely negative long-term consequences for the Serbian society, since they have strongly undermined confidence in the state, its institutions, and social justice.

One of the first attempts of the Serbian authorities to attract citizens' savings was the government loan for the economic renewal of Serbia, announced in June 1989. The launch of the public loan coincided with the nationalist rally in Kosovo and was accompanied by a lot of publicity, but the loan produced very meagre results. By the beginning of December 1989, only 2–5 per cent of the amount planned in foreign currency had been subscribed, while the part in dinars, although subscribed almost in full, was being devalued by rising inflation. A new media campaign began and a special commission was created in order to persuade enterprises to make contributions, but the total amount collected remained unimpressive (Dinkic, 1995, pp. 77–9).

Another measure with more long-term consequences was undertaken by SFR Yugoslavia's government in spring 1991, consisting of the official freezing of bank savings accounts of Yugoslav citizens, apparently justified by the general shortage of foreign currency. At that time, there was a substantial amount of foreign exchange, around DM 8.7 billion, deposited in Yugoslav banks on savings accounts of Serbian and Montenegrin citizens (Dinkic, 1995, p. 70). This created the problem of 'old foreign currency savings' which the Yugoslav government continued owing to its citizens for almost a whole decade. It is only after the radical political changes of October 2000 that the government would address the problem and subsequently also find a solution for repaying citizens their foreign currency savings lost in 1991.[12]

At that time, people also had substantial savings outside the banking system. Since state banks were not trusted, many people held their money at their homes under mattresses. According to some estimates, in mid-1991 the population still had about DM 8 billion in hoarded savings outside banks (Dinkic, 1995, p. 73). With galloping inflation in 1992–3, people were forced to supplement their regular incomes by selling their foreign currency savings. Using its monopoly over the printing of money and supply of dinars, the state had taken control over the foreign currency black market, and was continuously printing money to buy foreign currency through its own street dealers. Instead of openly appearing on this market, the state used a whole range of institutions and private persons to buy foreign currency on its behalf, including state banks, quasi-private banks (see below), private savings exchange offices and their street dealers (Dinkic, 1995, pp. 82–3). The continuous rise of the black market exchange rate induced citizens to keep on selling their foreign currency, but prices rapidly adapted to the new exchange rates. As hyperinflation increased, the time lag between the rise in prices and the exchange rate became even shorter.

In the meantime, more subtle methods were devised for squeezing out the remaining foreign currency from the population. In early 1991 a new private bank, the Karic Bank, started selling 30-day bonds at an annual interest rate of 45 per cent, at a time when state banks were paying a 10 per cent annual interest on dinar deposits. People rushed to convert their foreign currency into dinars in order to buy the bonds. The bank made enormous profits, while the people who bought the bonds lost their money because the interest paid on their deposits was never enough to keep up with inflation (Dinkic, 1995, pp. 70–3).

At the end of 1991 two other private banks appeared that were to perform the same function, by offering *monthly* interest rates on foreign exchange deposits comparable to *annual* rates in Western countries. In January 1991, Jezdimir Vasiljevic created the Jugoskandik bank which was offering a 10 per cent monthly interest rate on foreign currency deposits, paid in foreign currency (Dinkic, 1995, p. 31). In October 1991, the Dafiment Bank was founded by Dafina Milanovic which was offering even higher interest rates: in December 1992, monthly interest rates were 100–120 per cent on dinar deposits and 15–17 per cent on foreign currency deposits.

These two banks attracted a substantial amount of savings during the first months of their operations. For some citizens the monthly interest paid on their deposits was an important supplementary income. However, both banks would soon collapse. On the night of 7–8 March 1993, Jezdimir Vasiljevic left the country and Jugoskandik stopped all payments to depositors two days later. The Dafiment Bank savers were seized by panic, there were long queues of people wanting to withdraw their savings, the bank limited withdrawals and sought help from the state, and a month later the Dafiment Bank also ceased making payments to depositors.[13] Although these banks were not officially state banks, there are many indications that their operations were indeed organized by the authorities (Dinkic, 1995). Milosevic has used these banks quite literally to rob Serbia's citizens of their foreign currency earnings (Miljkovic and Hoare, 2005, p. 197). Through these pyramid schemes most citizens had lost whatever foreign currency savings they still had under mattresses. The government reacted only in June 1993, when it adopted a new Law on banks and other financial institutions, which introduced significant limitations on the free entry in the financial market by raising capital census on equity and increasing prudential control (CES MECON, 1993).

These episodes of clamorous fraud of the population in FR Yugoslavia were among the most terrifying events of those early 1990s, which have not been forgotten. The general mistrust of the government and of its institutions, which is still present in Serbia, dates back to those days. The following quotation from Mladjan Dinkic's book (1995), which describes these events in greater detail, is particularly revealing of the conditions prevailing in Serbia in the mid-1990s:

> The intensive application of destructive economic policies undermined the very foundations of Yugoslav society. People were robbed of their money and deprived of the right to lead a normal life. Completely abnormal phenomena became everyday occurrences. Sound economic logic was destroyed and the entire society slid into crime. People became accustomed to black marketeering and other illegal activities. In the absence of the rule of law, financial speculation and illegal transactions became far more lucrative than honest work, while bribery and corruption came to be seen as normal

by rich and poor alike. An insane atmosphere was created. People had grown used to queuing outside shops and banks, and had lost the habit of working for a living. They had become indifferent to cheating and injustice on the part of the state, and were prepared to withstand all hardship without asking themselves if there was any reason for doing so. The confusion was deliberately encouraged by the state-controlled media, which had no scruples about preserving the greatest national disasters as historical triumphs and tried to convince the public that the most insane economic policies were in fact highly rational and perfectly in tune with the sacred principles of the free market.

(Dinkic, 1995, pp. 249–50)

4
Post-Dayton: Slow Progress with Transition

After the war in Bosnia and Herzegovina had ended with the signing of the Dayton Peace Accords in late 1995,[1] a new phase seemed to emerge in FR Yugoslavia which promised major improvements on all fronts. There was peace finally after almost four years of conflict in neighbouring Bosnia and Herzegovina, the most severe international sanctions against FR Yugoslavia were soon to be lifted, and the prospects for economic recovery were encouraging. As will be seen, however, this period brought continuity rather than radical changes of the political and economic system, persistence of internal and international tensions instead of normalization of relations with neighbours and with the international community. This period of continued instability culminated with the Kosovo crisis in 1998–9 and the three-month-long NATO bombardments of FR Yugoslavia in spring 1999.

This chapter illustrates how the adverse political conditions in FR Yugoslavia which prevailed even after 1995 continued to negatively influence economic developments, resulting in unsatisfactory economic performance and very slow progress with reforms required by the transition to a market economy. A brief account is first given of the most important political developments, followed by an analysis of the macroeconomic performance of the Yugoslav economy during the 1996–2000 period. Throughout most of this period, economic performance of the Yugoslav economy has not improved much with respect to the early 1990s, whereas the 1999 NATO bombing had devastating economic consequences, aggravating the economic situation even further. There was also very limited progress with systemic changes, since the adoption of some new transition-related laws did not effectively translate into fundamental changes in the functioning of the Yugoslav/Serbian economy. This is illustrated by analysing, in particular, the results in the area of privatization and the related problems of corporate governance. The broader economic and social consequences of ten years of delayed transition are also highlighted.

4.1 Political environment: Peace without normalization

After the signing of the Dayton Peace Accords in December 1995 by Izetbegovic, Tudjman, and Milosevic, the presidents of Bosnia and Herzegovina, Croatia, and Serbia respectively, the internal political scene in Serbia and FR Yugoslavia did not change fundamentally with respect to the early 1990s. There was a further consolidation of the Milosevic regime, assured through the continued dominance of the Socialist Party of Serbia (SPS) in both the Serbian and the federal parliament, though with different coalition partners and frequent changes of the SPS leadership. Since after two terms Slobodan Milosevic could no longer be elected president of Serbia, in 1997 he was elected the president of FR Yugoslavia, changing the electoral law to assure the ruling parties in Serbia and Montenegro would gain an absolute electoral majority over the opposition (Thomas, 1999, p. 275).

A novelty on the political scene was the Yugoslav United Left (JUL), a new party created by Milosevic's wife, Mirjana Markovic, in 1994,[2] which would become extremely influential despite declining popular support. JUL was a thoroughly unreformed party which apparently rejected nationalist politics, but only in order to restore credibility of the regime. Mirjana Markovic was a central figure both in Serbian politics and the economy and her ultimate political purpose, as stressed by many, was the pursuit of power. The immediate political circle surrounding Mirjana Markovic, and through her also Milosevic, consisted of 'a clique of ultra-rich plutocrats whose business careers had been forged through the development of client-patron relationships with the state bureaucracy' (Thomas, 1999, p. 230).

This period was characterized by even sharper conflicts between the SPS and the opposition. Though the opposition parties continued to be represented in the parliament, they had very little effective power. The Serbian government continued with the harassment against the independent media and the use of violent means to resolve all confrontations; there were many cases of arrest, beating, and mistreatment of opposition leaders and their supporters. Though strong personal animosities continued to divide the opposition, the three main opposition parties – Zoran Djindjic's Democratic Party (DS), Vuk Draskovic's Serbian Renewal Movement (SPO), and Vesna Pesic's Civic Alliance of Serbia (Gradjanski Savez Srbije) – finally created a broad coalition 'Zajedno' (together) which initially organized joint rallies and later presented itself at the federal elections. The governor of the NBY, Dragoslav Avramovic, was to lead the 'Zajedno' coalition, expanded to include, upon his assistance, Vojislav Kostunica's Democratic Party of Serbia (DSS) and the Association of Free and Independent Trade Unions. However, at the very last minute Avramovic changed his mind and withdrew his participation, presumably for health reasons,[3] despite his enormous popular support. Opinion polls in autumn 1996 showed that Avramovic was considered the most popular political personality by 43 per cent of citizens, as compared to 29 per cent who expressed support for Slobodan Milosevic (Thomas, 1999, p. 279). In the November 1996 federal elections, the 'Zajedno' coalition was defeated by the 'leftist' parties (the SPS, JUL, and New Democracy); in the local elections, however, 'Zajedno' won in a number of major cities across Serbia, but the authorities tried to annul the results claiming irregularities.

This brought to the front the political conflict between the authorities and the opposition and the increasing social unrest in the winter of 1996–7. After the official non-recognition of the election victory of the opposition parties, mass demonstrations were organized throughout Serbia. The most remarkable were those in Belgrade in the winter of 1996–7, when several hundreds of thousands of people protested against the fraud in the elections for 100 days, at a temperature of –5. A popular movement of such dimensions had never been seen in Belgrade before: the young and the old, students and pensioners, intellectuals and workers, representatives of the Orthodox Church and ordinary citizens, took daily walks down the streets of Belgrade, blowing horns and whistles, yelling anti-government slogans, banging pots and pans, carrying puppets representing Milosevic dressed in a convict's uniform. Though the pretext for the mass protest was the theft of votes at the recent elections, it was much more than that. By that time, the population was profoundly miserable, fed up with Milosevic, with the political regime, with falling living standards, social injustice, general insecurity, crimes and murders, and continued isolation from the rest of the world. The police intervened several times using force to disperse the demonstrators.

The election votes were formally acknowledged only in early February 1997, after the intervention of an international mission of the Organization for Security and Cooperation in Europe (OSCE) that arrived in Belgrade, headed by the former Spanish Prime Minister Felipe Gonzales. Milosevic had to accept the electoral victory of the opposition as well as a series of concessions, including the post of mayor of Belgrade which was to be given to Zoran Djindjic. The opposition widened its demands for political and economic reform and renewed the calls for the liberalization of the media, but there were increasing tensions within the opposition. By mid-1997 'Zajedno' had fallen apart, failing to reach an agreement on the joint participation in the presidential and parliamentary elections in Serbia in September 1997. Most opposition parties boycotted these elections, while Djindjic was ousted from the position of mayor of Belgrade.

A further problem was that the end of the war in Bosnia and Herzegovina did not bring normalization of FR Yugoslavia's relations with international organizations. The official retreat of the Serbian government from support of the Bosnian Serbs led to the suspension of the most severe UN sanctions in November 1995, a day after the initialling of the Dayton Peace Accords, and to their official lifting on 2 October 1996 (UN Security Council Resolution 1074). Nevertheless, what remained thereafter was the 'outer wall' of sanctions, which effectively impeded the re-entry of FR Yugoslavia into the United Nations and the most important international financial organizations (these sanctions would be lifted only after the October 2000 radical political changes; see Chapter 5).

Moreover, as a reaction to Serbian policies in Kosovo, a new package of UN sanctions was imposed against FR Yugoslavia on 31 March 1998 (UN Security Council Resolution 1160), prohibiting the imports of armaments, which were reinforced on 30 March 1999 to include an air traffic ban and an oil and trade embargo. In an attempt to device sanctions to affect primarily the ruling political and economic elite, a visa ban was introduced in 1999 for some 300 senior Serbian politicians, army and police officers, and businessmen, which was extended to more than 700 individuals in late 1999 (Economist Intelligence Unit, 2000). The EU also invented 'selective sanctions' directed towards a selected group of Serbian enterprises (those that were considered to be collaborating with the authorities) which were put on the 'black list', prohibiting trade and other business transactions with them (Zucconi, 2000).

The situation in Kosovo had in the meantime progressively deteriorated. After the adoption of the new Serbian constitution in 1990 which centralized Serbia's power over Kosovo, the silent protests of the Albanians continued, but the confrontation between the Serb and the Albanian community became even more extreme after Yugoslavia's break-up in 1991. During the 1990s, Albanians were expelled from key positions in the police and army, there were massive layoffs of Albanian workers, and other forms of discrimination of the Albanian population. The Kosovars, on their part, boycotted political elections and created parallel health, educational, and other structures, as well as an Albanian shadow government and parliament.

At that time, however, the deteriorating situation in Kosovo remained overshadowed by the war in Bosnia and Herzegovina. The absence of the Kosovo issue from the agenda of the Dayton peace conference radicalized the Albanian national movement, pushing aside the parties and leaders like Ibrahim Rugova who advocated peaceful forms of struggle, and replacing them with more radical leaders who soon founded the Kosovo Liberation Army (KLA). The situation progressively deteriorated after April 1996, when the KLA began its campaign of armed attacks against the Serbian police and civilian targets (Thomas, 1999, p. xiii). In February 1998 the Serbian security forces began an offensive against the KLA, leading to further violent clashes between the Yugoslav National Army and the KLA. Several armed interventions of the Yugoslav National Army in the province followed. In April 1998 a referendum in Serbia rejected foreign mediation over the crisis in Kosovo.

The attempts to find a peaceful solution to the crisis in Kosovo through the Serbian – Albanian dialogue proved unsuccessful. In early 1999, after the failure of the negotiations with representatives of the Milosevic regime in Rambouillet,[4] the NATO military intervention in FR Yugoslavia started. Despite the lack of authorization on the part of the UN Security Council because of the veto of Russia and China, a number of countries – including the US, UK, France, Canada, Belgium, Netherlands, and Italy – considered the use of force necessary for preventing a 'humanitarian catastrophe' (Cassese and Gaeta, 2008, p. 44). The absence of the UN Security Council approval as a legal basis for the intervention led other countries – including Russia, China, Cuba, Ukraine, Namibia, and India – to strongly condemn the NATO intervention, sustaining that it was in contrast with the UN Charter and that the intervention undermined international law. The Italian public opinion and some political parties were against the war, but the Italian government nonetheless allowed NATO full use of Italian air bases.

The bombing of FR Yugoslavia would last for more than 11 weeks or exactly 78 days, between 24 March and 10 June 1999. During this period, NATO initially attacked primarily the Yugoslav military and the Albanian paramilitary forces in Kosovo, but proceeded with daily air raids of Belgrade, Novi Sad, and other Serbian cities. Civilian installations such as power plants, water processing plants, and bridges were intentionally targeted. The destruction of bridges over the Danube greatly disrupted shipping on the river for many months afterwards, causing serious economic damage to neighbouring countries as well. Industrial facilities such as the Zastava car factory in Kragujevac were also attacked, as were those of other Serbian towns. Probably the most controversial deliberate attack was the bombing of the headquarters of the Serbian television on 23 April, when at least 14 people were killed. NATO justified the attack on the grounds that the Serbian television was part of the Milosevic regime's propaganda machine. It was later revealed that the directors of the television had been forewarned of the attack, but ordered the employees to remain inside the building, since their death was to serve as anti-Western propaganda.

Although the NATO intervention was supposed to prevent the ethnic cleansing by the Serbian authorities in Kosovo, the bombing first prompted the regime to accelerate ethnic cleansing, then it succeeded in reversing it with Serbian army withdrawal and some KLA cleansing of Serbs. The costs of the war have been enormous, ranging from US$30 billion to 100 billion, depending on estimates (see section 4.2 below). As in all wars, the main victims have been the people, not only the Albanians but also the Serbs and other nationalities living in Kosovo. In Serbia, the NATO bombing was quite unexpected and was perceived by most citizens as an extreme and highly unjust measure, as a punishment of a whole nation for the criminal deeds of one man, Slobodan Milosevic, who in the meantime had become increasingly unpopular.

Irrespective of whether the NATO bombing was fair towards the Serbian people and other controversial issues, the NATO intervention has in no way facilitated, but has rather complicated, a permanent and effective solution for Kosovo. Ten years after the end of the war and more than a year since the proclamation of Kosovo's independence, the situation in Kosovo remains problematic, both for the economy in general and for the remaining Serbs in particular (Deimel and García Schmidt, 2009). UNMIK has not succeeded in creating a convincing system of local administration, in promoting economic reconstruction, or in halting the spiral of reciprocal obstructionist tactics and violations of minority rights (Bianchini, 2007, p. 12).

4.2 Sluggish macroeconomic performance

Within an essentially unchanged political environment, it is not surprising that macroeconomic performance of the Yugoslav economy during the second half of the 1990s remained unsatisfactory. Though there were a few attempts to move forward in different areas of economic reform, the results were short-lived and delusive, without bringing any major improvements in most economic indicators.

The government's macroeconomic policies continued to be characterized by stop-go measures and loose monetary and fiscal policies, which could not have provided more permanent macroeconomic stability. Although inflation never reached the dramatic proportions of the early 1990s, the Yugoslav economy continued to be characterized by high price fluctuations. After the implementation of the 1994 Avramovic programme of monetary reconstruction which eliminated hyperinflation (see Chapter 3), average annual inflation again jumped to 78 per cent in 1995 and rose further to 94.3 per cent in 1996. Some progress in monetary stabilization was achieved in 1997, when average annual inflation was reduced to 21.3 per cent, but it again increased to 29.5 per cent in 1998 and further to 37 per cent in 1999 (see Table 4.1). After the beginning of the NATO intervention in 1999, the government decreed a price freeze, forcing enterprises to bring down prices to their mid-October level. This measure was ineffective as it only provoked shortages, thus repressing inflationary pressures instead of reducing them.

Econometric results show that during this period of medium-to-high inflation in FR Yugoslavia (1994–8), the pass-through from the exchange

Table 4.1 FR Yugoslavia: Main macroeconomic indicators, 1995–2000

	1995	**1996**	**1997**	**1998**	**1999**	**2000**
Inflation (average) (%)	78.6	94.3	21.3	29.5	37.1	60.4
Growth in real GDP (%)	6.1	7.8	10.1	1.9	–19.0	10.7
Industrial production (%)	3.8	7.6	9.5	4.4	–24.4	11.1
Agricultural production (%)	4.1	1.5	7.3	–3.2	–2.0	–13.7
Public deficit (% of GDP)	–4.3	–3.8	–7.6	–5.4	–8.4	–3.7
Employed (in thousands)	2,379	2,367	2,507	2,504	2,298	2,238
Unemployed (in thousands)	775	819	814	838	811	806
Unemployment rate (in % of labour force)	24.2	25.4	24.1	24.6	25.5	25.6

Source: EBRD *Transition Reports*, various issues, and national statistics (Zavod za statistiku Republike Srbije). Note that these statistics are not fully comparable to those on Serbia reported in Chapter 6, since they refer to FR Yugoslavia.

rate to prices was also complete (equal to 1) as during the previous period of hyperinflation, the main difference being that it was delayed by six months (Mladenovic and Petrovic, 2009). Therefore, the exchange rate remained a very important determinant of increasing inflation also in the second half of the 1990s.

Similar to the situation in the first half of the 1990s, the Yugoslav government did not implement any substantial fiscal reforms. Though the public deficit of the Yugoslav federation throughout this period officially remained below 10 per cent, there was a hidden deficit not recorded in official statistics, such as subsidies to loss-making enterprises. After having been wiped out by the 1993 record hyperinflation, public debt increased continuously after 1994, so that by 1997 it had exceeded FR Yugoslavia's GSP by a substantial margin (Economist Intelligence Unit, 1998).

After the severe recession of the early 1990s there was gradual recovery of the Yugoslav economy (Table 4.1). During 1995–7, real GSP growth rates in FR Yugoslavia were frequently among the highest in SEE. In 1995, Yugoslav GSP grew by 6.1 per cent, in 1996 by 7.8 per cent, and in 1997 by 10.1 per cent; only in 1998 did it register a much lower growth rate of 1.9 per cent, primarily because of poor agricultural output due to a very bad harvest. Despite rapid economic recovery, these high growth rates were largely insufficient to compensate for the very deep recession of the early 1990s.

In addition, the 1999 conflict in Kosovo caused a notable worsening of all major macroeconomic indicators: real GSP declined by 19 per cent and industrial production by over 24 per cent. A whole decade of delayed transition and economic mismanagement had more than halved the country's annual production: by 1999, the country's GDP had come down to around 40 per cent of its 1989 level and was among the lowest in the SEE region.

The lifting of the most severe international sanctions in 1996 permitted the official renewal of foreign trade with most countries, which during the years of the embargo mainly took the form of illegal transactions. This permitted some recovery in foreign trade, despite the lack of concrete measures to liberalize the foreign trade regime. Yugoslav exports almost doubled, increasing from US$ 1.5 billion in 1995 to over US$ 2.8 billion in 1998, but imports rose even faster, to US$ 4.8 billion by 1998, determining a huge foreign trade deficit of almost US$ 2 billion (see Figure 4.1 and Table 4.2).

Following the 1999 NATO intervention, a very sharp fall was registered in both exports (almost 50 per cent), and imports (30 per cent).

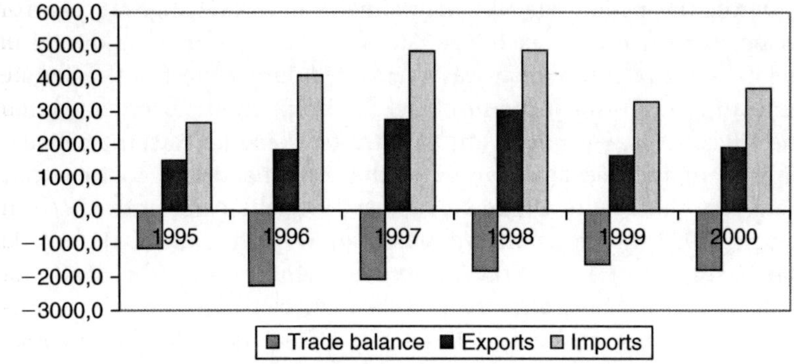

Figure 4.1 FR Yugoslavia: Exports, imports, and trade balance, 1995–2000 (million US$)

Table 4.2 FR Yugoslavia: External sector indicators, 1995–2000

	1995	1996	1997	1998	1999	2000
Trade balance (mln US$)	–1,135	–2,260	–2,431	–1, 991	–1,798	–1,900
Exports	1,531	1,842	2,368	2,858	1,498	1,700
Imports	2,666	4,102	4,799	4,849	3,296	3,600
Current account (mln US$)	NA	–1,670	–1,845	–1,238	–1,311	–1,319
Current account (in % of GDP)	NA	–10.7	–11.0	-6.7	–13.1	–12.6
FDI inflows (mln US$)	45	102	740	113	112	25
Foreign exchange reserves, excluding gold (mln US $)	260	306	288	173	130	Na
External debt (bn US$)	13.8	13.4	15.1	13.7	13.7	Na

Source: EBRD *Transition Reports*, various issues. The statistics on FDI, foreign reserves, and external debt are from the Economist Intelligence Unit (1999a, 1999b, 2000).

Unsatisfactory trends on the foreign trade account were accompanied by a rising current account deficit, at the level of around 11 per cent of GSP in 1996–7; though the deficit was somewhat reduced in 1998, it again exceeded 13 per cent of GSP in 1999.

During this period, the NBY maintained a fixed exchange rate regime. Given that the official exchange rate was adjusted only sporadically to the inflation rate, the dinar was overvalued during most of the period, generating a high and increasing black market premium. In order to bring the official exchange rate in line with the black market rate, the NBY did implement a few devaluations but with substantial delays, so the effects were very short-term. On 26 November 1995, the parity introduced in January 1994 by the Avramovic stabilization programme (DM1 = YD1) was changed to DM1 = YD3.3, and was maintained for the next two-and-a-half years. Only after the black market exchange rate had become more than three and a half times the official rate did the Yugoslav authorities implement another devaluation of the national currency, on 1 April 1998, when the parity was changed to DM 1 = YD 6. This dinar/DM official exchange rate was maintained throughout the next two and a half years and would only be changed after the October 2000 radical political changes (on 6 December 2000, see Chapter 5).

In 1997, foreign exchange reserves (excluding gold) of FR Yugoslavia were only around US$ 288 million, declining further to US$ 173 million in 1998 and to US$ 130 million in 1999 (see Table 4.2). Owing to the limited possibility to borrow on international financial markets, the country's gross external debt remained fairly stable during this period, even declining slightly from US$ 13.8 billion in 1995 to US$ 13.7 billion in 1999 (Economist Intelligence Unit, 2000, p. 7). Although in July 1997 the Yugoslav government's vice president tried to negotiate the rescheduling of foreign debt owed to the London Club of creditors, proposing the write-off of 80 per cent of total debt, no agreement was reached. Because of very low official reserves, a serious international liquidity crisis was expected in 2001 (Pitic et al., 1999).

The lack of normalization of FR Yugoslavia's relations with international financial organizations impeded the inflow of badly needed capital, not only loans of international financial organizations but also Foreign Direct Investment (FDI). Although there was an attempt to re-establish relations with the IMF in early 1996, there were increasing tensions between the Yugoslav National Bank governor Dragoslav Avramovic, the chief negotiator in the talks with the IMF, and the Yugoslav government. The government insisted that any agreement on IMF membership had to include the recognition of the 'continuity' between the FR Yugoslavia and the SFR Yugoslavia, in the hope that this would provide FR Yugoslavia the right to assets and membership in international organizations of the former country. On the contrary, Avramovic was proposing to accept the terms set by the IMF. Avramovic was soon removed as chief negotiator in the IMF talks and in mid-May 1996 was also forced to leave the NBY, after an unsuccessful initiative to propose a new privatization programme to the Yugoslav parliament (see below).

Owing to the country's unregulated status in international financial institutions and permanence of high political risk, there were extremely limited FDI inflows throughout the 1990s. Even in the second half of the 1990s, contrary to the experience of many other transition countries at that time, FDI has only marginally contributed to privatization in Serbia. During the 1993–2000 period, the stock of FDI into FR Yugoslavia amounted to US$ 1.3 billion (Kekic, 2003). The only important investment in the 1990s was the June 1997 privatization of 49 per cent of Serbia Telekom sold to the Italian STET (29%) and Greek OTE (20%), for a total of DM 1.57 billion, of which DM 1.25 billion was immediately collected in cash (Economist Intelligence Unit, 1998, p. 23). The main reason for the partial privatization of Serbia Telekom was the extremely unfavourable economic situation in 1997 and very low foreign exchange reserves. According to many analysts, the revenues from this privatization deal were spent primarily to buy social peace, paying pensions, and wages just before the elections in 1997, since by that time Milosevic already feared his political survival (Miljkovic and Hoare, 2005, p. 210).

The total FDI inflows to FR Yugoslavia during the 1990s of US$ 1.3 billion represented less than 1 per cent of the total invested in all transition economies. Although such a low level of FDI inflows was, in part, the consequence of the investment ban imposed by the international community in 1992 and maintained informally throughout most of the period, it also reflects limited interest of foreign partners to invest in Serbia due to the unsettled political situation and poor state of the economy.

The economic conditions in FR Yugoslavia greatly worsened after the Kosovo conflict in 1998–9, as the NATO bombing had devastating overall consequences. In addition to the loss of many human lives, the conflict brought physical damages of a large part of the country's industrial capacities, as well as of the transport, energy, and communications infrastructure. Serbia's road and railway connections had been seriously disrupted, while trade on the Danube after the war had almost come to a standstill. Serbia also had to face very serious heating problems, due to electricity and heating fuel shortages, though some energy provisions were provided by Russia (Uvalic, 2001a). In addition to direct costs, the war also had a number of indirect consequences, as it negatively affected macroeconomic stabilization and economic recovery.

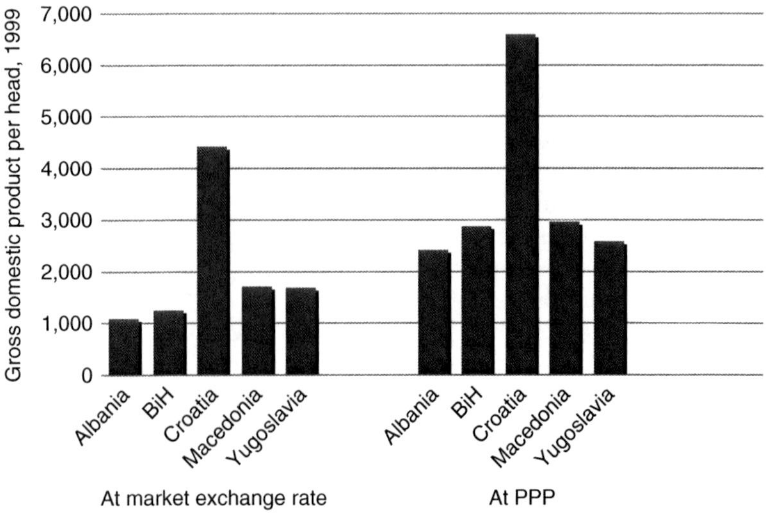

Figure 4.2 GDP per head in FR Yugoslavia and other SEE countries, 1999 (US dollars)
Source: Economist Intelligence Unit (2000).

The estimates of the overall costs for FR Yugoslavia of the Kosovo conflict vary widely, ranging from US$30–100 billion, the latter figure being the official estimate of the Yugoslav government while the former of the G17. According to the more realistic estimate of the G17, the direct costs incurred by physical damages were only around US$4 billion, of which the major losses referred to the destruction of industrial capacities (around 70 per cent of the physical damages), US$2.3 billion were losses of human capital, while the remaining US$23 billion were the losses of 'potential GSP' provoked by physical damages, expected to be felt over the next ten years (G17, 1999).[5]

By the late 1990s, FR Yugoslavia was probably the SEE country in the worst overall situation. It had an estimated GDP per capita at PPP of around US$ 2580 in 1999, being only marginally better off than Albania (US$ 2420) and behind all the other countries in the SEE region (Economist Intelligence Unit, 2000, p. 30). Figure 4.2 illustrates this unfavourable position of FR Yugoslavia with respect to other SEE countries in 1999.

FR Yugoslavia was not included in the Stability Pact for SEE adopted in Cologne on 10 June 1999, which raised serious problems both for FR Yugoslavia and for the implementation of the Pact itself. When the Kosovo conflict ended, the West toughened its stance saying that sanctions would stay in place as long as Milosevic did. Only humanitarian aid was given to FR Yugoslavia, but no major external resources were to be provided for undertaking economic reconstruction. EU humanitarian assistance was primarily to support refugees from Bosnia and Herzegovina and Croatia (around 500,000 persons), internally displaced persons from Kosovo (around 200,000), and other socially vulnerable groups (old people's homes, orphanages, hospitals), a total of almost one million persons.

In addition, some EU funds were offered through the G17 Plus project 'Energy for Democracy', providing energy to the democratically run Serbian municipalities where the democratic parties had won the elections. The EU supported a similar project on education, again restricted to those municipalities run by democratic parties. Russia also provided aid worth some US$70 million, including aid in kind (natural gas and other energy sources). But economic reconstruction of Serbia was impossible without a major inflow of foreign assistance, which was to arrive only after radical changes of the political regime in October 2000.

4.3 Slow pace of transition-related reforms

Progress with institutional reforms has been extremely slow and disappointing also during the second half of the 1990s. Strong anti-reform forces within the government remained influential and many vested interests impeded radical change. Milosevic was reluctant to initiate serious economic reforms since any diminution of state control over the social and economic apparatus would also diminish his personal and political power (Thomas, 1999, p. 164). Milosevic's wife's party, JUL, was only overtly hostile towards private property and the market, but its effective strategy was 'not to abolish the private sector in Serbia but to assert political control over it' (Thomas, 1999, p. 230). As observed by Gligorov (1999), the economic policy and institutional development pursued by the Yugoslav government during this period moved into the retrograde direction, having as its main features centralization, nationalization, anti-liberalization, anti-stabilization, and corruption. After 1996, in addition to the 'outer wall' of sanctions mentioned earlier, there was also an 'inner wall' impeding progress, namely the government's lack of willingness to implement any fundamental reforms (Popovic, 1997).

By the end of the decade, FR Yugoslavia was among the countries in transition that were lagging behind most in the implementation of market-oriented economic reforms. This is confirmed by the transition indicators prepared by EBRD for all countries in transition – the Baltics, CEE, Southeast Europe, and the Commonwealth of Independent States.

The EBRD indicators evaluate progress achieved in the various areas of reform, namely enterprises (small and large-scale privatization, enterprise restructuring, and corporate governance), markets and trade (price liberalization, trade and foreign exchange system, and competition policy), and financial institutions (banking reform and interest rate liberalization, securities markets and non-bank financial institutions). The EBRD scores range from 1 implying no reform in a given area, to 4+ implying a situation comparable to that of a developed market economy. Although for political reasons, in the late 1990s FR Yugoslavia's progress with transition-related reforms was still not officially reported in EBRD's publications, this was done subsequently.

As illustrated in Table 4.3, by 2000 FR Yugoslavia made no progress in most areas of reform (score 1), the only exceptions being small-scale privatization (score 3) and price liberalization (score 2+). During the 1990s, in some areas there have actually been reversals in systemic reforms and policies, eliminating or reducing elements of a market economy that existed in the late 1980s, as in the trade and foreign exchange system (score reduced to 1).

Within *enterprise reform*, limited progress was achieved in FR Yugoslavia in the area of privatization. Despite new privatization laws adopted in 1996–7 by the federal and Serbian governments (see section 4.4 below), only small-scale privatization had been partially implemented, thus meriting EBRD score 3. Still, privatization undertaken during the 1990s resulted mainly in widespread ownership by employed workers and managers who, given enormous losses of a large part of the economy, frequently owned worthless shares in highly undercapitalized enterprises. Large enterprises had not been privatized or restructured, the only major exception being Serbia Telekom, while some large monopolies in infrastructure had been nationalized. As a result, in 2000, the private sector contributed only around 40 per cent of GDP in Serbia, among the lowest shares among all transition countries. Owing to limited progress with privatization, Serbian enterprises were facing specific problems of corporate governance, essentially different in the social, mixed, and state-owned sector of the economy, as discussed below.

Regarding *markets and trade*, instead of liberalization the Yugoslav government continued to implement measures of strong administrative control. Price liberalization was very partial also in the second half of the 1990s and was on various occasions reversed by general or selective price freezes (as in 1998), thus the unsatisfactory EBRD score in 1999 of 2+. The foreign trade system remained highly protected by a number of measures, including a high level of average tariffs and associated

Table 4.3 FR Yugoslavia: EBRD transition indicators, 1989–2000

	Enterprises			**Markets and trade**			**Financial institutions**		
	Private sector share of GDP (in%) mid-year	***Large-scale privati-zation***	***Small-scale privati-zation***	***Governance and enterprise restructuring***	***Price liberali-zation***	***Trade and foreign exchange system***	***Competition policy***	***Banking reform & interest rate liberali-zation***	***Securities markets & non-bank financial institutions***
1989	10	1	3	1	3–	2	1	1	1
1990		1	3	1	4–	2	1	1	1
1991		1	3	1	4–	2	1	1	1
1992		1	3	1	4–	2	1	1	1
1993		1	3	1	4–	2	1	1	1
1994		1	3	1	3–	1	1	1	1
1995		1	3	1	3–	1	1	1	1
1996		1	3	1	3–	1	1	1	1
1997		1	3	1	3–	1	1	1	1
1998		1	3	1	2+	1	1	1	1
1999		1	3	1	2+	1	1	1	1
2000	40	1	3	1	2+	1	1	1	1

Source: EBRD online database (www.ebrd.com) and Chapter 2.

charges, widespread import and export licences, import quotas, and other quantitative restrictions. The foreign exchange system, despite the lifting of the most severe sanctions, continued to be subject to a series of restrictions and deficiences: the non-convertibility of the dinar, multiple exchange rates, inactive foreign exchange policy, and frequent rationing of foreign exchange. A competition law containing anti-trust legislation was adopted in 1997, but the law had no effect since the economy remained highly monopolized.

There was also no progress with *banking and financial sector* reforms. The entire banking system was permanently facing a serious liquidity crisis, since banks were heavily burdened by an enormous amount of bad loans. The unresolved problem of citizens' 'frozen' foreign currency savings from the early 1990s acted as a very strong disincentive against the placing of money in the banking system. Whatever savings citizens still had, if any, after the pyramid schemes of the early 1990s, they held under mattresses. This additionally prevented the badly needed recapitalization of banks. Although in the late 1990s a market for government securities was created, due to delays in privatization a stock exchange for enterprise shares was not operational.

There is no doubt that the main problem with the Serbian/Yugoslav economy in the late 1990s was lack of fundamental systemic changes, but it is also too simplistic to say that economic transformation never got started in Serbia. Some laws in line with the objectives of a market economy were formally there, either taken over from legislation of SFR Yugoslavia, or adopted during the 1990s. These include a company law enabling the commercialization of enterprises, several privatization laws, a bankruptcy and liquidation law, a competition law, a new law on foreign direct investment offering major incentives to investors, even a law on investment funds, while preparations also started for introducing a value added tax law (Federal Ministry, 1999).

Still, many of these laws contained provisions which pointed to the lack of willingness by the Serbian/Yugoslav government to abandon pre-1989 institutions and practices. In other cases laws were well prepared, but were simply never applied in practice. A large part of legislation in FR Yugoslavia in those times was implemented in a highly arbitrary and selective way, frequently to the advantage of state-owned and a dozen other state-protected private enterprises. Different criteria were applied to different segments of the economy, which had a number of very negative and far-reaching consequences, further contributing to the concentration of power in a handful of state-protected firms. For these enterprises, soft budget constraints were maintained through a number of direct and indirect privileges – selective bank credits, subsidised interest rates, exclusivity in getting import permits or access to foreign currency at the official exchange rate, relaxation or cancelling of tax or fiscal obligations.

A close relationship was established between the political and economic elite, providing for the overlapping of economic and political competences. In 1999, the directors of the 30 most important enterprises were at the same time key politicians, members of the Serbian parliament, ministers in the Yugoslav government, and closest political collaborators of president Milosevic. The elite in power had strong vested interests and was not interested, as a result, in any radical changes in the economic system.

4.4 Disappointing privatization results

The lack of systemic change in the Serbian economy can best be illustrated by looking further into the results achieved with privatization. Within the debate on privatization that took place in late 1995–early 1996, there were various proposals in Serbia on how to implement it further. The debate led to the adoption of two new laws, by the Yugoslav and by the Serbian parliament in 1996 and 1997 respectively, but these laws effectively led to only very limited changes in the property regime of the larger part of the economy.

4.4.1 The 1996 privatization debate and Avramovic's departure

In 1996, a new federal privatization law was to be adopted because of the constitutional obligation to replace all legislation of SFR Yugoslavia by new laws within certain time limits. The new federal privatization law was to serve as a framework law in both Serbia and Montenegro, leaving the elaboration of detailed provisions to specific laws of the two republics. Prior to its adoption, an intense debate took place focusing on the various privatization programmes which had been elaborated by all political parties, major research institutes, trade unions, employers' associations, individual experts, and the government. An attempt to find a compromise solution, also politically acceptable, was undertaken by the National Bank's governor Dragoslav Avramovic, who formed a working group on privatization in early 1996 (see Box 4.1).[6] The working group prepared a privatization programme based on common elements of the various proposals (Avramovic and Uvalic, 1996). The programme was based on a combination of various methods, including both sales and giveaways, but one of its most important features was that it envisaged

Box 4.1 Encounter with Avramovic

I met the governor of the NBY, Dragoslav Avramovic, in November 1995 at a conference on privatization in Belgrade. After my short presentation in front of a packed audience, he raised his hand and asked me the most amazing question: 'If you were the queen of Serbia and had all the power in your hands, what privatization model would you implement?' I never could have dreamed that Avramovic would actually offer me such an opportunity – to elaborate a privatization programme for Yugoslavia – only 5 months later, and that this short encounter would lead to probably the most exciting and intense, but also most distressing, month in my whole professional career. When Avramovic called me in early April 1996 to come to Belgrade, I was very happy to accept his invitation. Although I knew little about Avramovic as a person, the economic policies he was pursuing were for me a clear sign that he was pushing in the right direction. In Belgrade I found that we had similar views about specific problems in Serbia, similar approaches to economics, methodology, and working methods. I discovered a man who, despite his age, was one of the most brilliant persons I have ever met, lucid, up to the point, efficient, unusually quick in reasoning, while at the same time extremely modest and simple, very charming and kind. I discovered an idealist, a true believer in democracy (even in a country like Yugoslavia), an altruist, a convinced optimist. I fully identified myself with the cause for which he was fighting, with the objectives he was pursuing, though given the chaotic circumstances of increasing tensions between Avramovic and the government, the occasions for discussion were not many. My great admiration for all these values this personality contained, the positive energy that he transmitted to me, the importance of the task he had assigned me, are among the main reasons why I had thrown myself so wholeheartedly into writing his privatization programme.

On 14 May 1996, when our privatization programme was also to be discussed in parliament, Avramovic did not receive a sufficient number of votes and thus was forced to leave the NBY. I was struck by the injustice towards this man who had done so much for Yugoslavia, but I felt even more sorry for Yugoslavia, because without Avramovic the process of transition was bound to be substantially delayed. Still, the whole initiative was not futile, especially in the wider context of Avramovic's exposure of the true face of the governing elite. This experience has also left deep traces on me personally. In future difficult situations, I would always remember Avramovic – his optimism, determination, courage – and he has inspired me to carry my goals forward. That today I feel richer as a person, I also owe it to our encounter.

I had the occasion to discuss the political situation in Serbia with Avramovic in Sveti Stefan in November 1997. Although he had initially accepted to lead the opposition coalition 'Zajedno', he was very hesitant to return to politics, saying he could only trust a few people. I also saw him in Rome in June 1999, when we discussed at length the situation in Serbia and when I gave him my proposal for a 'technical' government of experts, with many names of people originally from Yugoslavia who were working abroad. Avramovic never returned to politics. He died in Belgrade at the age of 80. At his funeral in April 2001 at the New Cemetery in Belgrade, an important part of Serbia's history was also buried.

the obligatory privatization of all enterprises in the social sector within determined time limits.

Avramovic was aware of the fact that without radical changes in the property regime there would be no substantial improvements in the Serbian economy, that foreign capital inflows and large-scale privatization were vital for the revival of the economy, along with the renewal of membership in the main international financial institutions. Avramovic stressed that until 1996, only 'selective' privatization had taken place, in favour of the economic elite. The government wanted privatization only to a limited extent, so as not to undermine its control over the economy.

In spring 2006, privatization turned out to be the most burning political issue, 'the clash of all clashes': both Avramovic and the ruling SPS knew that the government would fall or stay in power over this issue (Cerovic, 1996). The proposal of the Avramovic group of radical reforms of the property regime encountered strong resistance, since it went much beyond what the government wanted. The political and economic elite was not ready to change the most fundamental features of the political and economic system (Uvalic, 1996). Avramovic faced increasingly fierce opposition to his reform proposals, particularly from JUL, since it was widely believed that any real economic reform which introduced a degree of transparency into economic life would undercut the power based on the financial oligarchy who held the positions of power (Thomas, 1999, p. 273).

At the parliamentary session of 14–15 May 1996, when the Avramovic privatization programme was also to be discussed as a counter-proposal to the draft law officially prepared by the Yugoslav government, Avramovic was not given a vote of confidence. Consequently, his privatization programme was not put on the agenda. On that occasion Avramovic spoke about his disagreements with the Yugoslav government regarding monetary and fiscal policies, negotiations with the IMF, official reserves of former Yugoslavia, systemic and property reforms. In his speech in the Yugoslav parliament, he detailed the fundamental weaknesses of the existing economic and political system. He openly attacked the government for the ignorant, short-sighted, and irresponsible policies which were, as he put it, suicidal and were likely to make Yugoslavia another Angola. He directly accused several key politicians of their ignorance, incompetence, and dishonesty, and he even disclosed some of the manipulations behind his back within the NBY (such as falsification of signatures, non-delivery of faxes, or payments of enormous dollar fees to external collaborators without his knowledge).

With his speech, Avramovic had discredited the political regime as probably no one had the courage to do until then. He was accused of 'illegal' actions, but the truth is that he was illegally forced to resign. He was forced to leave, simply because he wanted to pull the country out of isolation and backwardness. It is an irony that he did not get a sufficient number of votes that day in parliament primarily because of the betrayal of the leading Montenegrin party (Socialist Peoples' Party, SNP), which until the day before was one of his most faithful supporters. It is a pity that Avramovic was forced out of office; he had wide popular support within the country, even by pensioners despite his firm refusal to print money to provide them with pensions, in addition to his high international prestige and credibility. In purely political terms the demise of Avramovic was yet another demonstration of Milosevic's ability to dispose of subordinates who had outlived their usefulness, but in economic terms it was a major self-inflicted wound by which the government chose to sacrifice any credibility which they might have had with the international economic institutions (Thomas, 1999, p. 275).

Instead of Avramovic's programme, on 15 May the privatization law prepared by the Yugoslav government was adopted by one of the two parliamentary chambers. The new federal law envisaged voluntary privatization, leaving to the enterprise to decide whether, when, and to what extent it would privatize its assets, and therefore it in no way assured the elimination of 'social property'. The reluctance of Serbian authorities to abandon the concept of 'social property' led to solutions which prevented quick, comprehensive, and compulsory privatization, as proposed in 1996 by the Avramovic working group.

In the context of failed attempts to influence positive economic changes in Serbia during this period, another important initiative, which merits mention, was undertaken by the G17, originally a group of 17 Yugoslav/Serbian economists led by Mladjan Dinkic. In 1997, the G17 prepared a radical programme of economic reforms for FR Yugoslavia, proposing the urgent implementation of the most important transition-related reforms, including macroeconomic stabilization, liberalization, and privatization (G17, 1997). As in the case of the Avramovic privatization programme, however, the G17 proposal did not become operational due to the lack of political changes in the country.

Although these initiatives were not transformed into effective changes of the Yugoslav economic system, they were not futile. They served to prepare the ground for more radical economic reforms to be implemented later. It is from the G17 group that the G17 Plus was born, initially an influential non-governmental organization which was very active in preparing the September 2000 elections that brought an end to the Milosevic regime (see Chapter 5).[7] In late 2002, the G17 Plus was transformed into a political party with the same name, that has been part of the Serbian government since then (except for a very short period in Zivkovic's government in 2003). These initiatives illustrate there were serious attempts to positively influence economic reforms in FR Yugoslavia much before 2000, which however were blocked by strong interests of the governing elite to preserve the *status quo*.

4.4.2 Privatization after 1996

After the adoption of the federal law in 1996 of marginal importance, privatization in Serbia was re-launched through a new law adopted in 1997. Enterprises in the social sector were to be privatized 'autonomously', using methods which again offered employed workers and managers (insiders) the most favourable conditions in share subscriptions. In the first round, after the initial transfer of 10 per cent of shares to the Serbian Pension Fund, employed workers, pensioners, and ensured farmers had the right to receive a certain amount of shares of their enterprise free of charge, of a dinar equivalent of DM 400 for each year of employment, but the total amount distributed could not exceed 60 per cent of enterprise capital. In the second round, these same categories could purchase shares at a 20 per cent discount (plus 1% for each year of employment but not exceeding 60%) and repay them within 6 years, up to the limit of the dinar equivalent of DM 6000 per worker-shareholder, but employed workers had priority in bids. Proceeds from sales were to go to the Development Fund (50%), the Pensions Fund (25%), and the Employment Fund (25%). Unsold shares were to be transferred to the Shareholding Fund, which was to offer them on sale at the stock exchange.

These provisions of the 1997 privatization law did not cover all firms. Some 75 state-owned strategically important enterprises, which were among the largest and most profitable firms, representing 35 per cent of total capital of the economy, were excluded and planned to be privatized later, on the basis of a special government programme. In addition, another 514 state-owned enterprises were to be privatized with the approval of their founder, namely the Serbian government.

Despite the adoption of new legislation, the overall results of privatization in FR Yugoslavia were highly disappointing. At the end of 1998, the social (non-privatized) and mixed (partially privatized) sectors represented only 20 per cent of the total number of firms, though they jointly contributed more than 82 per cent of employment, over 80 per cent of fixed assets, and 62 per cent of revenue of the Yugoslav economy (see Table 4.4). There was a steady increase in the private sector's contribution to GSP – from 11 per cent in 1988 to 22 per cent in 1992, to 32 per cent in 1994, and to 37 per cent in 1998 – but in 1998, the private sector still employed only 15 per cent of non-agricultural workers, engaged 6 per cent of total assets, and realized 35 per cent of Yugoslav revenue. The four non-private sectors in FR Yugoslavia – social, mixed, cooperative, and state – in 1998 still contributed over 62 per cent of Yugoslav GSP.

Montenegro adopted its own privatization law already in 1992. The law was subsequently amended in 1997, but the results achieved were not very different from those in Serbia – by 1998, the contribution of the private sector to GSP in Montenegro was 33.4 percent, as compared to 37 per cent in Serbia (see Table 4.5). Despite the desire of Montenegrin authorities to implement privatization faster than in Serbia, problems were encountered with the sale of enterprises, as happened in many other transition countries.

Regarding the implementation of the 1997 Serbian privatization law, by the end of 1998 only 20 per cent of the socially owned enterprises to be privatized according to the new provisions had completed the capital valuation procedure (see Table 4.6). Privatization had thus proceeded at an even slower pace in the second half of the 1990s. The new 1997 Serbian law did little to restore confidence to potential buyers, or to

Table 4.4 Some indicators of different property sectors in FR Yugoslavia, 1998

Indicator & Property Type	Gross social product (mln of dinars)	In % of total	Number of firms	In % of total	Number of employees	In % of total	Fixed assets (mln of dinars)	In % of total	Revenue (mln of dinars)	In % of total
Total	127,189	100	81,821	100	1,625,939	100	279,627	100	326,737	100
Social	39,934	31.40	9,515	11.6	783,580	48.2	153,667	55.0	110,728	33.9
Private	47,957	37.70	62,219	76.0	238,136	14.6	17,313	6.1	114,977	35.2
Coop	1,210	0.95	2,530	3.1	26,235	1.6	2,727	0.9	5,457	1.7
Mixed	35,860	28.20	7,215	8.8	554,910	34.1	98,023	35.1	92,603	28.3
State	2,226	1.75	342	0.4	23,078	1.4	7,898	2.8	2,973	0.9

Source: Savezni zavod za statistiku Jugoslavije, 'Drustveni proizvod i narodni dohodak 1998', *Statisticki Bilten* no. 2259, 1998, Belgrade, p. 28.

Table 4.5 Contribution of various property sectors to GSP in FR Yugoslavia, Serbia and Montenegro, 1988–98

Sector	Year	FR Yugoslavia		Serbia		Montenegro	
		GSP (in million of 1994 dinars)	In % of total	GSP (in million of 1994 dinars)	In % of total	GSP (in million of 1994 dinars)	In % of total
Total GSP	1988	49,189	100	46,583	100	2,607	100
Social sector		43,838	89.1	41,477	89.0	2,362	90.6
Private sector		5,351	10.9	5,106	11.0	245	9.4
Total GSP	1992	29,226	100	27,641	100	1,585	100
Social sector		22,804	78.0	21,574	78.1	1,230	77.6
Private sector		6,422	22.0	6,067	21.9	355	22.4
Total GSP	1998	25,652	100	23,993	100	1,660	100
Social sector		16,201	63.2	15,096	62.9	1,106	66.6
Private sector		9,451	36.8	8,897	37.1	554	33.4

Note: Social sector includes all non-privatized or semi-privatized sectors (social, mixed, state, and cooperative).
Source: Savezni zavod za statistiku Jugoslavije, 'Drustveni proizvod i narodni dohodak 1998', *Statisticki Bilten* no. 2259, Belgrade, 1998, p. 11.

offer incentives for enterprises to start privatization, despite the even more favourable conditions with respect to previous legislation.

By the end of 1999 when the deadline for capital valuation expired, only 2218 enterprises (out of 7000 eligible for privatization) had started to value their capital; only 344 enterprises had begun the first privatization round of distributing free shares to workers; while even less, 202, had started the second round of share offers at a discount (see Table 4.6). During the next 11 months, by 20 November 2000, the number of firms that started privatization increased only marginally, to 412 enterprises.

There was an unexpected increase in the number of privatizing firms in Serbia by the end of the year, as in December 2000 another 350 enterprises decided to start privatization (Petrovic, 2003, p. 21). This happened not only because the new post-Milosevic government announced its intentions to change privatization legislation, but also because workers were able to benefit more from the provisions of the 1997

Table 4.6 Implementation of the 1997 Serbian Privatization Law (by December 1999)

	Number	In % of total eligible for privatization
Total number of firms	8,750	–
Firms eligible for privatization	7,000	100
Firms that completed capital valuation	2,218	31.7
Firms that started the first privatization round	344	4.9
Firms that started the second privatization round	202	2.9
Total number of enterprise employees	105,379	–
Total number of shareholders	139,180	–

Source: Federal Ministry of Development, Science and Environment (2000), p. 48.

privatization law after the dinar was devalued in mid-December 2000. Since the amount of free shares that workers could receive for each year of employment was the dinar equivalent of 400 DM, the devaluation of the dinar automatically increased the dinar value of free shares.

The 1997 privatization law remained in force in Serbia until the end of 2000. Enterprises that entered the process were allowed to complete privatization. Overall, by the end of 2000, some 778 enterprises (11% of the 7000 to be privatized) decided to start privatization according to the 1997 legislation, covering some 198,632 employees (Privatization Agency, 2005, p. 15). These were mainly small- and medium-sized firms. Very few large enterprises were motivated to start privatization, given the limits on the amount of shares that could be distributed and subscribed by employed workers and managers.

Until late 2000, therefore, enterprise shares in Serbia were most frequently subscribed at preferential terms, or distributed free of charge, to employed workers and managers. Insiders' enthusiasm to buy shares of their enterprise was greatest in the early 1990s, diminishing steadily with the passing of time. In the second half of the 1990s, privatization was initially blocked (and to a great extent cancelled) by the 1994 amendments requiring capital revaluation, and later by the lack of interest of firms to start privatization, despite the exceptionally generous provisions of the 1997 law. At that time, in the still unprivatized firms, there was a strong preference to maintain the *status quo;*

the standard of living had declined to such an extent that owning enterprise shares was the lowest priority for the average worker – even if they were given for free.

4.5 Specific problems of corporate governance

Owing to delays in privatization and the specific ownership structure of the Serbian economy, various problems of corporate governance were accumulating. By the end of the 1990s, many Serbian enterprises were still operating in the social sector, some had been transformed into state-owned enterprises, while those that had been privatized have done so using the method of sales at privileged terms or giveaways to employed workers and managers.

Owing to the incompleteness of the reform process, institutions typical of a market economy were still not in place in Serbia in the late 1990s. There were no traces of the Anglo-Saxon model of corporate governance, since capital markets were highly underdeveloped (Uvalic, 2001d). Control by large shareholders was also still not in place. Banks were in many cases the major institutional owners of firms, but they did not exercise any influence over firm policies as they were themselves undercapitalized, requiring restructuring and privatization. Small external shareholders had even less influence, as they were usually not organized and not protected by existing laws. Foreign owners played a marginal role since prior to 2001 little had been invested in the Serbian economy. The last category, insiders – workers together with managers and directors – have frequently been the main group controlling the typical Serbian enterprise, sometimes even with a minority share.[8]

The obstacles for activating effective systems of corporate governance in Serbia were of a somewhat different nature in each of the three non-privatized or semi-privatized sectors – social, mixed, and state – and can be traced to three groups of potential problems deriving from 'social property', insider ownership, and re-nationalization. Problems of corporate governance were much less present, if at all, in the new private sector, since at that time most private enterprises were small firms, frequently owned and managed by a single proprietor.

4.5.1 Social sector: Inherited 'social property'

The main problems of corporate governance in 2000 in the majority of Serbian enterprises derived from the system of 'social property'. Contrary to all the other successor states of former Yugoslavia that had officially abolished 'social property' by various forms of re-nationalization already in the early 1990s, in Serbia 'social property' had been maintained. This had far-reaching implications. According to the provisions of the 1994 company law, a socially owned enterprise was to be managed by its workers, while a mixed-ownership enterprise by both its shareholders (proportional to the share of invested capital) and employed workers (proportional to the share of 'social property'). Although the new company law adopted in 1996 substantially reduced workers' rights, imposing more government control through state representatives on management boards, this law and subsequent amendments still envisaged the existence of a socially owned enterprise which assured workers concrete rights.

The fact that workers in Serbia continued to have some say in decision making was clearly not in itself a problem. Forms of employee decisional participation are today practised in many countries throughout the world, through co-determination or other forms of employee involvement. The root of the problem in Serbia in 2000 was, as during four decades of self-management, the ambiguous definition of 'social property', as the property of 'everyone and no-one'. It has been argued that the modern corporation with diffused shareholding is also owned 'by everyone and no-one', but there is a fundamental difference. Contrary to the worker in a socially owned enterprise, a small shareholder of a corporation can sell his/her share on the stock exchange at any time. Since property rights of a socially owned enterprise in Serbia remained ill-defined, it is not surprising there were different interpretations (Uvalic, 1997a, pp. 56–8).

Some have argued that it is the employed workers in Serbia who collectively owned their enterprise, since they participate in management, have the right to use enterprise assets, and to appropriate their product. But workers rights remained limited for two reasons: first, they did not have the right to appropriate the proceeds from sales of social capital, which was to go to government funds, nor could they have decided to transfer property free of charge to a new owner; and second, workers' rights were collective and non-transferable, therefore limited to the period of employment in the firm.

Others have argued that it is the enterprise as a legal entity that holds all property rights (Kovac, 1996). This was said elsewhere in Poland, Russia, and the Czech Republic, but this is utter nonsense. Legal personality does not imply that the enterprise owns itself. Although the Serbian constitution and the 1994 revisions of company law have reenforced enterprise property rights, an enterprise is not and cannot be its own owner. The enterprise holds certain property rights while it is operational, but in case of bankruptcy or liquidation, what remains of its property goes to creditors and to the state.

The last and most convincing interpretation was that the real owner of the enterprise in 'social property' in Serbia is the state (Uvalic, 1992). This is because all proceeds from sales of social capital go to government institutions, while by definition, proceeds from sales of any good go to its owner. The problem is that not even the state in Serbia had all property rights over a socially owned enterprise, since the State could not decide to privatize it. According to the 1997 privatization law, the decision on privatization had to be taken by the General Assembly of the enterprise. Property rights in a socially owned enterprise remained highly ambiguous, divided among three collective agents – employed workers, the enterprise, and the state – where neither of them had full control and ownership over the whole bundle.

4.5.2 Mixed sector: Dominant insider ownership

The large majority of Serbian enterprises privatized until 2000 used the method of sales or giveaways to employed workers and managers. Most of these firms in 2000 were in the mixed property sector, since few firms were completely privatized. Insiders were frequently the dominant shareholders, since this was directly encouraged by privatization legislation. Two groups of potential problems occurred in such a context.

First, enterprises in mixed property still had some socially owned capital, which automatically raised the problems of ambiguous property rights previously stressed for the socially owned enterprise. Corporate governance in such firms was likely to be even more complicated, given that a mixed-ownership enterprise was to be managed by both its shareholders, proportional to invested capital, and employed workers, proportional to social capital. In comparison with the situation in 1989, the confusion regarding the distribution of property rights among the various agents – individual workers shareholders, external owners, foreign investors, workers collectives, banks, and the state – was surely even greater, since privatization had introduced new private owners of enterprises, without actually determining who were the old ones (workers, the enterprise, or the state). Second, dominant insider ownership could have posed specific problems because of the potential conflict of interest arising from the double role of insiders, as wage-earners and as shareholders. As argued frequently, workers would tend to distribute excessive wages, maintain above-optimal employment, underinvest, and would not undertake the necessary restructuring (World Bank, 1996). These problems were later reformulated by taking into account the distinction between minority and majority insider ownership, workers and managers, and ownership and control, suggesting that adverse effects would not necessarily prevail, except in the special case of a controlling interest being collectively in the hands of shareholding employees holding an individual share of company capital lower than their individual share in the company wage bill. For only in that case would shareholding employees gain more from higher wages as workers than they would lose as shareholders (Nuti, 1995; Uvalic, 1995).

An intense theoretical debate on insider ownership also took place in Serbia after 1996. One group of economists strongly criticized employee ownership, arguing that, in line with the Furubotn-Pejovich theory, workers would tend to eat up social capital by distributing excessive wages (Madzar 1996). Other economists argued, in line with Nuti's (1995) hypothesis on 'employeeism', that insider ownership will result in inefficiency only under certain conditions, and that it could even be desirable if it were to speed up transition (Cerovic, 1997, 1999; Uvalic, 1997a).

Empirical evidence from transition economies has not always supported the more pessimistic predictions about employee ownership. Firms owned and controlled by employed workers and managers often have been quite efficient (Uvalic and Vaughan-Whitehead (eds), 1997; Prasnikar and Svejnar, 2007). Some Serbian enterprises privatized through employee ownership have performed rather well, including Galenika, Hemofarma, and Metalac (Djuricin, 1994).

4.5.3 State sector: Re-nationalization

Many economists in Serbia have maintained that corporate governance had deteriorated in those firms that were re-nationalized by being transformed from social into state-owned firms (Kovac, 1996). These firms were once, under self-management, run relatively independently by workers and managers, while in the 1990s they were supervised and controlled directly by the government and its ministries. The creation of a state sector was evaluated as a step backwards, towards governance mechanisms that were abandoned more than half a century ago (Cerovic, 2000).

4.6 Broader consequences of delayed transition

Owing to the slow pace of transition in Serbia, by the end of the 1990s its economic system represented a mixture of very different economic systems. In 2000, the Serbian economy still had a number of similarities with the pre-1989 economic system, since many areas of reform had not even commenced. Nevertheless, elements of the capitalist economic system have also emerged in Serbia during the 1990s. Some transition-related features were introduced by explicit provisions of the government, but many other elements have appeared spontaneously, as a consequence or by-product of the rather unusual and unique overall conditions that prevailed in the country for over a decade. As noted by a Serbian sociologist, 'Serbian society entered the New Millennium as a considerably changed society' (Bolcic, 2003, p. 28). During the 1990s, new phenomena appeared in the Serbian society which could be characterized as elements of 'wild' or unregulated capitalism.

One of the most significant new features that emerged during the 1990s was *extreme social stratification.* The political events and accompanying economic crisis of the 1990s gave birth to a dramatic social differentiation within society: massive pauperization of large segments of the population, parallel with the fast enrichment of a thin layer of individuals, in part representing the new political and economic elite.

Poverty increased rapidly by the end of the decade. The percentage of the population considered to be living in poverty was already at 33 per cent in July 1998, increasing further to 63 per cent in September 1999, where the poverty level included all people with a monthly income equivalent to US$ 60 or less (the figure does not include Kosovo; see Economist Intelligence Unit, 2000). By December 1999, the average net Yugoslav salary declined to 95 DM (from DM 167 a year earlier), and was not even sufficient to buy half of the average basket of goods. Pensions and salaries were for years paid with several months delay, frequently in kind, while during the last few months in 1999 they were paid with coupons for electricity which, ironically, at that time was being rationed. The official unemployment rate was close to 30 per cent, but the figure neglects surplus labour (estimated at another 20 per cent) which was officially employed but effectively without work. Around 90,000 workers had lost their jobs only due to destruction of industrial facilities during the 1999 war. Although the decline of employment in FR Yugoslavia was rather gradual, this occurred simply because of postponed industrial restructuring (see Figure 4.3).

Parallel with the impoverishment of large segments of the population, a new economic elite was created, recruited among directors of the important Serbian factories, who were at the same time also the closest collaborators of President Milosevic and owed their positions primarily to

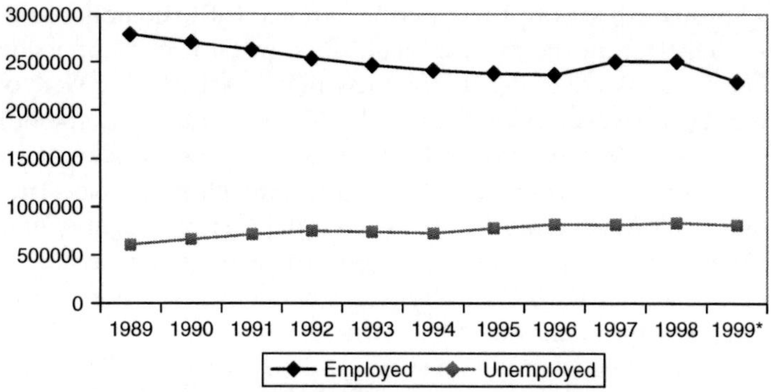

Figure 4.3 Employment and unemployment in FR Yugoslavia, 1989–1999
Source: National statistics (Savezni zavod za statistiku).

regime patronage. During Milosevic's first years in power, a small group formed around him drawn from different social categories – members of the communist party, directors of some of the most important state firms and banks; and owners of formally private enterprises, but working for the government (Miljkovic and Hoare, 2005, p. 195). This small political and economic elite was in charge of foreign trade during the years of sanctions, which ensured the accumulation of enormous amounts of money, thereafter transferred to private firms or personal bank accounts abroad. 'The Milosevic regime guaranteed the monopoly position of the Serbian economic elite, receiving in return a share of the material spoils' (Miljkovic and Hoare, 2005, p. 196).[9] This partnership resulted in an unchanged political regime for most of the 1990s, but brought economic autarky and continuous economic decline.

The secret of Milosevic's survival for so long was indeed his absolute control over the centres of financial power. The political and economic elite was deeply involved in illegal deals and with organized crime. The new economic elite has also been referred to as 'warlike entrepreneurs' (Babic, 2000), as it has enriched itself primarily during the wars in Croatia and Bosnia and Herzegovina, using various semi-legal and illegal channels. Economic sanctions had offered the government an excellent excuse to blame the West for the dramatic worsening of the economic and social situation, while also creating incentives for smuggling, illegal activities, organized crime, and 'war profiteering' (Babic, 2000).

These processes were accompanied by the diffusion of *criminality* in the society, frequent cases of robbery, kidnapping, even murders and false suicides, of which those responsible for these crimes have never been arrested, thanks to their 'good relations' with the police and the authorities. During the most difficult days, when it was impossible to get normal bank credit, it was the 'new rich' criminals that were offering money at weekly interest rates which were multiples of the official rates. Not surprisingly, there have been many cases of losses of entire family savings or of murders, following the inability to repay. There is a long list of assassinations of those who opposed the regime, or even prominent members of the elite who were eliminated because they were not considered obedient enough.[10] Numerous sanctions provided authorities with an alibi for the miserable situation in the society, but the sanctions affected only some firms and not others. The UN embargo provided strong incentives for the appearance of organized crime and war profiteers, as the state apparatus and organized crime had grown together (Babic, 2000).

Widespread *corruption* had also become a key feature of economic, political, and social relations. In 2000, FR Yugoslavia was considered one of the most corrupt among all transition countries. According to the report of Transparency International, in the late 1990s FR Yugoslavia was among the first ten most corrupt countries in the world and the most corrupt country in SEE, with a Corruption Perceptions Index of 2 (the index goes from 1 to 10, the highest score reflects no corruption). The greatest damage from these phenomena came from the destruction of traditional morals and rules of social conduct (Miljkovic and Hoare, 2005, p. 195).

Under such conditions, the *judiciary system* became highly inefficient, strongly weakening the rule of law, as the non-respect of regulations became diffused practice at all levels. Legality lost its respect and authority, as the courts were wholly deprived of any power to punish the guilty. Instead, they became pliable tools in the hands of those with the most political influence. Judges and lawyers had no choice but to toe the line or lose their jobs (Miljkovic and Hoare, 2005, p. 195).

Serbia also lost substantial *human capital* during the 1990s. Not only have the wars of the early 1990s taken many lives – the exact number of victims is not known – but there have been massive and continuous brain drain, frequently of the best experts, who have left their countries to seek employment opportunities abroad. Young people were escaping from being recruited for the wars in Croatia and Bosnia, older generations with professional contacts in the West left the country without the intention of returning home, and whoever had relatives in any possible country in the world bought a one-way ticket to leave Serbia forever, running away from poverty and misery. During the 1990s, some 600,000 people left Serbia to seek a better life abroad all over the world; in addition, some 30,000 university graduates left Serbia and Montenegro during the 1990s (Grecic, 2004). Serbia today has both absolutely and relatively a smaller population than it had in 1991, despite the influx of refugees from Croatia, Bosnia, and Kosovo (Miljkovic and Hoare, 2005, p. 194). In addition to massive brain drain, there has also been brain 'waste' in Serbia, as specialists have been leaving their professions for better paid jobs in the private and/or informal sector of the economy.

Both phenomena had very profound implications for Serbia's human capital stock, particularly for sectors such as education, science and technology, and research and development. The difficult economic situation has also brought public health institutions to the point of collapse. Although similar processes have taken place in other transition countries, their consequences have been much more dramatic in Serbia (Uvalic, 2005a).

The difficult economic situation and sanctions against FR Yugoslavia greatly contributed to the flourishing of the *informal (grey) economy*, which in the most difficult years had surpassed 50 per cent of GDP. Given that under economic sanctions, smuggling had become a very profitable activity and the main way to earn a living for many citizens; products which were scarce on the market were imported through illegal channels and offered on the open market, avoiding fiscal and other controls, thus also contributing to reduced government revenues. Over the 1990s, the ratio of the informal economy to registered GDP in FR Yugoslavia was approximately one-third; in 1999–2000 it was estimated at 36.4 per cent of measured GDP (Krstic and Sanfey, 2009).

Loss of confidence of the population in the government and its institutions was another important consequence of the 1990s, which still persists today. Most of the previously described phenomena – pyramid schemes, increasing corruption and criminality, and the absence of rule of law and of social justice – extensively contributed to widespread lack of popular support for any government. We should again recall that during the 1990s, the government confiscated a total of some 5–7 billion dollars of foreign exchange savings from Yugoslav citizens using various methods – starting from the 'freezing' of foreign exchange savings on individual bank accounts in 1991 in former Yugoslavia, government bonds for the reconstruction of Serbia whose value was eaten up by inflation, pyramid schemes by two major para-state banks, and the 1992–3 hyperinflation which forced citizens to pull out their last foreign exchange reserves held under mattresses, literally in order to survive (see Chapter 3). It is widely believed that clients with good political connections succeeded in recovering their foreign currency savings, but the largest part of the population was not as fortunate.[11]

A good example which illustrates these new times in Serbia is the well-known (and until recently possibly the richest) entrepreneurial family in Serbia, the Karic brothers (*braca Karic* in Serbian, so their various activities are known under the acronym 'BK', the Karic brothers business conglomerate). In the early 1970s, the Karic brothers invested in a factory in Kosovo thanks to a favourable bank loan, offered as part of the government programme to help the less developed regions. After 30 years of activity, they accumulated an enormous business empire, which has over the last ten years spread into all possible sectors. As can be seen from their publicity CD, the 'Astra Group' consists of 'a whole family of business stars' which operates in telecommunications (including one of the most important mobile networks and Internet providers), engineering (construction of buildings, roads, bridges, industrial complexes), media (TV channel, radio), banking and finance (Astra Bank, e-bank, e-Astra Insurance), trade (Astra Simit), services (transport and tourism), and education (BK University and Research Institute). The Karic brothers also have their foundation, which occasionally gives awards to citizens for their achievements in science, art, sports, and the like. With the political changes in 2001, an unseemly dispute took place between the Karic brothers and the new government, which was concluded to their disadvantage: they had to pay an enormous amount of money on behalf of the new extra-profits tax, while their Astra Bank has been closed because of illegal operations and insolvency.[12]

The various economic and social problems emerging in the 1990s were frequently presented by the Milosevic government and intellectuals close to the regime as proof that the transition had prevalently negative effects. This was used as a justification for the choice of a 'gradualist' strategy of transition in Serbia. Such positions were, in most cases, effectively hiding the unwillingness of the government and its supporters to introduce any more substantial economic reforms, which would have harmed vested interests.

Given all these characteristics of Serbia in mid-2000, the overall results after 11 years of transition were very modest. During the 1990s the economic system had changed little, and where change had taken place it was accompanied by new problems, frequently damaging instead of improving the functioning of the economy. The 'gradualist' strategy of transition, implemented selectively and in a highly distorted way, in reality was extremely costly for the largest part of the population.

5
Serbia's 'velvet' Revolution and Its Aftermath

The turning point of Serbia's recent history came in autumn 2000 when Milosevic was defeated at last, after having ruled the country for over ten years. The elections scheduled for 24 September 2000 brought the victory of Vojislav Kostunica, the presidential candidate of the Democratic Opposition of Serbia (DOS) for FR Yugoslavia. Radical political changes were to take place only after 5 October 2000 when, following Milosevic's non-recognition of the September 2000 electoral results, there was a general uprising of the Serbian population with thousands of people protesting on the streets of Belgrade. After two days of continuous demonstrations during which the parliament was also seized, Milosevic had to give in and recognize the electoral results. Kostunica became the new president of FR Yugoslavia and some of the main leaders of DOS were appointed ministers in the federal government.

This chapter describes the situation in Serbia/FR Yugoslavia just before and after the September 2000 elections. It recalls the atmosphere full of uncertainty preceding the elections and the principal factors that contributed to the overthrow of Milosevic, such as the active role of Non-Governmental Organizations (NGOs), a more united opposition, and the influence of Kostunica. The chapter then proceeds to describe the difficult political circumstances in the immediate aftermath of the elections. On the government agenda the tasks were already numerous, but their attainment was complicated further by the complex relationship between Serbia and Montenegro, the controversial issue of delivery of the indicted for war crimes to the ICTY, specific problems within the Serbian government, and the undefined status of Kosovo. After the 1999 bombing, FR Yugoslavia was badly in need of financial assistance from the international community, but receiving donors' aid required the prior regulation of the country's status in international organizations and the fulfilment of precise political conditions. These political issues hampered the quick implementation of many economic reforms and have also conditioned the contents of the initial transition strategy.

5.1 Uncertainty preceding the September 2000 elections

The first decade of transition in Serbia had brought most of the costs that have characterized other countries in CEE – a very deep recession, high inflation, poverty, social stratification, and corruption – but had delivered very few, if any, of the expected benefits. If freedom is the most important value that the transition to democracy and a market economy has brought to citizens of Eastern Europe after the fall of the Berlin Wall in November 1989 (Kekic, 2008), not even this objective has been realized in Serbia. On the contrary, with respect to one area – the freedom to travel abroad – there has even been a step backwards. After 1992, this important freedom that citizens in former Yugoslavia generally enjoyed from 1965 onwards has been limited by the introduction of visas for travelling to most countries throughout the world.[1]

On top of a decade of highly unfavourable general conditions – an undemocratic and repressive regime unwilling to implement any more radical economic and political reforms, a continuous fall in living standards, and international isolation – in the spring of 1999 came the 11-week-long NATO military campaign. Since the bombing did not bring any immediate political changes, in early 2000 there was a general and widespread sentiment among Serbian citizens that the country had entered a dead end street out of which there was no return to well-being and prosperity. It seemed that the regime was indestructible and that Milosevic would stay in power forever. Whoever had the possibility of going abroad left the country.

Moreover, the international isolation of FR Yugoslavia was not discontinued. The 'outer' wall of sanctions, including denial of access to international financial resources, was to remain in place as long as Milosevic was in power. In mid-1999, the Stability Pact for Southeast Europe was launched at the international conference in Sarajevo to help attract funds from potential donors for the economic reconstruction and political, economic, and security reforms in the SEE region, but without the official participation of FR Yugoslavia.[2] Soon after, the EU launched the Process of Stabilization and Association for the Western Balkan countries, but again excluded FR Yugoslavia. In early 2000, the EU granted autonomous trade preferences which significantly improved access of Western Balkan countries' exports to the EU market, but these trade concessions were not granted to FR Yugoslavia. The only exception was Montenegro's most important export item, aluminium, included among the goods with preferential access to the EU market, as a premium for what were considered positive political changes in Montenegro after the 1997 elections.[3]

In the summer of 2000 the Serbian population at large was deeply concerned about the uncertain prospects for the future, struck by the 'injustices' of the international community, disillusioned and without any hope that the situation could change for the better. The feeling of discouragement and hopelessness was present to such an extent that no one believed changes were possible. Even the most optimistic citizens who were actively engaged in preparing the electoral campaign hardly believed that their common goal – getting rid of Milosevic – could actually be realized. In case of Kostunica's victory, everybody was convinced that Milosevic would never be willing to give up his position.

Yet to the surprise of many citizens, radical political changes did take place. In early October 2000, following the presidential elections on 24 September and Serbia's 'velvet' revolution – the popular post-election demonstrations – Vojislav Kostunica became the new president of the Yugoslav federation. This was the final defeat of Slobodan Milosevic, who had dragged the country into what has been called 'the ghetto' (Curgus Kazimir, 2001). After October 2000, a new phase of Serbia's transition started which would gradually introduce democracy and a market economy. Although it was President Milosevic who decided to anticipate the presidential elections and also called for parliamentary elections with the hope of winning again,[4] he had overestimated his popularity. According to the DOS results, the presidential elections of 24 September, after the second round on 8 October, brought Kostunica 52.54 per cent of votes and Milosevic 35.01 per cent (though the Federal Electoral Commission official results reported a somewhat less convincing victory of Kostunica) (Cohen, 2002, p. 438). The DOS coalition also got the majority of seats in the federal parliament.

The outcome of the presidential elections in FR Yugoslavia was thus for many observers a surprise. The rather extraordinary events which followed the elections – the popular uprising of thousands of citizens which contributed to the recognition of the victory of Vojislav Kostunica as the new president of the Yugoslav federation – was perhaps an even greater surprise. The most common reaction to these events was astonishment; in one of the main Belgrade weeklies *NIN*, one could read 'Serbia has surprised itself.' There were many uncertainties regarding the elections, not only whether the democratic opposition could win but also whether Milosevic would be willing to step down voluntarily, but there were also a number of valid reasons supportive of a positive outcome.

5.2 Why did Kostunica win?

Many analysts have argued that it is primarily thanks to the 11-week-long bombing of Serbia that the population voted against Milosevic, therefore, the extreme measure implemented against Serbia had accomplished its main objective. Others have quite the opposite view, maintaining that the NATO bombing had re-enforced Milosevic, that the revival of nationalism in Serbia was stronger than ever, and that the democratic opposition to the regime had been killed.[5] Both views are only partial and very simplified explanations of the democratic outcome of the September 2000 elections. Other factors must be recalled, including the active role of NGOs, a more united opposition, the influence and personality of Kostunica, and the deep political, economic, and social crisis (Uvalic, 2001e).

5.2.1 Role of NGOs

The 'small October revolution', as the October 2000 demonstrations in Belgrade were sometimes called, was undoubtedly a spontaneous popular revolt, but it was organized by a number of opposition parties and NGOs, on the basis of a precise strategy that had one common objective – to get rid of Milosevic. The strategy was elaborated not only by the main opposition political parties – Zoran Djindjic's Democratic Party (DS), Vojislav Kostunica's DSS, and a number of other smaller parties – but also by numerous NGOs that have for years been active on the political scene in developing a civil society, political and social structures alternative to the official ones, as well as opposition trade unions and other organizations of citizens.[6] These organizations have given an extremely important contribution to the preparation of the September 24 elections, from trying to convince citizens to vote, to inventing humorous leaflets on why Kostunica should be their preferred candidate, diffusing information on the real face of the governing political and economic elite, and promoting the idea that only radical political changes could bring more permanent improvements of the economic, political, and international conditions of the country.

Initially concentrated primarily in Belgrade, these NGOs gradually became widespread and active throughout Serbia. In the spring of 2000, there were more than 150 NGOs involving around 25,000–30,000 volunteers organized under the umbrella 'Exit 2000', a campaign for free and fair presidential elections in 2000 (Minic and Dereta, 2007). Among the most active was the G17 Plus, an NGO grown out of the G17, a group of economists led by Mladjan Dinkic, which in 1997 prepared a programme of radical economic reforms for Serbia (see Chapter 4).[7] The G17 Plus had also launched useful initiatives such as the project 'Energy for democracy' through which financial support was obtained from the EU for importing energy only to those Serbian cities with democratic governments in place (such as Nis). A number of other NGOs were actively involved in preparing the elections, including the students' movement Otpor (Resistence), the Helsinki Movement for Human Rights, and the European Movement for Serbia.

The G17 Plus prepared *The White Book of Milosevic's Rule* (G17 Plus, 2000a), illustrating the dramatic economic consequences of the Milosevic regime for demographic trends, macroeconomic indicators, and living standard of the population. In the summer of 2000, the G17 Plus also prepared *The Programme of the Democratic Opposition of Serbia – For a Democratic Serbia* (G17 Plus, 2000b), offering guidelines on the economic policies and reforms to be undertaken by the first post-Milosevic government. Both documents were distributed to the population at popular meetings organized in Belgrade in August 2000. The *Programme of the Democratic Opposition of Serbia* was officially adopted by the DOS coalition as the main document that was to guide the forthcoming radical political and economic reforms.

These activities contributed further to increasing widespread sentiment against the ruling elite, also of those citizens who did not necessarily identify themselves with any of the main opposition parties. The numerous popular anti-government riots organized throughout the 1990s described earlier (see Chapters 3 and 4), which were ineffective in bringing radical and more permanent political changes, greatly contributed to the accumulation of social dissatisfaction and unrest. By mid-2000, Milosevic had become increasing unpopular. It is unfair to attribute to the whole Serbian nation 'collective responsibility' for the permanence of the Milosevic regime, as has often been done in the Western mass media or within academic circles. Many citizens have for years fought the regime in various ways, since they were very much in favour of a free, open, and democratic society for Serbia. They have fought for progressive political and economic changes in Yugoslavia, yet were blocked halfway or were cleverly outwitted. They voted against Milosevic on 14 September 2000.

5.2.2 A more united opposition

A positive transformation of the Serbian democratically oriented parties also contributed to the outcome of the September 2000 elections. At a meeting held in January 2000, the opposition parties agreed to fully cooperate, to begin joint protests on 9 March, and to demand early elections at all levels. Even more importantly, these parties presented themselves in a united coalition, proposing one presidential candidate, Vojislav Kostunica. After a decade of futile political struggle, continuous internal conflicts and political rivalries, the 18 parties united in the DOS coalition decided to act together, overcoming their previous internal disputes and the personal egos of their leaders, for the sake of achieving the final objective of overthrowing Milosevic. The only politician within the opposition who decided not to join the DOS was the leader of the Serbian Renewal Movement (SPO), Vuk Draskovic.

It should also be recalled that the 1996 elections had already brought victory to the opposition parties in some of the most important cities in Serbia, including Cacak, Kragujevac, Nis, Novi Sad, and Subotica, though with a delay due to the non-recognition of the electoral results (see Chapter 4). This enabled the spread of influence of some anti-Milosevic political parties, primarily the DS, well before 2000.

The close cooperation between the main democratic parties and the principal NGOs in Serbia was another important factor. Several key personalities in the most active NGOs were also the main politicians in the opposition parties, such as the president of the G17 Plus Miroljub Labus, who was also one of the most influential members of Djindjic's DS. Labus was to become a key figure on the political scene in Serbia, initially as deputy prime minister and minister for foreign economic relations in the new federal government appointed on 4 November 2000, and later, in autumn 2002, as candidate at the Serbian presidential elections running against Kostunica. An informal division of tasks between the DOS and G17 Plus was agreed upon: whereas Zoran Djindjic was considered the 'political manager' of the 2000 elections, Miroljub Labus and his group of G17 Plus experts were the 'technical brain' preparing the programme of radical political and economic reforms.

5.2.3 The influence of Kostunica

Vojislav Kostunica, the presidential candidate against Milosevic, was carefully chosen. Although Kostunica had been on the political scene of Serbia from the very beginning – he was one of the founding members of the DS, but in 1992 he decided to leave the DS and create his own party, the DSS – he was less exposed than the other main opposition leaders (Zoran Djindjic, Vesna Pesic, and Vuk Draskovic). This is one of the reasons why he seemed the right candidate at that time, more likely to win the elections than other opposition leaders who had also attracted widespread criticism. Kostunica was modest and honest, he was an intellectual (a professor of constitutional law) and his social background attracted votes of some undecided citizens who had abstained from voting throughout the 1990s. He was a strong supporter of democratic values, and contrary to some other opposition leaders in Serbia, he was considered to have been consistent in his political views.

But probably the most important reason why Kostunica attracted so many votes is that he seemed to promise the respect of traditional values so dear to many Serbian citizens, including Kosovo as the cradle of Serbia. Having acquired the label of being more nationalist than the other opposition leaders, he attracted votes of many citizens that were still infected by Milosevic's nationalism. However, contrary to Milosevic, Kostunica was considered a democratic nationalist, and was thus appealing to a large part of the electorate. For a long time – up until his departure from the political scene in 2008 – it is these traditional values that Kostunica gave importance to that made him very popular among the population.

5.2.4 Political, economic, and social crisis

All the above factors have given their impetus to the positive outcome of the 2000 elections, but we cannot but emphasize again the severe political, economic, and social crisis that accumulated for a whole decade in FR Yugoslavia. Particularly after the 1999 NATO military campaign, the economic conditions in the country were disastrous. There were continuous shortages of electricity, medicine, and heating; there were daily queues in front of stores for basic foodstuff; and half of the labour force was effectively without work, forced to invent strategies of survival by smuggling goods from neighbouring countries, and working in the grey economy. Corruption had become widespread at all levels, laws were not respected, and courts were ineffective. Milosevic's political and economic elite had strict control over the political and economic system, over the media, and over the judiciary. Under deteriorating living conditions, common people realized at last that they had been cheated and manipulated, that the goals proposed by Milosevic were false, that he had made empty promises he could never deliver.

5.3 The political difficulties of the immediate aftermath

The victory of the DOS opposition in October 2000 was only the first step towards more fundamental political changes in FR Yugoslavia and Serbia. Although Kostunica had won the elections, many remnants of the old regime were not eliminated. The political scene at that time was very complex for a variety of reasons. In autumn 2000, there were still a number of unresolved political issues which greatly slowed down, in some cases even blocked, the government's attempts to implement transition-related economic and political reforms. Within the federal government, the quick implementation of radical economic reforms was hampered by the existence of two different economic systems in Montenegro and Serbia, and the unstable coalition between the DOS and the political parties representing Montenegro. In the Serbian government, democratic changes took place only in January 2001 after Prime Minister Zoran Djindjic appointed his new cabinet, and the new government also had to address a number of specific problems.

5.3.1 One country, two economic systems

In the second half of the 1990s there was progressive deterioration in political and economic relations between Serbia and Montenegro. After 1997, for both political and economic reasons, Montenegro decided to distance itself even more from Serbia by adopting separate laws and implementing it own economic policies, as part of its project of political independence. This was motivated by the need for protection from the disastrous political and economic consequences of Milosevic's policies dictated by the Belgrade government, including currency instability, inflationary pressures, declining official reserves, and rising external imbalances.

At the October 1997 elections, Milo Djukanovic was elected president of Montenegro, defeating the pro-Milosevic candidate Momir Bulatovic, the representative of the Socialist People's Party (SNP) who in 1999–2000 was also the prime minister in the federal Yugoslav government. After the elections Djukanovic got strong national and international support, and his government introduced a series of measures which established independence from Serbia in most economic fields. Regarding privatization this was done much earlier, since Montenegro adopted its own law already in 1992. It was hoped that monetary, fiscal, and foreign trade independence would enable Montenegro to implement a swifter and faster transition to a market economy.

Montenegro achieved monetary independence through the creation of its own central bank and the introduction of the German mark, first as a parallel currency and after 3 November 1999 as the official legal tender, which in early 2002 was replaced by the euro.[8] In the area of fiscal policy, Montenegro implemented some major tax reforms and established control over most sources of fiscal revenues, the main exception being customs duties which remained under the federal state. Montenegro also adopted its own foreign trade law which in 2001 envisaged an average tariff on imports of only 3 per cent, while in Serbia it was still over 10 per cent (although Montenegro retained some quotas, while Serbia did abolish all quantitative restrictions as part of the liberalization measures implemented in 2001). From mid-February 2001, Montenegro also established five border crossings on the Serb-Montenegrin border, which produced long queues on the borders, creating traffic jams and stimulating the flourishing of the grey economy, smuggling, and corruption.

These measures led to the fragmentation of the Yugoslav common market and to the end of the monetary and customs union, with far-reaching political implications. Increasing tensions between the Montenegrin and federal authorities were also caused by restrictions of various transfers imposed on both sides, such as the Montenegrin block of transfers to the federal budget, or the federal government's restrictions on payments to firms which had not paid federal taxes and delays in paying Montenegrin pensions. The situation was aggravated further by the introduction of various duties on trade between the two Yugoslav republics.

As a result, the Yugoslav federation in late 2000 represented a rather specific and unique case: it was still one federal state, but without a full common market, or a customs union, or a monetary union, between its two constituent republics. Only some features of an economic union were present, such as free movement of labour (but not of goods, services, and capital), and coordination of some economic policies at the federal level. But it was no longer a monetary union (in addition to the dinar, the German mark, later euro, had become legal tender), nor a customs union (different external tariffs were applied by the two republics), and not even a free trade area (duties were imposed on inter-republican trade).

This anomaly of having two separate economies within one country, two distinct economic systems, two legal currencies, and two different types of monetary, fiscal, and foreign trade policies, was consolidated in late 2000. The tensions accumulated after 1997 between the

Montenegrin and the federal Yugoslav authorities represented a very unfavourable starting point for a swift implementation of the necessary economic reforms. Although Montenegro had in the meantime stepped back from organizing a referendum on independence,[9] it still wanted a revision of the terms of the Yugoslav Federation. The situation was further complicated by the unnatural coalition of political parties that formed the federal government in late 2000.

5.3.2 Federal government: The Socialist-DOS coalition

The fact that the DOS had won the September 2000 presidential and parliamentary elections did not mean the replacement of the entire federal government. Kostunica became the new president of the Yugoslav federation and many of the new federal ministers were from the DOS parties, but the Montenegrin part of the federal government was represented by the SNP, that for years had been Milosevic's faithful collaborator. This is because the Montenegrin leadership headed by Djukanovic announced that it would boycott the September 2000 federal elections, unless the two republics agreed on the future restructuring of the federal state.

Since no agreement was reached, the governing block in Montenegro supporting Djukanovic boycotted the September federal elections, allowing the pro-Milosevic Montenegrin socialist forces (SNP) to win. After the DOS victory in October 2000, DOS formed a coalition government with the Montenegrin SNP. In the new federal government appointed on 4 November 2000, the prime minister was Zoran Zizic from the SNP, while Miroljub Labus, representing the DOS, was the new vice prime minister. Other ministers and assistant ministers in the federal government were also representatives of the same Montenegrin coalition which, quite contrary to Djukanovic, was firmly for the maintenance of a common state with Serbia. Thus the SNP remained in the federal government, although at that time it was an opposition party in Montenegro, united with two other Montenegrin parties – the National Party (NS) and the Serbian National Party (SNS).

Such an unnatural coalition in the federation made cooperation within the federal government extremely slow and burdensome. Although effective power at the federal level was in the hands of President Kostunica and Deputy Prime Minister Labus, a part of the government represented by the SNP continued to exercise a substantial degree of influence.[10] This created enormous conflicts of interest within the federal administration, and also rendered cooperation with the Djukanovic-led Montenegrin government very difficult. Before the 2000 changes, the Montenegrin-Serbian disagreements essentially derived from Djukanovic's strive for political and economic independence, and Milosevic's opposite position, backed by Montenegrin politicians in the federal government in favour of maintaining the federation. These diametrically different positions resulted in increasing tensions, mutual distrust, and continuous deterioration of relations in 1999–2000 between Montenegro and the Yugoslav (federal) government, at that time still in the hands of President Milosevic.

A related issue which created further tensions in late 2000 was the existence of different positions within the federal government regarding collaboration with the ICTY. Given that the Montenegrin politicians in the federal government had for years closely collaborated with Milosevic, they could not but be against his extradition to The Hague. In addition, there was a split on the issue of the ICTY within the DOS part of the federal government, between President Kostunica and Vice Prime Minister Labus. Kostunica insisted on the respect of law and held a highly negative opinion of the Hague Tribunal, considering that the request for Milosevic's extradition did not constitute a priority and that justice would better be served if Milosevic first faced trial in Yugoslavia; in early 2001, opinion polls revealed that Serbs overwhelmingly agreed that Milosevic should be tried in Yugoslavia (Cohen, 2002, p. 7).

Although the Yugoslav authorities eventually permitted the ICTY to open an office in Belgrade and Kostunica agreed to meet the chief prosecutor Carla del Ponte, Kostunica wanted to continue with the indictment of NATO officials for the bombing of Yugoslavia, NATO's use of depleted uranium shells, and its alleged fabrication of the 1999 Racak massacre of Kosovo Albanians which had contributed to precipitating NATO hostilities against Yugoslavia (Cohen, 2002, p. 7). Kostunica's refusal to cooperate fully with the demands of the ICTY could have cost Yugoslavia the desperately needed foreign assistance and undermined the country's effort to obtain membership in international economic organizations. On the other hand, Labus's position was fully in accordance with Serbia's Prime Minister Djindjic's views of delivering Milosevic to The Hague as soon as possible.

The tensions within the federal government after October 2000 were therefore due to different issues. The federal government continued to be partly represented by the Montenegrin SNP that before late 2000 collaborated closely with Milosevic, but the SNP had a similar position as Kostunica regarding collaboration with the ICTY, as well as the future of the country. Like the SNP, Kostunica was also in favour of maintaining a common state, hoping that this would ensure the permanence of Kosovo in FR Yugoslavia. It therefore comes as no surprise that even after the political changes in October 2000, no agreement could be reached on a mutually acceptable solution for the country's future.

Although the Serbian and Montenegrin governments have implemented distinct economic policies in most areas, especially after 1998, in late 2000 there were still a number of issues that required their close cooperation. This was true for foreign economic relations – negotiations with the IMF, the World Bank, the EBRD, the Paris and London Club of creditors, and the EU – as well as certain areas still within the competence of the federal government, including foreign affairs, customs administration, the army, and telecommunication.

The political situation was extremely complicated also because of the parallel existence of three governments – federal, Serbian, and Montenegrin – with the triplication of many ministries and insufficient, if any, coordination among them. Internal political disputes within and between the three governments have greatly contributed to slow negotiations with international financial institutions, thus postponing the arrival of badly needed external funds. Political disagreements also complicated the process of stabilization and association with the EU as initially, three separate working groups had to be formed; and caused substantial delays in implementing the November 2000 trade preferences granted by the EU, because of the need to reach an agreement on what type of customs seal would be used for Yugoslav exports. All these problems limited the inflow of badly needed FDI, by perpetuating political risk and uncertainty.

5.3.3 Problems within the Serbian government

Following the federal presidential and parliamentary elections, and the local elections in Serbia held on 24 September 2000, all of which brought the victory of the DOS, the legitimacy of the unchanged Serbian government was brought into question. Under popular pressure the SPS government resigned, early elections were scheduled, and an interim government was formed. Negotiations between the DOS, the SPS, and the Serbian Renewal Movement (SPO) were concluded by the signing of an agreement on the formation of a transitory Serbian government on 16 October 2000, which would be in charge until after the Serbian parliamentary elections scheduled for 24 December 2000. The transitory Serbian government provided co-ruling of the former regime and the new democratic coalition; it was also called the 'three-headed' government since it established co-ministers, namely representatives of all three parties/signatories of the agreement. Decision making in the transitory Serbian government was to be based on consensus, which was clearly very difficult; thus it is not surprising that a major crisis arose in late 2000 when the SPS rejected to dismiss the head of the state security service requested by the DOS and the SPO.

The transitory Serbian government was replaced only after the official elections for the Serbian parliament on 24 December 2000, which brought the DOS 64.4 per cent of the votes and 70.4 per cent of the seats in the parliament. The new Prime Minister Zoran Djindjic formed his cabinet of ministers and on 25 January 2001 the pro-reform government was sworn in. Despite radical changes in the Serbian government, it should be recalled that the president of Serbia officially remained Milan Milutinovic, one of Milosevic's closest collaborators, since his presidential term was to expire only in December 2002. Although Milutinovic was not able to use his position as president because of the defeat of his party (SPS) and his indictment by the Hague Tribunal, he remained acting president until 2002.[11]

The ambiguous status of Kosovo was another major problem for the Serbian (and Yugoslav) government, since after the 1999 conflict FR Yugoslavia had lost effective sovereignty over this part of its territory. Although the UN Security Council Resolution 1244 proclaimed that Kosovo remains part of FR Yugoslavia, it was *de facto* the UNMIK that was in charge of the province. Within the government, there were very different views about policies regarding the status of Kosovo and the protection of Kosovo Serbs. The undefined status of Kosovo also complicated the government's negotiations with international organizations, as it was unclear whether the province would remain part of the country. The situation in Kosovo was far from stabilized. During the first half of 2001 there were disorders both in Kosovo and in the southern part of Serbia on the border with Kosovo. The Serbs in Kosovo strongly feared they would be abandoned in the case of an independent Kosovo, so their representatives were frequent visitors of the Belgrade governments in early 2001. In addition to all the delicate problems inherited from the Milosevic era, there were other severe problems the Serbian government had to urgently address during the winter and spring of 2001, such as the energy crisis that led to serious electricity shortages, and the bad harvest which put many farmers in a difficult financial situation.

5.4 FR Yugoslavia's return to the international community

Many issues on the economic agenda in FR Yugoslavia in 2000–1 depended directly on the prior resolution of key foreign policy objectives, from the renewal of membership in all international organizations, to the normalization of diplomatic relations with practically the whole world. The question of international donors' assistance to FR Yugoslavia, or the write-off of part of its external debt, could not even be addressed before the country's normalization of relations with the outside world.

The 2000 radical political changes did not automatically bring FR Yugoslavia membership in international organizations. FR Yugoslavia had to apply for membership, or ask for renewal of its status, in practically all existing international organizations. Formal procedures had to be initiated and support obtained for the country to be admitted to the World Bank and the IMF, to become a member of the EBRD, to become eligible for funding of the EU, to begin the process of negotiations with the World Trade Organization (WTO). These important tasks required time, a substantial amount of administrative work and diplomatic action – for the formal applications to be made, for the negotiations to be organized and launched, for the country's requests for admission/readmission to be approved. The Yugoslav minister of foreign affairs at that time, Goran Svilanovic, described well the complexity of these processes (Svilanovic, 2001).

On 1 November 2000, when the United Nations General Assembly adopted Resolution 55/12, FR Yugoslavia became a full-fledged member of the UN, which *de facto* initiated the process of regulating the country's membership in all specialized agencies of the UN system, international organizations associated with the UN, and other international organizations. In a relatively short period of time, FR Yugoslavia succeeded in regulating its membership in most UN specialized agencies and in signing, ratifying, or acceding to a large number of major international conventions adopted under the auspices of the UN.

From 1 November 2000 to September 2001, FR Yugoslavia obtained membership in 12, while admission procedures were under way in another two UN specialized agencies. In addition, FR Yugoslavia joined 9 European and regional organizations, including the EBRD, the Stability Pact for Southeast Europe, the Southeast European Cooperation Initiative, the Central European Initiative, and the Organization for Security and Cooperation in Europe, while the procedure for joining the Council of Europe was under way. During the same period, FR Yugoslavia also joined 9 other international organizations, such as Interpol, International Migration Organization, or the World Tourist Organization, while with the WTO and the Black Sea Economic Cooperation admission procedures were in course (Svilanovic, 2001, p. 15). An application to join the WTO was presented by the government on 23 January 2001.

The first international financial institution to officially admit FR Yugoslavia as a member was the EBRD. On 14 December 2000, the country's membership in the EBRD was approved, to become effective in January 2001. Soon after, on 20 December 2000, the IMF Board of Directors decided that FR Yugoslavia had met the necessary conditions for membership, a decision that came into effect retroactively from 14 December. On 20 December 2000 the IMF also approved a loan equivalent to SDR 116.9 million, under the IMF's policy on Emergency Post-Conflict Assistance in order to support the country's stabilization programme and reconstruction of the federal institutions and administration.

Contacts with the World Bank and the EIB were re-established with a view to getting these institutions operational in the country as soon as possible. Entering the IMF opened the doors for FR Yugoslavia's membership in the World Bank, but this required reaching an agreement on the US$1.7 billion debt that had accumulated since 1993, when membership of Yugoslavia was suspended. FR Yugoslavia was admitted to the World Bank on 8 May 2001, which was to pave the way for structural adjustment lending of the World Bank, supporting its stabilization and reform programme (see below).

Relations between FR Yugoslavia and the EU were intensified fairly quickly. The President of the EU Commission, Romano Prodi, visited Belgrade on 25 November 2000, when a Framework Agreement between FR Yugoslavia and the EU Commission was signed. The agreement represented the legal basis enabling the delivery of the first package of EU financial emergency assistance to FR Yugoslavia which was aproved in late 2000. In addition, in November 2000, the EU also extended the autonomous trade preferences previously granted to the other Western Balkan countries. In order to prepare the process of negotiations between the EU and FR Yugoslavia on its inclusion in the SAP devised by the EU in 1999 for all the Western Balkan countries, an EU Commission delegation headed by Katherine Day came on an official visit to Belgrade in March 2001. The European Agency for Reconstruction (EAR), in charge of delivering EU financial assistance to Serbia, started operating soon after.

Despite quick EU emergency assistance, it is only in July 2001 that FR Yugoslavia would be officially included in the SAP (see Chapter 8). The first joint Consultative Task Force (CTF) meeting between the representatives of the EU Commission and the Yugoslav, Serbian, and Montenegrin governments took place in Belgrade in July 2001. As envisaged by the EU SAP, it is through these CTF meetings that the process of negotiations regarding the future signing of an SAA was to be prepared.

One of the main reasons for the delays in organizing the first CTF meeting was the uncertainty regarding the future of the Yugoslav federation as well as the resulting political tensions between Serbia and Montenegro. Within the country, there were major disagreements on what was the most appropriate institutional framework and level for developing future relations with the EU, where the Montenegrin government was reluctant to accept any solutions at the federal level. In early 2001, the EU Commission was expecting a concrete proposal from the Yugoslav government on the creation of a ministry or an office in charge of specifically EU integration, but the political conditions in the country were still not ripe to allow the creation of such an office. The EU Commission was also hesitant to accept any solutions suggested by the federal government, fearing it would not be accepted by Montenegro.

After joining the Stability Pact for Southeast Europe on 26 October 2000, FR Yugoslavia fully supported and actively participated in all its initiatives. A special conference was organized by the Italian Ministry of foreign affairs in Rome in January 2001, to agree upon a concrete agenda of inclusion of FR Yugoslavia into all activities of the Stability Pact's Working Table II for economic reconstruction, cooperation, and development. In Geneva in January 2001, a Trade Policy Forum was organized by the Stability Pact, where FR Yugoslavia signed the Statement of Intent together with other SEE countries, confirming its willingness to liberalize trade with neighbouring countries in the region. This preliminary agreement led to the signing of the Memorandum of understanding on trade liberalization and facilitation in June 2001 in Brussels by foreign trade ministers of seven SEE countries (the then five Western Balkan countries, Bulgaria, and Romania). The Memorandum envisaged the conclusion of bilateral free trade agreements between the seven SEE countries, emphasizing that more liberal trade regimes could facilitate trade links in the SEE region, thus positively influencing trade flows and economic development. FR Yugoslavia actively participated at the Regional Conference of the Stability Pact for SEE in Tirana in May 2001, as well as in a number of other regional intiatiatives. After a decade of conflicts in the SEE region, these projects were very important for implementing regional cooperation among the SEE countries.

In addition to the urgent task of normalizing relations with all major international organizations, in late 2000 FR Yugoslavia also had to establish diplomatic relations with a number of countries worldwide, including neighbouring countries. In late 2000, FR Yugoslavia re-established diplomatic relations not only with the US, the UK, Germany, and France, which had been interrupted after the 1999 Kosovo conflict, but also with Bosnia and Herzegovina, Slovenia, Albania, and the other neighbouring countries. A dialogue was launched with all the successor states of former Yugoslavia on a number of open questions, which led to the Succession Agreement signed in Vienna on 29 June 2001. This important agreement regulated at last the division of assets of the former Yugoslavia that was pending since 1991, thus resolving one of the most disputed questions in their mutual relations. Talks on defining inter-state borders were intiaited with Bosnia and Herzegovina, Croatia, and Macedonia. The Yugoslav government also started talks on the return of Serbian refugess to Croatia and Bosnia and Herzegovina (Svilanovic, 2001).

As part of the renewal of diplomatic relations with the outside world, there were daily visits to Belgrade of high officials, politicians, diplomats, representatives of Western governments, international organizations, and NGOs.[12] In late 2000 and early 2001, FR Yugoslavia was offered an impressive amount of assistance and technical expertise by foreign governments and their development agencies, on all possible issues. Within the assistance packages, financial assistance was sometimes offered for projects which were not essential for attaining the most urgent objectives, but the resources were so scarce that any support seemed welcome. There was no way to distinguish in advance between essential and non-essential projects, since the name of an institution announced through a foreign embassy was not enough to know the purpose of the visit. In order not to miss a potentially important opportunity, whoever asked for an appointment was welcomed.

Under the pressure of numerous tasks that had to be accomplished, the government paid insufficient attention to diffusing information and explaining to the population at large what the concrete objectives of measures undertaken as part of radical economic reforms were. The main institution in charge of diffusing information – the Federal Secretariat for Information – would pass on information to the press almost exclusively according to what they considered important, frequently not giving sufficient credit to accomplishments of key politicians. This was one of the main reasons for lack of popular support for the transition-related reforms implemented during 2001. A large part of the population was not aware of the enormous amount of work that was being done behind the doors of the Federation Palace, where the federal government was located.

The government was literally working day and night, under extremely difficult working conditions, since the general state of the public administration inherited in late 2000 was disastrous. The Yugoslav government lacked not only basic technical facilities, such as computers, photocopying and fax machines, but there was even a general shortage of normal paper. A decade of international isolation, undemocratic political regime, lack of systemic changes, and continuous impoverishment of the country had left incredible traces on the public administration (see the appendix, Box 5.1).

5.5 The economic agenda: Aid-dependency and political conditionality

Given that in FR Yugoslavia, by late 2000, very limited progress had been achieved in most areas of reform required by the transition to a market economy, the number of tasks was enormous. Although the G17 Plus had prepared a general programme of economic reforms for the first post-Milosevic government which was endorsed by the DOS in October 2000 (G17 Plus, 2000b), many additional questions required concrete answers. The government had to determine the most urgent objectives and the sequencing of reforms, as well as the contents of specific programmes for the various areas of reform. It also had to coordinate the necessary economic changes to be undertaken by many ministries in the Federal, Serbian, and Montenegrin government.

In the aftermath of October 2000, the complex economic agenda was complicated further by important political issues, both internal and international. The earlier described political problems within the country greatly hampered the quick implementation of the most urgent economic reforms (like the Serb-Montenegrin relations, see section 5.3 above). In addition, the difficulties in setting up and implementing the government's economic agenda were closely related to international issues. In late 2000, there was an urgent need for substantial external financial assistance for the reconstruction of the economy after the 1999 bombing and the launch of radical economic reforms. However, in order to get financial support of international financial organizations and most important developed countries, FR Yugoslavia had to comply with the main political conditions, primarily its international obligations regarding cooperation with the ICTY. The country's extreme dependence on international donors' assistance also influenced the transition strategy adopted in 2001.

5.5.1 International donors' assistance

In late 2000, the tasks on the government's economic agenda were numerous, while the financial resources were extremely scarce. With a GDP at 47 per cent of its 1989 level, FR Yugoslavia was highly dependent on external donors' financial assistance. FR Yugoslavia hoped to get support from the IMF, the EBRD, the World Bank, the EU, and other donors, but in order to get financial assistance it first had to regulate its status and obtain membership in these institutions, which required the prior acceptance of its debt obligations that had not been settled after the break-up of former Yugoslavia in 1991. The government also had to start negotiations with its external creditors – the World Bank and the Paris and the London Clubs of creditors – in order to obtain the rescheduling and cancellation of a part of its huge external debt. An accurate assessment of FR Yugoslavia's outstanding debt had to be prepared and a plan to clear arrears had to be devised, as a precondition for World Bank membership. In addition, the government had to consider its financial obligations and prepare for negotiations with the other Yugoslav successor states regarding the division of assets and liabilities of the former Yugoslavia, an issue that was posponed for over a decade. All these issues were quite urgent and were subject to political conditionality.

Contrary to the naïve belief that donors' aid would arrive the day after the defeat of Milosevic, a large part of financial assistance to FR Yugoslavia was slow to arrive. The international community did support FR Yugoslavia almost immediately with emergency assistance, in order to facilitate the consolidation of power of the new democratic government during its first months of existence. The EU provided an emergency assistance package of some €200 million, as announced at the Biarritz European Council in October 2000. A Donors' Coordination Meeting was also organized by the European Commission – World Bank Office for Southeast Europe in Brussels on 12 December 2000, which secured an emergency aid package to cover the most urgent needs consisting of food aid, medical, and energy supplies to provide for the basic needs of the population during the winter 2000–1. In addition to assistance of the most important international financial institutions, many developed countries also offered generous bilateral financial aid almost immediately – including most EU member states, Switzerland, and Japan – but the needs were so enormous that the assistance received was simply not sufficient. The emergency package could only cover the short-term needs and was insufficient for launching major and urgently needed economic reforms. The more important donors' conference for

FR Yugoslavia, aimed at helping economic reconstruction and systemic economic transformation, was to be held only in June 2001.

When FR Yugoslavia resumed its membership in the IMF on 20 December 2000, it also received a loan under IMF's policy on emergency post-conflict assistance. However, the Yugoslav government channeled SDR 101.1 million, thus almost the entire amount of the IMF loan worth SDR 116.9 million, towards repaying the loan for bridging the time gap, that Switzerland and Norway had kindly granted to FR Yugoslavia for the purpose of settling its obligations towards the IMF (www.nbs.rs). In order to become eligible for IMF support, the Yugoslav authorities agreed to implement a stabilization programme that addressed the short-term needs, covering the initial period from December 2000 to March 2001. In addition, on 11 June 2001, the IMF approved an SBA of SDR 200 million as further support to the government's economic programme. This SBA provided a basis for conducting negotiations on Serbia and Montenegro's debt relief with the Paris Club creditors.

The procedure was very similar with the other international financial institutions. In the case of the EIB, new lending was conditional on FR Yugoslavia's acceptance and clearance of outstanding arrears of some €218 million as of the beginning of April 2001, stemming from relevant old loans to this part of SFR Yugoslavia. Similarly, only after FR Yugoslavia's arrears were settled with the World Bank, was it able to provide new loans. The Yugoslav authorities had to express their willingness to fulfil these obligations, following the example of all the other former Yugoslav republics (Commission of the EC, 2001).

The outcome of the donors' conference, planned to be held in June 2001 in Brussels, depended not only on the prior settlement of FR Yugoslavia's debt obligations towards major international organizations and creditors, but also on the resolution of pending political issues. International financial assistance to FR Yugoslavia was subject to very strict political conditionality. Although the government of Milosevic was no longer in place, this was not sufficient to obtain quick and comprehensive international support. A number of foreign governments and international financial organizations were unwilling to provide assistance to FR Yugoslavia unless the government complied with the demands of the ICTY. At that time, the main request was the imprisonment and delivery of Slobodan Milosevic.

There was a first externally imposed deadline for capturing Milosevic set for 31 March 2001. Although Kostunica took no measures to prevent Milosevic's imprisonment, it was Zoran Djindjic who ordered special police operatives under his personal control to arrest Milosevic. The deadline was respected and on 31 March 2001 Slobodan Milosevic was taken to the Belgrade central prison (Cohen, 2002, p. 8). The second deadline imposed from the outside regarded the international donors' conference for FR Yugoslavia, to be held in June 2001 in Brussels, when substantial financial assistance was to be pledged for Yugoslavia's economic reconstruction and transition programme. The amount that FR Yugoslavia was to get depended very much on whether Slobodan Milosevic would be delivered to The Hague.

On the evening of 27 June 2001, just one day before the donors' conference for FR Yugoslavia, Slobodan Milosevic was transported to the prison in The Hague. The plan of his delivery to The Hague prison was kept secret until the very last moment, in the fear of being discovered and undermined by conservative forces within the country. Thanks to the delivery of Milosevic, the amount for FR Yugoslavia's economic reconstruction programme pledged on 28 June 2001 in Brussels corresponded to what was initially announced, around US$ 1.34 billion (see Table 5.1).

Almost half of the financial assistance pledged at the donors' conference in June 2001 for FR Yugoslavia – US$ 637 million – was provided by the EU Commission, the EIB, and EU member states, while another US$ 206 million was offered by the EBRD. The World Bank provided US$ 150 million. Within bilateral assistance, the United States was the most important donor with US$ 181 million, followed by Italy (US$ 98 million), Germany (US$ 67), Japan (US$ 50), and Russia (US$ 48). Since the donors' assistance to FR Yugoslavia required the prior settlement of all its financial obligations, a part of the money in the donors' aid package was used to repay debt that FR Yugoslavia owed to the World Bank, the EIB, and other creditors. The donors' conference thus also served to clear FR Yugoslavia's debt obligations. It is not possible to establish exactly which part of the donors' assistance were grants, loans, or the amount automatically deducted for covering Yugoslavia's debt obligations.

5.5.2 The transition strategy

After the October 2000 political changes in FR Yugoslavia, the federal government quickly embarked on far-reaching economic reforms in those areas within the responsibility of the federal authorities. After January 2001, the new Serbian government implemented similar measures regarding a number of specific areas of reform. While these economic reforms will be analysed in greater detail in Chapter 6, here

Table 5.1 Donors' conference for FR Yugoslavia, 29 June 2001: Financial assistance pledged for the economic recovery and transition programme (in million US$)

Countries & European Commission	845.25
Austria	28.33
Canada	11.31
Denmark	6.85
Estonia	0.05
Finland	2.88
France	18.20
Germany	66.95
Greece	45.67
Hungary	3.04
Italy	98.59
Japan	50.00
Korea	1.00
Luxembourg	5.56
Netherlands	5.83
Norway	18.82
Russia	48.00
Slovenia	0.62
Spain	7.49
Sweden	10.98
Switzerland	22.44
United Kingdom	14.21
United States	181.60
European Commission	196.83
International Financial Institutions & other	496.73
EBRD	206.25
European Investment Bank	128.37
World Bank	150.00
United Nations Development Program	1.70
UNICEF	5.50
Soros Foundation	4.92
Total EC & Member States	508.36
Total EC & Member States & EIB	636.73
Total	**1,341.98**

we will point to the most important features of the initial transition strategy.

During the first 100 days of the new political regime, a systemic reform of the monetary and fiscal systems was launched. In addition to a major devaluation of the dinar to the level prevailing on the black market and the introduction of a managed float regime (as of 1 January 2001), a package of 11 fiscal laws was adopted, including a law on independent budget auditing (Labus, 2003b). The disparities of prices for utilities and food were reduced, in line with the obligations undertaken under the arrangement with the IMF. The first measures aimed at trade liberalization were adopted in order to introduce greater transparency, deregulation, and simplifaction of the foregin trade system. A number of unnecessary administrative burdens were eliminated; thus enterprises involved in foreign trade were no longer obliged to register in a special register with the ministry for foreign economic relations, while the automatic licensing procedures were abolished altogether. In order to restore confidence in the banking system, the restructuring of the banking system was announced while from early 2001, citizens could start withdrawing their foreign currency savings lost in the 1990s in cash (though limits were set on the amount that could be withdrawn every three months), or they could be converted into government bonds (the issue was regulated more permanently in a law adopted in 2002). Preparations started for the negotiations for the rescheduling of Yugoslavia's foreign debt with the Paris and London Clubs of creditors. A new privatization law was drafted. The special tax for citizens travelling abroad was abolished.

Given the disastrous economic situation inherited in the autumn of 2000, FR Yugoslavia had to rely on external sources of finance provided by international donors. Compliance with political conditions was an inevitable part of the Western package of financial assistance to FR Yugoslavia in 2001, but there was also a less explicit part of the package which effectively led to the implementation of economic reforms and policies recommended primarily by the principle international donors. Although Stiglitz (2002) has forcefully argued that countries do have a choice in defining their economic policies, it is questionable whether the Yugoslav government in 2000, with the GDP at less than half of its 1989 level, really had many options. As stressed by the then foreign minister of Yugoslavia, Goran Svilanovic:

> The economic situation in which our country finds itself, necessarily, reduces the room for manoeuvre in international affairs. A state where even pensions, social security benefits and family allowances, as well as soup kitchens are financed through foreign aid, must set for itself highly realistic and limited foreign policy objectives.
>
> (Svilanovic, 2001, p. 4)

Although Svilanovic's message referred to foreign policy, it applies equally well to economic policies. In deciding economic measures to be implemented in 2000–1, policymakers in FR Yugoslavia had limited freedom of choice. The type of economic policies chosen was heavily influenced by the country's dependence on foreign assistance provided by the most important international financial institutions. Yugoslav authorities officially announced their intention to work closely with the IMF and the World Bank in implementing the transition strategy, since this was to open the doors for additional funding from other creditors and major donors.

The short-term economic programme of the Yugoslav government was strongly influenced by the agreement concluded with the IMF in December 2000. Disbursement of IMF funds approved to FR Yugoslavia in June 2001 was also conditioned upon successful implementation of the agreed terms. Among the IMF conditions for obtaining financial support were the standard conditions which were applied in other transition economies. Macroeconomic policies were to be based on very restrictive monetary and fiscal policies, including a reduction of the fiscal deficit and a wage freeze in the public administration, liberalization of prices and of the foreign trade system, banking sector reforms, and development of the private sector (IMF, 2001). Fiscal policy was to try and contain the overall fiscal deficits of the federal and republican governments to the amount available through foreign grants and loans. Net domestic assets of the NBY were to be kept at a constant level and base money was to be created only on the basis of increases in net international reserves, with the aim of substantially reducing inflation and providing for exchange rate stability. At the federal level, military and internal security spending was to be cut. The Serbia government was to aim at balanced budgets based on conservative revenue projections. The main points of the 'Washington consensus' were thus literally implemented, almost in full.[13]

The longer-term transition strategy implemented in FR Yugoslavia was also strongly influenced by the main international organizations, primarily the World Bank, since its assistance package was partly provided 'in kind' through expert technical advice. The World Bank, even before FR Yugoslavia settled the question of its membership, embarked on a programme of analytical and advisory services which it hoped to expand through trust funds. The key element of the programme, in partnership with the EU, was to develop with the Yugoslav government a medium-term transition programme. This objective brought World Bank expert teams to FR Yugoslavia to assess economic and structural reform objectives.

As a result, the World Bank in co-operation with the European Commission produced an 'Economic Recovery and Transition Programme' for FR Yugoslavia, Serbia, and Montenegro, presented in a two-volume report titled *Federal Republic of Yugoslavia. Breaking with the Past: The Path to Stability and Growth* (World Bank, 2001). The programme outlined a comprehensive structural reform agenda, including sectoral policy reforms and priority public investments. It also identified urgent balance of payments and budgetary needs for 2001. Although the programme was formally prepared in cooperation with the EU Commission and in consultation with the FR Yugoslav government and its draft was also presented to members of the Yugoslav, Serbian, and Montenegrin governments in April 2001, the fundamental parts of the document and its principle recommendations were prepared primarily by World Bank experts. The volume was officially published and presented at the donors' conference for FR Yugoslavia in Brussels in June 2001 as the basis for raising financial assistance.

The main elements of economic policies applied by the government during the first year of radical changes were very much in conformity with the IMF and World Bank recommendations (Labus and Dinkic, 2001). The overall results achieved regarding macroeconomic stabilization and institutional reforms were soon after evaluated as being highly satisfactory (IMF, 2002). Inflation was drastically reduced, the exchange rate was maintained stable, official reserves were growing, whereas public expenditure was cut so drastically that there was 'overshooting' regarding the set target – the fiscal deficit in 2001 was reduced to 2.4 per cent, instead of the planned 6.1 per cent of GDP. Prices and the foreign trade system were liberalized through the abolition of quotas and other quantitative restrictions, the reduction in the average level of tariffs, and introduction of more uniform tariff categories. In the banking sector, all banks were subject to a thorough financial solvency evaluation, which brought about the closing of 23 banks. Privatization was re-launched with the adoption of a new privatization law in mid-2001, envisaging commercial sales as the main method. By the end of 2001, the new institutions for implementing the new privatization law were in place and the first enterprises were to be privatized. A new labour law was adopted in December 2001, after several months of harsh disputes with the trade unions, which introduced flexibility regarding employment conditions, the hiring and firing of workers, and thus was labelled 'neoliberal' (Arandarenko, 2009a).

One of the consequences of the IMF-agreed package was that real GDP growth in 2000 and in the first quarter of 2001 remained far below expectations (Commission of the EC, 2001). Other elements requested by the IMF had a devastating impact on the standard of living of the population. For example, measures of price liberalization also included a substantial increase in electricity prices. This measure was a heavy burden on family budgets, particularly considering that electricity represents the main source of energy for domestic use. The gradual increase in electricity prices could not have been avoided, but alternative measures could also have been applied. For example, former price subsidies for all users of electricity could have been replaced by income subsidies for the poorer groups of the population, in this way obtaining greater efficiency without the cost of worse inequality.

Therefore, the new reform agenda in FR Yugoslavia included most elements typical of the hyper-liberal model implemented a decade earlier in many CEE countries, very much in line with the recommendations of the 'Washington consensus' (Williamson, 1990). The recommendations set out by the 'Washington consensus' included ten main elements: (1) fiscal discipline; (2) redirection of public expenditure towards neglected fields; (3) tax reform; (4) financial liberalization; (5) a unified and competitive exchange rate; (6) trade liberalization (7) removing barriers to FDI; (8) privatization of state enterprises; (9) deregulation; and (10) secure property rights (Williamson, 1990). Although FR Yugoslavia and Serbia at that time had the advantage of being able to draw lessons from the rich experience of other transition countries, this advantage was not sufficiently utilized.

Still, the hyper-liberal option seemed unavoidable in FR Yugoslavia at that time for two main reasons. First, because of ideological (but also pragmatic) reasons. After years of permanence of an essentially non-reformed economic system, a strong need was felt to quickly go in the opposite direction, in order to accelerate the process of reforms and make up for all the lost time during the Milosevic regime. Second, the hyper-liberal model was also imposed, though not explicitly, by the policies of conditionality of the main international financial organizations that were to provide the largest part of financial assistance to FR Yugoslavia.

Notwithstanding notable progress in many areas and particularly high speed in implementing some economic reforms over the first year of radical economic reforms, the positive effects of the transition were not visible for a long time. FR Yugoslavia in 2001 was still one of the poorest economies in Europe, with a GDP per capita at PPP of only US$ 2,955 (Economist Intelligence Unit, 2002). Even before the implementation of radical economic reforms in 2001, the unemployment rate was very high. The liquidation of the four loss-making banks has left some 9000 employees without work. The overall situation at the end of the first year of radical economic reforms was rather difficult.

Since by late 2000, the 'Washington consensus' package of policy measures had shown some of its major shortcomings, one would have thought that the policy prescriptions for a country like FR Yugoslavia would have been different; but what was actually recommended was not departing much from the prescriptions of the early 1990s. After years of postponement of more radical economic reforms in FR Yugoslavia, it was erroneously assumed that the country was starting from scratch. The overall achievements and failures of eight years of the post-2000 transition in Serbia confirm that there were many areas that were neglected in 2001, which should have been implemented from the very start (see Chapters 6 and 7).

Appendix

Box 5.1 The poor state of the public administration in late 2000

The enormous building where the federal government was located after the October 2000 changes, the Federation Palace in New Belgrade, had been abandoned for many years, since Milosevic preferred the alternative buildings in the centre of Belgrade. The Federation Palace hosted most of the 15 ministries of the federal government (except the Ministry of foreign affairs), including the Federal ministry for foreign economic relations. Its minister was Miroljub Labus, who was also federal vice prime minister of the Yugoslav government. Among the five departments of the Ministry for foreign economic relations were also two newly established departments I was in charge of, the department for the EU and the department for multilateral economic organizations.

The Federation Palace had not been modernized since the early 1990s. Elevators were so unsafe that employees preferred to take the stairs, as the risk was high of remaining blocked in them for hours. The staff complained about the outdated furniture, old carpets, and old-fashioned black telephones, but the worst of all was the total lack of technical facilities for normal work. In December 2000 and early 2001, the Federation Palace lacked not only computers, fax machines, and photocopying facilities, but even ordinary paper. On occasion of the first important visit of an EU delegation in March 2001, a document was prepared on ongoing reforms to be distributed to members of the EU delegation, but there was no paper to print it.

Computers were almost inexistent and the federal government had extremely limited resources for these purposes. At the Ministry for foreign economic relations, in late December 2000, my two departments literally had only two computers. In late January 2001, we got a third computer which was bought from the federal government's budget. The three computers were to be used by the 16 employees who worked in these two departments. Only much later, in May 2001, did a fourth computer arrive thanks to financial support of the UK government that financed Serbia's inclusion into the e-initiative of the Stability Pact for SEE. Additional computers for these two departments arrived only in autumn 2001, when I had already left.

Without access to information through the Internet, it was extremely difficult to teach my employees about the EU, its institutions, and its policies. The European Reconstruction Agency was to implement exclusively the projects carefully planned for FR Yugoslavia, but technical equipment of the public administration was not among the priorities. The EU delegation had no understanding of the need to provide equipment, although the practice in some CEE countries had been different (in Hungary, in the early 1990s, the EU did help its public administration by providing second-hand computers). It took me some time to realize that computers for the EU department would not be financed by EU funds, but through bilateral assistance. It is an irony that it was the ambassador of a non-EU member state that facilitated the provision of funds to buy computers for my employees in the EU department.

For the whole ministry for foreign economic relations that had some 100 employees – if we exclude Mr. Labus's office – there was only one fax machine, located in the room where all the confidential documents were also stored, and which had to be locked regularly at 3.30 pm. Thus sending a fax after 3.30 pm was simply not possible. There were clearly urgent faxes to be sent in those days, so urgent that they could not wait until the next day. In the midst of thousands of parallel problems, this was not considered a priority, although such poor working conditions inevitably reduced the efficiency of the administration. My continuous complaints at the end brought concrete results; in February I got a telephone/fax that was put in my secretary's office.

However, not having fax facilities throughout the day was not the worst of our problems. Much worse was the system of photocopying. Employees in the ministry for foreign economic relations had offices on the third floor, but were to use photocopying machines located on the first floor. Not only were the distances substantial – one would need at least ten minutes to go down and come back – but there was even a break of the services from 10 to 10.30 am, when the photocopying room was closed. The amount of time lost in getting a few pages photocopied was such a waste of both time and human resources. On this issue also I had to insist until I got a photocopying machine that I placed in my office. It was an old photocopying machine, but it worked and given the difficult times, it seemed such an important achievement.

In the restrooms of the Federation Palace mirrors were broken, the doors were without keys, the toilets without seats, there was no soap, paper towels, not even toilet paper. The general electricity switches assuring lights in the main corridor and stairways were regularly switched off at 3.30 pm, the end of official working hours. This caused unpleasant blackouts, also on occasion of visits of important officials. There was little to be done, since the main switches were in the room with the fax machine and confidential material, regularly locked after 3.30 pm. The labour law regulating official working hours had not been changed, so these regulations had to be respected.

In late 2000, part of the public administration had to be changed. Many top officials had to leave for political reasons, since they had been faithful collaborators of the Milosevic regime. Others left for much better paid jobs in the private sector or newly set up offices of foreign organizations. Most of the employees that remained to work in the public administration were those who had nowhere to go, although there were some new employees recruited from outside. While donors' assistance helped the Serbian government to somewhat increase salaries, nothing of this sort was available to the federal government. There were absolutely no means to raise salaries or pay overtime work, so the only way to increase efficiency of existing staff was to improve working methods by inventing informal rules. Since employees could not work overtime, particularly with the miserable salaries they had, I suggested to work in shifts. One group would work from 8 am to 3 pm, while another from 11 am to 6 pm, so all were there at the peak of the day when most work had to be done.

In late 2000, the two newly created departments for the EU and for multilateral organizations I was in charge of had literally only one secretary and one employee, a young economist who previously worked on EU-Yugoslav trade issues. There was also a second person who decided not to stay, since I was not ready to offer her a promotion to the position of director. An internal competition for the new departments was organized in order to recruit employees from within the federal administration. Given that the ministry had just closed down a special office issuing foreign trade permits, abolished as part of the trade liberalization reforms implemented in early 2001, there was a group of young and well-educated people that had arrived at the Ministry just a few months earlier. After a selection on the basis of degrees and interviews, quite of few of them were hired by the two new departments. Among the newly recruited employees, a few also came from other Ministries, while four had previously worked in research institutes. Most of the young employees who had been recruited were well educated on certain issues, but much less on the EU and its institutions, with some exceptions.

Given the incredible speed of events in those extraordinary times, many important tasks could not be well prepared, including important meetings with high-level officials. With numerous visitors from all over the world, particularly during the first few months, there were many last minute changes in the names of visiting delegations, unclear messages regarding who they were actually supposed to meet, lack of knowledge about the purpose of their visit or background of their institutions, and therefore an inability to prepare for the meetings in advance.

The numerous negative elements inherited from ten years of a repressive regime also included very unsatisfactory interpersonal relations. There was a high degree of mistrust among employees, no willingness to share information, or cooperate in daily working assignments. Employees were unwilling or unable to distinguish between government and personal property, as exemplified by the practice of taking along chairs and carpets when transferring to another office. Personal interests were often placed above professional duties or the country's interests. An important and very urgent letter would not leave for Brussels for ten days just because colleagues from another important ministry regarded its contents inappropriate. Only later did I understand that behind such manipulations were personal rivalries and revenges for misunderstandings and unsettled issues from the past.

Box 5.2 Some personal achievements

Although at the time of my work in the federal government in Belgrade it seemed that each task required triple the energy and time, and that much of my efforts had not brought any concrete results, thinking backwards I do realize I have contributed to some important projects. I organized the first encounter of high level representatives of the Bosnian, Croatian, and Serbian government, in Brcko in February 2001, which officially initiated the Sava river project, the very first concrete project on regional cooperation within the framework of the Stability Pact which was later considered one of its most successful initiatives. The meeting led to the signing of a Letter of Intent on 29 November 2001 by FR Yugoslavia, Bosnia and Herzegovina, and Croatia, and by the end of 2002 to an international agreement aimed to rehabilitate navigation on the Sava river and its main tributaries Una and Drina, to regulate best usage of Sava Basin water and related resources, to monitor and improve the quality of Sava water, to commonly manage flood control and disaster preparedness and prevention. I have actively promoted many other important initiatives of the Stability Pact for Southeast Europe, including the trade liberalization initiative launched in January 2001 (I represented FR Yugoslavia at the Trade Policy Forum in Geneva where the initiative was launched), or the setting up of the working group on Social Cohesion initiated at the Tirana Regional Conference of the Stability Pact (where I was again representing the FR Yugoslav government). Linked to the initiative on trade liberalization, I obtained FR Yugoslavia's inclusion into the World Bank project on trade liberalization and facilitation.

As part of my attempts to accelerate the process of negotiations with the EU, I prepared a draft project on how the institutional structure of the future EU office was to be set up in February 2001.

Although at that time the political conditions were such that it could not be approved by the government, the EU office set up later at the federal level was based on the initial project I had prepared. In March 2001, I prepared a matrix on the fulfilment of EU conditions by the Yugoslav, Serbian, and Montenegrin governments, identifying the necessary conditions and degree of compliance; this matrix has been used by the government in the forthcoming years.

Among the many other tasks, I would like to recall the intense work shared with my employees for over eight months. I have done my best to teach them something not only about the EU, but about working methods, ethics, and human behaviour. I am glad that some of them are still there today, working very efficiently in the Serbian government's European Integration Office.

6
Embarking on Transition for a Second Time

A notable acceleration of transition in Serbia came after the October 2000 fall of the Milosevic regime. The establishment of a democratic government, together with gradual reforms of political institutions, radical changes in a number of internal and foreign policy objectives, and renewal of the country's relations with the outside world and substantial inflow of donor's assistance, have also permitted a profound transformation of Serbia's economic system. From early 2001 until the end of 2008, the new policies have brought a number of positive results. Quite contrary to the 1990s, when the Serbian economy was characterized by high economic instability, declining output, little or no interest from foreign investors, and extremely limited systemic changes, the reforms implemented after late 2000 have permitted macroeconomic stabilization, economic recovery, inflow of foreign direct investment, and quick progress in many areas of institutional reforms. The post-2000 period has also seen substantial political instability, but for somewhat different reasons than in the 1990s.

In what follows, the most important political events of the 2001–8 period will be briefly recalled, as some of them have had a notable impact on the speed of transition-related reforms. The chapter proceeds to analyse the economic measures implemented by the Yugoslav/Serbian government and the country's macroeconomic performance after 2001. The principal results achieved in various areas of economic reform are also discussed in some detail, following the well-known transition indicators of the EBRD on enterprises' privatization and restructuring, prices and foreign trade liberalization, banking and other financial sector reforms, and infrastructure.

6.1 Political developments

An enormous burden for the effectiveness of economic reforms immediately after the October 2000 changes was presented by a number of unresolved political issues, as discussed in detail in Chapter 5. Also after 2001, the uncertain future of the Serb-Montenegrin state, slow collaboration with the ICTY, and the resolution of the final status of Kosovo continued to hamper a swifter implementation of economic reforms. In the meantime, only the first of these issues was definitively resolved with the split between Montenegro and Serbia in June 2006. The issue of Kosovo, after its unilateral declaration of independence in February 2008, remains controversial since as of April 2009 it has not been recognized by the United Nations and a number of countries, including five EU member states (Cyprus, Greece, Romania, Slovakia, and Spain). In early 2009, the Serbian government appealed to the UN and to the International Court of Justice, challenging the legality of Kosovo's declaration of independence (deliberations on the appeal began on 17 April). Serbia's collaboration with the Hague Tribunal also remains on top of the present government's agenda, since one of the main reasons that prevented (until early 2010) the application of the SAA with the EU was the non-delivery of general Ratko Mladic, indicted for war crimes in Bosnia and Herzegovina.

In addition to these complex problems inherited from the past, a few other events have contributed to political instability in Serbia during 2001–8. The most serious was the tragic assassination of the Serbian Prime Minister Zoran Djindjic, on 12 March 2003, allegedly by members of the Serbian security services. Djindjic's departure represented an enormous loss for Serbia. He was one of the most determined leaders and democratic reformers, and his assassination was a serious blow to the democratic forces in Serbia. According to many analysts, this event has crucially contributed to the slow-down of economic reforms in Serbia (Cerovic and Nojkovic, 2008). Some months before Djindjic's assassination, his government had decided to set up institutions that would combat organized crime and corruption,[1] which would have put the military at last under full civilian democratic control (Vejvoda, 2006, p. 44). Djindjic's tragic departure therefore delivered a very important message, on the missed opportunity to implement, at an early stage, radical reforms of police and of security agencies (Anastasijevic, 2008).[2] Djindjic also had a clear vision of Serbia's future: in January 2003, he launched an initiative to spur on the resolution of the Kosovo issue, taking a proactive, forward-looking approach that advocated a 'European, democratic, rational and de-emotionalised path towards resolution' (Vejvoda, 2006, p. 50), a policy that was later discontinued.

The post-2001 political scene in Serbia has also seen numerous government crises, frequent threats of smaller parties leaving the ruling coalition, disputes, and accusations among the main party leaders, long periods of negotiations and bargaining between potential coalition partners. During 2001–8, Serbia has had three parliamentary elections and another four presidential elections – in 2002, 2003, 2004, and 2008 – of which the first two proved unsuccessful, due to the low turnout of voters (see Table 6.1). Many months have been lost under 'exceptional' political conditions during which Serbia had no government and the Serbian parliament was unable to function. These periods dedicated to political bargaining frequently interrupted the process of ongoing legislative changes, slowing down economic, legal, and institutional reforms.

Another important issue that has greatly contributed to political instability in Serbia is the change of the country's status. During the post-2000 period, the country that Serbia was part of changed its name, status, and territory several times. On 4 February 2003, FR Yugoslavia (composed of Serbia and Montenegro) was transformed into the State Union of Serbia and Montenegro, and new structures were set up to replace the previous federal institutions. The number of ministries at the level of the State Union was reduced to only five (foreign affairs, defence, foreign economic relations, internal economic relations, and human and minority rights), while all other competences were transferred to the Serbian and Montenegrin governments. Further important changes took place after May 2006. At Montenegro's long-announced popular referendum on 21 May 2006, the majority of the population (55.5 per cent of voters) declared to be in favour of independence. This led to the dissolution of the State Union of Serbia and Montenegro and to the establishment of two independent states in June 2006. The most recent change of borders occurred after Kosovo unilaterally proclaimed its independence in February 2008, when Serbia effectively lost its southern province of Kosovo and Metohija. Although the UN Security Council Resolution 1244 recognized Kosovo as part of its territory, Serbia retained very little control over the province after 1999.

All the mentioned changes in the country's status and territory required a set of legislative measures to replace existing laws with legislation adapted to the new country. These legislative changes were clearly time-consuming and detracted attention from other important issues on the policy agenda, including transition-related economic reforms.

Table 6.1 Major political events in Serbia, 2001–8

Governments	Major political events	Date	Duration of government
First government (Zoran Djindjic)			
25 Jan. 2001–3 March 2004	First crisis of the DOS coalition, DSS leaves the government	August 2001	7 months
	Reconstruction of the government	Sept. 2001	18 months
	Assassination of Prime Minister Djindjic	12 March 2003	
Temporary government (Zoran Zivkovic)		18 March 2003	12 months
Technical government (Zoran Zivkovic)		13 Nov– 3 March 2004	3.5 months
	Parliamentary elections	28 Dec. 2003	
Second government (Vojislav Kostunica)			
3 March 2004–16 May 2007			37.5 months
	Government crisis	November 2006	
Technical government (Vojislav Kostunica)		10 Nov. 2006	6 months
	Parliamentary elections	21 Jan. 2007	
Third government (Vojislav Kostunica)			
16 May 2007–Sept. 2008	Conflicts within the government	Dec. 2007	15 months
Technical government (Vojislav Kostunica)		13 March 2008	6 months
	Parliamentary elections	11 May 2008	
Fourth government (Mirko Cvetkovic)			
July 2008–to date		July 2008	Still in power (April 2010)

Source: Compiled on the basis of information in Prascevic (2008), pp. 47–8.

In the meantime, Serbia has also had an intense debate on a new constitution that was to replace the one adopted way back in 1990, during the early days of Milosevic's rule.[3] After 2001, a number of drafts of the new constitution were elaborated by the main political parties – including the DS, the DSS, the G17 Plus, and the Belgrade Center – and publicly discussed, but it is only on 30 September 2006 that the new constitution of the Republic of Serbia was finally proclaimed by the Serbian parliament.[4] The new constitution was confirmed at a referendum on 28–9 October 2006 by a bare majority of the electorate, having received weak popular support. The preamble of the constitution not only defines Kosovo as an integral part of Serbia, but also establishes 'the statutory obligation for all state organs to support and defend Serbia's state interests in Kosovo and Metohija in all internal and international political relations' (Constitution of the Republic of Serbia, 2006, p. 8). This emphasis on the territorial integrity of Serbia clearly clashes with a very different territorial situation on the ground, since Kosovo has been governed by UNMIK after the end of the war (Bianchini, 2007, p. 18). Another interesting point in the 2006 Serbian constitution is that 'social property' as a concept has finally been abandoned.[5]

During the 2001–8 period, therefore, a number of important political problems have been in the centre of the government's agenda, contributing to political instability in Serbia. It should nevertheless be stressed that the overall political conditions have been rather different than in the 1990s, when the political scene was dominated by Milosevic's SPS and its nationalistic and anti-democratic ideology. Since 2001, Serbia has had governments consisting predominantly of the democratically oriented political parties that have overthrown Milosevic – including Zoran Djindjic's/Boris Tadic's DP, Vojislav Kostunica's DSS, and Miroljub Labus'/Mladjan Dinkic's G17 Plus.[6] The preferences of the Serbian electorate have also gradually changed. At the parliamentary elections in January 2007, the majority of the Serbian electorate voted for pro-European liberal parties.[7] The last Serbian government formed in July 2008 is led by the alliance 'For a European Serbia', dominated by the pro-EU DS, whose President, Boris Tadic, is also the president of Serbia. Despite all the difficult political problems, many inherited from the 1990s, Serbia's political scene is increasingly resembling other young democracies in Central and Southeast Europe.

6.2 Macroeconomic performance

After the political changes in October 2000, the new government of FR Yugoslavia implemented a number of economic measures at the federal level which were considered urgent for implementing the transition to a market economy (Uvalic, 2005b). The Serbian government pursued similar goals after January 2001. During the last eight years, remarkable results have been achieved in many areas of transition-related economic reform, permitting substantial improvements in the performance of the Yugoslav/Serbian economy.[8] We will first analyse Serbia's macroeconomic performance during 2001–8, pointing to the main achievements and key problems, and then present an overview of market-oriented economic reforms implemented so far. Some of the principal failures of the overall transition strategy adopted in 2001 are discussed in greater detail in Chapters 7 and 9.

6.2.1 Macroeconomic stabilization

One of the most urgent tasks of the Serbian/Yugoslav government in late 2000 was macroeconomic stabilization. In late 2000, prices of many goods and services were already liberalized, but at the time of the Kosovo crisis price controls were introduced for some basic commodities, energy, and transport. These prices had to be gradually liberalized in order to eliminate major price distortions. Prices of electricity, for example, had to be adjusted upwards, since in late 2000 they were much lower than world prices.

Table 6.2 Serbia: Main macroeconomic indicators, 2000–8 (in %)

	2000	2001	2002	2003	2004	2005	2006	2007	2008
Real GDP growth (%)	4.5	5.6	3.9	2.4	8.3	5.6	5.2	6.9	5.4
Retail price inflation (Dec. to Dec., %)	111.9	40.7	14.8	7.8	13.7	17.7	6.6	10.1	6.8
Retail price inflation (annual average, %)	70.0	91.8	19.5	11.7	10.1	16.5	12.7	6.5	10.9
Government balance (% of GDP)	−1.0	−6.2	−3.1	−1.1	0.9	0.8	−1.6	−1.9	−2.5
Government expenditure (% of GDP)	40.4	39.6	43.0	41.4	40.3	42.0	45.2	44.9	43.4
Gross fixed capital formation (% of GDP)	12.7	10.7	12.4	16.7	19.2	19.0	20.8	23.4	21.4

Sources: NBS (www.nbs.rs), Economist Intelligence Unit (2009b), EBRD (www.ebrd.com), and World Bank (2009).

Price liberalization initially led to very high inflation – in 2001, an average annual retail price inflation of over 90 per cent (or a year-to-year increase of 41 per cent) – but substantial disinflation was achieved thereafter. The trend in both measures of inflation has been positive. Although the year-to-year inflation was quite high in 2005 (17%), mainly due to higher oil and electricity prices, it was substantially reduced thereafter, to 6.8 per cent in 2008 (see Table 6.2 and Figure 6.1).

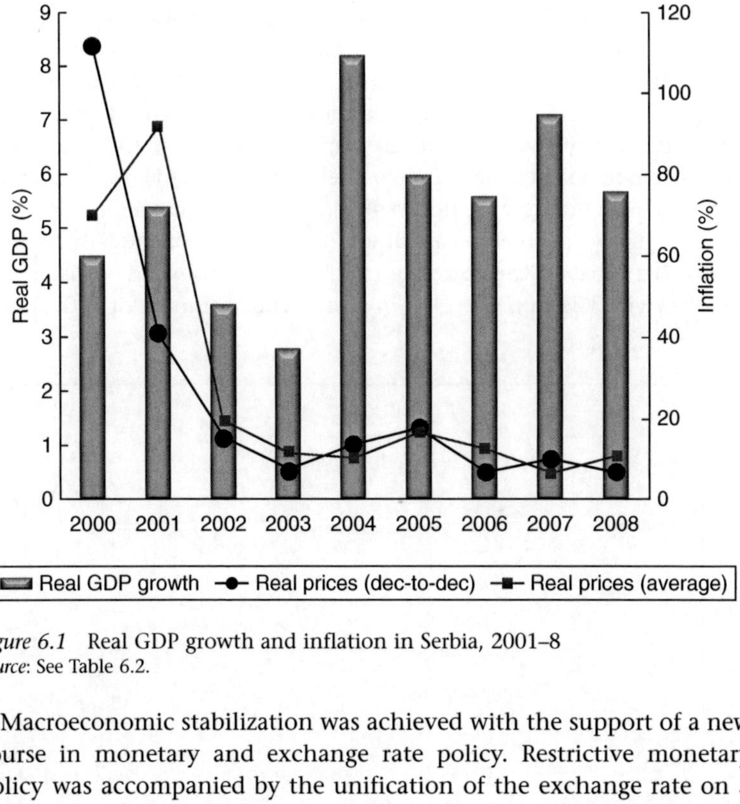

Figure 6.1 Real GDP growth and inflation in Serbia, 2001–8
Source: See Table 6.2.

Macroeconomic stabilization was achieved with the support of a new course in monetary and exchange rate policy. Restrictive monetary policy was accompanied by the unification of the exchange rate on 5 December 2000, when the Serbian dinar (RSD) was devalued to the level prevailing on the grey market rate (DM 1 = RSD 30). On 1 January 2001, a managed float regime was introduced to replace the previous fixed exchange rate, along with current account convertibility of the dinar. Various exchange rate restrictions were abolished, such as obligatory sales of foreign exchange by exporters and importers to the NBY. A new law on the central bank was adopted in order to ensure its autonomy. Although officially a managed float, the post-2000 regime has also been referred to as a 'near-pegged exchange rate' (EBRD, 2002, p. 146) since for two years the NBY intervened to keep the nominal exchange rate stable vis-à-vis the euro (Daviddi and Uvalic, 2006). After 2003, the central bank passed a more flexible exchange rate policy, and in August 2006 it switched to inflation rate targeting, which increased the use of the central bank's reference interest rate as the main instrument for reaching the targeted goal of inflation.

These policies have produced excellent results regarding monetary and exchange rate stability.[9] After the initial strong devaluation of the dinar at the end of 2000 and the passage to a more flexible exchange rate regime, the dinar has appreciated in real terms during most of the 2001–8 period (see Figure 6.2). Large real appreciation was experienced particularly during the first two years and again after 2006, when the NBS changed its exchange rate policy (Labus, 2009). There was even some nominal appreciation of the currency, the first experience of this sort in a long time, due to large inflows of foreign capital and the decision of the NBS to allow almost free float of the currency from mid-2006 onwards (Mladenovic and Petrovic, 2009, pp. 13–14). Only since the beginning of 2009, under

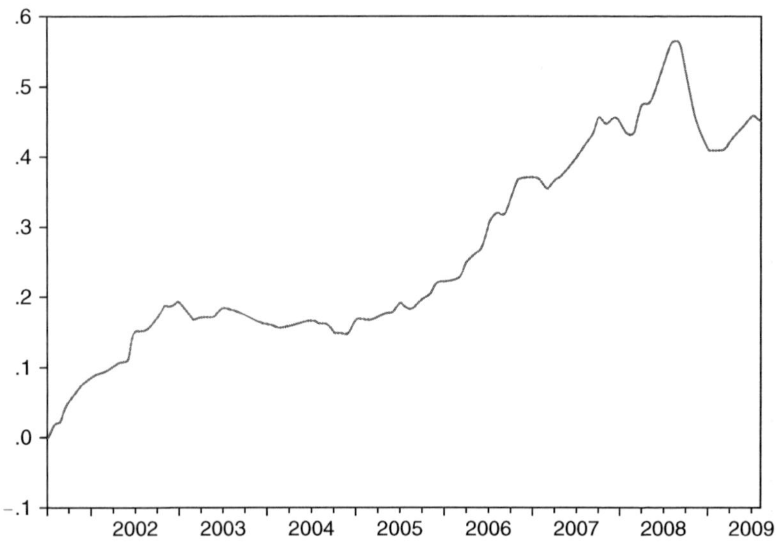

Figure 6.2 Real exchange rate in Serbia, July 2001–August 2009
Note: The figure depicts the real exchange rate: (*p-epe*), where *p* is log of retail price index and *epe* = *e* + *pe*, i.e. log of dinar/euro exchange rate (*e*) plus the log of foreign (EU) price level (*pe*). Thus an increase denotes real appreciation.
Source: Mladenovic and Petrovic (2009).

the pressure of the global economic crisis, has the dinar depreciated in real terms, though the trend was reversed in the summer of 2009.

Recent econometric evidence shows that the post-2001 monetary regime in Serbia led to a substantial decline in the exchange rate pass-through into domestic prices, in comparison to the 1990s when it was complete, supporting the hypothesis that improved monetary policy, facilitated by fiscal adjustment, can lead to a sizeable decline in pass-through even in a country with a long history of high inflation (Mladenovic and Petrovic, 2009, p. 22).

Some fiscal consolidation has also taken place in Serbia, though the overall results have not been very impressive. After the political changes in 2000, the practice of monetization of the fiscal and quasi-fiscal deficits, typical of the 1990s, was stopped. Serbia recorded a very high public deficit in 2001, of over 6 per cent of GDP. Thereafter the public deficit was cut to only 1.1 per cent in 2003 and was transformed into a surplus in 2004 and 2005. After 2006, however, fiscal policy was expansionary and the public deficit again rose to 2.5 per cent of GDP in 2008 (see Table 6.2).

In the meantime, radical reforms of the tax system have been implemented, including a major simplification of taxes, the passage to gross wages for social contribution purposes, broadening the tax base, and lowering the overall tax and contribution burden on wages. In mid-2001, a flat tax rate on personal income was introduced (Arandarenko, 2009a). Preparations for the introduction of value-added tax (VAT) began and VAT was introduced in 2005, with the standard rate of 18 per cent. The corporate profit tax is a uniform rate of 10 per cent, one of the lowest in SEE. A number of measures have been implemented to fight the informal economy, such as the obligation to issue receipts for all payments and fines if these regulations are not respected.

Along with reforms of the system of taxation, the structure and level of public expenditure has not changed substantially. The single-largest item of consolidated central government expenditure in 2008 were pensions, representing 30 per cent of public expenditure (or 11% of GDP), while health accounted for 15 per cent, and education for another 10 per cent of public spending (World Bank, 2009). Since 2001, public expenditure has remained over 40 per cent of Serbia's GDP, but this is a problem common to most other SEE countries, especially Croatia and Bosnia and Herzegovina that recently had even higher levels of public expenditure than Serbia.

The Serbian government did have plans to decrease public expenditure in sectors such as general public affairs, health, and national security, which would have enabled increasing expenditure and higher quality of services in some other areas, such as education (Government of Serbia,

2007). Among the items representing a heavy burden in the government budget, in addition to pensions, is Serbia's huge public administration. The Serbian government today consists of 24 ministries, another 15 specialized government agencies, and a number of offices in charge of specific issues (like the Office for Public Procurement). Recent reforms of the public administration have even introduced new public officials – the function of 'state secretary', in addition to the existing posts of ministers and assistant ministers. Since 2001, the number of employees in the public administration has actually increased. Not surprisingly, this was one of the main issues on the government's agenda in early and mid-2009, during negotiations with the IMF and discussions on how to rationalize public administration. Owing to the strong impact of the global financial and economic crisis, the Serbian government asked for IMF support in late 2008 and concluded a precautionary SBA in January 2009, that was replaced by another SBA in mid-May 2009 providing Serbia some US$ 4 billion (see Chapter 9).

Present plans for fiscal adjustment in 2010, among other measures, envisage downsizing of the public administration by some 10 per cent. The government also plans to eliminate redundancies in the health and education sectors, though reforms would be targeted to preserve the quality of public services provision. However, even a strong reduction of employment in the public sector cannot lead to substantial savings in the long run (Stamenkovic et al., 2009b). In order to reduce public expenditure more permanently, reforms of the pensions system will be necessary, as well as the further restructuring of large public sector enterprises.

6.2.2 Economic recovery

Serbia's growth performance has been impressive throughout most of the post-2001 period (see Figure 6.1 and Table 6.2). The average real GDP growth rate during 2001–8 was 5.4 per cent, despite a notable slowdown in 2002–3. Until the first negative effects of the global economic crisis in late 2008, growth was quite remarkable. Gross fixed investment has also gradually increased, from a very low 11 per cent of GDP in 2001 to 21 per cent in 2008 (see Table 6.2).

These high GDP growth rates have permitted some economic recovery and catching up. Still, rapid growth has been largely insufficient to compensate for the very substantial fall in GDP in Serbia during the 1990s. As a result, by mid-2008, Serbia had reached only around 72 per cent of GDP produced in 1989 (EBRD, 2009). Though only three of the six SEE countries had by 2008 surpassed their 1989 GDP level – Albania in 2000, Croatia in 2006, and Macedonia in 2008 – Serbia was by far in the worst position.

One of the less developed SEE countries, Bosnia and Herzegovina, had by mid-2008 arrived at 84 per cent of its 1989 GDP (EBRD, 2009).

The unfavourable position of Serbia in comparison with other transition countries is due to several factors. First, the recession in the years immediately after Yugoslavia's break-up was much more severe in Serbia than in the other successor states, since in addition to the loss of a common market, it was amplified by a longer and higher hyperinflation, greater fiscal imbalances, and the severe UN embargo in 1992–5 (see Chapter 3). Second, Serbia/FR Yugoslavia again experienced a very deep recession in 1999 – a 19 per cent drop in GDP – due to the NATO intervention (see Chapter 4). Consequently, by 1999, Serbia had reached only 45 per cent of its 1989 GDP, while rapid growth after 2001 was not sufficient to make up for the GDP lost in the 1990s.

Post-2001 economic recovery had permitted a substantial rise in living standards in Serbia. During 2005–8, Serbia had almost doubled its GDP per capita at market exchange rates (from US$ 3500 to US$ 6880) being third in the SEE region, after Croatia and Montenegro (see Figure 6.3). However, Serbia was the second-most developed SEE country by its GDP per head at PPP based on estimates of the Economist Intelligence Unit, which increased from US$ 8620 in 2005 to US$ 11,160 in 2008. In euros, Serbia's GDP per capita increased from €1723 in 2001 to €4500 in 2008, permitting some catching up with EU countries: from 21 per cent of the EU average GDP per capita (at purchasing power standards) in 2001 to 35 per cent in 2008 (Republicki zavod za razvoj, 2009, p. 11).

During 2001–8, average net wages in Serbia have increased more than four times, from €90 to over €400 (see Figure 6.4), much faster than productivity. The average growth rate of real net wages over the 2001–8 period has been 13.7 per cent, in comparison with average productivity growth of only 6.0 per cent. The rapid increase in real wages and pensions has led to some reductions in poverty, from around 14 per cent of the population in 2002 to less than 7 per cent in 2007 (according to the 2007 survey on living standards; see Republicki Zavod za Razvoj, 2009, p. 181). Rising earnings have permitted a fast increase in both consumption and imports, in this way contributing to the increase in the current account deficit.

6.2.3 Jobless growth

Post 2000 strong economic recovery in Serbia has not yet brought employment growth. Like many countries in CEE during the early years of transition, Serbia has also been characterized by 'jobless' growth, but the magnitude of the problem is undoubtedly much greater in Serbia. Over the 2000–8 period, the number of employed persons stagnated or

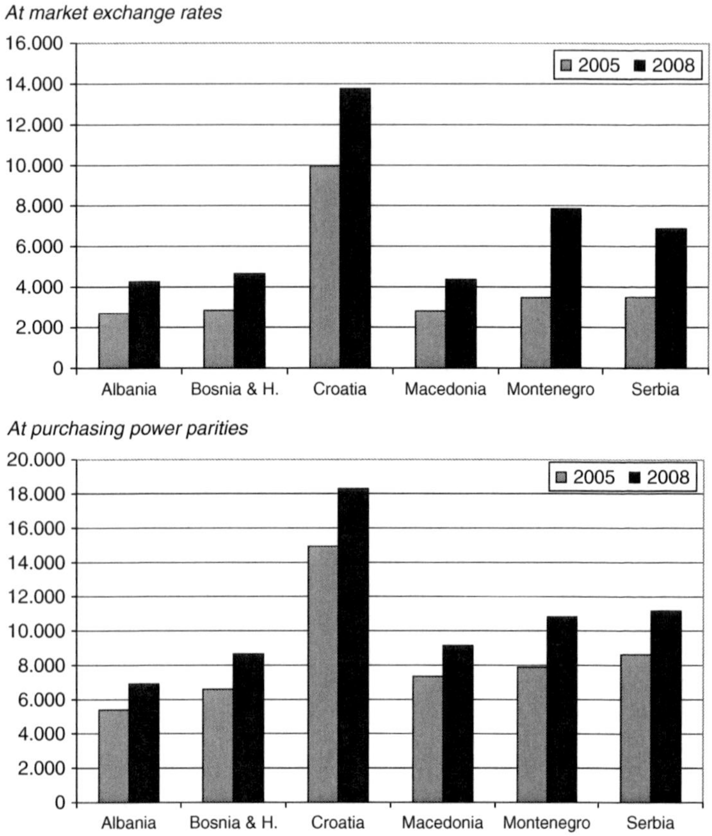

Figure 6.3 GDP per head in SEE, 2005 and 2008 (in US dollars)
Source: See Table A 6.1 (Appendix).

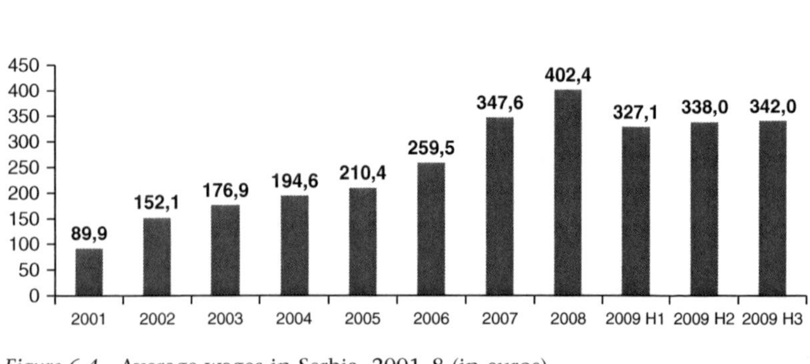

Figure 6.4 Average wages in Serbia, 2001–8 (in euros)
Source: Jelasic and Eric (2009) based on Serbian national statistics.

Table 6.3 Serbia: Employment, wages, and productivity

	2000	2001	2002	2003	2004	2005	2006	2007	2008
Employment (in thousand), LFS*	3,094	3,106	3,000	2,919	2,931	2,733	2,631	2,656	2,805
Unemployment rate (%), LFS*	12.1	12.2	13.3	14.6	18.5	20.8	20.9	18.1	14.0
Official unemployment rate (per cent)*	NA	21.8	24.5	26.1	23.9	25.3	26.6	24.4	21.4
Net wages (real growth, in %)	NA	16.5	29.9	13.6	10.1	6.4	11.4	19.5	3.9
Labour productivity (in %)	NA	5.2	5.4	3.7	7.8	4.7	7.5	8.1	5.6

*All figures refer to the situation on 30 September of a given year.
Source: Republicki zavod za statistiku Srbije (webrzs.statserb.sr.gov.yu) and Republicki zavod za razvoj (2009), p. 17.

declined, particularly after 2004 (see Table 6.3 and Figure 6.5). There was some increase in employment in 2008, but this was primarily due to new hiring in the public sector, and recent improvements in the Labour Force Survey (LFS) methodology, namely better coverage of various categories of informal employment – such as self-employment, employment of family members, and traditional agricultural employment (Arandarenko, 2009a, 2009b). After 2001, the unemployment rate (based on the LFS) has continuously increased, to 21 per cent by 2006, slightly declining only in 2007–8. Under the impact of the economic crisis in 2009, the LFS unemployment rate again jumped to 16.6 per cent by October 2009 (www.nbs.rs, April 2010).

The official unemployment rate has been much higher and has increased from 21.8 per cent in end-September 2001 to almost 27 per cent in end-September 2006, registering a decline to 21.4 per cent by end-September 2008, but again increasing to 23 per cent by September 2009. The long-term unemployment rate also increased continuously and reached 17.3 per cent in 2007, parallel with the decline in the employment rate from 59.7 per cent in 2001 to 51.5 per cent in 2007 (European Commission, 2009). The share of persons unemployed for more than one year has increased from 76.6 per cent in 2004 to 80.6 per cent in 2006 (Government of Serbia, 2007). Serbia's participation rate, though increasing, also remains relatively low (62.6 per cent) in comparison with the EU average (Arandarenko, 2009a).

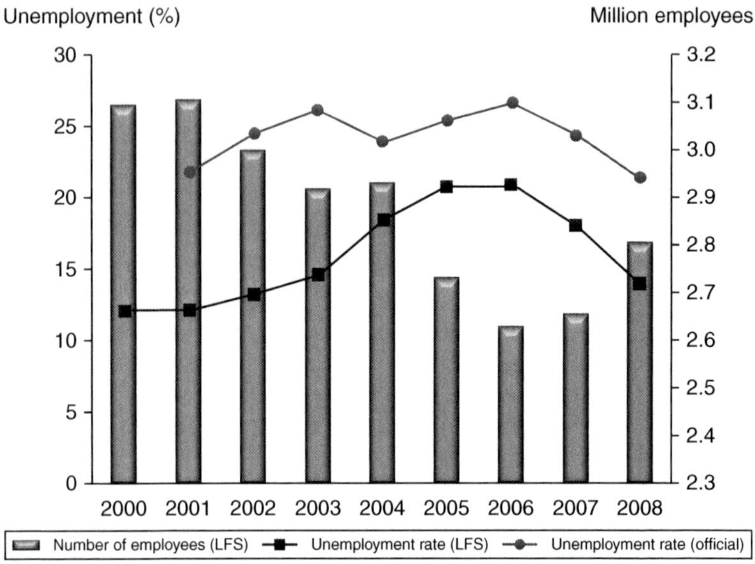

Figure 6.5 Employment and unemployment in Serbia, 2000–8
Source: See sources in Table 6.3.

These high unemployment rates do overestimate the effective number of jobless workers, since many individuals are still active in the informal economy. A recent study (Krstic and Sanfey, 2009) found that informal employment has actually risen: the size of the shadow economy in Serbia and Montenegro was estimated at 39.1 per cent of measured GDP in 2002–3, up from 36.4 per cent in 1999–2000 (Krstic and Sanfey, 2009, p. 2).

Numerous government measures over the last four years have been largely unsuccessful in reversing these negative trends. The government has implemented various labour market measures to stimulate an increase in employment. In 2006, these measures covered approximately 80 per cent of the total number of unemployed registered at the National Employment Service, and approximately 40 per cent more people found new employment than in 2005 (Government of Serbia, 2007). Nevertheless the policies so far have contributed only very marginally to alleviating the problem of unemployment. Although private sector employment has grown rapidly, the number of new jobs has not been sufficient to employ all redundant workers. The formal labour market in Serbia remains rather rigid and functions poorly, in contrast to its considerably more flexible informal part (Krstic and Sanfey, 2009). Given such high unemployment rates, GDP growth in Serbia has clearly been much lower than its potential.

Some of the problems on the Serbian labour market can be attributed to inadequate labour legislation. The first Labour law passed in 2001 was labelled 'neoliberal', while the new Labour law adopted in 2005 was somewhat more balanced, but fundamentally not very different from the first (Arandarenko, 2009a). These laws enforced major flexibility in labour relations. A single wage tax rate of 14 per cent was introduced and social insurance contributions were considerably reduced, down to 32.6 per cent of the gross wage, parallel with the introduction of a rather high minimum base of around 40 per cent of the average wage (Arandarenko, 2009a).

A very specific feature is the highly regressive wage taxation system introduced in 2001, which put a disproportionate tax burden on firms and sectors employing low-wage labour, as well as regions with under-average wages, thus perpetuating sectoral and regional wage differences. Such tax regulations have also, to a large degree, prevented the formalization of informal employment, since the marginal tax rate at the potential point of entry for small labour-intensive private firms was at least as high as the average labour tax rate, and have impeded job creation among the *de novo* private firms (Arandarenko, 2009a). Until the end of 2006, the tax burden for a person earning a very low income, amounting to 33 per cent of the average wage stood at 47.1 per cent; it stood at 42.2 per cent in case of workers earning average wages; while in the case of a worker whose salary was eight times the average wage, the tax burden was even lower, at 34.5 per cent (Arandarenko, 2009a). Although in 2007 a modest zero tax bracket was introduced and the minimum social security base lowered, thus finally cancelling regressivity in much of the wage distribution, the tax burden on low-wage labour has remained quite high, the tax wedge now standing at around 38 per cent of the minimum wage.

6.2.4 Increasing external imbalances

Recent growth in Serbia, as in many other East European countries, has been based on a model of credit-driven, consumer-led growth (Kekic, 2009b), largely funded by foreign capital inflows – foreign borrowing, workers' remittances, and FDI. During the 2001–8 period, domestic demand has increased much faster than GDP, as a result of fast growth in household consumption, facilitated by growing wages and pensions, increasing imports, and high government expenditure. Particularly during the last two years, Serbia has experienced rapid credit growth, driven by credit to households, increased government expenditure, and increases in real wages, which has further contributed to an increase in consumption. The availability of credit and investment from abroad has facilitated strong economic growth, but has also contributed to serious and growing imbalances in Serbia's external sector.

Serbia's external imbalances are primarily due to its huge and increasing trade deficit. Throughout the post-2001 period, imports have increased much faster than exports, leading to a continuous increase in the trade deficit, from US$ 1.6 billion in 2000 to over US$ 11 billion in 2008. Following a whole decade of falling or stagnant exports, due to the loss of markets, trade disruption caused by wars, and international sanctions, Serbia's volume of exports has registered an impressive increase, from a low US$ 1645 million in 2000 to almost US$ 11,000 million in 2008, but the volume of imports has regularly been higher by between 50 to 100 per cent than the volume of exports (see Table 6.4).

Serbia's foreign trade after 2001 has increased particularly with the EU, the country's main trading partner today, in 2008 representing 54 per cent of its exports and 53 per cent of its imports (see Chapter 8). The expansion in trade with the EU has been greatly facilitated by EU autonomous trade preferences extended to FR Yugoslavia in November 2000 and the process of trade liberalization implemented by the Yugoslav federal government in early 2001.

The extremely high trade deficit confirms sluggish export performance of Serbian enterprises, though the strong real appreciation of the dinar has also hampered export growth. The insufficient increase in exports is mainly due to the structural weaknesses of the economy, the limited restructuring and modernization of key industries which missed a whole decade of technological progress (see Chapter 7). As late as 2002, state and socially owned enterprises still provided 45 per cent of total exports (World Bank, 2004, p. 55). Another key feature that has contributed to such trends is the particularly fast growth of services, especially financial services and retail trade, while growth has been relatively modest in manufacturing and other tradable goods. Despite rapidly increasing trade volumes since 2001, Serbia's exports structure, dominated by agricultural and low processed manufacturing products, has changed only marginally (Kovacevic, 2008).

Table 6.4 Serbia: External sector indicators, 2000–8

In million US$	**2000**	**2001**	**2002**	**2003**	**2004**	**2005**	**2006**	**2007**	**2008**
Current account*	–153	280	–650	–1,532	–3,281	–2,194	–2,986	–5,285	–7,200
Trade in goods balance	–1,582	–2,308	–3,228	–4,021	–6,469	–5,290	–6,271	–9,130	–11,256
Exports of goods, FOB	1,645	1,821	2,212	3,319	4,082	4,970	6,442	8,756	10,957
Imports of goods, FOB	3,227	4,129	5,440	7,340	10,551	10,260	12,713	17,886	22,213
Current transfers balance	1,289	2,338	2,521	2,423	3,241	3,426	3,752	3,974	4,146
FDI, net	50	165	475	1,365	966	1,550	4,264	2,523	2,717
Foreign exchange reserves (end-year)	890	1,809	3,063	4,436	5,146	6,541	12,636	16,070	12,867
External debt stock (end-year)	11,659	12,609	10,768	10,857	10,354	13,064	14,884	17,789	21,800
In per cent									
Debt service, in % of exports of goods and services	2.7	4.4	6.2	10.3	17.5	26.0	20.2	16.6	NA
Current account balance (% of GDP)	–2.4	2.4	–4.1	–7.5	–13.5	–8.4	–9.8	–12.9	–17.3

*This is the reclassified current account, which takes into account the reclassification of one part of estimated remittances from the financial account to current transfers recorded in the current account. This was done in order to adjust completely the Serbian Balance of Payments Statistics used from the beginning of 2008 to the IMF methodology.

Source: NBS (www.nbs.rs.) and EBRD (www.ebrd.com).

The huge trade deficit is the main cause of Serbia's increasing current account deficit (see Figure 6.6). Despite some improvements after 2004, the current account deficit by 2008 again increased to over 17 per cent of GDP, being among the highest in the wider transition region. After 2001, the current account deficit has been covered by inflows of official donors' assistance of over US$ 3.1 billion during 2000–7, the largest part provided through the EU CARDS programme (see Chapter 8). A very important source of additional capital was emigrants' remittances, which totalled to US$ 16.8 billion over the 2001–8 period (annually corresponding to 9 per cent of GDP; see World Bank, 2009). FDI inflows of some US$ 12 billion after 2001 have also been important (see below). These capital inflows allowed an impressive increase in gross foreign exchange reserves, from only US$ 890 million in 2000 to over US$ 16 billion

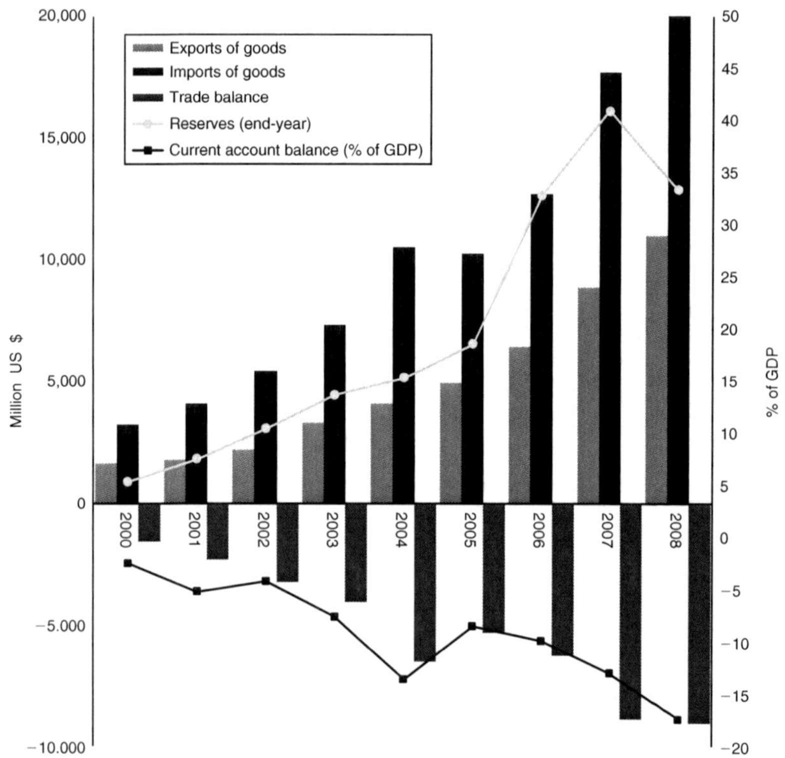

Figure 6.6 Serbia's external sector indicators, 2001–8

in 2007, though a decline was registered to US$ 12.9 billion by late 2008 (see Table 6.4 and Figure 6.6).

Serbia has benefited from several favourable write-offs of its external debt. In 2001, the Yugoslav government reached an agreement with the Paris Club on the consolidation and write-off of 66 per cent of its debt; the first phase of reduction of 51 per cent was implemented in March 2002, while the second phase of an additional 15 per cent was implemented in February 2006. An agreement was also reached with the London Club of creditors in July 2004 on the cancellation of 62 per cent of Serbia's debt and the rescheduling of the rest over the next 20 years.[10] In 2004, a large part of Serbia's debt to Russia was also written off.

These agreements have permitted a substantial reduction of Serbia's debt/GDP ratio, from 167 per cent in 2000 to 64 per cent in 2007 EBRD *Transition Reports*, 2006, 2008). There has been increasing borrowing on the world market, however, particularly after 2006, leading to nearly doubling Serbia's external debt, from US$ 11.7 billion in 2000 to almost US$ 22 billion in 2008, of which almost 70 per cent is private sector debt. Although in late 2008 Serbia was not among the most indebted transition economies – its net external debt/GDP ratio was 63 per cent, lower than in eight other countries in the transition region – debt repayment could emerge as a serious problem in the medium run.

6.2.5 Foreign direct investment

Serbia's post-2000 economic transformation has been facilitated by increasing FDI. Particularly after 2003, FDI has contributed both to compensating the increasing current account deficit and to the process of privatization. During the whole 1989–2007 period, the cumulative stock of net FDI in Serbia reached almost US$ 12 billion or US$ 1599 per head, but 88 per cent of the whole amount has arrived only after 2001. Serbia's cumulative net FDI inflows represent a respectable 28 per cent of total inflows into six SEE countries, but only 2.4 per cent of those into all 29 EBRD client countries (see Table A.6.2, Appendix).

Record FDI inflows in Serbia were recorded after 2006 – around US$ 4 billion in 2006 and more than US$ 2 billion annually in 2007 and in 2008, though the amounts remain relatively low in comparison with some neighbouring countries (see Figure 6.7). The countries that after 2000 have invested most are Austria (over US$ 2.6 billion, to a large extent due to the sale of a mobile operator in 2006), Greece, Norway, Germany, and Netherlands (over US$ 1 billion each), while close behind are also Italy, Slovenia, and France (see Table A.6.3, Appendix).

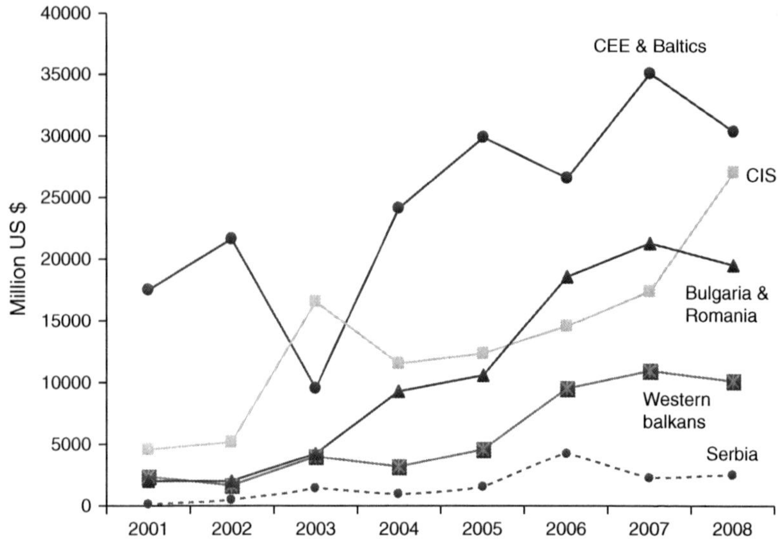

Figure 6.7 Foreign direct investment in transition countries and Serbia, 2001–8 (net inflows, in million US dollars)
Note: Data on the Western Balkans are inclusive of Serbia.
Source: EBRD (2008) *Transition Report 2008*.

The largest part of FDI in Serbia, as in other transition countries, reflects privatization deals in specific sectors – cement, tobacco, base metals, and more recently banking and telecommunications – and there has been very little greenfield investment, particularly in the industrial sector. Over the last three years, the banking sector recorded the largest FDI inflow (US$3.7 billion) followed by telecommunications (US$2.7 billion), while the manufacturing sector ranked third (US$1.8 billion). Among the companies that have invested in Serbia are US Steel, Phillip Morris, BAT, Microsoft, FIAT, Lukoil, Coca-Cola, Gazprom, Lafarge, Siemens, and Carlsberg. In the meantime, Serbia has also started investing in other countries; recently Telekom Srbija bought 65 per cent of Telekom Srpske (Bosnia and Herzegovina).

6.3 Systemic reforms: A radical break with the past regime

In addition to Serbia's improved macroeconomic performance after 2001, remarkable progress has been achieved in many transition-related economic and institutional reforms. We will consider the transition indicators of the EBRD prepared on four main areas of reform – enterprises, markets and trade, financial institutions, and infrastructure – which are used to evaluate progress of all East European countries, by scores going from 1 implying little or no reform, to 4+ implying a situation comparable to that of a developed market economy. The general conditions in late 2000 in Serbia were highly unsatisfactory, since it was among the least reformed countries in the whole transition region. At that time, the only three areas where some progress had been achieved in Serbia were small-scale privatization (score 3), price liberalization (2+), and infrastructure (2) (see Table 6.5).[11]

Only six months after the launch of radical economic reforms in late 2000, FR Yugoslavia was evaluated by the EBRD as the country where the most dramatic progress in structural reform in the past year had taken place, as the fastest reformer among all transition economies (EBRD, 2001, p. 20). Most reforms were initially indeed implemented very quickly. Where does Serbia stand today regarding each of these economic reforms?

6.3.1 Enterprise reform

Given the limited results achieved with privatization in Serbia in the 1990s (see Chapters 3 and 4), privatization of socially owned enterprises emerged as an important objective of the Serbian government in early 2001. A new privatization law was adopted in mid-2001, radically different from all previous laws, based on sales through public tenders and auctions as the primary privatization method, supplemented by limited give-aways to workers and citizens. Privatization of strategic enterprises is to be managed by the Privatization Agency, while all other enterprises are to implement privatization autonomously, usually initiating the process themselves. Around 300 large enterprises were planned to be sold at tenders, some 2000 firms at auctions, a slightly higher number was evaluated as loss-making firms likely to end in liquidation, while 50 large strategically important enterprises were to be restructured prior to privatization. The privatization of most state-owned enterprises, mainly in public utilities, was postponed to a later stage.

The intention of the new law was to attract strategic investors as majority owners. A firm was to offer up to 70 per cent of its capital on sale, or less if the buyer did not accept the offer, but the free transfer of shares to workers could be undertaken only if a majority of capital was sold. In autonomous privatizations, incentives were offered to implement privatization as soon as possible, since workers were to receive more shares in case of early privatizations – corresponding

Table 6.5 EBRD transition indicators: Serbia (2000–9) and SEE (mid-2009)

	Private sector share of GDP (in %) mid-year	Enterprises			Markets and trade			Financial institutions		Infrastructure
		Large-scale privatization	*Small-scale privatization*	*Governance and enterprise restructuring*	*Price liberalization*	*Trade and foreign exchange system*	*Competition policy*	*Banking reform and interest rate liberalization*	*Securities markets & non-bank financial institutions*	*Overall infrastructure reform*
Serbia, 2000–9										
2000	40	1	3	1	2+	1	1	1	1	2
2001	40	1	3	1	4	2+	1	1	1	2
2002	45	2	3	2	4	3	1	2+	2–	2
2003	45	2+	3	2	4	3	1	2+	2	2
2004	50	2+	3+	2	4	3	1	2+	2	2
2005	55	3–	3+	2+	4	3+	1	3–	2	2
2006	55	3–	4–	2+	4	3+	2–	3–	2	2
2007	55	3–	4–	2+	4	3+	2	3–	2	2
2008	60	3–	4–	2+	4	4–	2	3	2	2+
2009	60	3–	4–	2+	4	4	2	3	2	2+
SEE, mid-2009										
Albania	75	4–↑	4	2+	4+	4+	2	3	2–	2+
B&H	60	3	3	2	4	4	2	3	2–	2+
Croatia	70	3+	4+	3	4	4+	3↑	4	3	3
Macedonia	70	3+	4	3–	4+	4+	2+	3	3–↑	3–↑
Montenegro	65	3 ↓	4–	2	4	4	2↑	3	2–	2+↑
Serbia	60	3–	4–	2+	4	4 ↑	2	3	2	2+

Source: EBRD (2009), *Transition report 2009* and previous issues (www.ebrd.com). An arrow upwards indicates an improvement, while an arrow downwards a deterioration, with respect to the previous year.

to 30 per cent of the value of capital if privatization was undertaken within 18 months, 20 per cent if undertaken during the next 18–30 months, and only 10 per cent if undertaken after 30 months; and each worker was to receive, respectively, shares of the dinar equivalent of 400 DM, 300 DM, or 150 DM for each year of employment. In public tenders, shares corresponding up to 15 per cent of capital being privatized could be freely transferred, partly to workers (the dinar equivalent of 400 DM per worker for each year of employment) and partly to all 18-year old citizens. Proceeds from sales go to the Pensions Fund (10%), for compensation of nationalized property (5 per cent), and to the government budget for stimulating development, debt repayment, covering the costs of the privatization process, and other. Individuals can receive free shares only if they have not already been beneficiaries under the provisions of the 1997 law.

All socially owned enterprises earmarked for privatization were to start the process within a period of four years (by the end of 2005), otherwise they were to be privatized by the Privatization Agency. If any shares were left unsold, they were to be transferred to the Share Fund, a specialized financial state agency in charge of selling shares left over from partial or previous privatizations, state-owned minority share packages, and remaining stock packages of firms sold at auctions executed by the Privatization Agency. The Share Fund would offer them on sale until potential buyers were found, but all transferred shares were to be sold within six years, therefore by June 2007.

In order to facilitate privatization, the government adopted several amendments to the privatization law, in March 2003 and June 2005. In case of auctions, the procedure was simplified and the minimum price lowered to 20 per cent of the upper valuation. In tender sales, the relative importance of the criteria of the price offered had increased with respect to committed investment and redundancy programmes. Measures were also undertaken to ensure that insiders could not block the sale of their enterprise indefinitely, and that existing owners and managers could not artificially raise the cost of social programmes and redundancy packages to potential buyers (OECD, 2003). Since by late 2006 there were still around a 1000 socially owned firms that had not been sold, the Serbian government had to move the deadline for completing privatization to the end of 2008, and again recently to the end of 2009.

The largest number of enterprises was sold during the first two years (see Table 6.6). By the time the initial deadline for completing privatization expired at the end of 2005, some 1620 enterprises were sold out

Table 6.6 Serbian enterprises privatized according to the 2001 law, 2002–June 2009

Method	2002	2003	2004	2005	2006	2007	2008	2009	Total 2002–June 2009
Tenders (T)									
Sold	11	16	7	13	26	16	16	4	109
Broken contracts	1	3	2	3	5	2	3	0	19
Auctions (A)									
Sold	153	517	190	166	172	241	222	55	1,716
Broken contracts	54	163	67	35	37	41	4	0	401
Total sold at T & A	219	699	266	217	240	300	245	59	2,245
Total sold, excluding broken contracts	164	533	197	179	198	257	238	59	1,825
Share Fund sales of minority packages	48	117	65	294	307	348	248	59	1,486
Privatization revenues (in € mln)									
Auctions	36	177	93	155	118	286	191	40	1,096
Tenders	201	595	11	96	82	80	41	28	1,134
Share Fund	83	68	52	125	70	163	92	7	660
Restructuring	0	0	0.4	0.3	6.5	21.5	192.5	0.7	221.9
Total revenues	320	840	156.4	376.3	276.5	550.5	516.5	75.7	3,111.9
Cumulative revenues (in % of GDP)	–	6.9	7.7	10.2	17.4	20.2	21.4	NA	NA

Source: Annual Reports of the Serbian Privatization Agency and direct communications, except for privatization revenues in per cent of GDP which are from EBRD (2009, p. 218).

of around 2400 enterprises earmarked for privatization. However, there were also quite a few cases of broken contracts, so the actual number of privatized enterprises was lower. During the whole 2002–June 2009 period, 2245 enterprises were sold – 1716 at auctions and 109 at tenders – but considering that there were 420 broken contracts, the effective number of privatized enterprises comes down to 1825.

Parallel with privatizations at tenders and auctions organized by the Privatization Agency, the Share Fund has also been selling minority share packages at the Belgrade stock exchange of partially privatized enterprises. From 2002 until June 2009, the Share Fund sold 1486 minority share packages. Some enterprises have also been restructured in the meantime, or have been prepared for restructuring or liquidation.

Over the 2002 – mid-2009 period, government revenues from privatization have been quite substantial, totalling €3112 million, mainly from sales at auctions and tenders – €1096 from auctions and €1134 from tenders. The rest was cashed from sales by the Share Fund of minority packages on the stock exchange (€660 million) and of shares of enterprises in the process of restructuring. Privatization revenues have been a rather important source for covering the government's public deficit, as they have amounted to 2–7 per cent of Serbia's annual GDP, or by 2008 a cumulative 21.4 per cent of Serbia's GDP (see Table 6.6).

By mid-2009, the EBRD score for Serbia's small-scale privatization, already relatively high (3) in 2000, has increased to 4–, but it remains below the average in neighbouring countries (only Bosnia has a lower score and Montenegro the same; see Table 6.5). Since large-scale restructuring and privatization has been postponed until 2006, for this indicator Serbia has the lowest score (3–) among all SEE countries. Overall, Serbia's private sector share in GDP has registered a relatively modest increase – from around 40 per cent in 2000 to 60 per cent in mid-2009.

The private sector in Serbia, in almost nine years – mid-2001 to mid-2009 – increased its share in GDP by only 20 per cent, placing Serbia today among the least privatized transition economies. By mid-2009, there was one country, Bosnia and Herzegovina, that had the same share as Serbia of the private sector in GDP (60 per cent), while only other four among all 29 transition economies surveyed by the EBRD had a lower share – Belarus (30%), Tajikistan (55%), Turkmenistan (25%), and Uzbekistan (45%) (EBRD, 2009).

Unsatisfactory overall results in privatization, insufficient investment and restructuring in firms privatized through sales to domestic owners, the lack of respect of laws on corporate governance, maintenance of subsidies to large state-owned enterprises, and substantial delays in adopting and implementing bankruptcy legislation – are among the main reasons why Serbia in mid-2009 still had a rather low 2+ EBRD score in governance and enterprise restructuring. This EBRD score has remained the same since 2005, which is indicative of no improvements in enterprise governance and restructuring in Serbia over the last four years. The reasons are discussed further in Chapter 7.

6.3.2 Markets and trade

Measures directed towards the liberalization of internal and external markets and trade in Serbia have led to variable results. Since many prices were already liberalized in late 2000, additional price liberalization implemented soon after contributed to a high EBRD score 4 already in mid-2001 maintained up to the present, but reforms of Serbia's trade and foreign exchange system have been more gradual.

In 2001 the average tariff rate in Serbia's customs law was still relatively high (11%), but it has been gradually reduced to 6.3 per cent by 2007 along with a substantial simplification of the tariff structure. There are categories of goods that remain heavily protected (for example, tariffs for some agricultural products remain at 30%). In mid-2009 the EBRD upgraded Serbia's trade and foreign exchange system (score 4), thus today it is very close to the standards of a developed market economy. Serbia has implemented extensive trade liberalization with its neighbours in the SEE region, within the initiative on trade liberalization launched in 2001 by the Stability Pact for SEE.[12] Since mid-2001 Serbia has been negotiating with the WTO; it officially applied for WTO membership on 10 December 2004 and hopes to become a member in 2010.

By contrast, very limited results have been achieved in implementing competition policy. The EBRD score for Serbia in this area has remained 1 during the whole 2001–5 period, and has increased only slightly thereafter, to 2 by 2009. Only in 2005 was a new competition law adopted, which came into effect in September 2005. Thereafter, there were notable delays in setting up the new anti-trust authority, as it is only in May 2006 that the Serbian Commission for the protection of competition became operational (Government of Serbia, 2007). The de-monopolization of some sectors of the Serbian economy, such as energy, railways, or air transport, has been delayed as a consequence of the postponed restructuring and privatization of public utilities. In other sectors, such as wholesale and particularly retail trade, further concentration through mergers and acquisitions has taken place (see Chapter 7).

6.3.3 Financial sector reforms

A major banking reform was undertaken in FR Yugoslavia/Serbia soon after the political changes, that had taken place in May 2001. Banks were classified into four categories in order to distinguish between healthy banks and those that needed to be recapitalized, restructured, or simply closed down. This led to the closure of 19 loss-making banks in late 2001 and of another four largest banks in 2002, that represented 55 per cent of total assets of the Serbian banking sector. From 86 banks operating at the end of 2001, their number was reduced to 35 by the end of 2007, parallel with an increase in capitalization, the value of Serbian banks' balance sheets passing from 892 billion dinars in 2001 to 1562 billion dinars in 2007 (Dugalic and Matic, 2008, p. 246).

Though privatization of the banking sector was initially delayed, it speeded up after 2004. By mid-2006, 18 foreign banks were already operating in Serbia, foreign ownership accounted for 77 per cent of banking assets, while the remaining assets were in the hands of 19 domestic banks, 12 of which were state-owned (Zdrale, 2006). The share of state-owned banks in total assets of the banking sector was reduced from 50 per cent in 2003 to 37 per cent in 2004, further to 25 per cent in 2005 and to 15 per cent in 2006 (Government of Serbia, 2007, p. 28).

Thanks to the further privatization of banks in 2007–8, the share of state-owned capital has shrunk to negligible levels. Increasing concentration of the banking system has taken place, with the number of banks operating in Serbia reduced to only 32 by the end of 2008 (see Table A6.4, in the appendix). The 11 largest banks in Serbia (end-2008) held as much as 72 per cent of balance sheets of the total banking sector (see Table 6.7). Ten of these largest banks are private foreign-owned banks, including Banca Intesa, Raiffeisen, Eurobank EFG, Hypo Alpe-Adria, Unicredit, and Société Générale. The only bank that still retains a minority 42.6 per cent share of the Serbian government is the Komercijalna Banka, the second largest bank in Serbia (see Figure 6.8).

Despite these developments, some regulations regarding banking services are still less liberal and less transparent in Serbia than in most neighbouring countries (Prica and Backovic, 2009). From mid-2008, new regulations have been in force which have provided the full application of prudential supervision of banks according to Basel I standards, while the first steps were taken to implement the Basel II standards.

The lack of transparency in banking services in Serbia is reflected in the high net interest spread, which in 2005 was still 11 per cent, substantially higher than the SEE average of 7 per cent or the CEE average of 4 per cent (Commission, 2006b). The average interest rate on loans in Serbia during 2006 was still above 15 per cent; during 2007 it somewhat declined but remained over 10 per cent; and it again sharply increased after March 2008, to 20 per cent by November 2008. Interest rates on savings deposits, on average, have been around 5 per cent during the 2006–8 period,

Table 6.7 Eleven largest banks in Serbia, December 2008

Rank	Bank	Ownership features	Balance sheets (in thousands of dinars)	Share in total value of balance sheets of all 34 banks in Serbia (%)
1	Banca Intesa	Private, foreign	250,200,715	14.1
2	Komercijalna banka	Mixed, minority state	170,861,371	9.6
3	Raiffeisen	Private, foreign	160,895,536	9.1
4	Eurobank EFG	Private, foreign	124,029,267	7.0
5	Hypo Alpe-Adria	Private, foreign	114,398,731	6.4
6	Unicredit	Private, foreign	89,513,798	5.0
7	Vojvođanska banka	Private, foreign	86,711,705	4.9
8	Agroindustrijska komercijalna banka	Private, foreign	83,428,495	4.7
9	Société Générale	Private, foreign	71,893,224	4.0
10	ProCredit Bank	Private, foreign	64,808,057	3.6
11	Volksbank	Private, foreign	62,227,936	3.5
	Total			71.9

Note: These 11 banks are those that have balance sheets over 50 billion dinars.
Source: Compiled on the basis of Table A6.4 (Appendix).

determining a relatively high net interest spread, particularly after May 2008 of over 10 per cent (see Figure 6.9).

There are a number of factors which explain the high interest spread in Serbia. In addition to the recent NBS increase of the reference interest rate, other more fundamental reasons should be mentioned, such as regulations imposing very high official reserves on banks, unregulated interest rate policy, high banking charges, high premiums on insurance of deposits, regulations which discriminate against domestic banks, and insufficient financial liberalization (Vukovic, 2008; Prica and Backovic, 2009).

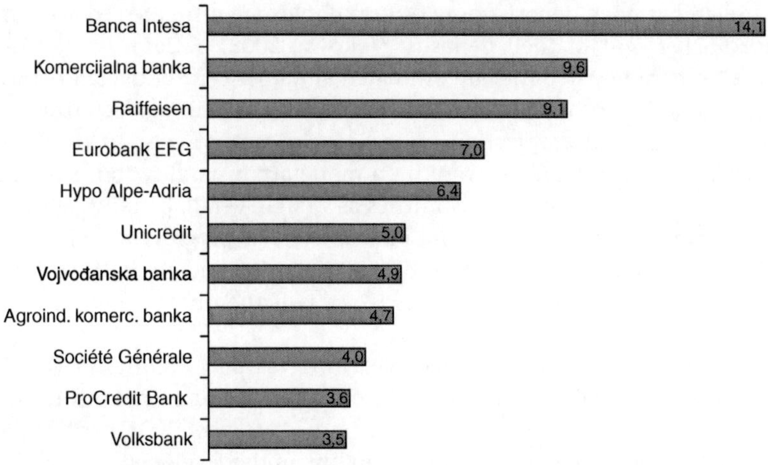

Figure 6.8 Banking sector concentration in Serbia: The 11 largest banks (December 2008)
Source: Table A6.4 (Appendix).

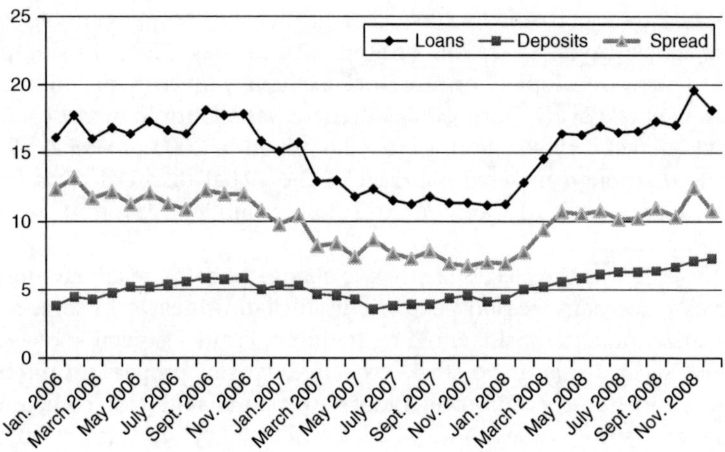

Figure 6.9 Interest rates on loans, deposits and interest spread in Serbia, 2006–8
Source: National Bank of Serbia (www.nbs.rs) and direct communications.

Citizens' foreign currency savings deposited in Serbian banks have grown continuously in recent years, which reflects an increase in confidence of the population in the banking sector. Still, currency substitution remains very high, though there are no accurate statistics.

Foreign currency deposits only of households are estimated to account for 98 per cent of their deposits (Vukovic, 2008, p. 265), while total foreign currency deposits are estimated at 68 per cent of overall deposits (Commission of EC, 2008). Serbia is therefore still characterized by a high degree of euroization, reflecting the lack of trust in the local currency after a decade of very high monetary instability (but this is a feature typical of other SEE countries as well). Overall, banking reforms and interest rate liberalization in Serbia have progressed well since 2001, particularly after 2005: in mid-2009, Serbia had an EBRD score 3, just like most other SEE countries (Croatia is the only exception with a score 4).

Far less progress has been achieved in developing securities markets and non-financial institutions, as in mid-2009 Serbia's EBRD score was only 2, the same as in 2003. In the immediate post-2001 period, the Serbian capital market remained highly underdeveloped, since the Belgrade stock exchange was dominated by trade of government bonds on frozen foreign currency deposits. The Serbian stock exchange has developed in the meantime (Commission of EC, 2006a). Enterprise shares have increased from only 6.9 per cent of traded securities in 2002 to 89.9 per cent in 2007, and further to 92.6 per cent in 2008 (Rebublicki zavod za razvoj, 2009, p. 42). In May 2006, three important laws were adopted: on the stock exchange, investment funds, and company takeovers. During 2003–8, there was a fourfold increase in the stock market capitalization, from €2.6 billion in 2003 to €18.2 billion in 2007, though under the impact of the global financial crisis there was a drop to €10.3 billion in 2008 (Rebublicki zavod za razvoj, 2009, p. 43).

Nevertheless the Belgrade stock exchange remains relatively underdeveloped. Many reasons explain it, including delays in large-scale privatization, lack of shareholding tradition, limited general knowledge about securities and the stock exchange, lack of proper institutional framework for the enforcement of laws, unreliability of companies' financial and business information, inefficiency of legal sanctions against management not respecting small shareholders' rights, low level of competence at brokerage houses and investment consulting firms, and lack of efficient practices regarding the resolution of financial disputes.

Some progress has also been made in the non-banking financial sector. The first investment funds started operating in 2007, founded by banks such as Raiffeisen, JUMBES, and Komercijalna Banka. Other banks, including Societé Générale, Unicredit, Volksbank, and Komercijalna

Banka have activated their custody function and are starting to operate as investment banks. By the end of September 2008, there were already 13 open-ended and two closed investment funds (Republicki zavod a razvoj, 2009, p. 43).

In the insurance sector, the NBS in 2008 withdrew licenses of a few insurance companies not satisfying required standards and privatization of socially owned insurance companies has continued, though delays have occurred in privatizing the main Serbian insurance company, 'Dunav osiguranje'. In May 2008, 21 insurance companies were operating in Serbia, including four greenfield companies that received operating licenses in 2007 and early 2008. The second biggest insurance company (DDOR of Novi Sad) was successfully privatized in 2007, sold to a EU-based insurance company. Foreign ownership of the insurance sector has increased to 62.8 per cent of total premium income in 2007, compared with 26.4 per cent a year earlier. During 2004–7, the premium income of non-life insurance almost doubled, while in the case of life insurance it nearly tripled. The insurance sector's share of capital in the total financial sector has increased to 6.9 per cent (Commission of the EC, 2008).

6.3.4 Infrastructure

Reforms of the infrastructure sector in Serbia have started only fairly recently, so by mid-2009 the overall EBRD score was still a low 2+. In part, this is due to the postponement of restructuring and privatization of most state-owned enterprises in public utilities, including the energy and transport sectors. This is again similar to the situation in other SEE countries, the only exception being Croatia which was evaluated with a score 3.

Over the past four years, some progress has been achieved in the area of roads (score 3–), thanks to the privatization in 2005 of 20 out of 26 maintenance companies. Similarly in telecommunications, Serbia has a score of 3–, thanks to the recent privatization of another mobile operator and the setting up of a regulatory authority. Reforms of the electricity sector and railways are still evaluated with a low 2+ score, while water and wastewater are with a 2– score (EBRD, 2009). It should be borne in mind that market-oriented reforms in infrastructure are a complex area of reform, requiring substantial financial resources and preparatory work. Reforms of public utilities have also been implemented very gradually in most developed market economies, sometimes not even successfully, as in the case of public transport in the UK.

6.4 Summing up

Serbia has achieved impressive results in implementing many transition-related economic and institutional reforms over the last nine years. Considering that Serbia in late 2000 inherited an essentially unreformed and distorted economic system, it has caught up quickly in many areas. By 2009, major convergence had taken place in Serbia's institutional setting with respect to not only other SEE countries, but also the wider transition region.

Despite fast progress in many areas, what clearly emerges from the analysis of the post-2001 economic transformation of the Serbian economy, whether one considers the main macroeconomic indicators or the situation in specific areas of economic reform, is that there has been *insufficient restructuring of the real sector of the economy*. Serbia's macroeconomic situation – a current account deficit that has increased continuously after 2001, to the level of over 17 per cent of GDP by late 2008, primarily due to the insufficient increase in exports – suggests that economic reforms implemented so far have not sufficiently contributed to the transformation and modernization of important segments of the Serbian economy.

A similar conclusion derives from the EBRD transition indicators for Serbia, which by 2009 indicate slow progress primarily in large-scale privatization (score 3–), the related area of infrastructure (2+), corporate governance and restructuring (2+), competition policy (2), and the resulting slow growth of the private sector.[13] It should again be stressed that Serbia, along with Bosnia and Herzegovina, still has among the lowest shares – 60 per cent – of the private sector in GDP. The limited restructuring of a substantial part of the Serbian economy can be traced to the overall transition strategy, in which the privatization model, in particular, has not delivered the expected results. These problems are discussed further in Chapter 7.

Appendix

Table A6.1 GDP per head in Southeast Europe, 2005 and 2008 (in US dollars)

	At market exchange rates		**At purchasing power parities**	
	2005	**2008**	**2005**	**2008**
Albania	2,690	4,260	5,400	6,920
Bosnia and Herzegovina	2,850	4,660	6,610	8,650
Croatia	9,970	13,760	14,940	18,290
Macedonia	2,820	4,370	7,350	9,140
Montenegro	3,480	7,850	7,880	10,800
Serbia	3,500	6,880	8,620	11,160

Source: Estimates of the Economist Intelligence Unit, June 2009.

Table A6.2 Net inflows of foreign direct investment in SEE, 1989–2008 (in million US dollars)

	Net annual inflows of Foreign Direct Investment									Cumulative net inflows 1989–2007		FDI inflows 2007
Country	**2000**	**2001**	**2002**	**2003**	**2004**	**2005**	**2006**	**2007**	**2008**	**Mln US$**	**Per head US$**	**In per cent of GDP**
Albania	143	207	135	178	324	258	315	641	484	2,655	830	5.9
Bosnia & H.	146	119	266	382	708	579	710	2,023	1,200	5,124	1,348	13.4
Croatia	1,105	1,398	553	1,927	732	1,551	3,212	4,644	4,806	18,515	4,168	9.2
Macedonia	175	441	106	118	322	94	424	321	434	2,234	1,117	4.2
Montenegro	na	10	84	44	63	482	585	717	827	1,986	3,009	20.6
Serbia	50	165	475	1,365	966	1,550	4,264	2,195	3,100	11,995	1,599	5.4
Total FDI in SEE-6	1,619	2,340	1,619	4,014	3,114	4,514	9,510	10,541	10,851	42,509	-	-

Source: Compiled on the basis of EBRD data.

Table A6.3 Serbia: FDI in cash (in 000 US$), by country

Country	2000	2001	2002	2003	2004	2005	2006	2007	2008	Total
Austria	183	1,421	33,876	93,747	146,104	201,189	520,356	1,161,096	475,613	2,633,585
Greece	334	1,280	12,496	62,268	52,968	249,536	923,698	336,401	48,456	1,687,437
Norway	0	2	74	280	0	29	1,546,993	3,187	6,135	1,556,700
Germany	6,152	9,788	82,801	75,708	51,985	187,320	905,824	69,530	88,882	1,477,990
Netherlands	0	102	2,248	598,963	102,008	92,113	–214,119	–27,958	510,400	1,063,757
Italy	2,006	594	7,553	21,325	10,149	18,316	52,752	155,363	485,884	753,942
Slovenia	33	11,254	9,561	29,036	15,706	183,563	201,241	92,856	112,189	655,439
France	0	81	87,489	7,858	24,022	62,347	159,085	84,391	78,345	503,618
Luxembourg	0	128	3,619	4,108	2,387	108,885	8,843	241,537	76,147	445,654
Hungary	0	275	1,167	4,224	16,567	24,677	244,045	31,494	31,030	353,479
Switzerland	35	86	2,913	12,559	29,401	56,990	–15,421	96,157	122,563	305,283
Croatia	0	1,096	5,243	34,446	10,806	40,484	25,240	35,944	143,148	296,407
Montenegro	0	0	0	0	0	0	12,946	209,288	73,900	296,134
Great Britain	0	1,225	6,618	20,631	79,620	63,330	135,915	–26,584	14,536	295,291
Bulgaria	0	0	133	129	9,910	655	54,270	46,916	21,884	133,897
USA	343	1,906	18,099	15,068	18,187	22,257	–29,612	31,825	55,336	133,409
Slovakia	3	10	10	18,342	0	25,447	19,325	3,084	1,471	67,692
Belgium	0	0	344	1,925	2,523	12,407	6,464	24,038	16,246	63,947
Russian Federation	736	3,581	2,556	3,359	538	14,324	15,992	488	12,629	54,203

(Continued)

Table A6.3 (Continued)

Country	2000	2001	2002	2003	2004	2005	2006	2007	2008	Total
Latvia	0	0	5	15,330	17,082	6,441	10,527	3,535	739	53,659
Israel	0	0	260	207	3,052	14,294	4,544	26,510	–712	48,155
Lichtenstein	0	216	57	2,162	2,974	–41,316	–17,538	–2,937	5,106	–51,276
Cyprus	762	2,045	41,717	31,581	16,310	71,551	–387,154	137,427	7,275	–78,486
Bosnia & Herzegovina	189	169	2,951	5,056	2,104	4,692	–16,750	–838,608	–60,804	–901,001
Other	476	129	4,664	13,098	182,000	21,175	118,913	109,317	36,122	485,894
TOTAL	**11,252**	**35,388**	**326,454**	**1,071,410**	**796,403**	**1,440,706**	**4,286,379**	**2,004,297**	**2,362,520**	**12,334,809**

Note: Since the NBS obtains data on FDI in cash from commercial banks, these data are classified by country of payment and not by country of investment. Data on FDI from Norway for 2006 does not include the license for Telenor (410 million) and from Austria for 2006 the third license (425 million US$) which, according to Balance of Payments methodology, is recorded under capital transfers, licenses, and patents.
Source: NBS (www.nbs.rs).

Table A6.4 Key features of the banking sector in Serbia (December 2008)

Bank name	Total Balance Sheets (in thousands of dinars)	Ownership structure Main shareholders (in per cent)	Key features Private/State Domestic/ Foreign
1. Agroindustrijska komercijalna banka AIK, Nis	83,428,495	ATEBANK 20.32% Julius Baer International Equity Fund 5.47%	Private, domestic
2. Alpha Bank Srbija, Beograd	58,319,687	ALPHA BANK A.E. 100%	Private, foreign (fully foreign owned)
3. Banca Intesa, Beograd	250,200,715	Intesa holding international 77.79% Intesa Sanpaolo SPA 15.21% IFC 7.00%	Private, foreign (majority foreign owned)
4. Banka Poštanska štedionica, Beograd	24,271,220	Republika Srbija 63.72% JP PTT Saobraćaja Srbija 30.28%	State (majority state owned)
5. Credy banka, Kragujevac	7,839,344	Republika Srbija 55.17% Beogradska banka, under bankruptcy 7.33%	State (majority state owned)
6. Čačanska banka, Čačak	17,784,698	Republika Srbija 38.84% EBRD, London 24.99%	Mixed, domestic/foreign (minority state owned)
7. Erste Bank, Novi Sad	49,187,125	Erste Group Bank AG 73.99% Steiermärkische Bank und Sparkassen AG 26%	Private, foreign (majority foreign owned)
8. Eurobank EFG štedionica, Beograd	124,029,267	EFG Eurobank Ergasias Athens 55.21% EFG New Europe Holding G B.V. Amsterdam 42.74%	Private, foreign (almost fully foreign owned)
9. Findomestic banka, Beograd	12,110,140	Findomestic Banka SPA 100%	Private, foreign (fully foreign owned)

(Continued)

Table A6.4 (Continued)

Bank name	Total Balance Sheets (in thousands of dinars)	Ownership structure Main shareholders (in per cent)	Key features Private/State Domestic/ Foreign
10. Hypo Alpe-Adria-Bank, Beograd	114,398,731	HYPO Alpe-Adria-Bank International AG Klagenfurt 99.89%	Private, foreign (fully foreign owned)
11. JUMBES banka, Beograd	7,022,039	Republika Srbija 21.17% Beobanka Beograd, under bankruptcy 6.98% SFR Yugoslavia 5.61% Hypo kastodi 5.10%	Mixed, domestic/ foreign (minority state owned)
12. Jugobanka Jugbanka, Kosovska Mitrovica	7,551,024	Jugobanka Beograd, under bankruptcy 51.25% Development Fund of Serbia – Beograd 30.63% Beobanka Beograd, under bankruptcy 10%	State (majority state owned)
13. KBC banka, Beograd	16,377,819	KBC Insurance NV 100%	Private, foreign (fully foreign owned)
14. Komercijalna banka, Beograd	170,861,371	Republic of Serbia 42.59% EBRD, London 25%	Mixed, domestic/foreign (minority state owned)
15. Kosovsko Metohijska banka, Zvečan	522,200	PKB-Orvin-Orahovac 2.51% Klinicki bolnicki centar Priština 2.09% DP 'Trepča' bat. Gnjilane 1.92% Semenarstvo Klina 1.76%	Private, domestic/foreign
16. Marfin Bank, Beograd	17,117,841	Marfin Popular Bank Public Co. Ltd 97.22%	Private, foreign (almost fully foreign owned)

(Continued)

Table A6.4 (Continued)

Bank name	Total Balance Sheets (in thousands of dinars)	Ownership structure Main shareholders (in per cent)	Key features Private/State Domestic/ Foreign
17. Meridian Bank-Crédit Agricole group, Novi Sad	35,381,063	Crédit Agricole S.A. 100%	Private, foreign (fully foreign owned)
18. Metals-banka, Novi Sad	18,633,289	DDOR Novi Sad 15.23% Zavarovalnica Triglav 5.02%	Private, domestic/foreign
19. Moskovska banka, Beograd	1,692,531	Akcionarska Komercijalna Banka – Moskovska Banka 100%	Private, foreign (fully foreign owned)
20. NLB banka, Novi Sad	39,389,883	Nova Ljubljanska Banka 99.50%	Private, foreign (fully foreign owned)
21. Opportunity banka, Novi Sad	4,521,296	Opportunity Transformation Investments Inc. 63.51% EBRD London 19.11% Nederlandse Financierings – Maatschappij Voor Ontwikkelingslanden N. V. 12.74%	Private, foreign (almost fully foreign owned)
22. OTP banka Srbija, Novi Sad	48,311,127	OTP Bank 90.43% Home Art & Sales Services 5.16%	Private, foreign (almost fully foreign owned)
23. Piraeus Bank, Beograd	31,556,256	Piraeus Bank Sapireus 100%	Private, foreign (fully foreign owned)
24. Poljoprivredna banka Agrobanka, Beograd	39,599,724	Republic of Srbija 20.07% Hypo Kastodi 46.45% Raiffeisen Zentralbank 5.45%	Mixed, state/ foreign (minority state owned)

(Continued)

Table A6.4 (Continued)

Bank name	**Total Balance Sheets (in thousands of dinars)**	**Ownership structure Main shareholders (in per cent)**	**Key features Private/State Domestic/ Foreign**
25. Privredna banka, Pančevo	6,312,647	Republic of Serbia 92.98%	State (almost fully state owned)
26. Privredna banka Beograd, Beograd	19,004,624	Republic of Serbia 19.41% Raiffeisen Zentralbank 5.90%	Mixed, state/ foreign (minority state owned)
27. ProCredit Bank, Beograd	64,808,057	ProCredit holding Frankfurt 83.33% Commerzbank Frankfurt 16.67%	Private, foreign (almost fully foreign owned)
28. Raiffeisen banka, Beograd	160,895,536	Raiffeisen International Beteiligungs 100%	Private, foreign (fully foreign owned)
29. Société Générale banka Srbija, Beograd	71,893,224	Société Génerale 99.99%	Private, foreign (almost fully foreign owned)
30. Srpska banka, Beograd	10,113,618	Republic of Serbia 96.52%	State (almost fully state owned)
31. Unicredit Bank Srbija, Beograd	89,513,798	Unicredit Bank, Austria 99.92%	Private, foreign (almost fully foreign owned)
32. Univerzal banka, Beograd	25,331,388	No major shareholder with more than 5% of voting rights	Private, domestic
33. Vojvođanska banka, Novi Sad	86,711,705	National bank of Greece 100%	Private, foreign (fully foreign owned)
34. Volksbank, Beograd	62,227,936	Volksbank international 96.90%	Private, foreign (almost fully foreign owned)
Total	1,776,919,418		

Source: Compiled from data of the NBS (www.nbs.rs), March 2009.

7
Transition Strategy Flaws: Privatization and Restructuring

Under the surface of remarkable progress in most areas of economic reform, there are fundamental problems remaining in the Serbian economy. The post-2001 transition strategy has not conduced to adequate restructuring of productive capacity within enterprises, nor to sufficient redeployment of human and capital resources across sectors. In a nutshell, a substantial part of the real sector of the Serbian economy has not been restructured, greatly contributing to slow and inadequate structural changes. This is to a large extent due to the chosen privatization model, and the neglect or postponement of other crucial reforms – such as the general hardening of budget constraints, facilitating the entry of private enterprises, effective competition policy, or efficient mechanisms of corporate governance. These accompanying reforms, complementary to privatization, are just as important for changes at the microeconomic level, as stressed by the 'post-Washington consensus' which emerged in the second half of the 1990s (Kolodko and Nuti, 1997).[1] These reforms on their own could have delivered many of the advantages expected of privatization. Although the first decade of transition in CEE has produced important lessons on neglected areas and the sequencing of reforms, the mistakes of other CEE countries seem to have been forgotten too easily in countries like Serbia, embarking on transition later (Nuti and Uvalic, 2003, p. 13).

The present chapter will analyse a few critical issues of the transition strategy adopted in Serbia in 2001, related to privatization and industrial restructuring. It will point to the main reasons why there has been insufficient microeconomic restructuring in Serbia. In addition to issues related directly to privatization, many policy failures that have contributed to limited microeconomic restructuring in Serbia were precisely in those areas of reform that are complementary to privatization.

The main macroeconomic consequences of delayed microeconomic restructuring are also analysed, namely inadequate structural changes characterized by a very fast expansion of primarily services. The chapter concludes by considering the principal shortcomings of the 2001 privatization model in reference to social property, the chosen methods, and attained objectives.

7.1 Limited microeconomic restructuring

There are many factors that explain the insufficient restructuring of Serbian enterprises, most of which are closely related, directly or indirectly, to the 2001 privatization strategy. The following are the most important reasons of limited microeconomic restructuring in Serbia:

- The slow implementation of the 2001 privatization law, along with many cases of unsuccessful privatizations;
- Delayed restructuring of the state sector;
- Over-optimistic expectations regarding FDI;
- Regulatory environment for firm entry and exit;
- Insufficient and selective hardening of budget constraints;
- Limited market competition and ineffective competition policy;
- Inadequate employment policy;
- Only gradual improvements in corporate governance.

Some of the factors responsible for slow microeconomic restructuring derive directly from the privatization strategy, while others are important areas of reform that were not given sufficient attention when privatization was re-launched in 2001. One of the most obvious consequences of these policy failures is the relatively slow growth of the private sector in Serbia.

7.1.1 Slow implementation of the 2001 privatization law

Privatization of state or socially owned enterprises was one of the most important elements of the transition in all post-communist countries, since the introduction of private property rights was regarded the best way to strengthen incentives at the microeconomic level. Also in Serbia, enterprise privatization was an essential part of the post-2001 transition, particularly considering the long and unsuccessful history of reforms in this area. Recalling that privatization in Serbia started already in 1989–90 (see Chapter 2), that the strategy was subsequently modified through two new privatization laws adopted in 1991 and 1997 (see Chapters 3 and 4), and that the overall results had been disappointing – by 2000, the private sector increased its share to about 40 per cent of GDP – privatization emerged as a high-ranking target of the Serbian government in early 2001. In order to enable a quick transfer of enterprise ownership into private hands, the 2001 privatization law was radically different from previous laws: it rendered privatization compulsory for all enterprises earmarked for privatization, and it changed the method, from the insiders model to cash-based sales (Vlahovic et al., 2003).

The implementation of the 2001 Serbian privatization law has lagged well behind the envisaged timetables. The delays were initially due to technical issues, such as the need to establish the accompanying institutions, but a more substantial reason was limited interest of potential buyers, domestic and particularly foreign. Since the best firms had already been privatized in the 1990s, enterprises offered on sale after 2001 were the less attractive ones. Even in the case of the more viable firms offered through tender sales, around 150 enterprises – instead of the 300 initially planned – were privatized during the 2001–8 period. Given limited interest, shares have sometimes been sold at very high discounts (20% book value), at Dutch auctions,[2] or in exchange for bonds of old foreign currency savings (Cerovic, 2009; see also Cerovic (ed.) 2006).

Although the initial deadline for completing privatization was set for 2005, as late as 1 May 2009, only 1828 enterprises within the Serbian Privatization Agency's portfolio (or 77% of the total) have been sold, while there were still 535 enterprises to be privatized, 272 of which were officially registered as socially owned firms (see Table 7.1). More than four months later, on 11 September 2009, the number of sold enterprises was actually lower (1810), while the number of firms in liquidation increased from 45 to 284. This can be explained by many cases of broken privatization contracts.

There has indeed been a remarkable number of broken privatization contracts – a total of 420 cases since 2001. Most frequently, the new owner was not able to fulfil the envisaged obligations regarding investment and social programmes, or was not even able to pay the agreed price. In other cases, contracts have been broken because of the illegal sale of enterprise assets, stop in the production process, or other irregularities. In a number of privatized enterprises, workers have not been paid wages, or payments of social security contributions have been greatly delayed, sometimes even for several years. These problems have contributed to an increasing number of strikes, particularly in 2009 when the credit squeeze brought many Serbian enterprises to the verge of collapse. Following the request of the Serbian trade unions in mid-2009, the government has promised to investigate all cases of dubious privatizations.

Table 7.1 Privatization of enterprises in Serbia on the basis of the 2001 law

Number of enterprises in privatization	By 1 May 2009	By 21 June 2009	By 11 September 2009
	2,363	2,123	2,116
Privatization method			
Auction	2,150	2,123	1,916
Tender	159	154	151
Liquidation	45	51	284
Restructuring	40	29	35
Preparation	14	13	13
Status of privatizing enterprises			
Sold	1,828	1,819	1,810
In per cent of total	*77*	*78.4*	*85.5*
Unsold	535	500	306
In per cent of total	*23*	*21.6*	*14.5*
Unsold enterprises, by legal status			
Socially owned enterprise	272	257	112
Limited liability company	56	46	36
Limited liability company (separated)*	32	32	20
Medical institutes	34	34	33
Public enterprises	22	22	20
Joint-stock companies	9	8	4
Socially owned agriculture firms	2	1	0
Unknown legal status	2	2	3

*These are limited liability companies which have been separated from public enterprises.
Source: Compiled on the basis of the Serbian Privatization Agency Database on Enterprises in Privatization (www.priv.yu), September, 2009.

These recent developments confirm not only the slow pace of privatization in Serbia, but also fairly unsatisfactory overall results. In privatizing enterprises sold to domestic owners, typically, little restructuring has taken place. The change in ownership was not sufficient to promote innovation, the introduction of new production programmes, or new investment. Owing to the lack of capital, privatized firms have often failed to undertake substantial investment and implement effective restructuring and modernization. Some enterprises were bought not with the intention of being restructured, but simply because it was the only way to get hold of land for new construction at favourable locations.[3] Existing legal regulations have also hampered faster enterprise restructuring. Contracts on the acquisition of capital of socially owned enterprises prohibit the sale of shares, as well as changes in the sector of activity, for a period of five years, without the approval of the Privatization Agency (Vlada Republike Srbije, 2006, p. 67). Such regulations have undoubtedly slowed down or even blocked the taking over of enterprises by potentially more competent owners.

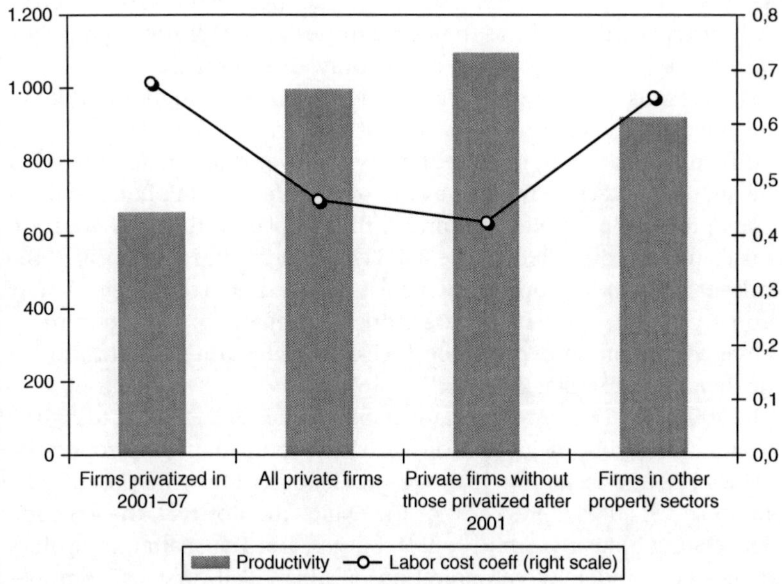

Figure 7.1 Productivity and labour costs in Serbia, 2007
Note: Firms in other property sectors include state, social and mixed property enterprises.
Source: Stamenkovic, et al. (2009a), p. 54.

Therefore, instead of the improvements in economic performance of Serbian enterprises expected after privatization, there have been many cases of unsuccessful privatizations which have delayed enterprise restructuring and slowed down economic recovery of the Serbian economy (Cerovic, 2009). These conclusions are confirmed by recent empirical evidence from Serbia, which show that the newly created private enterprises in Serbia have performed much better than firms privatized during the

2002–7 period (Stamenkovic et al., 2009a, pp. 180–4). The recent growth in private sector output in Serbia is due primarily to the contribution of the *ex novo* enterprises, much more than to enterprises privatized after 2001. Productivity has also been higher and labour costs lower in the *de novo* private firms than in those privatized after 2001 (see Figure 7.1).

7.1.2 Delayed restructuring of the state sector

An important reason behind the slow restructuring of the Serbian economy is that the 2001 privatization law deliberately excluded most public enterprises that were tacitly nationalized in the 1990s, which were planned to be restructured and privatized at a later stage.[4] These are mainly very large firms, frequently monopolies in public utilities and infrastructure. Most of these enterprises have still not been corporatized and their restructuring started only after 2006.

The reasons for delays are partly due to the late adoption (2006) of the new Serbian constitution, which at last removed the legal obstacles for the privatization of public enterprises. Previous norms specified that the Republic of Serbia was the owner of not only capital, but also of all assets/property of public enterprises, thus impeding their privatization (Arsic and Djokovic, 2006). The 2006 constitution has also clarified the concept of 'public property', which is now explicitly defined as state property: 'Public property is state property, property of the autonomous province, and property of the local self-governing unit' (Constitution of the Republic of Serbia, 2006, Article 86).

In 2006, the 17 most important public enterprises established by the Republic of Serbia included two electricity companies (Elektroprivreda Srbije – EPS and Elektromreza Srbije – EMS), other four enterprises in the energy sector (JP PEU Resavica for the exploitation of coal, the gas company Naftna Industrija Srbije – NIS, Srbijagas, and Transnafta), companies in transport and telecommunications (Serbian Railways, JAT Airways, Nikola Tesla Airport, Serbian Roads, Serbian Post and Telegraph, and Serbia Telekom), and other companies for skiing resorts, forestry, and water management (Skijalista Srbije, Srbijasume, Vojvodinasume, Srbijavode, and Vode Vojvodine) (Arsic and Djokovic, 2006).

By mid-2009, their number had increased further, as there were 33 public enterprises owned by the Republic of Serbia with 85,842 employees (without NIS and Telecom), while local communities owned another 598 public enterprises and had 66,139 employees (Ministarstvo Finansija, 2009). These are also among the most capital-intensive enterprises in Serbia.[5] In 2008, the 17 most important public enterprises represented 9 per cent of the total number of employees, 38 per cent of capital, 16 per cent of annual losses and only 4 per cent of net profits of the Serbian economy (www.razvoj.gov.rs).

The recent increase in the number of public enterprises in Serbia has occurred both because of the process of restructuring, since after 2006 some large companies have been split into smaller units, and because of the process of regional decentralization of the public administration. Over the last six years, the state sector has expanded according to other indicators as well. If we consider only non-financial enterprises (representing around 54% of gross value added), during the 2002–7 period the state sector has seen an increase in the number of enterprises (from 450 to 586), the doubling of workers employed (from 8 to 16% of employees in the non-financial sector), and the doubling of its share in gross value added (from 11 to 21%) (Stamenkovic et al., 2009a; see Table A7.3, Appendix). This notable increase in the relative importance of the state sector can also be taken as proof of poor performance of many enterprises privatized after 2001.

Although the state sector in Serbia includes a large variety of enterprises, the main problems are concentrated in a handful of large public enterprises that have been incurring enormous losses thus requiring continuous government subsidies. Since the corporatization of public enterprises has been delayed, these enterprises have not been able to attract private investment, badly needed for restructuring and modernization. These enterprises are still not run by independent profit-oriented managers, but by politically appointed company board members, who have been replaced continuously, following the very frequent changes in the Serbian government. This has greatly contributed to highly unprofessional management, lack of modernization, and absence of long-term restructuring strategies. Moreover, some of these public enterprises continue to perform important social functions, like providing cheap electricity, under-priced public transport, or other services. The government has been reluctant to undertake radical measures in this area, so a large part of the public sector has effectively been neglected after 2001.

The process of restructuring public enterprises started only in 2006, with the breaking up of large firms into smaller units and the separation of the core from secondary activities, settlement, or rescheduling of debt obligations, reductions of redundant labour, and price adjustments towards world prices. Some of the state-owned companies have recently been offered on sale or have also been successfully privatized. The JAT Airlines, after changing its legal status into a closed shareholding company and some restructuring (separation of *JAT tehnika*), was offered on sale in July 2008 through a call for a tender privatization of 51 per cent of its capital, but there were no interested buyers. For the Zastava car complex in

Kragujevac, an agreement on strategic cooperation between Serbia and the Fiat Group was signed in October 2008, which led to the foundation of 'Fiat Automobiles Serbia' with a 33 per cent share of the Serbian government (and 67 per cent of the Fiat group). In December 2008, 51 per cent of the Serbian oil and gas company (Naftna Industrija Srbije – NIS) was sold to the most important Russian state company Gazprom, at a price presumably much lower than its actual value, but the agreement also included the construction in Serbia of a new gas pipeline (the 'Southern Flow') and of a gas warehouse ('Banatski Dvor'). Four smaller public utility companies were privatized in 2006. Other state-owned enterprises are planned to be partially privatized in 2009–10, including the electricity company EPS, Telekom, the Nikola Tesla Belgrade airport, and the pharmaceutical company Galenika for which a tender sale was announced in October 2009. The global economic crisis which severely hit Serbia in 2008–9 is likely to interrupt some of the expected deals.

An important law was adopted in December 2007 related to the privatization of state-owned enterprises – the Law on the free distribution of shares in state-owned enterprises. According to the law, shares of six main state-owned enterprises planned for privatization will be freely distributed to all adult citizens who have not benefited from earlier privatizations (15%) and to former employees of these enterprises (2–5%). The companies are the oil and gas company NIS, Telekom Serbia, the electricity company EPS, JAT Airways, the Belgrade airport, and the pharmaceutical company Galenika. During 2008, all Serbian citizens who have not received enterprise shares in previous waves of privatization were able to submit their requests for receiving free shares of these state-owned enterprises.

7.1.3 Inadequate FDI

The expectations of Serbian authorities in 2001 regarding the arrival of FDI were overly optimistic. After years of isolation and adverse political conditions, it was believed that the change in the political climate would be sufficient to attract substantial FDI. The actual amount of FDI, particularly during the initial period, was rather disappointing. The US$ 12–13 billion (depending on source) invested in Serbia since 1989 corresponds to a relatively small amount of FDI invested in some other transition countries – only 26 per cent of Romania's, 24 per cent of Hungary's, 18 per cent of the Czech Republic's, and barely 12 per cent of Poland's cumulative FDI. Even in per capita terms, the amount of FDI invested in Serbia is low compared to the more advanced CEE countries, or Croatia and Montenegro. During the whole 2001–8 period, FDI inflows to Serbia have been lower, by some US$ 5 billion, than emigrants remittances (see Chapter 6). One of the reasons for limited FDI inflows are the relatively high labour costs in Serbia, burdened by excessive social contributions and an inadequate system of taxation (see Chapter 6).

FDI in Serbia has been an important source of additional finance, yet it has not brought some of the expected benefits. The structure of FDI in Serbia reveals that its prevalent part has concentrated in non-industrial sectors, mainly services (see Table 7.2). The largest proportion of investment has gone into sectors producing non-tradable goods, including banking, insurance, telecommunications, real estate, and wholesale and retail trade.

During 2004–7, as much as 34 per cent of FDI in Serbia has been in financial intermediation, another 20 per cent in transport and telecommunications, 13 per cent in wholesale and retail trade, 11 per cent in real estate and renting, and only around 18 per cent in the manufacturing industry. The structure of FDI has been similar in 2008: financial intermediation was the most important sector (52%) followed by real estate and renting (24%) and wholesale and retail trade (16%), while manufacturing represented only 23 per cent of total FDI (Republicki zavod za razvoj, 2009, p. 148). Owing to the concentration of FDI in trade and finance, multinational companies investing in Serbia may have contributed more to imports than to exports, as has often been the case in the CEE countries (Mencinger, 2003).

Table 7.2 Inward FDI in Serbia, by industry, 2004–7

Industry	**Total investment (in thousands of US$)**	**In per cent of total**
Financial intermediation	3,850,600	33.9
Transport and telecommunications	2,284,276	20.1
Manufacturing	2,111,239	18.6
Wholesale, retail, repairs	1,454,873	12.8
Real estate, renting	1,255,575	11.0
Construction	248,943	2.2
Hotels and restaurants	66,537	0.6
Agriculture	53,342	0.4
Mining and quarrying	38,049	0.3
Electricity, gas, and water	2,970	0.03
TOTAL	11,366,404	100.0

Source: Serbian Investment and Export Promotion Agency (SIEPA), www.siepa.gov.sr, November 2008.

The regressive labour tax system introduced in 2001 has most likely had a significant impact on the structure of FDI in Serbia, since it has favoured investment projects that involved wages much above average, and disfavoured those involving below-average wages. This has further reduced the chances for successful restructuring within labour-intensive sectors such as the textile, manufacturing, and food-processing industries (Arandarenko, 2009a). This partly explains why there have not been many cases of FDI in large Serbian industrial firms. The important foreign investment deals, all undertaken on occasion of privatizations, are the steel complex Sartid in Smederevo sold to US Steel (June 2003); two tobacco companies sold to Phillip Morris and BAT (August 2003); and the gas company NIS sold recently to the Russian state enterprise Gazprom. Three further acquisitions by foreign investors – by Stada, Carlsberg, and Interbrew – represent about half of total FDI in the Serbian industry. Stada bought Hemofarm, a pharmaceutical company from Vrsac that was first privatized in the early 1990s through privileged sales to insiders, and today is one of the most profitable enterprises in Serbia.

Moreover, there has been very little greenfield investment in the Serbian industry. Among the most important FDI deals in Serbia during 2002–9, only five were greenfield investments and all five were in services – telecommunications, retail and wholesale trade, and real estate (see Table 7.3). The greenfield investments undertaken in industry – for example Gorenje in Valjevo – have been much smaller, both in terms of capital and productive capacity.

Mencinger (2003) recalls the important difference between greenfield and privatizations-related FDI. While a strong link between greenfield FDI and capital formation is self-evident, acquisitions by foreign partners cannot be automatically considered as investment in real assets. Proceeds from privatization sales might be spent on current consumption and imports, in which case FDI would not directly contribute to the growth of productive capacities and to economic growth, but to an increasing current account deficit developing into foreign debt. Though Mencinger's arguments are based on the experience of the more advanced CEE countries in the 1990s,[6] the resemblance with the Serbian case is remarkable.

The relatively low FDI in industrial enterprises in Serbia and focusing on a very small number of sectors has meant that some key industries have not been able to benefit from modern technology, know-how, and other benefits of foreign investment. This is one of the reasons why many industrial enterprises in Serbia have not been modernized or restructured, while it is precisely the manufacturing industry that remains responsible for the predominant part of Serbian exports. The manufacturing industry

Table 7.3 Leading foreign investors in Serbia, 2002–2009

Leading Foreign Investors (2002-2009)				
Company	**Country**	**Industry**	**Investment Type**	**Investment Amount (EUR mn)**
Telenor	Norway	Telecommunications	Privatization	1,602
Gazprom Neft	Russia	Energy	Privatization	947
Philip Morris	USA	Tobacco	Privatization	611
Mobilkom	Austria	Telecommunications	Greenfield	570
Intesa Sanpaolo	Italy	Banking	Acquisition	508
Stada	Germany	Pharmaceutical	Acquisition	475
AB InBev	Belgium	Food	Acquisition	427
National Bank of Greece	Greece	Banking	Privatization	425
Mercator	Slovenia	Retail	Greenfield	240
Fondiaria SAI	Italy	Insurance	Privatization	220
Lukoil	Russia	Energy	Privatization	210
Airport City Belgrade	Israel	Real Estate	Greenfield	200
Blok 67 Associates	Austria & Serbia	Real Estate	Greenfield	180
Holcim	Switzerland	Construction	Privatization	170
OTP Bank	Hungary	Banking	Privatization	166
Carlsberg	Denmark	Food	Acquisition	152
U.S. Steel	USA	Metal	Privatization	150
METRO Cash & Carry	Germany	Wholesale	Greenfield	150
Coca-Cola	USA	Food	Acquisition	142
Lafarge	France	Construction	Privatization	141

Source: SIEPA

Source: Serbian Investment and Export Promotion Agency (www.siepa.sr.gov.yu), December 2009.

contributes around 15 per cent of gross value added, but as much as 95 per cent of total Serbian exports (Jakopin and Bajec, 2009).

FDI should also have brought positive spillover effects to the Serbian economy. Substantial FDI in banking and finance, by providing more credit at lower cost for investment, should have brought important benefits to the whole economy. This has not been the case, judging from the very high interest rates still prevailing in Serbia despite the sale of the almost entire banking sector to foreign banks. Mencinger's (2003) warnings about the unfounded glorification of positive spillover effects of FDI in reference to the CEE experience are also worth recalling, as they are very relevant for Serbia. Productivity spillovers can be weakened by the small size of an economy and the fact that a single company often represents the whole industrial sector; foreign companies often purchase raw materials and spare parts from foreign, rather than local suppliers; and instead of increasing competition, large foreign companies often force small newly emerging domestic firms out of business (Mencinger, 2003, p. 507).

7.1.4 Business environment, enterprise entry and exit

It has frequently been stressed that the regulatory environment in Serbia is still quite burdensome for entrepreneurs. Although since 2001 there have been remarkable improvements in the business environment, in some areas reforms have been very slow. The most recent World Bank *Doing Business Survey* for 2010 indicates that Serbia has improved its position with respect to the previous ranking in 2009, now being 88th among the 183 countries, thus slightly above average (see Table 7.4).

The 2010 Report also points to two important reforms implemented in Serbia in 2009: simplification of the registration of enterprises, as this will soon be done at a single counter (the 'one stop shop'); and improved access to information on credit worthiness. Serbia has significantly improved its rank regarding access to credit (4th), though it ranks very poorly regarding construction permits (174th) which still involve 20 procedures and an average require 279 days, paying taxes (137th), registering property (105th), or enforcing contracts (97th).

Within the SEE region, conditions for doing business during the last year have improved less in Croatia (now ranked 103d), Bosnia and Herzegovina (116th), and Kosovo (113th), though the situation is much more favourable in Macedonia (32d) and Montenegro (71st). It ought to be stressed that these World Bank indicators give only the *relative* position of a country in a given year in comparison with other countries – a downgrade in a country's ranking does not necessarily mean that its conditions for doing business have worsened, but simply that those in other countries have improved more.

Contrary to the recent improvements in the World Bank overall business environment in Serbia and much better conditions for starting a business, those regarding the closing of a firm are among the

Table 7.4 Doing business indicators: Serbia and SEE countries, 2009–10

Ease of doing business in SEE countries	**Doing business 2009 rank**	**Doing business 2010 rank**	***Change in rank 2010/09***
Albania	89	82	+7
Bosnia &Herzegovina	119	116	+3
Croatia	110	103	+7
Macedonia	69	32	+37
Montenegro	77	71	+6
Serbia	90	88	+2
Kosovo	107	113	–6
Ease of doing business in Serbia			
Starting a business	108	73	+35
Dealing with construction permits	172	174	–2
Employing workers	87	94	–7
Registering property	99	105	–6
Getting credit	12	4	+8
Protecting investors	70	73	–3
Paying taxes	126	137	–11
Trading across borders	67	69	–2
Enforcing contracts	95	97	–2
Closing a business	102	102	0

Source: World Bank Doing Business Indicators (www.doingbusiness.org).

worst – Serbia in 2010 ranked 102nd. In large part this is due to the very late adoption of new bankruptcy legislation. The problem of loss-making enterprises was not addressed immediately, though among enterprises earmarked for privatization in 2001 there were many heavily indebted loss-making firms. These problems were postponed due to the need to revise bankruptcy legislation, so the procedures for firm exit remained unclear for years. Many insolvent firms had to wait for a new bankruptcy law which was adopted only in 2004. The related question of the write-off of enterprise debt owed to the government or to other firms was also not resolved at an early stage, but was clarified only in 2006 in amendments to the privatization law and further changes in the bankruptcy law. In many cases, unclear obligations regarding enterprise debt have blocked or greatly delayed their privatization. In 2008, revisions of the bankruptcy law were again underway.

As a result of late adoption of bankruptcy legislation, the bankruptcy unit of the Privatization Agency still has a number of socially owned enterprises in its portfolio, most of which have now been pending for years. Although the 2004 bankruptcy law at last enabled the closure of some of these firms – about 25 per cent of cases were closed within one year and another 20 per cent within two years – the number of pending cases remains very high – 651 at the end of 2007 (Commission of the EU, 2008, p. 27). In addition, there were also some socially owned enterprises planned for restructuring that have been incurring substantial losses: by 2005, out of 100 such enterprises, only 15 had started the process (Vlada Republike Srbije, 2006, p. 65).

Although the regulatory environment for both enterprise entry and exit has improved in recent years, the overall results are not quite satisfactory. Recent data on firm entry and exit show that during 2006–8, the annual number of newly created firms has practically stagnated, while the number of enterprises closed has doubled (see Table 7.5). The rate of entry, measured by the share of new in the total number of active enterprises, has declined, parallel with an increase of the rate of exit. The net effect – the ratio of the rate of entry and the rate of exit – shows that for every closed enterprise, eight new enterprises were created in 2006, but only four in 2008 (Jakopin and Knezevic, 2009, p. 7). The deceleration in the speed of firm entry is rather discouraging, considering that the process of creation of *de novo* enterprises has played a fundamental role in the overall transformation of many transition economies. For the private sector to grow, privatization needs to be accompanied by a substantial lowering of entry barriers, so that *de novo* private firms become the major driving force behind the recovery of output, employment, and labour productivity (Brixiova and Egert, 2009). According to recent NBS data based on enterprises financial reports, the annual number of newly created enterprises has recently declined further – from 9483 in 2007 to 8918 in 2008 (NBS, 2009a). Moreover, most newly created enterprises are micro enterprises, employing up to 5 workers.

Table 7.5 Entry and exit of enterprises in Serbia, 2006–8

	2006	2007	2008
Number of newly created enterprises	11,536	11,902	11,248
Number of closed enterprises	1,528	2,027	3,068
Rate of entry (new enterprises in % of total active firms)	15.1	14.1	12.5
Rate of exit (closed enterprises in % of total active firms)	2.0	2.4	3.4
Net effect (rate of entry/rate of exit, in %)	7.5	5.9	3.7

Source: Jakopin and Knezevic (2009), p. 7, based on data of the Republicki Zavod za Razvoj (Serbian Development Bureau).

7.1.5 Selective hardening of budget constraints

In addition to the late adoption of bankruptcy legislation, firm exit has also been slowed down by the insufficient hardening of budget constraints. A number of state and socially owned enterprises continue to be subsidized directly by the government, some are in a better position than private firms regarding access to bank credit or tax relief, while still others continue to be sheltered from competition from abroad through non-tariff barriers; thus the import ban on refined petroleum products was still in place in 2008, protecting the domestic refinery industry from foreign competition (Commission of the EU, 2008, p. 30). State influence on competitiveness has declined, but remains substantial.

Some years ago, budget subsidies to large loss-making firms in Serbia were among the highest in the SEE region; according to a World Bank survey, 12 per cent of Serbian firms in 2003 faced no competition on the local market (World Bank, 2004, p. 34). Government subsidies have declined in the meantime, from 2.9 per cent of GDP in 2004 to 1.9 per cent in 2006 (Republicki zavod za razvoj, 2009, p. 162). Still, the government continues to subsidize a number of state and socially owned enterprises (World Bank, 2009). In 2008, subsidies to non-privatized state and socially owned enterprises still represented 22 percent of central government subsidies, and included severance payments financed from various government funds (the Development Fund, the Transition Fund, and the Solidarity Fund), and credit lines and soft loans to socially owned enterprises for restructuring. The level of enterprise subsidies (excluding subsidies to railroads) has increased in nominal terms over the last four years. Indirect subsidies, in the form of tax and contribution arrears, have also been frequent (World Bank, 2009, pp. 54–5). The highest subsidies are extended to large state-owned enterprises that incur losses, primarily in the mining industry (Resavica and Bor)[7] and Serbian railways. The Development Fund provides subsidized financing (interest rate about half the market rate) for various programmes – economic and regional development, SMEs, increased competitiveness, but a large part of its funding has supported socially owned enterprises. In 2008, €33 million was spent on 114 loss-making enterprises in transport, metal, metallurgy, textiles, chemicals, electrical machinery, non-metals, construction, wood, tourism, and some other industries (World Bank, 2009, p. 55).

7.1.6 Limited market competition

Competition policy has also been substantially delayed, though it has been on the agenda for a long time. Foreign trade liberalization implemented after 2001 has been important for increasing competition in many sectors, but policies promoting competition on the domestic market have officially started being implemented only recently. A new law on the protection of competition was adopted only in 2005. The Commission for the protection of competition was set up in 2006, though it has not been very effective. Further improvements took place in 2009, when a new law on the control of state aid was prepared in line with EU directives, which for the first time regulates direct and indirect subsidies.

As a result of all the problems discussed so far, market conditions in many sectors in Serbia have not become sufficiently competitive. The breaking up of monopolistic structures in public utilities has started only in 2006, as indicated earlier. Other indicators suggest a further concentration of ownership in the Serbian economy, as the number of so-called large economic systems – holding companies embracing a group of smaller daughter companies – has increased from 476 in 2006 to 732 in 2008, involving an increasing number of linked enterprises (2191 in 2008) and employing an increasing number of workers (35% of total employment in 2008) (Jakopin and Knezevic, 2009, p. 8). Some of these holding companies represent the most profitable enterprises in Serbia today.[8]

In the Belgrade retail trade sector, the market for food products is particularly concentrated. During the last few years, instead of increased competition, the retail trade sector has experienced an increase in concentration, so smaller suppliers today depend directly on the larger trade chains (Cerovic, 2009). The anti-competition authority created in 2006 has not been very effective. There was an interesting case of mergers of a few Serbian retail trade companies that was judged illegal by the Serbian Commission for the protection of competition, but the Serbian Supreme Court annulled the decision (Labus and Cullen, 2008).

7.1.6 Inefficient employment policy

The lack of an adequate employment policy has also contributed to limited restructuring of the Serbian economy. During the whole post-2001 period, employment policy was not given the right attention in Serbia, both conceptually, since it was treated as exogenous to the core reform agenda, and in terms of resources, since expenditures for active labour market programmes were on average only 0.1 per cent of GDP (Arandarenko, 2009a). 'Employment policy, understood in its wider definition as a consistent mix of various sectoral economic policies aimed at employment generation, was basically treated as exogenous to the reform process and reduced to a supporting legislative labour market reform that was aimed at bringing more labour market flexibility, in order to support the core processes of market liberalization and privatization' (Arandarenko, 2009a). The earlier discussed regressive labour tax system has also greatly contributed to these problems, by impeding faster job creation in the *de novo* private firms, in this way delaying redeployment of labour.

This does not mean that the Serbian government has not adopted a number of measures to facilitate employment generation. In order to create new employment opportunities, considerable support has been provided to facilitate the development of the new private sector, particularly through various credit lines for small- and medium-sized enterprises – such as the Development Fund, a start-up programme for beginners, micro credits for employment, credits for support of women entrepreneurship, and the like. The government has also adopted legislation on the establishment of business incubators, on financial support and consultancy services to future entrepreneurs, and other types of measures meant to facilitate the setting up of firms. However, considering the enormous problems of unemployment in Serbia discussed earlier (see Chapter 6), these measures have clearly done very little to absorb a substantial part of redundant workers.

In recent years, the principal segments of employment that have increased, in addition to employees in the state sector, are informal employment, illegal work, self-employment, work by contributing family workers, and traditional agricultural employment. By contrast, wage employment in the private sector is relatively low, in 2007 including less than 950,000 workers (out of almost 5 million of working age population and total employment of 2,650,000) (Arandarenko, 2009a). Non-agricultural self-employment, including small entrepreneurs, has almost doubled to the current 600,000, but this increase was mostly driven by push factors (people entering the sector as a last resort) rather than pull factors, so the quality of jobs in self-employment is rather poor. Agricultural employment, comprising small farmers and family members who assist them, has also slightly increased in recent years to almost 600,000 people (Arandarenko, 2009a). The informal labour market in Serbia remains much more flexible than the formal market.

7.1.7 Poor corporate governance

Many Serbian enterprises continue to be characterized by ineffective systems of corporate governance, due to both problems inherited from the 1990s and new problems that have emerged after the recent wave of privatizations. In late 2000, the situation regarding corporate governance in Serbian enterprises was particularly confusing, because of ambiguous rights of various stakeholders – workers, managers, enterprises, the state, and banks as lenders – and the parallel existence of social, state, mixed, cooperative, and private property (see Chapter 4). Since the clarification of property rights in a number of Serbian enterprises has still not been completed, effective systems of corporate governance are still not in place.

There have been some improvements after 2001, following the privatization of a number of socially owned enterprises. Given that the 2001 predominant model envisaged sales to a strategic owner, the standard problem of corporate governance – the separation of ownership from management[9] – should not have been present, since in a number of Serbian enterprises privatized after 2002, the new owner is also the firm's manager. In the meantime, the 2004 new Serbian company law has incorporated the principles on corporate governance of the OECD and EU directives. In 2006, Serbia also adopted new laws in the area of finance, such as the law on investment funds, that have facilitated the development of the capital market (see Chapter 6).

Despite these positive developments, privatization has frequently not been conducive to effective corporate governance mechanisms, nor to enterprise restructuring. There is ample evidence that in many privatized firms in Serbia the change of ownership has not led to improved corporate governance. The new owners of privatized enterprises, particularly those bought at auctions, have often lacked the necessary skills to run the firms efficiently or to control managers. The new regulations on corporate governance, though in conformity with EU/OECD standards, have frequently not been respected.

A survey of 214 Serbian joint-stock companies undertaken in 2008 reveals the persistence of poor corporate governance in many enterprises (Center for Liberal Democratic Studies (CLDS), 2009). Corporate governance was found to be satisfactory in companies owned by foreign companies, but much less in locally owned firms. The prevalent privatization model implemented after 2001 – the sale of a majority share to a single investor – has benefited the new majority owner, who has both the ways and means to control management, but minority shareholders are not well protected. The new owners have had the opportunities to expropriate minority shareholders, due to poor legal protection of their rights and weak judiciary. The board of directors, elected by the single majority owner, was indicated as responsible for the control of the company by 44 per cent of the respondents, but the problem is that it does not have effective power to control the company due to inadequate access to information.

In 90 per cent of surveyed companies, at least one board member declared that he/she still did not understand who manages the company (CLDS, 2009, pp. 3–5).

Another problem is that the Serbian 2001 privatization law automatically transformed all enterprises into open joint-stock companies, irrespective of the firm's size. Small firms were also obliged to introduce the same complex legal form as large enterprises. This is regarded as the main reason why companies do not raise new capital on the market; instead, they trade in shares to change their status from an open joint-stock company to a limited liability company, which is much simpler and thus less costly to operate (CLDS, 2009, p. 3). Among the other problems revealed in the survey is the incomplete understanding of new laws on corporate governance in Serbia, the aspiration of controlling owners to increase their share package, and the desire of employees (minority owners) to dispose of their shares since they have no control (CLDS, 2009). This has led to a further concentration of ownership: some 52 per cent of the surveyed companies have a single owner holding over two-thirds of the company's shares. The survey also showed that the self-management model has been marginalized: in only 4 per cent of surveyed enterprises do the employees still have control, namely in those firms privatized according to the 1997 law based on the insiders' model.

The activation of effective mechanisms of corporate governance in Serbia continue to be impeded by the incompleteness of the reform process. A cluster of institutions typical of a market economy are still not in place, including a well-functioning stock exchange and developed capital market that would provide for enterprise valuation, a competitive market for managers that would impose greater managerial discipline, or the effective implementation of laws that protect small shareholders, assure transparency in share dealings, or impose penalties for the use of insider information for personal benefits. Since radical reforms of the judiciary in Serbia have been very slow, it is not surprising that many important laws that should lead to improvements in corporate governance are not yet effective.

7.1.8 Slow growth of the private sector

Most features of the post-2001 economic transition in Serbia that have contributed to limited microeconomic restructuring are also directly responsible for the relatively slow growth of the private sector. According to EBRD estimates, the share of the private sector in GDP increased from 40 per cent in 2000 to around 60 per cent in 2009, placing

Serbia today among the six least privatized transition economies (see Chapter 6).

The 20 per cent increase in the private sector's contribution to GDP that Serbia achieved in eight years has taken place much faster in most CEE countries in the 1990s. The private sector's share in GDP increased from 40 to 60 per cent in just one year in the Czech Republic (1993–4), in two years in Estonia (1993–5), in three years in Hungary (1992–5), Bulgaria (1994–7), and Romania (1994–7), and in four years even in countries that adopted more gradual privatization strategies, like Poland (1991–5) and Slovenia (1993–7) (EBRD). Moreover, if we consider that in 1989 the private sector contributed around 15 per cent of Serbia's GSP (see Chapter 2) and that by 2000 the share had increased to 40 per cent (see Chapter 4), it turns out that, paradoxically, the private sector expanded more during the 1990s, the decade of repressed transition, than in these last eight years of accelerated institutional changes. This is also due to the transformation of some socially owned enterprises into state-owned firms after 2001.

The question is not simply one of speed, but of the overall privatization strategy which in Serbia failed to address, at an early stage, other important issues of crucial importance for microeconomic changes stressed earlier – market competition, enterprise entry and exit, corporate governance, or the restructuring of non-privatized parts of the economy. In enterprises earmarked for privatization, restructuring and improved corporate governance was seen as a simple by-product of privatization. Similarly, new employment generation was seen as a buy-product of privatization, that would come along with the growth of the emerging private sector.

Although accurate and up-to-date national statistics are not available on the contribution of the various property sectors to GDP (see Appendix), there are indications that the non-privatized social and state enterprises still generate a relatively large part of Serbia's output. According to estimates of the Serbian Ministry of Finance (2008), the private sector in 2007 contributed 58.3 per cent of GDP, 50.2 per cent of exports, and 65 per cent of total employment. According to estimates of the Serbian Development Bureau, in 2007 small- and medium-sized enterprises represented 99.8 per cent of the total number of firms, but some 598 large enterprises still contributed more than 40 per cent of gross value added, 45 per cent of total profits, and employed 30 per cent of workers in the non-financial sector of the Serbian economy (Republicki zavod za razvoj, 2009, p. 20). If we consider only enterprises in the Serbian non-financial sector that have submitted their financial reports to the NBS (they represent around 54 per cent of total gross value-added), those in the private sector have increased their contribution to gross value added from 21.5 per cent in 2002 to 64.3 per cent in 2007 (see Table A7.3, Appendix). Private enterprises have a major role in retail and wholesale trade and most other services, but they remain relatively weak in many industrial sectors. A competitive and dynamic private sector has still not developed sufficiently in Serbia.

Private sector employment has grown faster than private sector output, increasing from 49 per cent in 2001 to 74 per cent in 2008 of total employment (see Figure 7.2). Within the non-financial sector enterprises, private sector employment has increased from a low 20.3 per cent in 2002 to 62.5 per cent in 2007 (see Table A 7.3, Appendix). As indicated earlier, however, much of the new employment created in the private sector has been non-wage employment – like self-employment – that does not have any potential for further expansion and thus cannot be a major driver of economic growth (Arandarenko, 2009a).

The structure of profits by enterprise size also suggests that the emerging private sector is relatively weak (though this indicator should be considered with caution, since tax evasion through the underreporting of profits has been a frequent phenomenon in Serbia). In 2007, large enterprises still contributed 45 per cent of overall profits, while the micro- small- and medium-sized enterprises, prevalently in the private

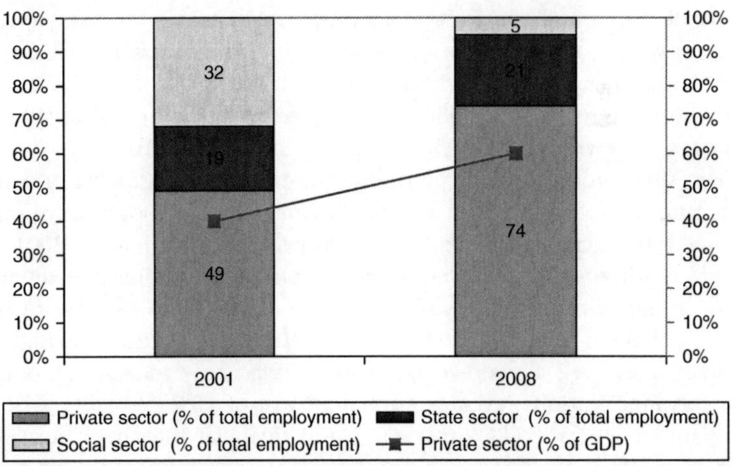

Figure 7.2 Private sector growth in Serbia: Changes in employment and output, 2001–8

Source: Employment data: Jakopin and Knezevic (2009), p. 4, based on estimates of the Serbian Development Institute (Republicki zavod za razvoj); contribution to GDP: EBRD (2008).

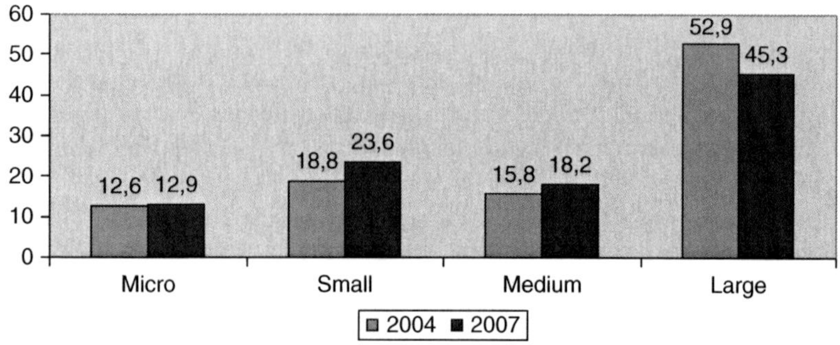

Figure 7.3 Profits in Serbia, according to enterprise size (in % of total), 2004 and 2007
Source: Republicki zavod za razvoj (2009), p. 20.

sector, have increased their share in profits rather marginally during the 2004–7 period (see Figure 7.3).

7.2 Capacity restructuring: Inadequate structural changes

All transition countries have experienced radical structural changes during the last 20 years, which have brought a notable decline in the share of agricultural value added; de-industrialization with falling absolute employment and output in all branches of industry, particularly manufacturing and energy; and a substantial expansion of the services sector, which remained underdeveloped during socialism (Cornia, 2009). Similar structural changes have taken place also in Serbia, but there are reasons to believe they have favoured the expansion of services somewhat excessively, at the expense of industry.

The slow process of microeconomic restructuring in Serbia and the resulting limited changes in the real sector of the economy have contributed to such imbalances. Rapid growth registered after 2001 in Serbia has been rather uneven across sectors, much stronger in services than in agriculture or industry, leading to a very rapid increase in the relative share of primarily services. During the 2001–8 period, the highest growth rates, well above average, were in services – transport, storage, and communications (average annual growth of 15.9 per cent), wholesale and retail trade (14.6 per cent), and financial intermediation (9.3 per cent). These three sectors were the main drivers of growth and have increased their share in gross value added from less than 18 per cent in 2001 to 30 per cent in 2008 (Stamenkovic et al., 2009b). The non-service sectors have registered slower than average annual growth rates: agriculture (0.3%), manufacturing industry (1.5%), and total industry (1.6%), while only construction grew somewhat faster (4%).

As a result, the relative share of productive sectors in the formation of Serbian GDP has declined quite substantially. Over the 2000–8 period, the share in gross value added of agriculture declined from 14 to 11.8 per cent, while of industry even more markedly from 26.7 to 20.4 per cent (see Table 7.6). The share of manufacturing industry has also substantially declined, from 21 per cent of gross value added in 2000 to around 16 per cent in 2008. In the meantime, the share of services increased very fast, from 55 per cent of gross value added in 2000 to 64.2 per cent in 2008.

EUROSTAT reports an even higher – 69 per cent – contribution of services to gross value added in Serbia in 2006–7 (Commission of the EC, 2009, pp. 61–2).[10] In comparison with the EU-27 share of services of 71.6 per cent in 2007, Serbia's share does seem rather high, considering

Table 7.6 Structure of gross value added in Serbia, 2000–8 (in % of total)

	2000	2001	2002	2003	2004	2005	2006	2007	2008
Agriculture	*13.9*	*15.8*	*15.3*	*14.1*	*15.5*	*14.1*	*13.2*	*11.4*	*11.8*
Industry	*26.7*	*25.0*	*24.3*	*23.2*	*22.9*	*22.0*	*21.7*	*21.2*	*20.4*
Mining	2.0	1.7	1.7	1.8	1.7	1.7	1.6	1.5	1.5
Manufacturing industry	20.9	19.6	19.0	17.7	17.8	16.9	16.8	16.6	15.8
Production of energy & water	3.8	3.7	3.6	3.7	3.4	3.4	3.3	3.2	3.0
Construction	*4.6*	*3.8*	*3.5*	*3.8*	*3.7*	*3.6*	*3.6*	*3.8*	*3.6*
Services	*54.8*	*55.4*	*56.9*	*58.8*	*57.9*	*60.3*	*61.5*	*63.6*	*64.2*
Wholesale & Retail trade	6.8	7.2	8.3	9.2	9.9	11.5	12.0	13.5	13.6
Hotels & restaurants	1.2	1.1	1.1	1.1	1.0	0.9	0.8	0.8	0.8
Transport, storage, & communications	7.1	8.1	8.2	8.9	9.6	11.2	13.7	15.4	16.4
Financial intermediation	4.3	3.9	3.8	3.7	3.6	3.9	4.1	4.4	4.6
Real estate	16.2	15.9	16.1	16.4	15.4	15.2	14.9	14.3	14.1
Other services	19.3	19.2	19.4	19.6	18.4	17.6	16.1	15.2	14.7
Gross value added	**100**	**100**	**100**	**100**	**100**	**100**	**100**	**100**	**100**

Source: Direct communications of the Serbian Development Bureau (Republicki zavod za razvoj).

its much lower level of economic development (Serbia is at about a third of the EU-27 average GDP per capita). Much of the recent growth in other SEE countries, including Bosnia and Herzegovina, Montenegro, and Kosovo, has also taken place in services, but Serbia presently has the highest relative share of services in GDP of all SEE countries.

The sharp decline of the share of industry requires an additional comment. Although in 1989, as other communist countries, Serbia probably also had an oversized industrial sector, in the 1990s industrial output experienced a continuous and remarkable decline. The process of de-industrialization was most intense in the early 1990s due to Yugoslavia's break-up which affected all Yugoslav successor states, but in Serbia it was further amplified by the UN trade embargo imposed in May 1992, and again by the 1999 NATO bombing. Despite the dramatic decline in Serbian industry throughout most of the 1990s, employment in industry was reduced by only about 35 per cent. Since 2001, industrial output has grown at a slower pace than GDP and its rate of growth has been lower in Serbia than in other transition countries, contributing to insufficient structural adjustment (Jakopin and Knezevic, 2009). Owing to the remarkable decline in industrial output during the 1990s and its slow recovery after 2001, industrial production in 2008 was only at 51 per cent of the level in 1990 (see Figure 7.4).

In many industrial branches, recent economic recovery has not been sufficient to make up for the sharp economic decline in the 1990s. Although investment in fixed assets has doubled during the 2001–8 period, this has been largely insufficient to compensate for the low rates in the 1990s. More than 76 per cent of Serbian industry is in

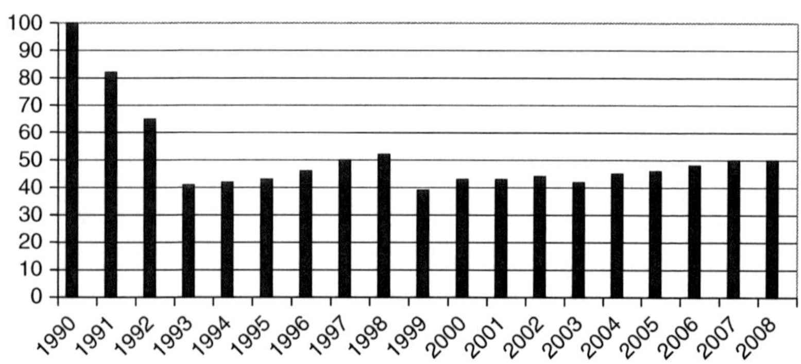

Figure 7.4 Industrial production in Serbia, 1990–2008 (1990 = 100)
Source: National statistics (Republicki zavod za statistiku Srbije).

Table 7.7 Serbia: Contribution of tradable goods sectors to GDP (in %)

Sector	2000	2001	2002	2003	2004	2005	2006	2007
GDP	**100**	**100**	**100**	**100**	**100**	**100**	**100**	**100**
Tradable goods, total	**40.7**	**37.6**	**29.5**	**25.8**	**26.9**	**25.2**	**25.2**	**24.6**
Agriculture, forestry, fisheries	18.6	17.8	13.1	11.4	11.8	10.3	9.6	8.8
Manufacturing industry	22.1	19.8	16.4	14.4	15.0	14.9	15.6	15.8

Source: Stamenkovic et al. (2009b), p. 9.

manufacturing, where a number of sectors have registered a decline in recent years, including textiles, leather, shoes, and wood. Serbia's manufacturing industry still consists of many traditional sectors with a low technological input. During 2004–7, an increase in gross value added and employment was registered primarily in low-tech and medium-tech manufacturing industry. Thus in 2007, low-tech sectors still represented 51 per cent of value added of manufacturing industry, another 25 per cent was in medium low-tech, while only 7 per cent was in high-tech sectors (Republicki zavod za razvoj, 2009, p. 23).

The much faster expansion of services with respect to industry has also negatively influenced Serbia's export structure. The contribution to GDP of sectors producing tradable goods has declined quite remarkably, from around 41 per cent in 2000 to less than 25 per cent in 2007; within the manufacturing sector, tradable goods have reduced their share from 22 per cent in 2000 to less than 16 per cent in 2007 of gross value added (see Table 7.7).

Since Serbian manufacturing products represent the most important part – as much as 95 per cent – of total exports, such trends have greatly contributed to unsatisfactory export performance, thus also to the increasing trade deficit, which represents one of Serbia's most acute problems. The structure of investment has also not been adequate, since investment in tradable goods has grown less than total domestic demand, thus not providing the foundations for stable economic growth in the future (Stamenkovic et al., 2009b, p. 11).

7.3 Shortcomings of the privatization model

The limited microeconomic restructuring, the slow increase in the private sector's contribution to GDP, and the resulting inadequate structural changes of the Serbian economy, are all closely related to the privatization strategy adopted in 2001. Regarding, more specifically, the 2001 privatization law, three issues, in particular, have not been addressed adequately: social property, reliance on sales as the exclusive method, and the criteria of social justice.

7.3.1 Social property

Owing to the very slow implementation of the 2001 privatization law, social property has survived in Serbia well beyond the set deadlines. Although one of the principal objectives of the 2001 law was to eliminate the ambiguous concept of social property, the new law did not abolish social property but relied on its privatization. Although unsold socially owned enterprises were, in principle, to be liquidated, the number of such enterprises has greatly surpassed the initial expectations. Today, after more than eight years, the process of eliminating social property has still not been completed.

If before 1989, social property could have been considered an advantage of former Yugoslavia with respect to other communist countries where enterprises were state property, by the end of the 1990s it did become a disadvantage. Because of the ambiguous system of property rights in SFR Yugoslavia, all successor states as well as Montenegro (within FR Yugoslavia) decided first to eliminate social property through various methods of 're-nationalization' and proceed with privatization later. The Serbian authorities also should have addressed this issue immediately, in order to draw a definite line between rights on the basis of labour, and rights on the basis of capital.

There was, however, a legal obstacle to the abolition of social property in Serbia. Article 56 of the 1990 Serbian constitution, which was still in force in 2001, guaranteed equal protection to all property forms (social, state, private, and cooperative). The new Serbian constitution, adopted only in 2006, at last addressed some of the issues regarding social property. Although the principle of 'equality' among various property forms was not abandoned – article 86 ensures 'Equality of all property forms' – the forms which are now legally protected are limited to private, cooperative, and public. The same article of the new constitution also specifies that the 'remaining social property is (to be) transformed into private property' (Constitution of the Republic of Serbia, 2006, article 86), suggesting the intention to definitely eliminate remaining social property.

The government has continuously stressed that the time limits for privatizing socially owned enterprises must be respected. According to the set deadlines, social property ought to have disappeared from Serbian enterprises initially by 2005; the deadline was then postponed to 2007; and another time it was moved to the end of 2008; but by autumn 2009, there were still some socially owned enterprises which had not been sold. The legal uncertainty posed by the ambiguous concept of social property thus remains, 20 years since privatization started in Serbia. Serbia is the only part of former Yugoslavia which still has social property. This is a major shortcoming of the privatization strategy adopted in 2001.[11]

7.3.2 Privatization method

A related criticism to the 2001 law regards the chosen dominant privatization method – sales of a majority stake to strategic buyers. In many countries in transition, such investors were the 'best' private owners, who brought in capital, modern management and know-how, and were most likely to restructure firms and improve the system of corporate governance. Empirical evidence from many transition countries has often confirmed this, particularly in case of acquisitions by foreign owners. However, it is not a coincidence that the method of commercial sales has been used as the dominant method of privatization in only a few transition countries, primarily in Hungary and Estonia (World Bank, 1996). Because of low purchasing power of local potential buyers and limited interest of foreign investors, most countries in transition have decided to use other, less conventional, methods as dominant rather than sales, including mass privatization through vouchers, sales at privileged conditions or give-aways to insiders, or a combination of the two, while commercial sales has been used only as a supplementary method.

Considering the general economic conditions in Serbia in 2001, one could have anticipated that strategic owners would not be numerous. On the domestic scene, potential investors could only have been those individuals who used dubious methods to enrich themselves by illegal, sometimes war-related, activities in the 1990s, relying heavily on special political privileges and close connections with the governing elite. On the international scene, it was unlikely that Serbia would immediately see a massive influx of foreign investors. The main risk, therefore, was that many Serbian enterprises would end up being bought by the 'new rich' oligarchs, individuals who gained their wealth under the exceptional conditions which prevailed in the 1990s, during long years of isolation and international sanctions. This outcome – the tycoon method of privatization, anticipated more than eight years ago (Uvalic, 2001b) – has in the meantime indeed become a reality. A part of Milosevic's economic elite has not only survived, but has strengthened itself through recent privatization deals, becoming a dominant player in the Serbian economy.

The main method chosen – commercial sales to strategic investors – has definitely not facilitated either a fast, or a fair process of privatization. Although there were proposals in Serbia in 2001–2 to diversify the privatization model (Cerovic, 2009), sales remained the only method. Instead of relying exclusively on sales, the Serbian authorities should have adopted a multitrack privatization strategy based on a combination of various methods,[12] including the free distribution of enterprise shares to insiders. Workers and managers having the skills and capabilities to transform their firm into a viable enterprise would have been awarded as they would become the new owners. Even if this could have led to a number of new insider-owned firms, this would have been a highly pragmatic means of implementing the process of privatization. Employee ownership has been a frequently used privatization method also in the more successful transition countries, like Slovenia (Prasnikar and Svejnar, 2007) or Poland (Nuti, 1997).

Sound banking institutions could have played an effective monitoring role in the corporate governance structure of insider-controlled firms, as proposed by Aoki (1995).[13] The problem of corporate governance – of the separation of ownership and control – could potentially have been much less acute in firms owned by employees, because of the reduced need for managerial monitoring (Hansmann, 1990, p. 1768). In the traditional firm, investors of capital are often widely dispersed and are frequently not in a position to control the firm's management; by contrast, in a firm with employee ownership, workers have a personal stake in the capital of the firm and also dispose of important information about the firm simply as a by-product of their employment. As in many other transition economies, employee ownership would most probably have been a transitory form of organization, eventually leading to a shift in ownership from insiders to outsiders (Nuti, 1997, p. 179).

A more decentralized model of privatization would have led to a faster clarification of property rights, as it would have enabled either the gradual recovery of the enterprise, or further sales of shares on the stock exchange, or its liquidation, if none of the other possibilities were possible; the only disadvantage would have been lower budget revenues (Cerovic, 2009). A strategy based on the combination of various privatization methods, including employee ownership, would have provided some continuity – instead of a radical break – with the past and the heritage of self-management (Uvalic, 2004). Such a multitrack strategy therefore could have been a socially more acceptable solution.

Advocating employee ownership does not contradict our earlier criticism of social property. Despite their apparent resemblance, there are important differences between social property and employee share-ownership. The fundamental difference is that in the pre-1989 Yugoslav firm the most essential element – individual employee ownership – was non-existent since employed workers had no individual private capital stakes in their firm. What the self-management system gave workers in former Yugoslavia were *usus fructus* rights – the right to use socially owned assets and to appropriate the proceeds – together with substantial decision-making rights, but even these rights were severely restricted by government regulations (Uvalic, 1992). Following the debacle of the Western private ownership model in the continuing global financial and economic crisis, the employee ownership model has again emerged as a viable alternative to closure of companies facing difficulties.

Within a privatization strategy based on a multitrack approach, two other important issues, so far not resolved in Serbia, could have been addressed. The first is the problem of restitution of property nationalized during communism. There are about one million people who have claims on nationalized property in Serbia, who for years have been waiting for the long-announced adoption of the law on restitution. Although a draft law on restitution was prepared some years ago during the Kostunica government, the newest 2008 version was under public debate only in autumn 2009; since the law still needs to be adopted by the Serbian parliament, the earliest it may start being implemented is mid-2010. The draft law envisages the restitution of claimed property in kind (whenever possible), or payments in cash and in government bonds. Although the issue of property restitution is very complex – nowhere in the transition region has it been implemented without difficulties – Serbia is the only country, to our knowledge, in the SEE and CEE region that still has no legislation in this domain. Moreover, this is one of Serbia's obligations towards the Council of Europe, since in 2003 it has ratified its convention on human rights which also includes the clarification and security of individual property rights.

The other important issue regards the use of urban land, which is closely related to the problem of restitution of property to former owners. Since 2001, there was no clear government policy in this area, permitting local 'entrepreneurs' to rent urban land also for construction purposes, or to rent buildings for subcontracting apartment space, in this way earning fortunes and living of enormous rents. How to regulate the use of urban land was also under discussion in 2009. Although the 2006 Serbian constitution removed the obstacles for its privatization, there are no reasons why urban land ought to be privatized. The government should rather introduce adequate regulation regarding the use of urban land that could benefit primarily the local community and prevent its misuse by 'privileged' individuals, as has been the case to date in Serbia.

7.3.3 Social justice? Few winners, many losers

Who are the winners and the losers of the privatization process in Serbia? In 2001, the 'politically correct' model of privatization was chosen, strongly recommended by World Bank experts, based on the method of commercial sales to strategic owners, with the aim of privatizing some 2400 socially owned enterprises in a relatively short period of time. The results have been unsatisfactory also from the perspective of the trade-offs between the objectives of the different privatization routes (see Table 7. 8).

Four objectives were considered important for privatization in transition economies – improved corporate governance, speed, public revenues, and fairness (World Bank, 1996). Of the four objectives, the only one that has been realized in Serbia through the 2001 privatization law is substantial government revenues. The new approach was justified by arguments of economic efficiency, rather than social justice which mainly guided previous privatization laws in Serbia.

The privatization strategy has not been fair, since it has benefited primarily those companies and individuals who had some capital to invest in Serbian enterprises – in addition to a handful of foreign firms, the new oligarchs. Although the 2001 law did envisage some shares being distributed freely to workers and citizens and social programmes were incorporated into the legislation regarding redundant workers, these benefits in favour of workers and citizens were clearly secondary.

Table 7.8 Trade-offs among privatization routes

Objective **Method**	**Better corporate governance**	**Speed and feasibility**	**More government revenues**	**Greater fairness**
Sale to outside owners	+	–	+	–
Management-employee buyout	–	+	–	–
Equal-access voucher privatization	?	+	–	+
Spontaneous privatization	?	?	–	–
Serbian 2001 route	*Partial* (20% of economy)	–	+	–

Source: Based on World Bank (1996), p. 52, except for the Serbian route, added by the author.

Improvements in corporate governance mechanisms have been rather limited considering that the post-2001 privatization process has involved enterprises representing only around 20 per cent of Serbia's GDP, also confirmed by recent evidence on poor corporate governance in Serbia reported earlier. The Serbian authorities also counted on speed – the initial deadline for completing privatization was four years – but this has definitely not been a feature of the Serbian privatization route, as confirmed by continuous postponements of the set deadlines.

That the 2001 privatization strategy was not fair either to workers or to the population at large has been a frequent complaint in Serbia in recent years. With the newest wave of privatizations of state-owned enterprises, which started in 2006, free shares are to be distributed to all citizens who have not benefited from previous privatization laws. It is yet to be seen, however, how much individuals will actually receive on this basis. The delays which occurred in the distribution of free shares of NIS to the citizens, which were due in August 2009, provide a cautionary example which shows that this process may be difficult.

Considering the overall privatization results, many people are dissatisfied with the outcome of privatization in Serbia. According to an opinion poll in 2003, 32 per cent of the surveyed thought that privatization has been 'pure theft'; another 31 per cent considered privatization necessary, but stressed that it has been implemented in the wrong way (*Ekonomist*, 17 November 2003, p. 20). More recent opinion polls confirm similar dissatisfaction of the public with privatization in Serbia. Particularly in the summer of 2009, under the impact of the global economic crisis, an outburst of social unrest and an increasing number of strikes in many Serbian factories brought to the surface fundamental problems in a number of privatized firms. The new owners have often not been able to fulfil their obligations not only regarding investment and social programmes, but also regarding the regular payment of wages and social security contributions. Given that the implementation of privatization has lasted so long and has not benefited workers and the population at large, it is not surprising that popular dissatisfaction has grown.[14]

7.4 Summing up

Despite many achievements, some transition-related economic reforms after 2001 in Serbia have not brought all of the expected results. Privatization has provided the badly needed budgetary revenues, but not a quick transfer of property rights, nor rapid enterprise restructuring. As a result of the slow process of privatization of socially owned enterprises, delayed restructuring of the state sector, unfavorable sectoral structure of FDI, insufficiently dynamic process of entry of new private firms, slow adoption of legislation on firm exit, insufficient and selective hardening of budget constraints, and inadequate employment generating policies, a large part of the real sector of the Serbian economy has not been sufficiently restructured and the contribution of the emerging private sector to GDP remains fairly low. Despite major similarities to other transition countries, Serbia still retains certain features which explain why its post-2000 transition has been more complex than initially anticipated. Some of the additional reasons are discussed further in Chapters 8 and 9.

Appendix

Box 7.1 How large is the private sector in Serbia?

In trying to verify the EBRD figure of the private sector's contribution to GDP in Serbia, estimated at 60 per cent in mid-2008, various national sources have been consulted. Until 2005, the Serbian Office of Statistics continued to publish data on the contribution of the various property sectors – social, private, cooperative, mixed, and state – to GSP, similar to those published in the 1980s in SFR Yugoslavia (see Table A7.1). These statistics were interrupted in 2005, as indeed were all other statistics on national accounts which were based on the material concept of GSP. These statistics show that during 1999–2003, there was a decline in the contribution of the social sector (from 29 to 17%), a slight increase in the mixed sector (from 24 to 25%), a surprisingly small increase of the private sector, covering both enterprises and individual shops (from 43 to 46%), and a fivefold increase in the state sector (from 2 to 10%) in Serbia's GSP. However, these statistics probably underestimate the role of the private sector, since the aggregate concept of GSP excludes most 'non-material' services.

The Serbian Office of Statistics also publishes data on registered legal entities, which cover not only enterprises in various sectors including services, but also financial institutions, the public administration, political organizations, and non-governmental organizations. Since 2005, the number of entities in the social and mixed sector has declined quite substantially, though an increase was registered in the number of entities in the state sector (see Table A7.2). By March 2009, 66 per cent of the total number of legal entities were in the private sector.

Another source of information is financial reports of Serbian enterprises, which are now deposited with the department for registers and solvency of the NBS. A recent NBS publication (NBS, 2009a) reports some of the information. In 2008, there were 105,748 enterprises and cooperatives that were obliged to submit their financial reports, of which only 92,832 (88%) actually did. These enterprises employed 1,118,771 workers, but the large majority are very small firms: 26 per cent had no employees, 21 per cent only one employee, 19.9 per cent had 2–5 employees, 9.7 per cent had 6–10 employees, 10.3 per cent had 11–50 employees, 2.9 per cent from 50–250 employees, and only 0.6 per cent had over 250 employees. Regarding sectors, the largest number of firms is in retail and wholesale trade (40.1%), manufacturing industry (20.6%), and real estate (14.6%), while around two-thirds of workers are employed in three sectors: manufacturing industry (35.2%), wholesale and retail trade (19.2 per cent), and transport and communications (10.6%). The NBS also receives financial reports of entrepreneurs in Serbia (NBS, 2009b): in 2008 there were 22,066 entrepreneurs who had submitted their financial reports to the NBS, employing 52,590 workers.

A recent study by Stamenkovic et al. (2009a) has analysed in detail all financial reports of Serbian enterprises submitted to the NBS during 2002–7. These are enterprises in the non-financial sector, which represent around 54 per cent of gross value added (the other sectors being the financial, government, and household sector). In 2007, private enterprises were by far the most numerous (93% of the total); they represented 60 per cent of non-financial sector employment, and contributed 64 per cent of gross value added (see Table A7.3).

These statistics offer only partial insights into the varying importance of the different property sectors in Serbia during the last eight years. They are not fully comparable, as they are based on different sources and methodologies. What they do indicate is that after 2001, the private sector has expanded continuously and that by 2008 it has become dominant in terms of not only the number of enterprises (as it was in 2000), but also employment and somewhat less, gross value added, parallel with the decline in the social and mixed property sector. Along with these changes, the state-owned sector has grown in size.

Table A7.1 GSP in Serbia, by property sector, 1999–2003 (in million dinars and in % of total)

Property Sector	1999		2000		2001		2002		2003	
	GSP	% of total	GSP	% of total	GSP	% of total	GSP	% of total	GSP	% of total
Social	43,169	28.67	71,831	22.78	134,156	24.25	142,735	20.35	141,047	17.46
Private	65,359		140,384		235,238		303,951		370,902	
Firms		17.62		19.18		15.85		20.15		23.88
Shops		25.79		25.33		26.66		23.18		22.03
Cooperative	2,213	1.47	4,478	1.42	7,222	1.31	8,904	1.27	9,184	1.14
Mixed	36,754	24.41	85,239	27.03	152,921	27.64	195,906	27.93	204,984	25.37
State	3,071	2.04	13,456	4.27	23,768	4.30	49,977	7.12	81,896	10.14
Total	150,565	100.00	315,389	100.00	553,304	100.00	701,473	100.00	808,012	100.00

Source: Republicki zavod za statistiku Srbije, 'Drustveni proizvod i narodni dohodak Srbije', December 2000, November 2001, December 2002, May 2004, and April 2005.

Table A7.2 Enterprises and other legal entities in Serbia, by property sector, 2005–9

Property form	2005	2006	2007	2008	March 2009
Social	4,237	3,736	3,188	2,972	2,678
Private	202,074	85,988	94,471	103,623	106,889
Cooperative	5,915	6,115	6,124	6,249	6,284
Mixed	3,351	4,281	1,949	2,158	2,011
State	3,901	4,946	7,193	6,795	5,546
Unspecified	44,270	47,852	53,660	59,251	38,708
Total	263,748	152,918	166,585	181,048	162,116

Note: Except for 2009, all data refer to 31 December. These statistics include all registered legal entities in Serbia – enterprises in industry, agriculture and services, including banks and non-bank financial organizations, the public administration, the judiciary, political organizations, various non-governmental organizations, and association of citizens.
Source: Republicki zavod za statistiku Srbije, *Saopstenje*, various issues (online).

Table A7.3 Enterprises in the non-financial sector in Serbia, by property type, 2002–7

Property sectors	2002	2003	2004	2005	2006	2007
Number of firms						
Social	3,885	3,210	2,737	2,050	2,763	2,751
Private	57,182	64,198	66,411	68,495	69,808	77,867
Cooperative	2,384	2,686	2,755	2,433	1,898	1,814
Mixed	2,977	3,177	3,119	1,967	1,190	1,095
State	450	559	455	485	575	586
Total	66,878	73,830	75,477	75,430	76,234	84,113
Number of employees						
Social	473,284	300,246	222,700	143,965	145,653	93,466
Private	263,340	328,061	407,700	607,030	607,763	685,913
Cooperative	18,633	16,639	18,070	13,498	12,861	10,127
Mixed	429,359	403,874	371,566	170,323	148,570	132,659
State	108,663	160,862	162,908	183,076	181,735	175,748
Total	12,932,79	1,209,682	1,182,944	1,117,892	1,096,582	1,097,913

(*Continued*)

Table A7.3 (Continued)

Property sectors	2002	2003	2004	2005	2006	2007
Gross value added (in % of total)						
Social	30.7	17.7	12.5	9.0	8.1	3.4
Private	21.5	28.0	35.5	57.6	59.5	64.3
Cooperative	0.8	0.8	1.2	1.0	0.9	0.8
Mixed	36.3	34.6	31.3	12.9	12.5	10.7
State	10.7	18.9	19.5	19.5	19.0	20.8
Total	100	100	100	100	100	100

Source: Based on data of enterprise financial reports of the NBS, reported in Stamenkovic et al., 2009a, p. 187 and own calculations of shares.

8
Integrating Serbia into the EU

The transition in Serbia has also been slowed down by the exceptionally unfavourable international conditions that have prevailed during most of the last 20 years. Some of the problems are specific to Serbia, while others are common to all countries in the region of SEE. The process of Serbia's economic and political integration with the EU therefore needs to be analysed within the broader context of EU policies towards the whole SEE region. In EU terminology, the SEE region is usually referred to as the 'Western Balkans', which until 2006 comprised five states: Albania, Bosnia and Herzegovina, Croatia, the Former Yugoslav Republic of Macedonia (FYR Macedonia), and FR Yugoslavia (Serbia, Montenegro, and Kosovo), although its wider definition also includes Bulgaria and Romania.

This chapter will discuss EU policies towards the SEE countries during the 1990s following the disintegration of SFR Yugoslavia, as well as after 1999 when the SAP was launched specifically for the Western Balkan countries. The main achievements and failures of the new EU approach implemented after 2000 will be assessed. Within such a wider context, specific factors that have hampered Serbia's path towards the EU are discussed in detail. After the difficult 1990s, the October 2000 democratic changes in FR Yugoslavia promised accelerated integration with the EU. However, despite progress on many fronts, it has taken more than seven years for Serbia to sign an SAA and its implementation was for long blocked due to Serbia's non-compliance with EU political conditions. Serbia still has the status of 'potential candidate' for EU membership and the overall results have been rather disappointing.

8.1 EU policies towards SEE in the 1990s

Contrary to today's ten EU member states from CEE[1] that have established contractual relations with the EU by signing association agreements relatively quickly after the fall of the Berlin Wall in 1989, the SEE countries were not able to intensify their relations with the EU until after 2000. This was the direct outcome of the exceptional conditions that prevailed in the region throughout the 1990s, due to the disintegration of SFR Yugoslavia, the multiple military conflicts that accompanied it, the inward-oriented policies of the newly created states, and the various types of embargoes – FR Yugoslavia was under severe UN and EC sanctions throughout most of the decade, while FYR Macedonia was under a Greek embargo. These events have not only left profound and long-lasting economic, political, and social consequences on all SEE countries, but have also greatly delayed their integration with the EU. The military conflicts in the area of former Yugoslavia directly contributed to the lack of an EU long-term strategy for the SEE region during the 1990s. At the same time, the EU foreign policy was inconsistent, since very different types of policy instruments were used vis-à-vis the individual countries (Uvalic, 1997b).

8.1.1 Lack of long-term strategy

After the outbreak of the first armed conflicts in former Yugoslavia in the early 1990s, the EU failed to elaborate a clear, comprehensive, and long-term strategy for the whole SEE region (Uvalic, 2003b). The EC imposed an embargo on the import of arms by Yugoslavia in July 1991, a month after the proclamation of political independence of Slovenia and Croatia. In November 1991, the EC suspended the Trade and Economic Cooperation Agreement concluded with SFR Yugoslavia in 1980. It also removed the country from the General System of Preferences and the new programme of financial assistance offered to post-communist countries from Eastern Europe, PHARE.[2]

Owing to uncertainty in defining a clear EU position towards the war-affected SEE countries, EU intervention and assistance policies were mainly shaped in response to emerging crises, most frequently on an *ad hoc* basis. Given the conflicts in the 1990s – in Croatia, Bosnia and Herzegovina, and Kosovo – the EU countries were involved in the war-affected Balkan countries primarily through their military presence (via NATO), provision of humanitarian assistance, and the EC/EU civilian monitoring mission,[3] which remained in the region throughout the 1990s.

It is only in 1996 that the EU announced its 'Regional Approach', intended to promote economic reconstruction, democracy, and regional cooperation among the SEE countries. The EU Council of Ministers officially launched the 'Regional Approach' in 1997, which established political and economic conditionality for the development of bilateral relations with the Western Balkan countries. Though called the 'Regional Approach', Bartlett observes that 'there was little in the way of a common regional policy towards them. Its essence was, in fact, to differentiate assistance towards the five countries on the basis of a set of political and economic conditions' (Bartlett, 2003, p. 73).

The 'Regional Approach' failed to bring any substantial results, either in terms of political stabilization or substantial economic development. Not only were the EU instruments backing the approach vague and inadequate, but also the internal conditions in most SEE countries were still not ripe to enable any meaningful regional cooperation (Lopandic, 2001). There was no willingness, in particular, on the part of two key countries – Croatia and FR Yugoslavia – to apply any form of regional co-operation (Uvalic, 2001c).

Owing to the break-up of former Yugoslavia and the political events that accompanied it, the Western Balkan countries benefited only to a limited extent from the main EU programmes meant to support the transition to a market economy and multiparty democracy offered to the CEE countries after 1990. The EU implemented a differentiated approach also within the SEE region. The military conflicts strongly conditioned the type of EU policies applied towards the successor states of former Yugoslavia. Consequently, though perhaps not always intentionally, EU policies regarding financial assistance, trade preferences, and contractual relations in the 1990s were more generous towards Albania, Bulgaria, and Romania, than towards the SEE countries originating from former Yugoslavia (Uvalic, 2003c and 2008).

8.1.2 EU financial assistance

Albania, Bulgaria, and Romania were among the SEE transition countries that were offered support by the EC almost immediately after the fall of the communist regimes. They received substantial financial assistance through the PHARE programme – Albania (after 1991) €385 million, Bulgaria €539 million, and Romania €726 million (Mayhew, 1998, p. 140). SFR Yugoslavia was also included among the beneficiaries of the PHARE programme for a short period in 1990–1 and received €35 million in 1990. In comparison to PHARE funds allocated to Poland or Hungary, this was not much – 7 per cent of PHARE resources in 1990.

Still, the amount given to SFR Yugoslavia was similar to what was allocated in 1990 to Bulgaria (€24.5 million), Czechoslovakia (€34 million), or Romania (€15.5 million). However, the PHARE funds for many of these countries almost tripled in 1991, but for SFR Yugoslavia they were sharply reduced, to €14.5 million or less than 2 per cent of PHARE resources in that year (Samardzija, 1994, pp. 167–8).

After the exclusion of SFR Yugoslavia from PHARE in 1991, Slovenia was the only country among its successor states that was able to benefit from the programme starting from 1992. Although Croatia was also offered €26 million within PHARE in 1992, these resources were never used, since Croatia was in the meantime suspended from the programme (Samardzija, 1994, p. 168). All successor states of former Yugoslavia other than Slovenia also received a very small amount of financial assistance provided by the G24 to the transition countries in CEE and SEE. During 1990–5, the four countries of former Yugoslavia received €4780 million, or only 5.5 per cent, of the overall package of G24 financial assistance to transition countries (Mayhew, 1998, p. 158, and Table 8.3).[4]

The stabilization of the political conditions in the SEE region after the end of 1995 led to some positive changes in EU policies of financial assistance, but not towards all countries. The PHARE programme was extended to Bosnia and Herzegovina and to FYR Macedonia in 1996, but not to the other countries. Croatia was temporarily included in the PHARE programme between 12 June and 4 August 1995, when it was again suspended as the EU reacted angrily to perceived human rights abuses following the Oluja offensive in the Krajina (Bartlett, 2003). Similarly, FR Yugoslavia was not included into the PHARE programme for political reasons. After the UN and EU sanctions against FR Yugoslavia were lifted in early 1996, the EU announced the political conditions for the further development of relations with FR Yugoslavia in April 1996, but the dispute over Milosevic's non-recognition of local election results in late 1996 (see Chapter 4) effectively blocked most forms of EU financial assistance (Lopandic, 1997, p. 133).

A specific EU programme of technical assistance – the Obnova programme[5] – was set up by the EU Council in July 1996 for the war-affected SEE countries, amended in 1998 and 1999, providing €400 million for the 1996–2000 period. Although the package was formally open to Bosnia and Herzegovina, Croatia, FR Yugoslavia, and FYR Macedonia, the resources were allocated very unevenly. Within the initially approved Obnova package of €218 million, as much as 64 per cent was used in Kosovo (Commission of the EC, 2002). During

1998–9, FR Yugoslavia did receive some €166.6 million from Obnova, but these funds were used almost exclusively in Kosovo (€135 million) and Montenegro (€27 million).

The overall EC financial assistance during 1991–9 to the five Western Balkan countries amounted to some €4.8 billion, but was very unevenly distributed. As much as 43 per cent was allocated to Bosnia and Herzegovina, 21 per cent to Albania, 20 per cent to FR Yugoslavia (mostly Kosovo in 1998–9), while Croatia and FRY Macedonia received the least (see Table 8.1).

Table 8.1 EC assistance to the Western Balkans, 1991–9 (€ million)

Country	1991–4	1995	1996	1997	1998	1999	Total
Albania	368.1	90.2	55.3	96.4	54.3	321.7	986
Bosnia and Herzegovina	495.5	216.4	445.2	358.9	297.6	250.8	2,064.4
Croatia	204.9	38.7	29.6	27.0	24.1	24.5	348.8
FYR Macedonia	96.6	34.4	25.0	73.7	25.5	166.8	422
FR Yugoslavia	170.6	40.0	24.5	18.1	311.8	385.8	950.8
Total							4,772

Source: European Commission, DG External Relations, 24 March 2000.

Looking into the type of EU assistance provided to the Western Balkans in the 1990s, by far the largest part was humanitarian assistance. Out of the overall commitments on the part of the EU from 1991 to early 1999 totalling €4185 million (see Table 8.2), almost 50 per cent (€1909 million) was provided under the European Commission's humanitarian ECHO office,[6] directed towards victims of the military conflicts and the socially vulnerable groups. If we exclude the PHARE resources given to the Yugoslav federation before its break-up, as mentioned earlier, only three countries benefited from PHARE – Albania, Bosnia and Herzegovina, and FYR Macedonia.

The Western Balkans received additional funds through bilateral assistance from EU member states of around €3277 million. During 1990–7, Croatia received substantial bilateral aid from EU member states (€1166 million) as well as loans from the EBRD worth €511, while FR Yugoslavia got €712 only from EU member states (see Table 8.2 and Bartlett, 2003, p. 73). The EBRD provided a further €792 million for private sector development projects to all countries except FR Yugoslavia. As to assistance of the EIB, due to the problem of unsettled debt obligations of former Yugoslavia and its successor states to the EIB,

Table 8.2 EU assistance to the Western Balkans, 1991–8 (commitments, € million)

	Albania	*Bosnia & Herzegovina*	*Croatia*	*FR Yugoslavia*	*FYR Macedonia*	*Total **
PHARE	616.4	754.5	49.6	41.7	236.7	1,708.6
Humanitarian Aid	41.2	1,032.1	290.8	262.8	45.7	1,908.7
Food	16.5	–	–	–	–	16.5
Balance of Payments	20.0	60.0	–	–	40.0	120.0
EIB	46.0	–	–	–	–	46.0
Other	122.8	221.2	9.3	17.5	2	385.1
Total EC-EU	862.9	2,067.8	349.7	322	324.4	4,184.9
EU Bilateral**	712.8	507.9	1,165.9	712.4	178.2	3,277.2
Grand Total	1,575.7	2,575.7	1,515.6	1,034.4	502.4	**7,462.1**
EBRD	68.0	70.0	511.0	0.0	143.0	792.0

*Including EC multi-country programmes (total 258.2 Million Euro).
**1991–7.
Source: EU Press Release PR 33/99 May 1999, in Bartlett (1999).

the only country that was able to benefit from its loans in the 1990s was Albania.

EU financial aid to FR Yugoslavia mainly consisted of humanitarian assistance (see Table 8.2) and a few projects aimed at facilitating the development of democracy. During the 1991–8 period, €263 million was provided to FR Yugoslavia to support refugees from Bosnia and Herzegovina and Croatia, internally displaced persons from Kosovo and other socially vulnerable groups. Still, the largest part of these funds, particularly in 1998–9, was allocated for Kosovo. Serbia also received some EU funding for specific projects in 1998–99. A sum of €6 million was given to the Serbian independent media to help resist repression by the Milosevic regime and to the civil society sector; and after October 1999 heating oil worth €8.8 million was donated to 34 Serbian municipalities that at that time were in opposition to the Milosevic regime, within the 'Energy for Democracy' programme prepared by the G17 Plus.[7] The pilot project was for Nis and Pirot, but in February 2000 it was extended to other cities – Kragujevac, Kraljevo, Novi Sad, Sombor, and Subotica. In July 2000, the EU Commission supported a similar programme, 'Schools for a Democratic Serbia' with €3.8 million, aimed to support education institutions under the responsibility of the 34 democratically run municipalities.[8]

8.1.3 EU trade measures

An even more important form of support that the EU offered to post-communist countries in the early 1990s were measures of trade liberalization. Also in this area, the EU applied very different types of policies towards the individual countries (see Table 8.3).

Bulgaria and Romania were able to sign Association Agreements with the EU already in 1993, which enabled gradual trade liberalization and the duty-free entry of most industrial products into the EU. Slovenia also signed an Association Agreement with the EU, though somewhat later than the other CEE countries, in June 1996, due to the dispute over borders with the Italian government. The Association Agreements greatly facilitated their gradual economic integration into the EU and the later implementation of pre-accession strategies and European partnerships,

Table 8.3 EU measures to support transition in SEE countries in the 1990s

	Multilateral financial assistance			**Trade arrangements with the EU**
	Year of inclusion in PHARE	***Total PHARE 1990–5***	***Total G24 assistance (mln ECU) 1990–5***	***Type of trade agreement* & year of conclusion***
Albania	1991 onwards	332	1,585	TECA: 1992
Bulgaria	1990 onwards	476.5	3,981	AA: March 1993
Romania	1991 onwards	607.7	8,191	AA: Feb. 1993
SFR Yugoslavia	1990–1	49.5		
Slovenia	1992 onwards	69 (1992–5)	870	TECA: 1993; AA: June 1996
Bosnia & Herzegovina	1996 onwards	(166)**	(4,780)**	ATP: 1992, 1996
Croatia	1995 (shortly)			ATP: 1992
Macedonia FYR	1996 onwards			TECA: June 1996
Yugoslavia FR	–			ATP: 1997 (withdrawn in 1998)

*TECA: Trade and Economic Cooperation Agreement; AA: Association Agreement; ATP: Autonomous Trade Preferences, mainly taken over from the 1980 Trade and Cooperation Agreement with SFR Yugoslavia.

**The four countries of former Yugoslavia, other than Slovenia. Over the 1990–5 period, these four countries received a cumulative total of 166 million ECU within PHARE and 4780 ECU within G24 assistance (including PHARE).

Source: Compiled by the author on the basis of various sources, in particular Bartlett (1997), Uvalic (2001c), and Mayhew (1998), pp. 157–8.

preparing the ground for their accession to the EU in 2004 (Slovenia) and 2007 (Bulgaria and Romania). Albania was offered a Trade and Economic Cooperation Agreement with the EU which was signed in 1992 and which is less extensive in scope than the Association Agreements, but still allowed preferential access of most Albanian industrial products to EU markets in the 1990s.

Regarding the countries of former Yugoslavia, in December 1991 the EC Council adopted the Declaration on Positive Measures, which reintroduced trade preferences for all the Yugoslav successor states previously included in the Trade and Economic Cooperation Agreement signed with SFR Yugoslavia in 1980, that had been suspended a month earlier. However, the UN and EC sanctions imposed in May 1992 against FR Yugoslavia due to its involvement in the war in Bosnia and Herzegovina interrupted the application of these EU trade preferences.

After the signing of the Dayton Peace Accords in late 1995, these autonomous trade preferences were renewed in 1996 for Bosnia and Herzegovina and Croatia, and in April 1997 also for FR Yugoslavia. FYR Macedonia was able to conclude a Trade and Economic Cooperation Agreement with the EU in 1996 which entered into force in 1998, similar to the one concluded with Albania in 1992.

At first, FR Yugoslavia was not able to benefit from the EU autonomous trade preferences because of the embargo introduced in late 1991 and reinforced in May 1992. After the most severe sanctions were lifted in October 1996, the EU did prepare, in November 1996, autonomous trade preferences also for FR Yugoslavia, but due to Milosevic's unwillingness to accept the victory of democratic parties at the local elections their adoption was delayed until April 1997. On that occasion, additional political conditions were imposed on FR Yugoslavia regarding democratization, improvement of the conditions in Kosovo, and respect of the Dayton agreement (Lopandic, 1997, p. 133). Since in the meantime the political situation in Kosovo worsened, these autonomous trade preferences were not renewed in 1998 and 1999.

The autonomous trade preferences offered interruptedly to countries of former Yugoslavia did little to facilitate their faster economic integration with the EU. The break-up of SFR Yugoslavia ended many traditional trade links and contributed to a drastic reduction in the overall level of trade of the newly created states, which throughout the 1990s remained highly depressed (see Figure 8.1).

Despite low levels of trade in the 1990s, the majority of SEE countries gradually reoriented their trade from previous trading partners in former Yugoslavia or the CMEA, towards primarily the EU. Already in

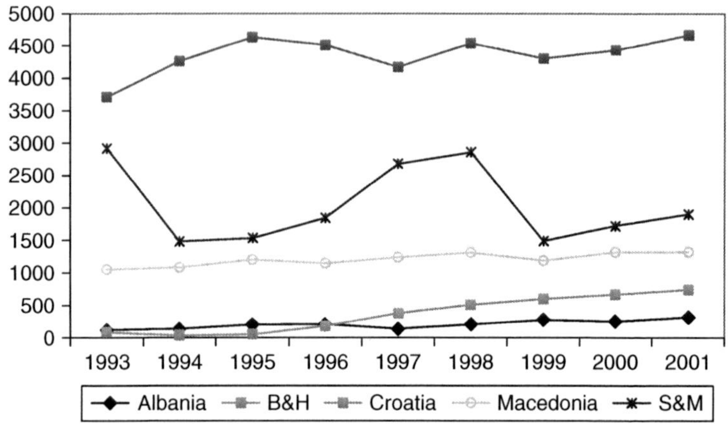

Figure 8.1 Western Balkan countries value of exports, 1992–2001 (million US$)

1998, export shares going to the EU were quite high for most countries, including Albania (89 per cent), Bulgaria (52 per cent), Romania (65 per cent), Slovenia (65 per cent), even Croatia and FYR Macedonia (in both cases close to 50 per cent). On the contrary, in 1998 only 22 per cent of Bosnian exports and 33 per cent of Yugoslav exports were directed towards EU markets (see more in Uvalic, 2001c).

8.1.4 EU policy instruments

Owing to the highly unfavourable political circumstances which characterized the war-affected SEE countries in the 1990s, EU policies were frequently based on the use of the 'stick' rather than the 'carrot'. Particularly towards some of the key SEE countries, Croatia and FR Yugoslavia, the EU used primarily the 'stick', often in the form of the withdrawal of the 'carrot' – such as exclusion from the PHARE programme or other types of EU programmes, or delays in extending trade preferences. However, in comparison to all the other Western Balkan countries, Croatia did receive an important 'carrot' soon after the break-up of former Yugoslavia – the visa-free travel regime to most EU countries.[9]

As an expression of disapproval of Serbian/Yugoslav politics, FR Yugoslavia was particularly subject to the EU policy of 'sticks', as it was under economic and political sanctions throughout most of the 1990s. EU member states also actively participated in the NATO military intervention of FR Yugoslavia in 1999. Despite strong political motives underlying this type of policies, they did not bring many tangible results, but frequently were counterproductive.

Instead of putting pressure on the regime to adopt more democratic policies, the severe international sanctions actually contributed to Milosevic's hold on power (Crnobrnja, 1994, p. 232). Instead of punishing Milosevic, the UN and EU sanctions in many ways reinforced him. The decade-long isolation of the country facilitated the strengthening of an authoritarian regime and contributed to the accumulation of internal tensions, which reached their peak in 1999 with the Kosovo crisis and the NATO intervention (see Chapters 3 and 4). Within Serbia, the international sanctions were perceived as highly unjust, in large part due to the brain-washing capabilities of the regime-controlled media (Crnobrnja, 1994, p. 232). This feeling of 'EU unjustice' towards Serbia has remained in the minds of many citizens also after the political changes in 2000, in part due to the slow pace of improvement of EU-Serbian relations and the maintenance of the burdensome visa regime.

Instead of using primarily the 'stick', at a time when it was already too late to essentially influence the Yugoslav break-up and accompanying wars, the EU should have used other measures, such as offering the country association status at an early stage, much *before* the escalation of the conflicts, under strictly defined political conditions focused on a peaceful transformation of the Yugoslav federation. Discussing the inappropriate timing of EU measures towards SFR Yugoslavia, Susan Woodward observes: 'In moving from the carrot of economic aid and association with the EU in May (1991) to the stick of punitive sanctions and withdrawal of aid during July and early August, however, the two organizations (the EC and the Conference for Security and Cooperation in Europe) only compounded the division within Yugoslavia between those who saw options outside of Yugoslavia and those who, out of a realist assessment or objection to the consequences of rapid westernization, sought some alternative within an independent Yugoslavia' (Woodward, 1995b, p. 175).

In the late 1980s, the EU greatly underestimated the political crisis in SFR Yugoslavia. For a long time, the EU and the United States appeared unwilling to recognize that Yugoslavia was disintegrating and that the presidents of its republics were not capable of regulating this process in a peaceful manner (Glenny, 1992, p. 177). The EU ignored the origins of the conflict rooted in economic decline and quarrels over the necessary political reforms to transform the Yugoslav federation, accepting the representation of the problems and possible solutions as presented by radical nationalist governments in Croatia, Serbia, and Slovenia, in this way depriving the non-nationalists, like the prime minister Ante Markovic (Woodward, 1995b, p. 169).

The EU also had other much more important issues on its agenda at that time, so 'the Balkans were uninteresting both from a political and economic point of view' (Glenny, 1992, p. 177). In 1989, the history of Europe was radically changing, with the fall of the Berlin Wall in November 1989 and German unification, the collapse of communist regimes throughout Eastern Europe, and soon after the break-up of the USSR and the disintegration of the CMEA. In addition, the preparations of the Maastricht Treaty were already very much in course. 'For the Europeans ... European security lay with the fate of the Soviet Union and its nuclear arsenal and with the outcome of the Maastricht Treaty, not with conflict in the Balkans' (Woodward, 1995b, p. 177). These events of unprecedented historical importance for Europe overshadowed the political and economic crisis that was developing in SFR Yugoslavia.

In 1990–1, the EU failed to elaborate a longer-term strategy for all the Balkan countries, which perhaps could have prevented some of the tragic consequences of its break-up. The German decision to recognize Croatia, pushed through in December 1991 by the foreign minister Genscher against the wishes of the European Commission and the United States, has been widely criticized, though also credited with ending the war (Lampe, 2000, p. 372). The decision ended the war in Croatia, but it directly contributed to the explosion of the military conflict in Bosnia and Herzegovina that would last up until the end of 1995. The recognition of Slovenia and Croatia, that put a definite end to SFR Yugoslavia, left Milosevic and Tudjman to pursue their nationalistic goals further. In this way, the opportunity was lost to prevent the bloody wars among the peoples of Yugoslavia. Even if SFR Yugoslavia was bound to break-up under the impact of its many contradictions, it could have done so in a peaceful way and the EU could have helped as mediator.

8.2 The new EU approach: Stabilization and association

A fundamental change in the EU and international strategy towards the SEE region took place after the end of the Kosovo conflict in mid-1999, when a new, more comprehensive, and longer-term strategy for the whole SEE region was formulated under the wide-ranging SAP.

In June 1999, the 'Stability Pact for Southeast Europe' was adopted by the EU, its member states, major international organizations, and other participating countries.[10] Its principal aim was to help mobilize donors' assistance for the economic reconstruction of countries negatively affected by the Kosovo war, not only the Western Balkans, but also Bulgaria and Romania (Stability Pact, 1999). Its main mechanism was the Regional Table, which coordinated the work of three Working Tables in charge of different sets of issues – Democratization and Human Rights; Economic Reconstruction, Development and Co-operation; and Security. After having operated for almost nine years, in February 2008 the Stability Pact was replaced by the Regional Cooperation Council with headquarters in Sarajevo.

Even more importantly, in May 1999 the EU Commission announced a new approach towards the Western Balkan countries, as a follow-up of its 1996 'Regional Approach' – the Stabilization and Association Process – devised specifically for the five SEE countries (Finnish Presidency and the European Commission, 1999). The SAP's main objective is to support economic and political transition, stabilization, and integration efforts of the SEE countries through a series of measures, including economic and financial assistance, privileged trade access to EU markets, political dialogue, approximation of EU legislation, contractual relations, and even prospects of future EU membership. Positive internal developments in two key countries contributed to the implementation of the announced new strategy – in Croatia, President Tudjman's death in January 2000, and in Serbia, the replacement of Milosevic's regime by a democratic government in October 2000. SAP was officially launched at the EU–Western Balkan summit held in Zagreb in late November 2000.

The SAP offered the five SEE countries the possibility to establish contractual relations with the EU through the signing of an SAA, similar to those signed with the CEE countries in the 1990s. Moreover, for the first time since 1989, these SEE countries were also offered prospects of joining the EU, though without any precise timetable. The speed of EU integration is determined by how quickly a country meets the political and economic accession criteria. These criteria were formulated at the European Council Summit in Copenhagen in 1993, and were used in the late 1990s for assessing the readiness of the CEE countries to join the EU (Nuti, 1996). The Copenhagen criteria consist of three groups of requirements that the acceding countries need to fulfil:

- Stability of institutions guaranteeing democracy, the rule of law, human rights, and respect for and protection of minorities;
- Functioning market economy and capacity to cope with competitive pressures and market forces within the Union;

- Ability to take on obligations of membership *(acquis communautaire),* including the aims of political, economic, and monetary union.

These criteria were further clarified in 1995 at the Madrid European Council, when a fourth criteria was added regarding EU's capacity to integrate new members. The EU needs to ensure that its institutions and decision-making processes remain effective and accountable; it needs to be in a position, as it enlarges, to continue developing and implementing common policies in all areas; and it needs to be in a position to continue financing its policies in a sustainable manner.

In addition to the Copenhagen criteria, the Western Balkan countries must also fulfil two additional groups of requirements, which were formulated at the European Councils in 1997 and 1999 specifically for the war-affected SEE countries (Commission of the EC 1997 and 1999):

- Countries must demonstrate their willingness to implement regional cooperation with neighbouring states; and
- Countries must fulfil all their international obligations, including collaboration with the ICTY in The Hague, the Dayton Peace Accords, and the UN Security Council Resolution 1244.

The SAP offered SEE countries privileged access to EU markets even before the conclusion of an SAA. In early 2000 the EU granted autonomous trade preferences to the SEE countries, but not to FR Yugoslavia (an exception was made only for aluminium products from Montenegro). After democratic changes in Belgrade in October 2000, on 1 November 2000, these preferences were also extended to FR Yugoslavia. The EU trade concessions provide for the elimination of duties and quantitative restrictions for around 95 per cent of goods from the Western Balkans entering the EU market, including agricultural and sensitive industrial products, with only a few exceptions.[11] In the case of Croatia and FYR Macedonia, these trade provisions were incorporated into the SAAs signed in 2001, which until ratification were governed by the Interim Agreements. The EU autonomous trade preferences were recently renewed until the end of 2010 (Commission of the EC, 2006b, p. 7).

Another important element of SAP was a new programme of financial assistance, Community Assistance to Reconstruction, Development and Stabilisation (CARDS), which provided over €5 billion of aid to the five SEE countries over the 2000–6 period (€5385 million with Croatian pre-accession funds in 2005–6; see Commission of the EC (2000) and Table 8.4). In order to increase the efficiency in aid delivery, the EU also

Table 8.4 CARDS programme allocation for 2000–6 (million €)

	2000	2001	2002	2003	2004	2005	2006	TOTAL
Albania	33.4	37.5	44.9	46.5	63.5	44.2	45.5	315.5
Bosnia and Herzegovina	90.3	105.2	71.9	63.0	72.0	49.4	51.0	502.8
Croatia (transferred to pre-accession after 2005)	16.8	60.0	59.0	62.0	81.0	–	–	278.8
FYR Macedonia	13.0	56.2	41.5	43.5	59.0	45.0	40.0	298.2
Serbia and Montenegro	650.5	385.5	351.6	324.3	307.9	282.5	257.5	2,559.8
Interim Civilian Administrations	10.0	24.5	33.0	32.0	35.0	36.0	35.0	205.5
Regional	20.2	20.0	43.5	31.5	23.0	47.9	43.5	229.6
Other	141.5	118.0	11.0	17.0	22.5	19.7	16.1	345.8
Macro-Financial Assistance (grants)	70.0	120.0	100.0	15.0	16.0	33.0	50.0	404.0
TOTAL	1,045.7	926.9	756.4	634.8	679.9	557.7	538.6	5,140
Croatia, pre-accession 2005–6	–	–	–	–	–	105	140	245
TOTAL including Croatia, 2005–6	–	–	–	–	–	662.7	678.6	5,385

Source: Commission of the EC (2002).

established the European Agency for Reconstruction (EAR) in charge of managing the implementation of economic reconstruction in FR Yugoslavia (Serbia, Montenegro, and Kosovo) and FYR Macedonia, officially inaugurated in Thessaloniki in March 2000.[12]

The EU strategy was reinforced at the Thessaloniki EU–Balkan Summit in June 2003. An important new instrument was introduced for the Western Balkan countries – the European Partnership, similar to the Accession Partnership designed earlier for the CEE countries – which identifies the main priorities and checklists (Commission, 2004a). In addition, the Thessaloniki provisions announced the opening of various EU programmes which previously were reserved only for EU candidates, including 'twining', TAIEX, ISPA, SAPARD, and FP6,[13] and reconfirmed the EU's commitment to EU–Balkan integration.

In July 2006, the European Council established a new instrument – the Instrument for Pre-accession Assistance (IPA) – which replaced all the previous assistance instruments available for the EU candidate and potential candidate countries from the Western Balkans and Turkey (Obnova, PHARE, ISPA, SAPARD, CARDS, and the financial instrument for Turkey). IPA assistance is provided on the basis of the European Partnerships of the potential candidate countries, and the Accession Partnerships of the candidate countries. It is intended as a flexible instrument, providing assistance which depends on the progress made by the beneficiary countries and their needs as shown in the Commission's evaluations and annual strategy papers. The total pre-accession funding for the current EU financial framework (2007–13) is €11.5 billion.

IPA offers support to five main components: (1) transition assistance and institution building; (2) cross-border cooperation; (3) regional development; (4) human resources development; and (5) rural development. However, the possibility of using the various IPA components depends on the country's status in the EU integration process – whether it is a candidate or a potential candidate for EU accession. Whereas the candidate countries can benefit from all five components of IPA, the potential candidates can only use the first two. The status of a country is therefore fundamental, as it determines whether it can access all, or just a few, of the components of IPA funds.

Political dialogue is another important part of recent EU–Western Balkan relations. Joint Parliamentary Committees were established in 2004 between the EU and the two more advanced countries, Croatia and FYR Macedonia, while regular inter-parliamentary meetings were held with Albania, Bosnia and Herzegovina, Serbia, Montenegro, and Kosovo. In order to improve the quality of the EU accession process, various other instruments have also been used, such as impact assessment of accession in key policy areas, estimates of budgetary implications of specific measures, evaluation of a country's integration capacity, the use of benchmarks, and so forth.

8.3 Results of the new EU approach

The new EU strategy for the Western Balkans has brought a number of positive results, though some countries have moved forward faster than others. Some of the achievements include increasing financial assistance, harmonization of legislation, establishment of contractual relations, initiatives in regional cooperation, fast economic integration, and growing internal support of the EU integration process.

8.3.1 EU financial assistance

The Western Balkan countries have received an increasing amount of EU financial assistance. From barely €1.4 billion in 1991–4 and €3.1 billion in 1995–9, EU financial assistance increased to over €5 billion in 2000–6 (Uvalic, 2001c), and to €11.5 billion in 2007–13 period (now also including Turkey). After 2000, additional financial assistance was collected at the various donors' conferences organized by the Stability Pact for SEE. Serbia has also been one of the major recipients of EU financial assistance since 2001. According to recent calculations, during the whole 1991–2006 period the Western Balkan countries have received from the EU a total of €12 billion, or an average of €444 per capita (Travaglino, 2009, p. 173).

Although the amount of EU financial assistance provided to the Western Balkan countries has progressively increased, it has been relatively low if compared to what the ten CEE countries received during the decade prior to EU membership. Moreover, the quality of EU assistance to the Balkans is different with respect to the CEE countries, since 60–80 per cent of total financial aid to the Balkans consists of technical assistance, without the possibility of using these funds for more important projects such as infrastructure. In the Western Balkans, the quality of transport or energy networks are way below European standards, representing a serious impediment to faster economic development (Travaglino, 2009, pp. 173–4). Present budgetary constraints in the Balkan countries are such that they cannot easily finance extremely costly infrastructure projects. A major access to EU funds for these purposes, possibly co-financed by international financial institutions, could substantially contribute to economic development of not only the single countries, but of the whole Balkan region.

8.3.2 Harmonization of legislation

The EU has provided a strong anchor for the process of economic, political, and legal reforms in all the Western Balkan countries. The EU model and the *acquis communautaire* has been an important blueprint for institutional reforms. The EU integration process has prompted and accelerated the process of internal reforms also in Serbia in many areas, even before the signing of a SAA. Thanks to many technical meetings between the EU Commission and the Yugoslav/Serbian government, many new laws have been adopted in conformity with EU norms.

The EU has also made major efforts to follow much more closely, the political and economic developments in the region. Starting from 2002, Annual Reports on SAP have started being prepared, including individual country's SA Reports, individual country's CARDS Strategy Papers, and Regional CARDS Strategy Papers. After the entry of ten CEE countries into the EU, its Enlargement Directorate General is exclusively

Table 8.5 SAAs signed by the EU and SEE countries

Country	Date of signature	Entry into force
FYR Macedonia	9 April 2001	1 April 2004
Croatia	29 October 2001	1 February 2005
Albania	12 June 2006	1 April 2009
Montenegro	15 October 2007	Ratification process not complete
Serbia	29 April 2008	Ratification process not complete
Bosnia and Herzegovina	16 June 2008	Ratification process not complete

dedicated to the candidate and potential candidate countries, prevalently from SEE (in addition to Turkey and Iceland).

8.3.3 Contractual relations

The Western Balkan countries are presently at very different stages of the EU integration process. Only two countries were able to sign a SAA with the EU at an early stage – FYR Macedonia in April 2001 and Croatia in October 2001. Albania signed an SAA only in June 2006 and Montenegro in October 2007. The last two countries to sign an SAA were Serbia, at the end of April 2008, and Bosnia and Herzegovina, in June 2008 (see Table 8.5). By end-2009, Croatia was the only candidate negotiating EU membership, FYR Macedonia was a candidate but accession negotiations have not yet commenced, Montenegro and Albania have applied for candidate status which needs to be approved, Bosnia and Herzegovina and Serbia are still potential candidates, while Kosovo has a special status under the so-called tracking mechanism.[14]

Despite their present very different status, by 2008 all the Western Balkan countries have, at last, signed an SAA, thus becoming associated to the EU (except Kosovo). The SAAs provide a framework of *mutual* commitments on a wide range of political, trade, and economic issues, and not simply unilateral measures decided by the EU, as were various measures provided to the Western Balkan countries in the 1990s.

8.3.4 Economic integration

Over the past eight years, all Western Balkan countries have become increasingly integrated with the EU economy (Uvalic, 2007b). Thanks to the political stabilization of the region and more substantial EU trade preferences, there was an enormous increase in EU trade with the Western Balkan countries after 2000. In only five years, there was a threefold increase in trade volumes. The EU has had an increasing surplus in its trade with the Western Balkan region. The EU has become the main trading partner of all countries, in 2007 accounting for 55–80 per cent of both Western Balkan countries' imports and exports. The positive trade effects are particularly evident for those countries like FR Yugoslavia (Serbia and Montenegro) which before 2000 were granted no or limited EU trade preferences.

After 2000, there has also been a substantial inflow of FDI to the Western Balkan countries, mainly by firms from EU member states. During 2000–8, the six Western Balkan countries have attracted around US$ 48.1 billion of FDI (see Table 6.5, Chapter 6). Increasing FDI has fundamentally contributed to closer economic links of the Balkans with the rest of Europe (Uvalic (2003a).

Balkan–EU integration has also taken place through increasing integration of financial and capital markets, additionally prompted by the privatization of the banking sector. Major EU banks today own 60–95 per cent of banking assets in most Western Balkan countries. Although foreign ownership of banks in the SEE countries has fundamentally contributed to the process of bank restructuring and privatization, it has also increased their vulnerability to the global financial crisis of 2008–9 (Uvalic, 2009a).

8.3.5 Regional cooperation

An important objective promoted by the EU for over a decade in the Balkans, that also represents an official criteria of EU accession, is regional cooperation among the SEE countries. Since the launch of the Stability Pact for SEE, there have been numerous initiatives aimed at stimulating cooperation among the SEE countries – in addition to the Western Balkans, also involving Bulgaria and Romania before their entry into the EU in 2007. The widespread perception until recently was that regional cooperation might be at the expense of the individual country's prospects of joining the EU, creating an antagonism between the bilateral and regional approach (Bojicic-Dzelilovic, 2001, p. 240). The initial scepticism has, to a large extent, been overcome, and many regional initiatives have been implemented successfully.

One of the most important is the intra-SEE trade liberalization process, which started with the signing of the memorandum of understanding on trade liberalization and facilitation by all SEE countries in Brussels in June 2001. The memorandum led to the conclusion of bilateral free trade agreements among the SEE countries from mid-2001 onwards, which in December 2006 were incorporated into the Central European Free Trade

Agreement (CEFTA), thus creating a free trade area in SEE. The process of trade liberalization has led to increasing trade among the SEE countries, helping economic recovery and growth (Uvalic, 2009b). There has been steady progress with regional cooperation in many other important areas such as energy, which led to the signing of the SEE Energy Treaty in October 2005, or a number of political and security issues.

Moreover, as of 2008 regional initiatives are governed primarily by the Western Balkan countries themselves. The long-promoted 'regional ownership' of the process of regional integration has finally been attained with the February 2008 transformation of the Stability Pact for SEE into the Regional Cooperation Council based in Sarajevo. The responsibility and 'ownership' of regional policies was at last passed to the SEE countries.

8.3.6 Support of the EU integration process

EU integration has become a political priority of all the Western Balkan countries, leading to the adoption of EU resolutions, national strategies of EU integration, and other important documents. This has been the case also with countries lagging behind in the EU integration process, including Serbia. The Serbian parliament adopted a Resolution on EU Accession in October 2004, an Action Plan and Strategy on EU integration was implemented shortly afterwards, followed by other important documents.

Most Balkan countries have also experienced rising popular support of EU integration. According to an opinion poll of the Serbian European Integration Office, Serbia's membership in the EU received support of 61 per cent of the respondents in December 2008 (even more by the younger generations), which is somewhat higher than comparative figures for Croatia, Bosnia and Herzegovina or Montenegro, though a bit lower than those for Albania and FYR Macedonia (www.seio.gov.rs). In May 2009, when asked whether they would vote in favour of Serbia joining the EU in case of a referendum, as many as 79 per cent of the respondents expressing an opinion replied positively (www.seio.gov.rs).

8.4 Some failures of EU policy: Two facets of the integration process

Despite the discussed positive results of the new EU approach, the Western Balkan countries are presently at very different stages of their EU integration process and there is high uncertainty about their eventual EU membership. Croatia is the only candidate negotiating EU accession, while in the case of all the other Western Balkan countries progress has not been quick enough.

Why has the success of CEE not been replicated in the Western Balkans? The obvious reason is that the overall political and economic conditions in the SEE region in 2000 were fundamentally different than those in CEE in 1990. The legacy of the 1990s, when the region experienced military conflicts and high political instability, has left a heavy burden on most Balkan countries, including delicate problems of borders, country status, return of refugees, and minority rights. Recalling these historical legacies, there is no doubt that the principal reasons for the slow pace of EU–Balkan integration are to be sought on the side of the SEE countries. Moreover, countries have still not adopted many important reforms and need to fulfil the necessary conditions. Progress in the EU accession process of the two potential candidate countries, Bosnia and Herzegovina and Serbia, has been particularly slow.

Nevertheless part of the responsibility for the slow pace of EU–Balkan integration also lies with the EU. Three issues need to be stressed in this regard: current problems within the EU, EU policy of very strict conditionality, and specific policies applied towards some countries like FR Yugoslavia/Serbia (to be discussed in section 8.5).

8.4.1 EU integration capacity

There is high uncertainty on the part of the EU about its enlargement commitments. The Dutch and French rejection of the EU Constitution, the difficulties in adopting the Lisbon Treaty, the long-forgotten 'fourth' criteria referring to EU's readiness to absorb new members, the often stressed problem of enlargement fatigue, have all added to increasing uncertainty regarding the EU commitments towards the Western Balkans and Turkey. Although during Finland's Presidency of the EU in the second half of 2006, the EU member states agreed to a renewed consensus on enlargement, more recently some countries have taken the view that Croatia should be the last country to join the EU. Today there seems to be a new consensus among politicians and citizens of the Western Balkan states, that the road to EU membership has become longer and less certain (Teokarevic, 2009).

The situation has become even more complicated after Iceland's decision to present an application for EU membership in mid-2009, which was welcomed by the President of the Commission, José Manuel Barroso, and was strongly supported by the Nordic EU member states, including Sweden as the incoming EU Presidency. Whether this may favour future EU enlargements also to the Balkans is yet to be seen.

8.4.2 EU conditionality

During the last decade, the EU has tried to improve its instruments of accession for the SEE countries. On the one hand, the EU Commission has directly drawn on the rich experience gained during the accession process with the CEE countries. Most instruments that have been employed for the CEE countries in their pre-accession integration process are presently used in the SEE countries, which has undoubtedly contributed to raising the quality of the EU–Balkan integration process. On the other hand, however, the development of more sophisticated EU instruments has also brought changes in its conditionality policies, which for the Western Balkan countries renders the EU integration process more complicated and more burdensome than it was for the CEE countries. While the pre-accession process itself is immensely complex, the Balkan countries are subject, for several reasons, to *stricter* EU conditionality than the one applied to the CEE countries.

First, the EU conditions for the Balkan countries are more numerous. In addition to the three groups of Copenhagen criteria, the Balkan countries also have to demonstrate that they have participated in regional cooperation initiatives, and that they comply with all international obligations, particularly cooperation with the Hague Tribunal. The last two criteria are justified insofar as they aim at more permanent political stability in the region after a decade of wars, but they still represent additional criteria that the Balkan countries need to fulfil. Moreover, it is precisely these additional criteria which in most cases have been the most important for delaying progress in relations with the EU. The Copenhagen criteria have often been criticized as not being sufficiently precise, thus leaving room for discretion on the part of the EU in its evaluation of a country, but this is even more the case with the criteria requiring 'the compliance with international obligations'. Too often has this criteria been used in an arbitrary way, depending on the opinion of individual experts or, as in the recent phase regarding Serbia, of the position of one country (the Netherlands).

Second, the phases envisaged as part of the EU–Balkan integration process are more numerous. Except for FYR Macedonia and Croatia that were able to sign an SAA already in 2001, the procedure for the other Balkan countries has been much longer. The process of preparations for signing an SAA envisages the setting up of a joint EU–Balkan country Consultative Task Force (CTF) which is to meet regularly to assess progress in various areas of reform, in the case of Serbia and Montenegro promoted in 2003 into 'Enhanced Permanent Dialogue' (EPD) meetings. After a series of CTF/EPD meetings, the EU Commission is to prepare a positive Feasibility Report, confirming that a country is ready to start negotiating an SAA. After the completion of the process of negotiations on the SAA, the signing of an SAA takes place, when the country becomes associated with the EU. The SAA also needs to be ratified by the parliaments of the country in question and all EU member states. Once a country has signed an SAA, it can apply for the status of EU 'candidate', which must be approved by the European Council. The final stage involves the launch of negotiations on EU accession, during which each of the many chapters of the EU's *acquis communautaire* needs to be opened and negotiated, and an agreement has to be reached on temporary provisions and derogations in specific sectors.

Third, for the Western Balkan countries it is the political criteria that have played the most prominent role, particularly the 'compliance with international obligations'. The countries are formally assessed for all the other criteria, including the economic ones, but these criteria are of far minor importance. The transition indicators of the EBRD, which measure progress of all East European countries in various areas of reform, show that by mid-2009 most Western Balkan countries have also completed many important economic reforms required by the transition to market economy (see Chapter 6). Even if today most Balkan countries are not lagging much behind some of the present EU member states, this is unlikely to greatly accelerate their future EU membership.

Given strict EU conditionality, it is of no surprise that for some countries the process of concluding an SAA has taken so long. In the early 1990s, it was sufficient for the CEE countries to declare that they wanted to implement the transition to multiparty democracy and market economy in order to be offered Association Agreements (AA) with the EU. The AAs were indeed signed fairly quickly – from December 1991 to June 1995 – with all the CEE countries except Slovenia, signed in June 1996. The first CEE–EU AAs were signed in late 1991, at a time when the EU membership criteria were not even known, as they were specified only at the Copenhagen European Council in 1993. The signing of AAs was therefore not subject to any EU conditionality, quite contrary to the signing of SAAs with the Balkan countries. Had the CEE countries been required, at that time, to demonstrate the fulfilment of certain conditions, including the administrative capacity to implement the *acquis*, most of them would probably have had serious problems in fulfilling them.

This important incentive – *the status of association with the EU* – was offered to the majority of SEE countries (all except Croatia and Macedonia) only after a very long and burdensome process of technical meetings, negotiations, assessments, and feasibility reports, not to mention a series of country-specific conditions, as has been the case with FR Yugoslavia and later Serbia (see below).

8.5 Serbia's slow progress towards EU membership

FR Yugoslavia was not included in the SAP when it was launched in November 2000, due to the lack of fundamental political changes in Serbia. At that time Milosevic was still in power, impeding the country's access to international financial assistance and EU programmes devised to help transition and reconstruction of the SEE region. With the change to a democratic regime in October 2000, political relations between FR Yugoslavia and the EU quickly intensified, as described in detail earlier (see Chapter 5). The first package of EU financial aid arrived in October 2000, while a month later the EU autonomous trade preferences were extended to FR Yugoslavia. In March 2001, a high-level EU–FR Yugoslavia meeting was held in Belgrade in order to prepare the ground for the forthcoming first CTF Meeting, scheduled for July 2001.

Since the official launch of the SAP for FR Yugoslavia in July 2001, there has been steady progress in many areas, regarding financial assistance, legal harmonization and trade, while the visa regime was also finally lifted at the end of 2009. However, substantial delays have taken place in establishing contractual relations between the EU and Serbia, since the signing of the SAA was delayed up until 2008 and its full implementation was blocked until late 2009 (see below).

8.5.1 EU financial assistance

Serbia has received a substantial amount of EU financial assistance during the last eight years. The EU helped FR Yugoslavia with an Emergency Assistance Programme of almost €200 million in October 2000, which was to help consolidate democratic changes during the winter 2000–1. The EU Commission, its member states, and the EIB were the largest donors at the June 2001 donors' conference for FR Yugoslavia in Brussels, providing a total of US$ 636.73 million out of the US$1.3 billion package (see Chapter 5). During the 2000–6 period, the EU helped the ongoing economic, political, and legal reforms in Serbia and Montenegro through the CARDS programme with some €2.6 billion, out of a total of €5.1 billion allocated to the SEE (see Table 8.4). During 2007–9 Serbia received EU assistance through the new programme IPA, amounting to some €572 million. By far the largest part

Table 8.6 EU financial assistance to Serbia: Multi-annual indicative financial framework, 2007–9 (in million €)

Component	2007	2008	2009	2007–9
Transition assistance and institution building	178.5	179.4	182.6	**540.5**
Cross-Border Cooperation	8.2	11.5	12.2	**31.9**
Total	186.7	190.9	194.8	**572.4**

of IPA funds for Serbia (€540) is for transition assistance and institution building, while a minor part (€32 million) is for cross-border cooperation (see Table 8.6).

8.5.2 Legal harmonization

Serbia has also adopted legislation in conformity with EU laws in many areas, as envisaged by the European Partnership. After the first EU–FRY CTF meeting was held in July 2001, numerous political and technical meetings have been organized to discuss progress in various sectors of reform in FR Yugoslavia/Serbia – some 5 CTF meetings in 2001–2 and 22 Enhanced Permanent Dialogue (EPD) meetings from July 2003 until the end of 2008, while another 9 EPDs were planned for 2009. Progress on Serbia's reform priorities has been encouraged and monitored by the Enhanced Permanent Dialogue process.

The new Serbian pro-European government elected in May 2008 identifies EU integration as its top foreign policy priority. The European Council in 2008 adopted a new European Partnership for Serbia. The Serbian administration has prepared the National Programme for EU Integration (NPI) which covers the main European Partnership priorities, that was adopted by the government in October 2008. The European integration structures were strengthened through the formation of coordination bodies, including a policy coordination body chaired by the deputy prime minister and an expert working party comprising 35 working groups covering all areas of the *acquis*. The Serbian European Integration Office was also reinforced. Most ministries and agencies continue their efforts to draft legislation in the area of European integration.

The first report on the implementation of the NPI of the Serbian government adopted in February 2009 showed that the process of legislative changes has been very slow, though somewhat faster than during the previous years. The results have been much better for the July–September 2009 period. The fulfilment of the NPI in the third quarter of 2009 was 96 per cent, as out of 81 planned acts, 78 were actually adopted. The Serbian government fulfilled its plan by 69 per cent, while the parliament fulfilled it by 222 per cent, due to the adoption of law proposals shifted from the previous period (www.seio.gov.rs). This is a remarkable improvement, though clearly the real problem is not in adopting legislation, but in implementing it effectively.

8.5.3 Economic integration

Serbia has also become increasingly integrated with the EU economy through a rapid increase in FDI, financial integration, and trade. Enterprises from EU member states have been the main investors in Serbia; only in 2007 net FDI from EU countries in Serbia were around €2.3 billion. The most important banks in Serbia are also from the EU, as described earlier (see Chapter 6). Trade has also increased significantly, after the EU granted autonomous trade preference to FR Yugoslavia in November 2000 (see Table 8.7).

By 2008, Serbia's exports and imports of goods and services to and from the EU increased to 54 per cent of Serbia's total exports and 53 per cent of its total imports, compared with 53 per cent and 49 per cent respectively in 2006. However, Serbia has had a large and increasing trade deficit with the EU (see Figure 8.2).

Serbia's main exports to the EU consist of agricultural products (sugar, raspberries, corn), tyres, iron, steel, and machinery, while the main goods imported from the EU are vehicles, diesel fuels, and medicaments. Despite increasing trade volumes after 2001, Serbia's exports structure has not changed substantially, as it continues to be dominated by

Table 8.7 Serbia's trade with the EU, 2000–8 (in € and in million US$)

Year	Value in thousands of EUR			Value in thousands of US$		
	Exports	Imports	Balance	Exports	Imports	Balance
2000	911,441	2,223,147	–1,311,706	848,834	2,054,164	–1,205,330
2001	1,103,796	2,739,547	–1,635,751	1,006,375	2,455,475	–1,449,100
2002	1,304,474	3,529,958	–2,225,484	1,234,913	3,350,336	–2,115,423
2003	1,315,518	3,842,160	–2,526,642	1,477,453	4,364,366	–2,886,913
2004	1,603,828	5,000,660	–3,396,832	1,998,149	6,238,611	–4,240,462
2005	2,116,272	4,577,138	–2,460,866	2,631,593	5,668,389	–3,036,796
2006	2,932,244	5,696,263	–2,764,019	3,692,132	7,175,712	–3,483,580
2007	3,602,784	7,437,797	–3,835,013	4,935,153	10,220,694	–5,285,541
2008	4,028,406	8,243,402	–4,214,996	5,953,520	12,188,903	–6,235,383

Source: Republicki zavod za statistiku Srbije (Serbian Office of Statistics).

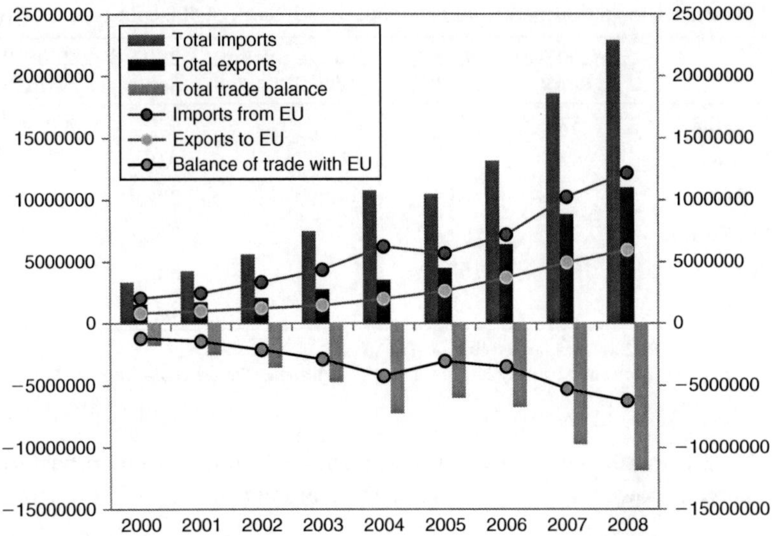

Figure 8.2 Serbia's trade, total and with the EU, 2001–8 (in thousand US$)

agricultural and low processed manufacturing products. Still, there was a sharp decline in food and animals (from 23% in 2001 to 15.3% in 2007) and an increase in industrial products (from 71.8% in 2001 to 74.2% in 2007). Within the category of industrial goods, the share of machines and transport equipment has remained roughly the same (around 14% both in 2001 and 2007), chemical products increased from 7.7 per cent in 2001 to 10.4 per cent in 2007, and finished products declined from 20.8 per cent in 2001 to 14.5 per cent in 2007, while the largest increase was registered in products classified by material (SMTC-6), from 29.3 per cent in 2001 to 35 per cent in 2007, but these are mainly various low processed manufactured products (Kovacevic, 2008, pp. 131–2).

Serbia's import structure has changed less during 2001–7. The Serbian economy remains dependent on imported minerals and energy (SMTC–3, over 17% of total imports in 2007, particularly oil). There was an increase in imports of machines and transport equipment (mainly cars), from 21 per cent in 2001 to 28.6 per cent in 2007 of total imports (Kovacevic, 2008, p. 133). The dominant products imported by Serbia are oil and gas, cars, and medicine.

According to the competitiveness index calculated by the World Economic Forum (see Table 8.8), Serbia has somewhat improved its position in recent years. From the 91st rank in 2007–8, it advanced to

Table 8.8 Global Competitiveness Index 2007–9: Rank of SEE countries

	2007–8 Rank	2008–9 Rank	Change in rank (2008–9/2007–8)	2007–8 Score	2008–9 Score
Croatia	57	61	−4	4.2	4.2
Montenegro	82	65	+17	3.9	4.1
Serbia	91	85	+6	3.8	3.9
Macedonia	94	89	+5	3.7	3.9
BiH	106	107	+1	3.6	3.6
Albania	109	108	+1	3.5	3.6

Note: The US in 2008–9 is ranked first, with a score 5.74.
Source: World Economic Forum (2008), *Global Competitiveness Report 2008–2009*.

the 85th in 2008–9. Serbia's relative position in the SEE region has not changed, however, since it remains third among the six SEE countries.

8.5.4 Visa regime

An extremely important recent achievement is the visa regime for Serbian citizens. The maintenance of visas has been highly counterproductive in Serbia, directly slowing down the process of democratization and EU integration.[15] The 2004 and 2007 EU enlargements have created further dividing lines, since some of the remaining visa-free travel regimes between the Western Balkan countries and the future new EU member states had to be eliminated (Uvalic, 2008).

The visa facilitation and readmission agreements between the EU and Serbia entered into force in January 2008, permitting a dialogue on visa liberalization. In May 2008 the Commission presented a roadmap on visa liberalization to Serbia. In September 2008 Serbia presented the Commission with a detailed report of measures undertaken in the framework of visa liberalization, including the issuing of new passports, identity cards, and licence plates in line with the highest EU and world standards (completed by the end of 2009). These measures were necessary in view of the debate over the issue of visas for Serbian citizens in Kosovo, and Kosovo citizens with Serbian passports. The EU Commission finally proposed, on 15 July 2009, visa-free travel to Schengen countries for citizens of three SEE countries – FYR Macedonia, Montenegro, and Serbia – confirmed on 30 November, which started being implemented at the end of December 2009.

The elimination of visas will have a number of positive effects, greatly facilitating travel, studying abroad, the re-establishment of business, and other contacts with EU member states. In December 2008, opinion polls in Serbia showed that 87 per cent of the respondents consider entering the White Schengen list is important for Serbia (www.seio.gov.rs). According to the opinion polls undertaken in May 2009, 85 per cent of the respondents indicated they have not travelled to a country where a visa is required in the past year (up from 80 per cent in May 2008).

8.5.5 Delays in signing the Stabilization and Association Agreement

Despite progress in all the discussed areas, contractual relations between Serbia and the EU have advanced extremely slowly. Two key issues have hampered a quicker intensification of relations between FR Yugoslavia and the EU. The first is regarding the difficult political relations between Serbia and Montenegro, described in detail in Chapter 5. The second concerns Serbia's cooperation with the Hague Tribunal. Both issues have involved specific EU conditions imposed on FRY/Serbia which have greatly delayed the signing of the SAA.

From 2001 onwards, the EU insisted on the maintenance of one state – first of the Yugoslav federation with its two republics (Serbia and Montenegro), and after 2003 of the State Union of Serbia and Montenegro. Such an EU stance delayed, quite substantially, Serbia's path towards the EU, perhaps as much as the other sensitive political issues. Although president Djukanovic wanted to organize a referendum on Montenegrin independence already in late 2000, under EU's pressure the referendum was postponed. Due to increasing tensions between Serbia and Montenegro, on 4 February 2003 FR Yugoslavia was transformed into the State Union of Serbia and Montenegro, which was not very functional. Montenegro pressed further for independence and finally, in May 2006, organized its popular referendum, which led to the establishment of two independent states in June 2006.

The EU Commission also insisted on the full harmonization of a number of economic laws, which already in 2001 were quite different in Serbia and Montenegro. Since FR Yugoslavia (later the State Union) was to remain one country, it was also to have a common market and the same foreign trade policy. One of the laws which proved impossible to fully harmonize was the foreign trade law, since in 2002 the average tariff in Montenegro was 3 per cent, while in Serbia it was still 9 per cent (Uvalic, 2002b). After a long and burdensome process of negotiations in 2002–3, most tariffs were harmonized, except for 56 agricultural products. An Action Plan on Harmonization of the Internal Market was adopted, but it ended up being a total failure. The process was stalled by the inability to find a mutually acceptable solution, since Serbia and Montenegro had very different economic interests. Unlike Montenegro, Serbia has strong interests in agriculture and thus was not willing to reduce tariffs on these agricultural products.

It was only in 2004 that the EU decided not to insist any longer on the harmonization of economic legislation, but to proceed with the 'twin track' approach – namely deal separately with the two republics on policies which Serbia and Montenegro conduct separately such as trade, economic, and sectoral policies, while continuing to work with the country as a whole where it is the State Union that is the competent authority (international political obligations or human rights). The change in the EU position allowed the re-launch of the Feasibility Report on an SAA with the State Union of Serbia and Montenegro, which was approved by the Council of Ministers on 25 April 2005.

On 3 October 2005, the European Council approved the beginning of negotiations on an SAA between the EU and Serbia and Montenegro, and negotiations started soon after separately with Serbia and with Montenegro. Again due to the insufficient collaboration with the ICTY, however, the signing of the SAA was postponed. In May 2006, negotiations on the SAA with the EU were called off again due to the lack of progress on Serbia's cooperation with the ICTY and a related government crisis.

Serbia finally signed the SAA and the Interim Agreement on trade and trade-related issues with the EU on 29 April 2008. As is standard practice, the SAA is to enter into force only after its ratification by the EU Council of Ministers, the European Parliament, Serbia, and all EU member states. Since the process of ratification of the SAA is a lengthy process, taking between two to three years, the Interim Agreement should provide Serbia access to most of the benefits of the SAA ahead of its ratification by EU member countries. The full liberalization of Serbia's trade with the EU should be completed by 2014.

However, in contrast with usual practice, this agreement could not be implemented, nor could the long process of ratification of the SAA commence, until EU member states agreed unanimously that Serbia is cooperating fully with the ICTY. This was the price of securing Dutch assent for the signing of the Serbian SAA. The arrest of Radovan Karadzic, a former Bosnian Serb leader, by Serbian authorities in July 2008 after nearly 13 years, drew EU praise for the new pro-Western government in Serbia. However, this was not enough to unfreeze the Interim EU Agreement, since the Netherlands insisted until recently that general Mladic also be delivered (Economist Intelligence Unit, 2009a).

The SAA with Serbia was signed immediately prior to the parliamentary elections, which greatly helped the Democratic Party-led pro-European coalition win the elections, illustrating how EU incentives can positively influence internal political processes. In the meantime, the Serbian parliament ratified the SAA on 9 September 2008. The Serbian government also decided, in October 2008, to implement the Interim Agreement as of January 2009, in order to demostrate its commitment to advance rapidly towards EU membership. As a result of Serbia's decision to start implementing the provisions of the Interim Agreement, the access of EU exporters to the Serbian market have substantially improved from the beginning of 2009.

Nevertheless, after the signing of the SAA Serbia has not been given a clear membership perspective, nor have the trade-related parts of the SAA (the Interim Agreement) been implemented by the EU. EU ministers agreed to submit the SAA to their parliaments for ratification and the EU agreed to implement the Interim Agreement, but only after the Council decides that Serbia is fully cooperating with the ICTY. This happened only on 7 December 2009, so the Interim Agreement finally entered into force on 1 February 2010.

The alleged insufficient collaboration of Serbia with the ICTY regarding the delivery of the people indicted for war crimes to The Hague is what was, as late as early December 2009, blocking the full implementation of the SAA, more than a year and a half after it has been signed. It is primarily the non-delivery of general Ratko Mladic to The Hague that is blocking faster progress of Serbia towards the EU, much more than lack of readiness to fulfil the other criteria. It ought to be stressed that Serbia has made significant progress in improving cooperation with the ICTY. In June 2008, Stojan Zupljanin was arrested near Belgrade and transferred to The Hague, in addition to Karadzic. Only two remaining fugitives, Ratko Mladic and Goran Hadzic, have not yet been arrested.

Considering Serbia is a key element of stability in the Balkan region, the political conditions that have blocked the full implementation of the SAA and its submission for ratification need to be reconsidered. If general Mladic has not yet been delivered to the ICTY, this does not mean that the Serbian government has not undertaken measures to find and arrest him. Mladic continues to be protected by the most nationalistic political forces in Serbia, but not by the majority in the present Serbian government. Capturing Mladic is not only a question of political will of the Serbian authorities, but also of the government's capacity to find him.[16] The government's capacity to arrest Mladic probably involves facing up the most reactionary forces within Serbia, that seem to have remained outside the government's control even after the tragic assassination of Zoran Djindjic in 2003. Addressing these issues is of fundamental importance for Serbia, irrespective of whether Mladic will ever be found.

Relations between the EU and Serbia have also been negatively affected by Kosovo's unilateral declaration of independence in February 2008. In October 2008, the UN General Assembly voted in favour of a resolution tabled by Serbia, seeking a non-binding advisory opinion from the International Court of Justice (ICJ) on the legality of the Kosovo declaration of independence. Serbia opposed the deployment of EULEX, the new EU justice and law mission in Kosovo, unless authorized by the UN Security Council. The EULEX officially became operational on 9 December 2008, but its deployment was delayed by six months owing to opposition from Serbia. Serbia demanded assurances that EULEX would be neutral as regards Kosovo's status and would not implement the plan of the former UN envoy Martti Ahtisaari for Kosovo's supervised independence (Economist Intelligence Unit, 2009a). Serbia received the assurances it sought when the UN Security Council adopted a six-point plan for the reconfiguration of the UNMIK, which envisaged the deployment of EULEX under the status-neutral umbrella of the UN. The EULEX deployment was preceded by demonstrations in Pristina, against what was seen by many Kosovo Albanians as a rollback of Kosovo's independence. In Serbia, some opposition parties (Kostunica's DSS) also remain strongly opposed to the EULEX deployment. In any case, scepticism remains about EULEX and the prospects of stabilizing Kosovo (Economist Intelligence Unit, 2009a).

According to recent opinion polls in Serbia, the main reason for the slow progress in Serbia's integration with the EU is the continuing policy of conditionality. In late 2008, there was a general perception – 62 per cent of the respondents – that the EU constantly imposes new conditions for accession of Serbia to the EU, thereby placing Serbia in an unfavourable situation with respect to the other countries (www.seio.gov.rs). As many as 47 per cent of the respondents, however, do consider acceptable the EU condition of completion of the cooperation process with the Hague Tribunal. Moreover, as indicated earlier, in May 2009, almost 70 per cent of the surveyed were in favour of Serbia joining the EU.

8.6 Preparing for EU membership

Almost seven years since perspectives of EU membership were promised to the Western Balkan countries at the Thessaloniki summit in 2003, it's time for 'Thessaloniki 2' (Teokarevic, 2009). The primary responsibility for speeding up the current EU integration and accession process of the Western Balkans lies with the countries themselves. As was the case with the CEE countries, the Balkan countries also need to meet the accession criteria set by the EU in order to be invited to join the EU-27. However, a large part of the responsibility also lies with the EU. While the countries concerned should speed up their compliance with EU membership criteria which is also to their own benefit, the EU should speed up the process of their integration and accession.

Although political conditionality will necessarily remain the main EU instrument for implementing its policy objectives, it should be applied in a flexible way in order not to undermine the attainment of other important objectives. Given the very different stages of EU integration of the individual Balkan countries, the EU needs to demonstrate a stronger commitment to their future EU integration, offering additional incentives particularly to 'potential candidates' – Albania, Bosnia and Herzegovina, Montenegro, Serbia, and Kosovo under UN Security Council Resolution 1244.[17] The current rather uncertain prospects of EU membership may not be sufficient as an anchor to the reform process.

One way to strengthen incentives for the countries lagging behind is to change their status from potential candidates into candidates, without necessarily proceeding with negotiations on EU membership. Such a change in status would automatically enable them to have access to all five components of the IPA, which would be extremely important for their economic development. Despite strong growth in the Balkan countries over the 2001–8 period, which has permitted some catching up with respect to the EU average income, the process has been very slow and has been interrupted by the global economic crisis, that has severely affected all SEE countries from mid-2008 onwards. Except for Croatia, at 63 per cent of the EU-27 average in 2008, all the other Balkan countries are much further behind. Accepting all Western Balkan countries as EU candidates would also represent a strong political message that the EU is committed to their European future.[18]

A further measure to improve the accession framework for the Western Balkans could consist of defining a matrix of more articulated conditionality linked specifically to the negotiating chapters of the *acquis* (the 'stick'), together with a programme similar to the 'Agenda 2000'[19] that would provide the Western Balkan countries more substantial resources for infrastructure (the 'carrot') (Travaglino, 2009, p. 174). A new mechanism capable of connecting even more directly the reforms undertaken in the Western Balkan countries with a visible and clear advancement in European integration needs to be worked out (Teokarevic, 2009). The EU should also launch a major campaign to raise public opinion awareness in the EU member states about the benefits of enlargement to the Western Balkans.

The alternative scenario of the continuation of the *status quo*, without clear commitments on their EU entry, risks a reversal in progress achieved so far. Political will must therefore be employed to accelerate the EU–Balkan integration process. The EU enlargement to the Balkan region, with its 20 million inhabitants and economies which are already strongly integrated with the EU, could be absorbed by the EU relatively easily. Although unanimity for the most important decisions in the EU now implies that any state can block decisions regarding enlargement (and other issues, such as the budget), the entry of the small Balkan countries is unlikely to significantly change the present power relations within the EU.

Letting the Western Balkan countries into the EU would help resolve some of the remaining political problems in the SEE region, thus contributing to more permanent stability in the Balkans. Although EU membership is not a magic wand, the easiest way to overcome existing tensions over borders, status, statehood, refugees, minority rights, and sovereignty, is to let the Western Balkan countries join the EU as soon as possible. This is the safest way to secure lasting peace and stability in the Balkans, and more generally in Europe. After two decades of continuous fragmentation of the Balkan region, their entry into the EU would contribute to a further unification of Europe.

9
The Way to a Better Future: Remaining Challenges

The global financial and economic crisis of 2008–9 that began in August 2007 with the sub-prime loans crisis in the US, affected Serbia very seriously, but with a delay of over a year. Like most countries in Eastern Europe, Serbia initially seemed resilient to the global financial crisis, but from mid-2008 it began to feel the effects very strongly. With the global financial and economic crisis, what emerged to the surface was not only the fragility of Serbia's economy, due to the model of credit-driven growth and the resulting high dependence on capital inflows from abroad. The global economic crisis also revealed more general flaws of the transition strategy pursued in Serbia after 2001.

The global economic crisis hit Serbia at a moment when many economic problems were becoming unsustainable. For years consumption has been much higher than production and has been financed by foreign savings and investment, there has been an increasing trade account deficit, huge and increasing unemployment, limited enterprise restructuring, insufficient growth of the new private sector, mounting problems of many state-owned enterprises, and inadequate structural changes that had favoured primarily the fast expansion of services. The global economic crisis therefore raises the question whether the economic model pursued in Serbia after 2001 has been the best among the feasible policy options.

This concluding chapter will discuss the effects of the global financial and economic crisis on the Serbian economy and prospects for the future. In view of the strong impact of the crisis, it will consider the critical elements of the transition model pursued by the Serbian government after 2001, the new conceptual framework emerging as a consequence of the global crisis, and possible blueprints for Serbia's policies in the future. The chapter will conclude by considering the specific features of Serbia's 20-year transition and remaining challenges for a better future.

9.1 The strong impact of the global financial and economic crisis

The global financial and economic crisis has seriously affected Serbia through similar transmission channels as in other Central and Southeast European countries (Uvalic, 2009a). Serbia was also hit primarily by two external shocks – the greatly reduced capital inflows from abroad and the collapse of export demand. By the end of 2008, the Serbian economy was deeply affected by the credit crunch on international financial markets, declining FDI, and the sharp reduction in export demand in the EU as its main trading partner (Prica and Uvalic, 2009).

Although Serbia is not yet a member of the EU, its economy has become increasingly integrated with the other European economies through trade, FDI, financial flows, and the banking system, today prevalently owned by large European multinational banks. Since 2001, the Serbian economy has grown fast, but it relied heavily on the influx of foreign capital – official financial assistance, foreign investment, foreign loans, and emigrants' remittances – to cover its increasing current account deficit, which by late 2008 was one of the highest in the entire transition region (see Figure 9.1). During 2001–8, internal demand grew by an annual average growth rate

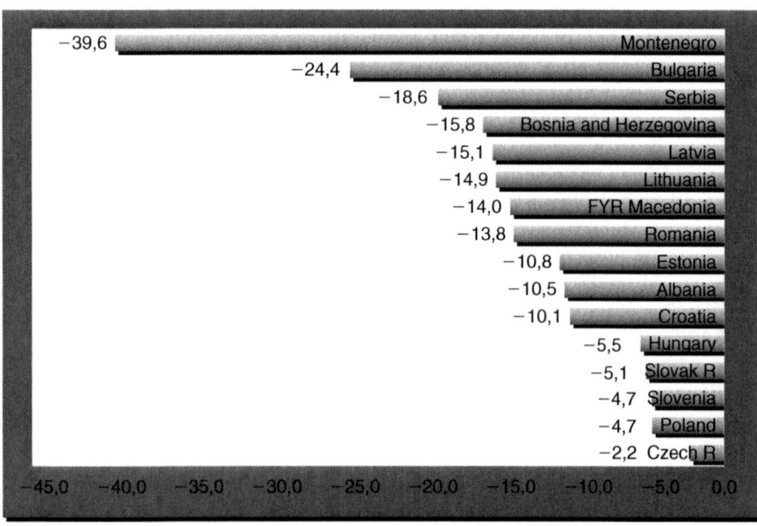

Figure 9.1 Current account deficits in Central and Southeast Europe, October 2008 (in % of GDP)

Source: Compiled on the basis of data of the IMF World Economic Outlook, October 2008.

of 7.5 per cent, therefore much faster than GDP which registered an average annual growth of 5.4 per cent.

Like many other countries in the region, Serbia has also implemented a growth model based on a strong credit boom, as foreign-owned domestic banks have extended an enormous amount of loans to local clients, especially to households. Domestic credit to the private sector almost doubled in five years, increasing from 21 per cent of GDP in 2003 to 39.7 per cent of GDP in 2008. The increase in domestic credit was particularly marked in the case of households – from only 2.6 per cent of GDP in 2003, it went up to 13.9 per cent of GDP in 2008 – of which mortgage lending represented 5.7 per cent of GDP (EBRD, 2009, p. 218). In per capita terms, household debt in Serbia increased from only €12 in 2001 to over €580 at the end of 2008 (Jelasic and Eric-Jovic, 2009).

The effects of the global financial and economic crisis began to be felt in Serbia from mid-2008 onwards (Ministarstvo Finansija Vlade Srbije, 2008). The banking sector was affected by reduced foreign capital inflows and the abrupt halt in cross-border credits from foreign sources. This caused a sharp fall in banks' lending activity and brought the first withdrawals of foreign currency deposits, in the last quarter of 2008 amounting to over €1 billion (Petrovic, 2009). By late 2008, there was a very sharp fall in credit availability. The increment of total credit dropped from € 2210 million in the third quarter of 2008, to only €287 million in the last quarter, while domestic credit, at the level of €1193 million in the third quarter, became negative (–€29 million) in the last quarter (Petrovic, 2009).

The dinar exchange rate was under pressure already from early October 2008. In order to prevent the withdrawal of foreign currency deposits, in October 2008 the NBS raised the guaranteed level of savings deposits from a low €3000 to €50,000. The NBS also tried to defend the exchange rate by selling foreign currency, which led to a monetary contraction and rapid fall in foreign exchange reserves, but without preventing the depreciation of the dinar. From 1 October 2008 until the peak on 30 January 2009, the dinar depreciated strongly (from €1 = RSD 76 to €1 = RSD 96), followed by a period of high volatility (until end-April), some appreciation (May–June) and stabilization in the autumn of 2009, at around €1 = RSD 94.

The NBS overall foreign exchange reserves, which reached a peak at the end of 2007 of over US$ 16 billion, by the end of 2008 declined to less than US$ 13 billion. In the meantime they have recovered and were again over US$ 15.6 billion at the end of September 2009 (www.nbs.rs). The NBS initially also tried to tighten monetary policy by increasing the reference interest rate on deposits in October 2008 (from 15.75 per cent to 17.75 per cent), but this measure had no effect (this was to be expected, since higher interest rates cannot bring back capital in a recession). Expectations of further depreciation led to increasing euroization. In the meantime, fiscal policy remained expansionary, particularly in the last quarter of 2008.

In addition to problems in the financial sector, Serbia also experienced a substantial fall in FDI inflows. In comparison to net FDI inflows of US$ 2.36 billion in 2008, similar to the amount received in 2007, during the first nine months of 2009 net FDI inflows were down to US$ 1.26 billion (www.nbs.rs). This is in line with a remarkable drop in FDI predicted on the global scale (Kekic, 2009a).

The sharp reduction of credit availability to enterprises and households was almost immediately transmitted to Serbia's real sector, with a sharp contraction in production and aggregate demand. Although real GDP for the whole of 2008 grew by 5.4 per cent, this was much lower than in 2007 and was mainly due to high growth in the earlier part of the year. Industrial production during August–December 2008 declined by some 15 per cent, while the fall was even sharper in processing industry that provides the dominant part of Serbian exports (see Figure 9.2). The trend of declining industrial production continued in early 2009 reaching the lowest point in April, when it was almost 20 per cent lower than in August 2008.

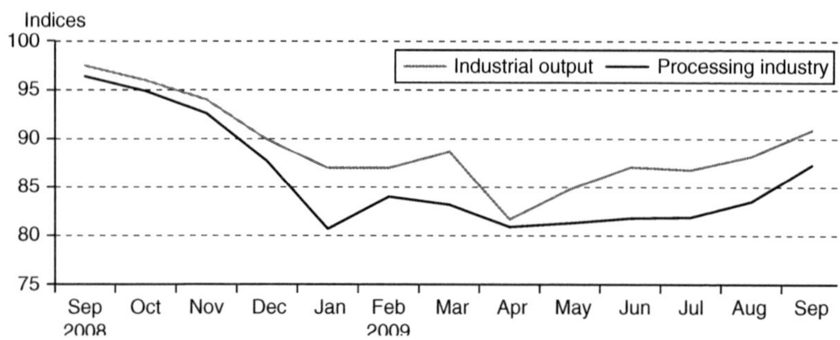

Figure 9.2 Serbia: Industrial output (seasonally adjusted data, 2008 = 100)
Source: Jelasic and Eric-Jovic (2009).

Foreign trade followed a similar declining trend. During the last quarter of 2008, exports dropped by 24 per cent and imports by 26 per cent. The contraction in exports stopped in January 2009 and thereafter stagnated, but imports continued to decline (see Figure 9.3). With falling exports and imports, the current account deficit in 2009 is likely to be greatly reduced, to less than 7 per cent of GDP (Economist Intelligence Unit, 2009b).

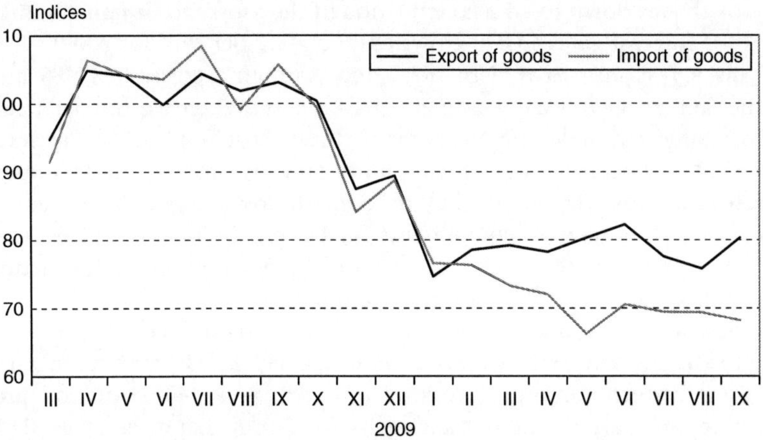

Figure 9.3 Serbia's foreign trade (seasonally adjusted data, 2008 = 100)
Source: Jelasic and Eric-Jovic (2009).

In the second half of 2008, there was a slowdown in all economic sectors except agriculture. A further deterioration was registered during the first two months of 2009, when all sectors except agriculture and services registered negative growth (see Figure 9.4). Since the beginning of 2009, estimates of annual GDP growth have been revised downwards continuously, overall by some 7–8 percentage points. While in mid-January 2009 a positive 3.5 per cent was still announced by some Serbian government officials, in October 2009 the estimated GDP

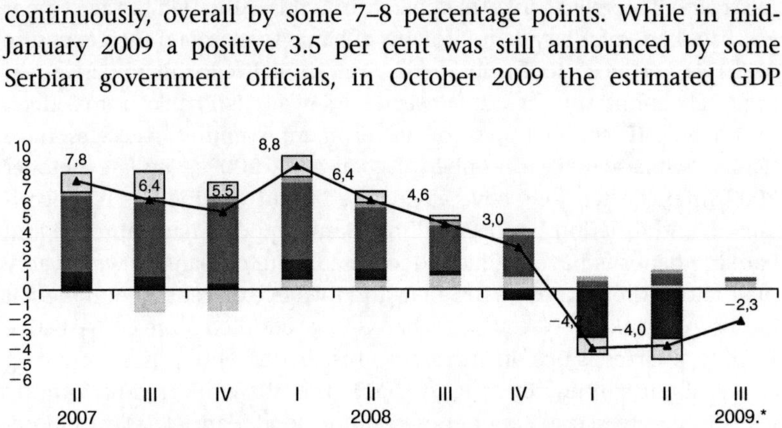

Figure 9.4 Contribution to year-on-year GDP growth in Serbia (in %)
Source: Jelasic and Eric-Jovic (2009).

growth was down to –4 per cent (though the most recent January 2010 EBRD forecast gives a GDP growth rate of –3.1 per cent for 2009).

As a response to the financial and economic crisis, the NBS and the Serbian government implemented a comprehensive financial sector support programme and several stimulus packages. The measures included subsidized loans for liquidity and investment, lower interest rates on banks' credits for buying domestic durable goods, relaxation of some NBS reserve requirements for banks, the bailing out of large firms, rescheduling of enterprise debt obligations, public infrastructure projects, and measures to stimulate employment.

Serbia also asked for support from the IMF. In January 2009, the IMF mission and the Serbian government reached a first agreement, on a 15-month economic programme supported by a €402.5 million precautionary SBA for strengthening its foreign exchange reserves. This arrangement was replaced by a new 27-month SBA, whose terms were broadly agreed in March 2009. On 15 May 2009, the Executive Board of the IMF completed the first review of Serbia's performance under the SBA and increased IMF support to about €2.942 billion (US$4 billion), equivalent to 560 percent of Serbia's quota or close to 10 per cent of its GDP. The IMF extended the SBA by one year to mid-April 2011.

In addition to substantial financial support, in early May 2009 the IMF also sponsored the so-called Vienna Initiative, which ensured an agreement with 31 foreign banks that operate in Serbia. Although the agreement was based on voluntary commitments of banks to maintain their exposure to Serbia and keep their subsidiaries well capitalized, this initiative was important for preventing capital withdraws by foreign banks from Serbia.

Timely IMF support and the government stimulus packages have helped Serbia achieve a number of goals (IMF, 2009c). By late October 2009 financial tensions have eased, the output decline has been contained, and inflation has been falling. Bank liquidity has improved and banking deposits have gradually recovered. Foreign banks have broadly maintained their exposure to Serbia and the large current account deficit has been shrinking. Nevertheless banks have adopted more conservative lending policies, since an increasing number of enterprises are facing financial difficulties. By August 2009, the share of non-performing loans has increased to about 10 per cent of total loans (Jelasic and Eric-Jovic, 2009). The most recent IMF forecast gives a GDP decline of 3 per cent in 2009, with a modest recovery of 1.5 per cent in 2010.

Owing to the sharp fall in output, government revenues have been lower than expected, which will probably lead to the non-fulfilment of the fiscal deficit target in 2009 (though all the other targets under the

IMF programme have been met). In early November 2009, an agreement with the IMF was reached to raise the fiscal deficit target to 4.5 per cent of GDP and to aim at a 4 per cent fiscal deficit in 2010 (IMF, 2009d). The latter goal requires maintenance of most of the fiscal measures put in place in 2009, such as the freeze in public sector wages and pensions. Several structural reforms have been announced by the Serbian government in the areas of public employment and pensions.

The structural reforms will be very difficult to implement and are bound to be highly unpopular. The envisaged cuts in public sector employment, the closing down of insolvent enterprises, and the further restructuring of state-owned firms will inevitably lead to further increases in unemployment and closure of unviable enterprises. In view of these demanding tasks and other important areas of reform to be completed, Serbia may not be able to benefit fully from the economic recovery of the more developed EU economies and return to its path of strong economic growth. This is why the Serbian government must seriously consider its policy options for the future.

9.2 Serbia's transition model: Lessons *not* learnt

Following the radical turn in the course of transition in Serbia after the October 2000 political changes, most economic reforms of the 'first generation' have been completed, while progress has been slower in areas more difficult to implement similarly as in other transition countries, like the development of the stock exchange, setting up of non-banking financial institutions, or reforms of infrastructure. Over the last eight years, Serbia's institutional model has converged to the other transition and post-transition countries, as its EBRD transition scores today are close to or at the level of the 2009 average for all 29 EBRD transition countries (see Figure 9.5).

This could lead to the conclusion that Serbia's transition path has been quite similar to that of other countries in transition, the main difference being that in Serbia it was implemented a decade later. This interpretation is only partly correct, since it disregards other important features of Serbia's transition. There are a number of similarities between Serbia's post-2001 transition strategy and those implemented in a large majority of CEE countries in the 1990s, but also important differences.

The principal similarity lies in the initial reform package, which in Serbia in 2001 also included the main elements typical of the hyper-liberal model, in line with the prescriptions of the 'Washington consensus' (see Chapters 5 and 6). The Serbian transition strategy focused on macroeconomic stabilization, the liberalization of prices

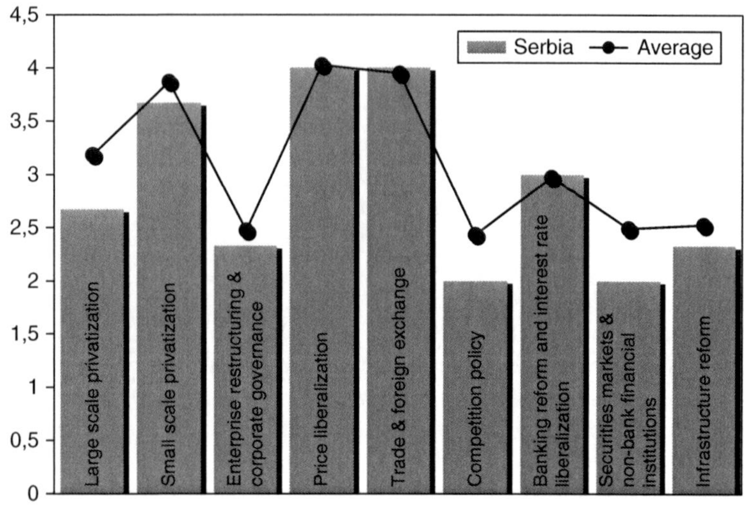

Figure 9.5 EBRD transition indicators: Serbia and average scores of all EBRD countries, 2009
Source: EBRD transition indicators (www.ebrd.org), November 2009.

and of the foreign trade system, exchange rate stability, current account convertibility, and substantial fiscal reforms, including the introduction of a flat-tax rate on personal income. The strategy relied on privatization of a large number of socially owned enterprises that were to be sold in a relatively short period of time to strategic owners. Financial sector reforms were also important, which began with the restructuring of the banking system in 2001–2 and accelerated after 2006, with the privatization of almost the entire banking sector sold to foreign banks and substantial liberalization of interest rates. The institutional framework based on the liberalization of markets, in a stable macroeconomic environment in which enterprises are assigned clear property rights through privatization, was supposed to lead to quick economic recovery and capacity restructuring.

The differences in Serbia with respect to the more successful transition economies regard both the specific contents and speed of implementation of some of these reforms. Since transition in Serbia in 2001 was identified primarily with liberalization, stabilization, and privatization, the new agenda of the 'post-Washington consensus' was ignored. The main elements of the 'post-Washington consensus' emerged in the second half of the1990s, in part based on the Polish experience (Kolodko and Nuti, 1997; Kolodko, 1999). The new consensus stressed the importance of the 'organic' growth of the private sector through the expansion of *de novo* enterprises, not just privatization of existing firms; the importance of corporate governance, as opposed to the sheer transfer of property titles; and the negative consequences of neglect or discriminatory penalization of the state sector. A reassessment of policies in a number of transition countries also indicated very high costs, in terms of slower growth, of excessively restrictive macroeconomic policies, or of sterilization policies (Kolodko and Nuti, 1997, pp. 49–52).

At a time when the invisible hand of the market continued to be glorified, the post-Washington consensus stressed the new role of the state and active government policies, not just *less* government but *a different role* of the government. In particular, the importance of industrial policy was pointed out, for example in promoting investment in certain sectors, improving access to credit for small and medium enterprises, encouraging innovation, or in introducing and protecting quality and technical standards. If a country has *no* industrial policy, its industrial policy will simply be the residual of other policies, for example liberalized foreign trade, high interests rates, and an appreciating real exchange rate (Kolodko and Nuti, 1997, p. 38). Such a 'residual industrial policy' can be detrimental for industrial sectors requiring protection if tariffs are lowered excessively, or can prevent new investment and modernization of key industrial sectors, as indeed has been the case in Serbia.

Serbia in 2001 had the advantage of being able to learn from the rich experience with transition gained in CEE in the 1990s, an advantage that was not sufficiently utilized. If we recall our analysis in Chapter 7, which provided ample evidence on limited enterprise restructuring and slow growth of the private sector in Serbia, this can indeed be attributed to the neglect or substantial delays in implementing policy measures that should have accompanied privatization from the very start and that could have delivered some of the benefits expected from privatization. These complementary reforms stressed by the 'new Washington consensus' – including competition policy, hardening of budget constraints, and effective corporate governance – were known at the end of the 1990s, yet they were not sufficiently considered in Serbia in 2001.

Why were some of the messages of the 'post-Washington consensus' not taken into account in Serbia in 2001? The long-awaited political changes in late 2000 finally opened the doors for a fundamental change of the unreformed economic system, where the hyper-liberal model seemed the safest way to radically break with the past. It should also be recalled that in 2001 the international financial institutions were guiding quite closely economic reforms in Serbia, not least because of

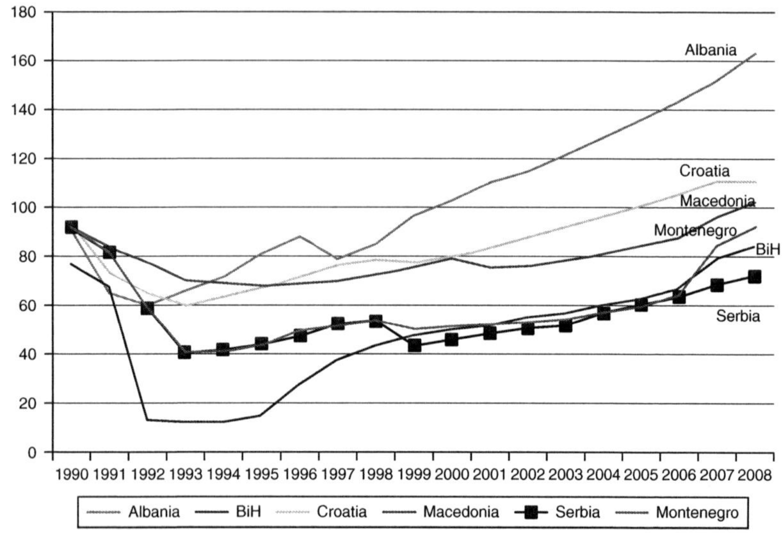

Figure 9.6 Real GDP growth in Serbia and SEE countries, 1990–2008 (1989 = 100)
Source: Based on EBRD (www.ebrd.org), November 2009.

the government's high dependence on their financial and technical assistance (see Chapter 5). The adoption of the hyper-liberal package of reforms was therefore to a great extent intentional. What was not necessarily intentional was the neglect of other reforms that were substantially delayed, whether due to too many tasks on the government agenda, ideological rejection, or simply naïve conviction that the simple recipe – liberalize, stabilize, and privatize – would be sufficient to stimulate restructuring, modernization, and increasing enterprise efficiency.

One of the main consequences of various policy failures in Serbia is that it has still not made much progress in catching up with the EU average income. Serbia remains one of the transition countries in the worst position regarding its present level of GDP as compared to 20 years ago. In 2008, Serbia was still almost 30 per cent below its 1989 GDP level, in the worst position among all SEE countries (see Figure 9.6). Though this gap may be an over-estimate, it is indicative of Serbia's relative underdevelopment and slow process of catching up (Uvalic, 2009c).

9.3 The emerging new policy framework

In reconsidering its future transition course, Serbia ought to take into account the emerging new policy framework. The global crisis of 2008–9 has set in motion a new transition in advanced market economies, towards a reconsideration and revaluation of the role of the state, of active fiscal and monetary policy – right down to zero, and even negative, nominal interest rates, in place of the previous dogma of positive real rates – and government regulation and control, especially of financial markets (Nuti, 2009a). The policy responses to the crisis of Western governments have consisted in major support programmes of the financial sector in the form of bailing out banks and their nationalizations, together with major stimulus packages to the real sector through expansionary fiscal policies. Within the EU, fiscal policies in 2009 have been expansionary to such an extent that by early October 2009, 18 of the 27 EU member states were no longer able to respect the fiscal obligations set by the EU Stability and Growth Pact.

All post-socialist economies will have to adjust their transition course towards these new, moving targets, often undoing some institutional developments that had been regarded as important transition achievements (Nuti, 2009a, 2009c). Countries that by the old standards have achieved the transition to the market economy successfully and fast, will now have to reconsider where they have arrived and where they want to go next. We are witnessing the emergence of a new consensus which goes beyond even the 'post-Washington consensus' in its emphasis of the important role of the state and active economic policies.

An unexpected change in policy prescriptions of the major international organizations – such as the EBRD or the IMF – has also taken place. The EBRD President, Thomas Mirow, warns that 'The region will need to change its growth model – away from reliance on easy finance and commodities, towards the development of domestic financial markets, strong institutions and a diversified production base' (Wagstyl (2009), *Financial Times*, 28 September). As observed by Nuti (2009a), quite uncharacteristically, the IMF has recommended easing monetary policy and lowering interest rates to advanced economies experiencing the global recession and has also called for 'a timely, large, lasting, diversified fiscal stimulus' (Nuti, 2009a). Consequently, the IMF could not but recommend the same policies to transition economies in crisis, though along with stronger warnings about the negative side effects of exceeding fiscal deficits.

Since conditions imposed by the IMF on many transition and developing countries, as part of SBAs, have frequently been criticized as responsible for the deeper than necessary recessions (Stiglitz, 2002), the IMF has recently tried to revise its conditionality policy. In late March 2009, the IMF announced a major overhaul of its lending and conditionality framework (IMF, 2009a). 'Modernizing conditionality' is among the key elements of the new IMF policy framework[1] which has been described as follows: 'The IMF aims to ensure that conditions linked to IMF loan disbursements are focused and adequately tailored to the varying strengths of members' policies and fundamentals. … This modernization is to be achieved by relying more on pre-set qualification criteria (ex-ante conditionality) rather than on traditional (ex post) conditionality. In addition, structural reforms will from now on be monitored in the context of program reviews, rather than through the use of structural performance criteria' (IMF, 2009a, p. 3).

The global financial and economic crisis has also put into doubt the transition model pursued in Serbia after 2001, as it has brought to the surface many problems which have accumulated during these last eight years. Some key policymakers in Serbia are fully aware that the current model is no longer viable, like the 2009 governor of the NBS (who resigned in March 2010): 'High GDP growth rates, based on sizeable growth of non-tradables and driven by domestic demand (high wages, credit boom and foreign borrowing) is no longer viable. The decline in domestic demand cannot be substituted fully by additional government borrowing. Prior economic growth can be restored only if export-driven. To have an export-driven economic growth, we need to cut current and increase investment budgetary spending. Without a GDP increase of at least 5 per cent annually, foreign debt financing is not sustainable in the medium and long term. … We also need a competitive labor force, a good infrastructure, a stable political and macroeconomic environment, and strong strategic partners' (Jelasic and Eric-Jovic, 2009). Irrespective of whether the growth model based on financial globalization and capital inflows has been irrevocably broken or could be revived, finding an appropriate set of policies for Serbia during the next few years will not be an easy task.

9.4 Transition towards where? Some blueprints for Serbia

Factors that have made transition economies vulnerable to the global financial and economic crisis, including trade openness, economic and financial integration, are precisely the factors that will reinforce recovery trends when the global economy recovers (Nuti, 2009b). In the case of Serbia, however, there are reasons why its economy may receive limited benefits from the incipient global recovery.

The first reason is that Serbia, in comparison to most CEE and SEE countries, is not a very open economy. The remarkable increase in Serbia's exports after 2001 has also led to a gradual increase in its trade/GDP ratio, from about 54 per cent in 2003 to 68 per cent in 2007, but this is still very low in comparison to the 2007 trade/GDP ratio of Hungary (159%), Bulgaria (149%), Slovenia (141%), Macedonia (129%, Croatia (96%), or even one of the least open East European economies, Romania (73%) (Republicki zavod za razvoj Srbije, 2009). Serbia's exports in 2007 represented only 22 per cent of its GDP, again substantially lower than those of Hungary (80%), Slovenia (70 per cent), or Croatia (44 per cent), thus much more similar to those of some old EU member states, including Italy and France.

The second reason is that FDI inflows, a major factor contributing to Serbia's recent growth, are likely to be substantially lower, as already confirmed by a substantial decline of FDI in 2009 with respect to 2008 reported earlier. Despite remaining privatization opportunities, the growth model largely driven by FDI will not be available to Serbia over the next few years. The global economic and financial crisis has had a major impact on recent FDI flows. After declining in 2008 by 17 per cent to US$1.73 trillion (from US$2.09 trillion in 2007, the high point of a four-year long boom in cross-border mergers and acquisitions and FDI), global FDI inflows are forecast to plunge by 44 per cent to less than US$1 trillion in 2009, despite the improvements in the global economy in recent months (Kekic, 2009a).

This is why the Serbian government will need to tackle a number of problems before the global upturn can be expected to pull its economy out of recession or stagnation. The Serbian government must use this occasion to consider the implications of the shortcomings of the post-2001 transition strategy. In particular, it must address those problems which became evident before the outburst of the current economic crisis, related to the increasing trade and current account deficit and insufficient restructuring and modernization of a large part of the real sector of the economy (see Chapters 6 and 7). Given Serbia's low export base, a largely non-modernized manufacturing industry which provides the dominant part of exports, and its undersized private sector, perhaps economic closeness could be used to its advantage, serving for achieving much faster growth in the future. The government should re-examine both its macroeconomic policies and its longer-term transition objectives.

9.4.1 Macroeconomic policies

Macroeconomic policies in Serbia after 2001 have produced important results, primarily substantial macroeconomic stabilization, an objective of particular importance for a country that has experienced hyperinflation since the late 1980s. This has been achieved primarily through prudent monetary policies, while fiscal policies have remained expansionary. Through restrictive monetary policies, the Serbian government has progressively reduced inflation to a one-digit figure. At present, there is probably room to somewhat relax monetary policy, especially in view of the highly recessionary impact of restrictive monetary policy in recent years in Serbia (Labus, 2009).

As shown by recent econometric evidence, the risk of the return of inflation in Serbia has been substantially reduced: the pass-through from the exchange rate to prices is much lower than in the 1990s, inflationary inertia has decreased, and a policy regime change towards credibly low inflation does seem to have occurred (Mladenovic and Petrovic, 2009). Indeed, despite substantial depreciation of the dinar since autumn 2008, inflation has declined further in 2009. These adjustments of the exchange rate in Serbia have reduced the costs of the current economic crisis, in comparison with countries with more rigid exchange rate regimes, like the Baltic states or Bulgaria. The most recent changes in monetary policy have indeed moved in the direction of relaxing monetary policy, with the lowering of the key policy rate by one per cent, from 11 per cent in September 2009 to 10 per cent in early November.

Restrictive monetary policies, which have provided appreciation of the domestic currency particularly after 2006, have frequently been blamed for the poor export performance of the Serbian economy. The recent depreciation of the dinar should, in principle, facilitate increasing exports of Serbian enterprises once the EU economy fully recovers from the ongoing crisis, but more permanent improvements in export performance must be sought in other types of measures. The Serbian government must concentrate on the more fundamental problems of the real sector and the related aspects of institutional reforms that have not yet been implemented successfully.

While monetary policy has been restrictive, fiscal policies since 2001 have remained expansionary (see Figure 9.7). Despite good results obtained in the reduction of the fiscal deficit, even its transformation into a surplus (as seen in Chapter 6), public expenditure has remained a high percentage of the increasing GDP and its structure has not changed substantially, characterized by high spending on various types of transfers.

The Serbian government has done little to address the structural problems of budgetary expenditure, primarily very high spending on pensions, health, and education. In late September 2009, the Serbian government convened a working group for reforming the pensions system that should come up with concrete proposals. A new draft pension law was planned to be ready for submission to the Serbian parliament in December 2009. In launching more radical reforms in these areas, Serbia must not forget the experience of other transition countries, which

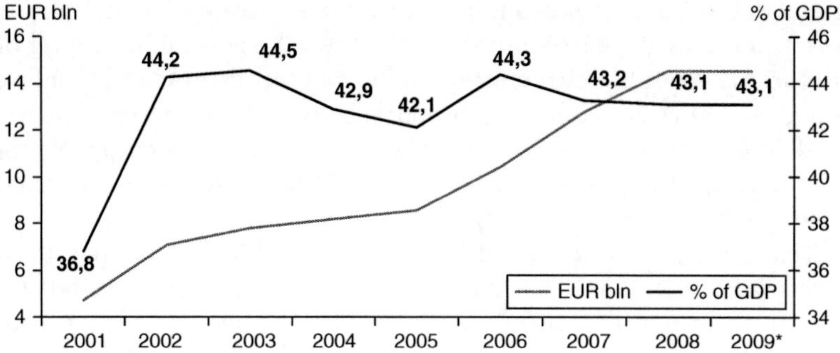

Figure 9.7 Public expenditure in Serbia, 2001–8
Source: Jelasic and Eric-Jovic (2009).

frequently have uncritically adopted solutions that have been costly and inefficient (Eatwell et al., 2000). The Serbian government must also avoid other types of mistakes, such as reducing excessively the size of the state below the essential minimum, as has been the case in some SEE countries like Albania or Macedonia.

State-owned (public) enterprises are another major problem presently on the agenda of the Serbian government. Most of these enterprises have not been corporatized, not many have been restructured or privatized, while some have been incurring enormous losses requiring continuous state subsidies (see Chapter 7). The ongoing economic crisis has worsened the prospects of privatizing the more viable state firms through sales to foreign investors. Nevertheless all state-owned enterprises will need to be corporatized, restructured, and recapitalized, and not necessarily through sales of majority stakes to foreign investors. Another problem is the unsold socially owned enterprises, including those earmarked for restructuring, that have also been kept afloat with the help of government subsidies, but this is a minor problem in comparison to the huge state sector. Instead of closing them down, the government could give them free of charge, possibly along with a one-off start-up loan, to workers willing to take them over, as has been done frequently throughout CEE (Uvalic and Vaughan-Whitehead 1997).

9.4.2 Transition-related reforms: Strengthening institutions

In some areas of institutional reforms, the results in Serbia have been below expectations. To a large extent, this is because some fundamental reforms have not accompanied liberalization, stabilization, and privatization, which are essential for improving the institutional framework of a market economy – including measures facilitating the entry and growth of new private enterprises, the general hardening of budget constraints, restructuring public enterprises instead of bailing them out, effective competition policy, active labour market policies, and improvements in corporate governance (see Chapter 7). Serbia will need to strengthen many of its institutions that are fundamental elements of a market economy.

That institutions are a critical dimension of transition has been stressed for at least a decade (Stiglitz, 1997). A special emphasis today is put on the *quality* of institutions, in the first place government institutions, in enforcing laws, collecting taxes, or supervising the financial sector (Berglof and Zettelmeyer, 2009). The quality of institutions is important also with respect to non-state institutions. Markets will not function well if they are not competitive and if there are barriers to entry. Corporations will not function well if corporate governance is poor and minority investors are not protected. These differences are driven by the presence (or absence), and the quality of supporting state institutions, such as a functioning legal system to enforce contractual obligations, or competition authorities to ensure a competitive market structure. 'In sum, transition should be about redefining the state as opposed to simply minimising it, and improving the quality of both state and private institutions' (Berglof and Zettelmeyer, 2009, p. 4).

These issues are extremely relevant also for Serbia, particularly today when transition policies must be carefully reconsidered. The Serbian government also needs to redefine the role of the state and improve the quality of its state and non-state institutions. The restructuring of a large part of the real sector of the Serbian economy has not taken place because of a number of policy failures on the part of the government, not because of market failures. Some important reforms were deliberately postponed since they were regarded secondary, while others were neglected because positive changes were expected as a by-product of liberalized market conditions.

9.4.3 A new role of the state

In order to define a new and better role of the state and devise appropriate government policies for the future, it seems appropriate to start from the most fundamental problem of the Serbian economy: the insufficient restructuring and modernization of large segments of the Serbian economy. The slow restructuring at both the micro and macroeconomic level has contributed to inadequate competitiveness of enterprises on foreign markets thus increasing external imbalances, to an undersized private sector, to high unemployment, and economic growth below potential. In view of all these problems, three areas of closely related economic policies seem particularly important for Serbia today: industrial policy, employment policy, and R&D policy.

1. Serbia needs an *industrial policy*. Such a policy should not involve the government in 'picking winners' in the sense of arbitrary support for individual enterprises, but rather in picking winning sectors or winning typology of enterprises – export oriented, innovative, or high value-added firms – in line with the current EU policy for enhancing competitiveness. The Serbian government cannot count on increasing FDI in a climate where FDI is predicted to fall by some 40–50 per cent at the global scale. Even if and when FDI picks up, judging from the experience of the last eight years it is highly unlikely that foreign firms will take up the modernization of large parts of the Serbian industry. It is the government that needs to implement measures to facilitate enterprise restructuring, to strengthen and diversify the industrial base. The main task of economic restructuring lies with the government and its agencies, not with the market as it has functioned so far in Serbia (Economics Institute, 2009, p. 16). These arguments are even stronger if we consider that the very extensive process of de-industrialization in Serbia during the last two decades has led to the decline of industrial output to 50 per cent of its 1989 level.

   The automotive industry has recently been chosen for specific government support after the conclusion of the Fiat – Zastava agreement, which builds upon the decades-long cooperation between the two firms that started in the early 1950s. There are other sectors that would merit government support, as the pharmaceutical industry or some branches of agriculture or the food industry. Serbia has to develop its specific attractiveness in certain sectors in order to be recognized for certain brands of goods on foreign markets. The options must not only be assessed – this has already been done in serious studies evaluating Serbia's comparative advantages (Jovicic ed., 2002) – but also translated into concrete policy measures that would ensure the implementation of the chosen options. Serbia cannot lose time waiting for foreign investors to modernize branches of its industry that may potentially be competitive on world markets.
2. *Employment policy* needs to be given a much more prominent role and be fully integrated within the overall economic development strategy. Considering Serbia's huge problems of unemployment, its undersized private sector, and its still very large informal economy, special

attention must be given to policies promoting private sector wage employment. A very thorough reform of the entire tax and social contributions system seems essential for lowering enterprise labour costs, in order to make them more competitive, stimulate more investment, facilitate new employment, and encourage the formalization of the informal economy (Arandarenko, 2009a). Government measures aimed at facilitating the growth of small and medium sized enterprises must be carefully combined with employment programmes and national priorities. Particularly considering that the ongoing economic crisis will lead to a further increase in unemployment in 2010–11, the government needs to critically examine why the numerous labour market measures implemented since 2001 have not been effective. Active labour market measures must receive more government attention and more funding than has been the case to date.

3. A related area is *R&D policy* and investment in human capital. Policies must be implemented which could raise economic competitiveness in the long run, through more investment in science, education, skills, life-long training, and re-qualifications. The objectives put forward by the EU Lisbon strategy, of making the EU the most competitive knowledge-based economy and society, are extremely relevant also for Serbia (Uvalic, 2005a, Djelic, 2006). There is a huge literature stressing the importance for long-term economic growth of the 'knowledge triangle' – Research, Education, and Innovation. Serbia also needs to place human capital development as a top government objective. One of the main constraints on growth now is the supply of skilled labour to meet the demands of new foreign investments and the new technology which it brings. The lack of innovative capacity within domestic firms hinders their effective engagement with foreign-owned companies and with new export market opportunities in the EU. There is a mismatch of labour supply and labour demand because of lack of skills of certain professions, and this is one of the main obstacles to developing new branches of the economy.[2] The Serbian government should implement new policies to build domestic competitiveness, raise the skills of the workforce, and provide incentives to boost innovation and knowledge transfer (Bartlett and Uvalic, 2008). According to international criteria, the Serbian economy is presently at the very beginning of these processes, without an organized system and concrete solutions for stimulating innovative activities and networks.

In addition to these three important areas which deserve a very high rank in Serbia's government policies, two issues of more general relevance must also be stressed. The first is *statistics*. Economic policies cannot be effective unless the government knows with some certainty what the country produces, how much it spends on specific programmes, and which percentage of the labour force is effectively unemployed. Statistics on many aspects of the Serbian economy remain unsatisfactory. The main institutions producing statistics in Serbia, the Serbian Office of Statistics and the NBS, have extremely competent experts, but more financial resources must be provided for statistical services, for collecting data on important indicators, improving methodologies, modernizing existing data bases, publications, and online websites. A country aspiring to become a member of the EU must have accurate statistics on its main macroeconomic indicators,[3] and should introduce standard indicators published by EUROSTAT, including those on the knowledge-based economy, starting from the basic indicator on how much is spent on R&D (GERD – General Expenditure on Research and Development).[4] The lack of fully reliable official statistics has led to the proliferation of statistics by different institutions within Serbia, which is not very helpful.

Serbia also needs a *coordinated strategy of development*, that would encompass the various strategies produced so far – the Strategy for Employment, the Strategy of Economic Development for the 2006–12 period, the Poverty Reduction Strategy, the National Programme for Business Incubators and Clusters Development for 2007–10, the National Innovation Strategy, the Strategy for the Development of Small and Medium-sized Enterprises until 2012, the most recent Strategy of Scientific and Technological Development of Serbia for 2009–14 (and probably quite a few others).[5] These strategies are important as they demonstrate the interest of the government to improve policies in all these areas, but there have been too many documents of this kind. Serbia needs a consistent and long-term economic and social development strategy that would incorporate all of these different, but clearly interlinked, separate strategies. The Strategy of Economic Development needs to be linked to the Strategy for Employment and to the Strategy of Scientific and Technological Development, which in turn cannot have positive results unless it is implemented in coordination with reforms in the sector of education. Although the Serbian Strategy of Economic Development for the period 2006–12 is an extremely valuable analysis of the current situation in Serbia, the strategy's weakness lies in its extensive treatment of all possible issues and the resulting unavoidably long list of numerous objectives. A strategy striving to accomplish too much normally becomes unfeasible in its implementation.

9.5 Is Serbia still different?

Given the overall results of market-oriented economic reforms implemented so far, how different is Serbia today with respect to other countries in transition? Only eight years ago, Serbia was lagging behind most transition countries and was frequently compared with the other laggards in SEE or the Commonwealth of Independent States (CIS) (Nuti, 2004, p. 184). In the meantime, from being a laggard Serbia has caught up in many areas of reform, even surpassing some SEE and many CIS countries. The Serbian economy today is characterized by the coexistence of ingredients of various economic systems, but this is true of most transition and post-transition countries. Elements of traditional socialism include soft-budget constraints, subsidies to loss-making social and state-owned firms, and monopolistic practices; those of the self-managed market economy are the last cases of socially owned enterprises. There are a number of elements of 'wild' or unregulated capitalism, such as the inefficient judiciary, gaps in market regulation, insecure property rights, or corruption and criminality, as well as those of hyper-liberal capitalism, like current account convertibility, banking sector privatization, and emphasis on a balanced budget.

While these same elements were also there in 2001 (Uvalic, 2002a), what has changed in the meantime is their relative weight, as the capitalist components have gained importance. Today, the dominant paradigm in Serbia is the capitalist model. The remnants of the previous economic systems – the pre-1989 market socialist and the post-1989 socialist-capitalist system – have been marginalized. Most importantly from the aspect of systemic transformation, the radical turn towards a market economy taken in late 2000 can now be considered irreversible, since political changes could influence the speed of transition, but not its general direction.

Despite major similarities, Serbia still retains certain specific features which explain why its post-2000 transition has been much more complex than initially anticipated. This is due to essentially four groups of factors: its socialist legacy, the negative heritage of the 1990s, resistance to change, and international factors.

9.5.1 Socialist legacy

What has remained of Serbia's 1989 specific economic features, reflected at that time in a number of advantages but also disadvantages (see Chapter 2)? The main advantage of a shorter reform agenda has mainly been lost, due to the unwillingness of the pre-2000 governments to radically change the economic system, reversals in transition-related economic reforms, and measures that implied abolishing, rather than introducing, the principles of a market economy (Uvalic, 2007a).

Other advantages may not have been entirely lost, however. One such advantage, latent during many years of isolation and sanctions which has re-emerged in Serbia after 2001, is the rich experience accumulated during several decades of intense contacts with the West – of enterprises, commercial banks, government institutions, and individuals. Contacts with Western institutions have proved to be a valuable asset for re-establishing relations worldwide after 2001.

Another advantage is the high quality of human capital in Serbia, despite delays in implementing reforms in the areas of science and education, and ambivalent results of some surveys done also for Serbia – such as PISA for education (OECD, 2006) or the Global Entrepreneurship Monitor (GEM). The GEM's index TEA, on Total Early Entrepreneurial Activity, suggests a high value of the index for Serbia in 2008, in line with results for other countries that early entrepreneurial activity is particularly present in low income countries with high unemployment, thus driven primarily by poor living conditions (Republicki Zavod za Razvoj Srbije, 2009, pp. 89–92). In the 1990s, the daily difficulties in Serbia were so pronounced for the average citizen, that he/she had to develop an entrepreneurial spirit, inventing strategies to survive not only materially but also psychologically. People were not able to travel to the West for 20 years, but they were forced to adapt quickly to highly deteriorating living conditions. Virtually overnight, a professor of philosophy would switch to selling buttons on the open market, an architect would convert into an electrician, a political scientist and writer would start earning a living primarily as a musician playing for a tip in restaurants.

As to Serbia's disadvantages, one of the elements of the pre-1989 economic system that has robustly survived these 20 years of transition in Serbia is 'social property'. The same systemic feature that was a burden in 1991 – ill-defined property rights – has remained a burden today, though to a very marginal extent as the last socially owned enterprises are likely to disappear soon.[6] The other disadvantage present in 1989 – resistance to change – may still today be more present in Serbia than in many other transition countries, but for somewhat different reasons than 20 years ago, as further discussed below.

9.5.2 Legacy of the 1990s

The transition in Serbia has proved to be rather complex not only because of the survival of some pre-1989 economic features and the postponement of radical change for a whole decade, but because of the numerous problems which emerged after 1991. The 1990s was not simply a lost decade from the standpoint of transition (Begovic and Mijatovic eds, 2005); it was a decade of particularly unfavourable overall conditions associated with wars, isolation, a non-democratic political regime, hyperinflation, and reversals in economic reforms, which left profound traces on all segments of Serbia's society. The general conditions for re-launching transition in Serbia in late 2000 were consequently far worse than those in CEE in 1989, when the transition first started.

The legacy of the 1990s inherited from the Milosevic regime has produced many obstacles at all levels which have impeded quicker systemic changes. The retrograde political and economic system set up in 1991 and a decade of political and economic mismanagement have left many negative consequences, some of which are still felt today – in the behaviour of the still non-privatized enterprises, in the criminal and semi-criminal networks that made up much of the Serbian economy in the 1990s and have proved very difficult to dismantle, in the highly non-transparent and still insufficiently reformed public administration, in the inefficient judiciary, in workers' mentality and their reluctance to accept that the days of self-management are over, in the use in politics of traditional communist methods and highly non-democratic culture, and in citizens' mistrust of the government and of the transition.

Though features of continuity with the old regime are not an exclusivity of Serbia – also in other post-communist countries discontinuities with the old regime have frequently been more apparent than real (Kekic, 2000) – in Serbia the element of continuity has probably been even stronger. Because of substantial delays in radical economic and political reforms and the very negative heritage of the 1990s, these elements of continuity are proving more difficult to eradicate.

9.5.3 Resistance to change and popular dissatisfaction

The issue of inherited legacies is closely linked to the previously mentioned resistance to change, as one of the factors that hampered more rapid economic reforms in SFR Yugoslavia and Serbia in 1989 (see Chapter 2). Resistance to change in Serbia is present not simply because, as in many other countries, the losers from transition are numerous, even after nine years of a new start in market-related economic reforms.

Despite a continuous and notable increase in living standards during these last eight years, the degree of popular dissatisfaction in Serbia, for various reasons, is rather high. There is still widespread nostalgia for the pre-1989 days, when the standard of living was apparently higher, employment more secure, pensions were paid regularly, travel abroad did not require burdensome visas, and the country was respected worldwide. However, there is occasionally also nostalgia for the 1990s: there are citizens who recall with sympathy some features of those times, such as the possibility of earning extra income in the fully tolerated informal economy, or subsidized prices of electricity, bread, and milk. The illusion that the clock could miraculously be turned backwards has somehow still not faded away, explaining the reluctance or inability of many people to fully accept the new realities. Resistance to change in Serbia also derives from the unfulfilled expectations associated with false promises of nationalism, continuous manipulations of facts by the pre-2000 government and the state-controlled television (if not all media), and populist policies which for years have intentionally postponed the necessary adjustments, making today's costs of transition in Serbia particularly high.

EBRD's fascinating publication *Life in Transition* (EBRD, 2007), reporting recent perceptions of Serbian citizens, confirms some of these conclusions. Household ownership of consumer goods and access to public services are, by SEE standards, both relatively high in Serbia, but very few people believe that the economic and political situation is better than in 1989. All age and income groups show more dissatisfaction than satisfaction with life today, with 70–80 per cent of the surveyed disagreeing or strongly disagreeing that the economic situation today is better than in 1989. Somewhat more favourable are the views on the present political situation in Serbia, as 55–70 per cent disagree or strongly disagree that the political situation is better than around 1989. Only 20–30 per cent are satisfied with their life now, all things considered. There is general support for both democracy and a market economy, but less among the elderly. Corruption is generally seen as worse than in 1989, though the degree of 'irregular payments' to public officials is reported to be very low. Trust in society has dramatically fallen: 60–70 per cent of respondents consider people could be trusted in 1989, while today only 25–35 per cent. Trust in public institutions is generally weak, except for the armed forces and the presidency (EBRD, 2007, pp. 72–3).

9.5.4 International factors

International factors have also contributed to delays in systemic changes in Serbia. The apparent ambivalence and slowness in embracing change in Serbia is the result of another key difference between Serbia and CEE countries which concerns the underlying drivers of transition and associated attitudes to the West. In the early 1990s, the geopolitical and national interests in CEE coincided with those of political and economic transition, since anti-Russian and pro-European sentiment strongly facilitated the post-1989 changes. By contrast, in Serbia the international geopolitical changes ran counter to its national interests, in particular the negative impact of the break-up of the country for Serb minorities outside Serbia (Kekic, 2000). Moreover, during the 1990s, the prevailing negative attitudes in the West towards Serbia, which culminated in NATO's bombing in 1999, have been seen by many in Serbia as fundamentally hostile to Serb interests (Kekic, 2000). Serbian citizens have lived a whole decade in international isolation, under sanctions and the veil of false promises of the Milosevic regime, in a world of unrealistic expectations. These factors explain, in part, why until recently a third of the voters in Serbia were still not ready to accept the new direction taken in late 2000, towards a capitalist market economy and full integration with the rest of Europe.

After October 2000, the political climate has fundamentally changed, many reforms have been implemented at accelerated speed, yet EU–Serbian political relations have progressed very slowly. The EU policy of very strict political conditionality has delayed the conclusion of an SAA with Serbia for almost seven years. Although finally signed in end-April 2008, the SAA has not been implemented because of the alleged insufficient collaboration of Serbia with the Hague Tribunal. Serbia remains a 'potential candidate' of the EU, despite the substantial progress it has made in many areas of economic and political reforms. The divisions between Serbia and the EU were further perpetuated by the maintenance of the visa regime for Serbian citizens, finally removed only in late December 2009. The reserved Western attitudes have not facilitated the ongoing process of political and economic reforms in Serbia.

The initial exclusion of countries of former Yugoslavia from major EU programmes of assistance offered to other transition countries has not only delayed the process of their integration with the EU, but has also contributed to the slower pace of economic and political reforms and slower economic development, rendering the process of their catching-up with the other transition countries even more demanding. If a country like Serbia is today less ready for EU membership – economically, politically, and institutionally – it is also because it has not received the same type of political, financial, and technical support as many other transition countries. The international isolation of Serbia, while most pronounced during the 1990s due to severe UN and EU sanctions, has continued after 2000 through strict EU conditionality. The hesitation and unreadiness on the part of the EU to do more for Serbia has very significantly influenced the internal processes of democratization and political transformation within the country, since it has been used by conservative, nationalist, and anti-EU parties to distance Serbia even more from the EU.

9.6 Towards a better future

Although transition to a market economy and multiparty democracy in Serbia has proved to be rather complex and in many ways unique, Serbia is beginning to resemble other transition countries more and more. During the 2001–8 period, it has become a more open market economy with dominant private ownership; it has liberalized its trade with the EU and with its non-EU neighbours; it has reformed many of its institutions; its financial sector is now dominated by foreign-owned banks, and there is an emerging stock exchange. After 2001, Serbia has been one of the fastest growing transition economies, it has reached substantial macroeconomic stabilization, it has had a stable or appreciating internally convertible domestic currency, it has accumulated substantial foreign exchange reserves reducing the risk of external insolvency, it has at last attracted some FDI, and privatization opportunities still abound.

These features have characterized the Serbian economy during much of the 2001–8 period. The global financial and economic crisis, which hit Serbia in the second half of 2008, has interrupted the process of institutional and economic catching up with other countries in transition. Unlike countries in the CEE region, Serbia may not be able to fully benefit from the forthcoming recovery of the world economy. With the 2008–9 economic crisis, many problems that have accumulated during the last eight years have come to the surface, making today an excellent opportunity for the government to reconsider future policy options. Among the numerous challenges, the most important is to further increase competitiveness on world markets through more substantial enterprise restructuring and modernization and fast completion of all those reforms that were considered secondary in 2001, yet have proved to be major impediments for faster transformation of the real sector of the economy. Serbia needs to reconsider the role of the state and improve the quality of government supportive institutions, in order to take full advantage of ongoing reforms and the return to normality of a country that has remained isolated from the rest of the world for too long.

The more difficult challenges lie in the political domain. The first is regarding Serbia's difficult relations with the EU. Considering Serbia's negotiations with the EU has been a powerful engine of institutional change towards EU standards, political will must be employed to substantially accelerate further progress of Serbia towards EU membership. The second issue is Kosovo, since its declaration of independence in February 2008 has further complicated the history and geography of the Balkans.[7] The Serbian government should forcefully and consistently implement its pro-reform and pro-Europe agenda, reconcile with its difficult past and look primarily towards the future, despite of its formal constitutional obligations. The Serbian government submitted its application for EU membership on 22 December 2009, and hopes its application will be evaluated positively, since it has put in lots of efforts to carry forward market-oriented reforms, introduce democratic institutions, implement European standards, renew relations and build new bridges with its neighbours and with the EU. It is now up to the EU to accept Serbia into the European family.

Postface

The book was completed on 9 November 2009, the twentieth anniversary of the fall of the Berlin Wall, commonly taken as the date of the collapse of communism in Eastern Europe, when its citizens at last conquered freedom, after 40 years behind the Iron Curtain and the dictatorship of the Soviet Union. Two years later the USSR disintegrated and began its own transition. For Serbia/Yugoslavia the fall of the Berlin Wall had a somewhat different meaning, although it did pave the way for the first multiparty elections that soon took place in all the Yugoslav republics. Before the fall, Serbia/Yugoslavia was not behind the Iron Curtain but right in front of it, somewhere in between the two parts of Europe. Until then, Yugoslavia was still a communist country, but it was not a member of the CMEA or of the Warsaw Pact, it was a non-aligned country with privileged relations with the West. Despite remaining communist, Yugoslavia departed from the traditional East European model in many ways: it had economic democracy due to the system of workers' self-management, more political liberties, and more personal freedoms, as its citizens could freely travel abroad. It had experienced 40 years of economic reforms that had gradually introduced elements of the market economy to replace administrative allocation of resources, it had increasing trade with the European Community to replace trade with members of the CMEA, it had open instead of repressed inflation, and many of its workers could escape unemployment by emigrating abroad.

In 1989 Serbia/Yugoslavia was a vanguard, different and ahead of other East European countries. In November 1989, SFR Yugoslavia was already experiencing hyperinflation after a decade of unsuccessful stabilization policies. On 18 December 1989, the last government of Ante Markovic adopted a bold macroeconomic stabilization programme based on the 'shock therapy' recommended by Jeffrey Sachs, the very first of this kind implemented in Eastern Europe (a few weeks later, a similar 'shock therapy' stabilization programme would also be adopted by the Polish government). Owing to its privileged relations with the West, its specific economic system, and a less rigid communist regime, the revolutionary transformations that spread all over Eastern Europe were much less revolutionary in a country like SFR Yugoslavia and Serbia.

On reflection, the overall balance of these 20 years of transformation is not very positive. Serbia is an example *par excellence* of a country that has not taken advantage of the revolutionary changes of the early 1990s. During the first decade of transition, the government's political objectives led to multiple military conflicts, international sanctions, and isolation, together with economic policies that brought high macroeconomic instability, a reversal of many market-oriented economic achievements, and economic backwardness with an increasing development gap instead of catching-up. By subordinating economic to political objectives and choosing wrong policy options, Serbia lost much of its good starting position and the comparative advantage it had with respect to many other countries embarking on transition in 1989.

After the political turn in late 2000, Serbia sought to catch up quickly for the missed opportunities of the 1990s, by adopting economic policies and institutional reforms that had characterized other CEE countries and enabled them to become members of the EU. One of Serbia's advantages in 2001 was precisely that it could learn from the decade-long experience of the CEE countries. Despite remarkable progress in many areas of reform, Serbia did not draw many lessons from the economic policies implemented by the CEE governments in the 1990s, but repeated some of the same mistakes. It was naively assumed that the Serbian transition was starting from scratch in 2000, that the policy package recommended by the 'Washington consensus' still had its full appeal, and that the success of CEE could be replicated in Serbia albeit a decade later. In addition, political reforms in Serbia were much slower and less radical than economic reforms, delaying a more profound transformation of its institutions and postponing an open public debate on many important issues that should have been addressed early on.

The responsibilities for the missed opportunities during these last 20 years do lie with the Serbian authorities. Nonetheless the EU could have done much more for Serbia, particularly immediately after the fall of the Milosevic regime. Slow changes in Serbia's political environment are also due to wrong or hesitant policies on the part of the EU. Since 2001, EU policies towards Serbia have radically changed for the better, but Western attitudes towards Serbia often do not differ much from those prevailing ten years ago. Serbia continues to be pressured not only for the delivery of all indicted war criminals, but also for acknowledgement of and apology for the actions in Kosovo, without sufficient recognition that violence has taken place on both sides.

Twenty years after the fall of the Berlin Wall, there are practically no border controls between a large part of Eastern and Western Europe, between countries that were on either sides of the iron curtain. Although in 1989 Serbia/Yugoslavia was not behind the iron curtain, 20 years later the perception in Serbia is that it is today. A new wall has been built during these last 20 years that is proving difficult to bring down. On 30 November 2009, the EU Councils of Ministers approved the request of Serbia, Macedonia, and Montenegro for the abolition of visas, which has been interpreted as the restitution of dignity, since it will terminate humiliating queues in front of foreign embassies. The Schengen Wall has been brought down for three countries, but the wall is still there for Albanians, Bosnians, and Kosovars. Not only that, there is an even higher wall dividing the western Balkans from the EU regarding a set of conditions for EU membership. Facilitating Serbia's membership in the EU, together with the entry of all other SEE countries including Kosovo, would be the best way to bring down the new walls that have been created after 1989. Letting all Balkan countries join the EU would ensure a new era of more permanent peace and stability not only for the Balkans, but for the whole of Europe. It should not be forgotten that the Balkan region is an integral part of Europe.

Notes

1 Introduction

1. I owe this accurate description of Serbia's complicated history to Veljko Vujacic.
2. The Interim Agreement, which covers trade and trade-related issues and can be applied before the ratification of the SAA, finally entered into force on 1 February 2010.
3. See, for example, van Meurs (ed.) (2003).
4. For a well-documented and detailed legal context of Yugoslavia's disintegration, see Trbovich (2008).
5. Contrary to the situation in other countries in Central and Eastern Europe, before 1991 citizens of the SFR Yugoslavia could freely travel abroad; they had passports valid for five years and did not need visas to go to any European country. The EU visa regime was lifted for Serbia only recently, at the end of 2009.
6. When I inquired with the Serbian Statistical Office in early 2001 why the concept of Social Product continued to be used in some of its publications, I got a rather unsatisfactory answer that 'Serbian enterprises request statistics on the Social Product'. Although the concept of Social Product may have certain advantages, in times of structural changes such as those occurring during the transition, it can be highly misleading.

2 Serbia on the Eve of Transition

1. Even before the adoption of specific legislation on joint ventures, cooperation contracts with foreign partners were permitted; one of the oldest examples dates back to 1954, when the first cooperation agreement was concluded between the car manufacturer Zastava (in Kragujevac, Serbia) and Fiat (Torino, Italy).
2. Social compacts were agreements concluded between representatives of the political authorities, trade unions, enterprises, and other organizations, on policies in specific fields, such as prices, income distribution, employment, and foreign trade. Self-management agreements regulated relations between enterprises and other organizations in areas of mutual interest, such as terms for the foundation of firms and banks, or joint investment projects (Uvalic, 1992, p. 7).
3. These reforms are described in greater detail in Uvalic (1992).
4. The working group in charge of preparing the foundations of the programme included, among others, Kiro Gligorov, Dragomir Vojnic, Aleksandar Bajt, Oskar Kovac, Zoran Pjanic and many others, while as members of the various subgroups, that were to prepare concrete proposals of reforms in the various areas, practically all existing economics professors in the country were engaged.

5. The detailed programme of economic reforms and some 19 new laws (or amendments to existing laws) adopted in 1988–9 were published in a special government volume: see Savezno izvrsno vece, Sekretarijat za informacije (1990).
6. EEC regulation no. 460/70, Official Gazette of the EC no. 58 of 13 March 1970; see more in Lopandic, 1997, pp. 93–9.
7. An initial EIB loan financed the extension of the high-tension electricity network and its connection to the Greek and Italian networks, while a second loan financed the trans-Yugoslav motorway (CEC, 1979).
8. Susan Woodward therefore rightly notes how the underlying theme in the entire literature on Yugoslavia, namely the differences with respect to the Soviet bloc, distracts from all the similarities (Woodward, 1995a, p. 34).
9. Gross Social Product, or Social Product in Yugoslav terminology, corresponds to Gross Material Product: it is the value added of the 'productive' sectors of the economy, thus excluding most 'non-productive' sectors such as education, health, defense, banking, and other services. In this sense it is similar to the concept of Net Material Product that was used in other socialist countries, but differs from such a concept because it is gross of depreciation.
10. The private sector was much more important in Kosovo than elsewhere because of the large share of agriculture and small-scale crafts, both predominantly in private hands. These shares have been calculated on the basis of data on GSP in constant 1972 prices, in Statistical Yearbook of Yugoslavia 1991 (Savezni zavod za statistiku Jugoslavije, 1991), Table 205–1, p. 475.
11. The ambiguity of the concept of 'social property' has given rise to endless debates about its real meaning. In the 1974 Yugoslav constitution, it was explicitly stated that social property was property 'of everyone and no-one'. Enterprise property rights were limited since an enterprise did not have the right to sell its assets and appropriate the proceeds; on the contrary, it was obliged to maintain the value of its assets through obligatory and prescribed rates of depreciation.
12. These unemployment rates were calculated on the basis of data provided in the Savezni zavod za statistiku Jugoslavije (1991). The unemployment rates reflect only the number of persons formally registered as seeking work with the employment agencies, and thus are underestimates of the effective rates of unemployment. Because there were no household surveys in Yugoslavia in those times, these are the only available statistics. On the various problems of calculating the unemployment rate in Yugoslavia, see more in Woodward (1995a) pp. 194–208. Somewhat different figures are found in various OECD publications, where it is reported that the registered unemployment rate was 6.9 per cent of the domestic labour force in 1976, rising to 8.4 per cent by 1980 and further to 11 per cent by 1989 (OECD, 1982, p. 14; OECD, 1990, p. 21).
13. The stabilisation programmes were strongly influenced by Jeffrey Sachs who at that time was advisor to both SFR Yugoslavia and Poland.
14. According to the law, it was up to the enterprise's workers' council to decide to start privatization, but all proceeds from sales were to go to special Republican Funds. In this way the law recognized that the seller and hence real owner of capital was the state. Since the law had been interpreted as 'tacit nationalization', no enterprise decided to start privatization. Although some

economists like Aleksandar Bajt (1988) have sustained that social property had actually been transformed into group property of workers employed in the enterprise, the way privatization was implemented in all countries of former Yugoslavia confirms that social property had remained effectively state property.

15. Due to institutional arrangements specific to Yugoslavia, the NBY had only a limited influence on commercial banks' interest rate levels and structure. In addition, as mentioned earlier, commercial banks were conceived as service agencies of enterprises.
16. There are advantages which only applied to the country as a whole. For example, in the late 1980s, SFR Yugoslavia was the largest, most populous, and most developed country of the four Southeast European countries (Albania, Bulgaria, Romania, and SFR Yugoslavia). In addition, the privileged position in international relations was lost after its disintegration, since each of its successor states had to re-establish its relations with all international organizations.
17. This was also intended to dilute the numerical preponderance of Serbs in Yugoslavia, thus to prevent a possible resurgence of Serbian domination on the basis of its size, as it was the most populous and largest republic (Crnobrnja, 1994, p. 94). It has frequently been argued that the creation and status of the two provinces was part of Tito's deliberate policy to weaken Serbia and the influence of Serbs as the most populous nation within Yugoslavia; thus a weak Serbia was to ensure a strong Yugoslavia.
18. The more developed parts of the Yugoslav federation included the republics of Slovenia and Croatia, Serbia proper (central Serbia, without the two autonomous provinces) and one of its autonomous provinces, Vojvodina; while the less developed were the republics of Bosnia and Herzegovina, Macedonia, and Montenegro, and the other autonomous province of Kosovo (part of Serbia).
19. The Memorandum stressed the presence of a system of 'unequal exchange' in Yugoslavia which was supposedly highly unfavorable for Serbia because of adverse terms of trade, further aggravated by the 'penetration' of the developed republics' capital into Serbia, making Serbia increasingly dependent on them.
20. The 1974 Yugoslav constitution did considerably increase the powers of Serbia's two provinces, Kosovo and Vojvodina, giving them a high level of autonomy, in many areas comparable to that of the republics. Nevertheless, the complaint on Serbia's limited sovereignty over its provinces was clearly exaggerated, since only some years later, in 1989, Serbia would adopt amendments to its constitution which effectively reinforced its rights over Kosovo (for further details, see Trbovich, 2008, pp. 232–3).
21. Some of the economic consequences of rising nationalism in Yugoslavia are examined in Dallago and Uvalic (1998).
22. The Battle of Kosovo, held in 1389, signaled the beginning of the final destruction of the independent medieval Serbian kingdom, completed in 1459. Although Serbia lost, thereafter remaining under the Ottoman Empire for almost 500 years, the legend of this battle became a myth and epic verses about Serb heroes were narrated for many centuries. Kosovo has always been considered the cradle of Serbia and of Serbian culture. The oldest Serbian monasteries built during the 11th–14th century are located in Kosovo.
23. Nationalism has always been regarded as a major threat to the 'fraternity and unity' of communist Yugoslavia. As a response to the requests of a group

of key Croatian politicians for more decentralized political power along national lines in 1971, Tito accused them of separatism, 'counterrevolution', and betrayal, forcing them to resign. Soon after in Serbia, a group of Serbian politicians proposed major decentralization of power and more liberal economic policies, but were soon replaced by politicians more loyal to the Yugoslav idea.

24. Tudjman openly declared the continuity of the Croatian state, which included the infamous Ustasha Independent State of Croatia which during World War II was responsible for mass murders of Serbs, Jews, and other populations. Tudjman restored some of the Ustasha symbols, as the one adopted on the new flag; and in the new Croatian constitution, Serbs were no longer considered a nation (Crnobrnja, 1994, p. 151).

3 The Early 1990s: Political and Economic Instability

1. The parties represented in the Serbian parliament included the Serbian Renewal Movement (SPO led by Vuk Draskovic), the Serbian Radical Party (SRS led by Vojislav Seselj), the Democratic Party (DS led by Zoran Djindjic), the Democratic Party of Serbia (DSS led by Vojislav Kostunica), and the Democratic Movement of Serbia (DEPOS), to name just the most important.
2. There were other extreme parties, such as the Serbian Unity Party (SSJ) created by Zeljko Raznjatovic known as Arkan, a criminal who formed paramilitary forces which fought in Croatia and Bosnia.
3. For the definition of GSP, see note 9 in Chapter 2.
4. Mainly based on *Yugoslav Survey* (2001), pp. 29–35 and Lopandic (1997), pp. 102–4.
5. Mainly based on *Yugoslav Survey* (2001), pp. 29–35.
6. Seigniorage can be defined as the revenue deriving from the state monopoly to issue money, usually measured as the real value of the increase in nominal money supply.
7. The Olivera–Tanzi effect reflects a specific situation during a period of high inflation, which results in a decline in the volume of tax collection and a deterioration of real tax proceeds being collected by the government. The actual real tax proceeds gathered by the government, after adjusting for inflation, will be less than in a period of normal inflation, due to both increased operating costs and decreased tax revenues; see Olivera (1967) and Tanzi (1977).
8. On 14 November 2008, Zimbabwe's annualized inflation rate was estimated at 89.7 sextillion per cent (10^{21}). This placed Zimbabwe's hyperinflation as the second highest hyperinflation in world history. In April 2009, Zimbabwe abandoned printing of the Zimbabwean dollar, and the South African and the US dollar became the standard currencies.
9. Although Serbia in August 1991 had access to US$ 3.8 billion, or 85 per cent of total US$ 4.5 billion official reserves of SFR Yugoslavia, these reserves rapidly declined to less than US$ 1.3 billion by the end of 1992. Some official reserves were blocked abroad after the introduction of the UN sanctions, so by early 1994 Yugoslav official reserves amounted to only about US$ 350 million (Dinkic, 1995).

10. See 'Zakon o sredstvima u svojini Republike Srbije', *Sluzbeni glasnik Republike Srbije* 53/1995, 3/1996, 54/1996, and 32/1977.
11. The Gini coefficient is a measure of inequality of income or wealth, ranging from 0 to 1. A low Gini coefficient indicates a more equal distribution of income, with 0 corresponding to perfect equality, while higher Gini coefficients indicate more unequal distribution, with 1 corresponding to perfect inequality.
12. Starting from early 2001, citizens could start withdrawing their foreign currency deposits in cash, though there were limits on the amount that could be withdrawn every three months; or they could opt for their savings to be converted into government bonds. The issue was regulated more permanently in a law adopted in 2002, on the settlement of all liabilities arising from citizens' frozen foreign currency savings. The 2002 law converted all citizens' frozen deposits into government bonds (Official Gazette of FR Yugoslavia no. 36, 2002).
13. Dafina Milanovic died in the meantime, while Jezdimir Vasiljevic was arrested at last in April 2009 in Austria.

4 Post-Dayton: Slow Progress with Transition

1. The Dayton Peace Accords were initialed in Dayton (USA) on 21 November 1995 and were signed in Paris on 14 December 1995.
2. The JUL was created from the transformation of a party of retired communist officials and military officers called the League of Communists – Movement for Yugoslavia – SK-PJ. Apparently JUL rejected nationalist politics to restore credibility of the regime, had a Marxist and anti-Western orientation, but held communist China as an example for Serbia to emulate.
3. Rumours suggested that Avramovic was forced by Milosevic to leave politics; in exchange, he was allowed (contrary to other citizens) to withdraw his foreign exchange savings, which he needed for curing his health (dialysis); others suggested he was pressured by some Western diplomats in Belgrade not to participate in the elections. Judging from a conversation I had with him in Sveti Stefan in autumn 1996, I believe Avramovic was simply disappointed and fed up with Serbian politics. After having been used, manipulated, cheated, and fired at last by the governing coalition in May 1996, there were very few people he trusted on the Serbian political scene, even within the opposition.
4. For a detailed background of the Kosovo crisis and account of the talks in Rambouillet, see Simic (2000).
5. It should nevertheless be stressed that even these lower estimates have been considered unrealistic by experts of the Economist Intelligence Unit.
6. Avramovic was the chairman of the working group, while the secretary was the author of the present book.
7. The leaders of G17 Plus, Mladjan Dinkic and Miroljub Labus, would become key politicians in the new post-2000 government: Dinkic was the governor of the Yugoslav National Bank, and Labus the federal minister for foreign economic relations and vice prime minister of the federal government.
8. This emerged from some interviews undertaken in several privatized firms in Belgrade in early 2001; see Uvalic (2001d).

9. For further details about the new economic elite in Serbia and careers of its typical representatives, see Miljkovic and Hoare (2005), pp. 197–202.
10. For further details on some of these murders, see Miljkovic and Hoare (2005), pp. 204–17.
11. As already mentioned, it is only after the political changes in October 2000 that this issue has been addressed by the then appointed new governor of the Yugoslav National Bank, Mladjan Dinkic.
12. In the meantime, the Karic business conglomerate has mostly disappeared, as part of the family has also left the country.

5 Serbia's 'velvet' Revolution and Its Aftermath

1. By November 2009, EU member states had still not granted visa-free entry to Serbian citizens, although this policy finally changed by the end of the year (see Chapter 8).
2. A delegation of the Serbian opposition, headed by Dragoslav Avramovic, was present at the conference in Sarajevo, but FR Yugoslavia as a country was not officially represented nor included into the Stability Pact for Southeast Europe on that occasion.
3. In this way Montenegro was also able to benefit from these EU trade concessions, while Serbia was excluded. Although still part of the Yugoslav federation, after the 1997 elections when Milo Djukanovic became prime minister, he declared openly to be against the Milosevic regime. This is when Montenegro gained substantial support of the Brussels administration.
4. Milosevic's term of office was due to expire only in July 2001.
5. Although Milosevic was becoming increasingly unpopular, the NATO military campaign created a feeling of national unity. It is only normal that the NATO bombing of Serbia provoked patriotic sentiments among its citizens, as the most natural reaction of any nation being attacked by an external enemy. Patriotism must not be confused with nationalism. The opposition in Serbia was certainly not dead, but was restless after several months of bombing and exhausted by ten years of futile efforts in fighting the Milosevic regime. If the opposition was not speaking up more loudly, it was also because in mid-2000, opposition supporters feared for their lives.
6. For a detailed analysis of NGOs in Serbia, see Minic and Dereta (2007). For a detailed list of activities of NGOs and various organizations which in the 1990s represented civil alternatives, see also Curgus Kazimir (ed.) (2001), pp. 373–418.
7. The G17 Plus would become a political party in December 2002. Its first president was Miroljub Labus, while Mladjan Dinkic was its vice-president. When Labus resigned from his position of deputy prime minister on 3 May 2006, after the EU suspended enlargement talks with Serbia over the issue of cooperation with the ICTY, he also resigned from the position of the president of the G17 Plus. Mladjan Dinkic became the president of the G17 Plus and has maintained this position ever since.
8. The expectations from unilateral eurozation in Montenegro were only partly successful. The monetary reform did drastically reduce inflation, though not immediately since it was still double-digit in 2001. Moreover, the introduction

of the euro as legal tender did not return confidence of the population in financial institutions; some estimates indicate that around two-thirds of the money in circulation in 2001 was still held under mattresses, while around half of all economic transactions were in cash, avoiding the mediation of official financial institutions.

9. At that time, Djukanovic was not sure whether the majority of citizens would actually vote for Montenegro's independence; opinion polls showed that about 40 per cent of the population still favoured the union with Serbia. Montenegrins were deeply divided on the issue of independence because of the ethnic affinity between the two nations. This is because many Montenegrins view themselves a part of the wider Serb nation (Economist Intelligence Unit, 2000). In addition, there was pressure from US and EU officials on Montenegro to remain part of the Yugoslav federation.
10. Some of the political problems encountered during those times within the Yugoslav federal government are described in detail in Labus (2006).
11. When his term expired, Milutinovic surrendered to the ICTY where he was tried for various war crimes. He was found not guilty on all charges on 26 February 2009.
12. While working for the Yugoslav government I had the privilege to meet a number of important personalities, including Romano Prodi, Danuta Hubner, Katherine Pak, Katherine Day, Johannes Linn, and many others.
13. The 'Washington consensus' refers to a set of common recommendations most often given by the main international financial institutions based in Washington – the IMF, the World Bank, and other lending institutions (Williamson, 1990). It was originally intended to address the economic problems of Latin America, but was also proposed to the post-communist East European countries in the late 1980s (Kolodko and Nuti, 1997).

6 Embarking on Transition for a Second Time

1. Legislation was prepared to introduce special courts to deal with organized crime and war crimes and in January 2003 the heads of the Serbian secret service were changed. The final step in these radical reforms was supposed to be the appointment of a new federal minister of defence who was to be voted on 13 March 2003, but Djindjic was assassinated just the day before (Vejvoda, 2006).
2. Discussing the complexity of the situation in Serbia, a well-known journalist notes: 'one needs to look into the darkest shadows of Milosevic's legacy: his secrete police, powerful and unaccountable, which outlived not only Milosevic's downfall but also three consecutive democratic governments, and is likely to outlive the fourth' (Anastasijevic, 2008).
3. The Constitution of the Republic of Serbia was adopted on 28 September 1990.
4. There were a number of controversial issues in the proposed drafts of the Serbian Constitution on which there was no consensus among the leading political parties. A detailed discussion of these controversial issues can be found in Labus (2003a).
5. We should recall that social property was introduced in the early 1950 along with workers' self-management, to replace the more traditional form of state property. Given that social property was vaguely defined in

the 1974 constitution as 'property of everyone and no one', there was no agreement on who was the real owner of enterprise assets. The ambiguity of the concept of social property created difficulties in the privatization process in the late 1980s, but it remained one of the guaranteed property forms in the Serbian constitution adopted in 1990 (see Chapter 2).

6. Miroljub Labus was the first president of the G17 Plus when it was founded in December 2002, but he decided to leave politics in mid-2006. Previously he was one of the founding members and vice president (1994–7) of the DS. In late 2002 he officially ran for president of Serbia.
7. At the parliamentary elections in January 2007, Boris Tadic's DS got 23 per cent, Kostunica's DSS-New Serbia 16.5 per cent, and G17 Plus 7 per cent of the votes. These parties by far surpassed that of the right-wing SRS that got 28 per cent. In fact, considering the votes for other smaller parties, two-thirds of the voting public supported some form of pro-European option (Rajkovic, 2007).
8. The initial achievements of the first post-2000 Serbian/Yugoslav government are described in Labus (2003b). One of the most extensive overviews of economic reforms implemented during 2001–5 is Begovic and Mijatovic (eds) (2005).
9. On exchange rate regimes in the Western Balkan countries, see Daviddi and Uvalic (2006).
10. The London Club debt stems from the 1980s, when Serbian enterprises took out attractive loans through foreign commercial banks mostly from EU countries.
11. This assessment of Serbia's economic reforms by the EBRD was done retrospectively (after 2006), since in 2000 Serbia was still part of FR Yugoslavia.
12. FR Yugoslavia signed free trade agreements (FTA) with seven SEE countries, as envisaged by the Stability Pact's Memorandum of understanding on trade liberalization and facilitation of June 2001. These FTAs have in 2006 been transformed into one agreement under the framework of the CEFTA.
13. Another very low EBRD score (2) is on securities markets, but the still underdeveloped capital market is in great part the consequence of delays in privatizing large-scale enterprises.

7 Transition Strategy Flaws: Privatization and Restructuring

1. In 1997, drawing from the experience with the Latin American economies and those in Eastern Europe and the former Soviet Union, the new agenda was presented as the 'post-Washington consensus' (Kolodko and Nuti, 1997; Kolodko, 1999).
2. In a Dutch auction, the auctioneer offers an enterprise on sale at a set price, which in case of no interested buyers is subsequently lowered until some participant is willing to accept the offer.
3. Unregulated land issues have indeed greatly hampered privatization, particularly in case of sale to foreigners. The new Serbian constitution adopted in 2006 has removed the obstacles for private ownership of urban land, but the issue of how to regulate the use of urban land is still under discussion.

4. Only one large state-owned enterprise was partly privatized already in 1997, Serbia Telekom, sold to Italian and Greek partners (see Chapter 4).
5. Among the top 20 Serbian enterprises with the largest capital stock in 2008 are also 7 state-owned enterprises. Two are at the very top of the list (EPS and Serbian Railways), while others are the state-owned companies in charge of roads (JP Putevi Srbije), water and drainage (JKP Beograski vodovod i kanalizacija and JP Vode Vojvodine), forests (JP Srbijasume), and electricity (JP EMS) (see www.nbs.rs).
6. Mencinger's regressions gave a somewhat surprising result, of a negative impact of FDI on economic growth in eight CEE countries. The results are explained by the fact that FDI were predominantly acquisitions related to massive and often politically motivated privatizations, while proceeds from sales were spent on consumption and imports (Mencinger, 2003, p. 504).
7. Resavica is a complex of nine mines employing 4195 people across 8 municipalities; of the nine mines, a maximum of one-third are viable, while one mine has been out of operation since the late 1980s. Direct subsidies for Resavica in 2008 amounted to €22 million or 0.06 percent of GDP (World Bank, 2009, p. 54).
8. The 15 'large economic systems' in 2008 included *Sintelon AD* Bačka Palanka, *Fabrika duvana AD* Niš, *Invej DOO* Beograd, *Telenor DOO* Beograd, *Hemofarm AD* Vršac, *IM Matijević DOO* Novi Sad, *Lafarge BFC AD* Beočin, *APA AD* Apatin, *TCK AD Kosjerić* Kosjerić, *Coca cola HBS AD* Beograd, *Tetra pak production DOO* Beograd, *Koncern Farmakom MB DOO* Šabac, *Agromarket DOO* Kragujevac, and *Delta M* Beograd i *Autoritas Invesment DOO* Novi Sad (Jakopin and Knezevic, 2009, p. 8).
9. Corporate governance functions through mechanisms assuring shareholders' control over managerial discretion, either through direct monitoring and control exercised by one or several large shareholders (the German–Japanese model), or in countries with developed financial markets and institutions, through the threat posed to managers by the potential taking over of a controlling interest (the Anglo-Saxon model). The separation of ownership from management can lead to problems of asymmetric information and moral hazard. The solution is to combine ownership functions with control functions, or to otherwise align the interests of owners and managers, for example through performance related pay schemes.
10. The World Bank Development indicators provide somewhat different statistics on structural changes of the Serbian economy during 2000–7: a decline of the share of gross value added in agriculture from 21 to 13 per cent and in industry from 31 to 28 per cent, while an increase in services from 48 to 59 per cent.
11. Although many arguments have been put forward by Horvat (1982) and a number of other scholars in favour of social property, the way this form of ownership was implemented in SFR Yugoslavia did not provide the right incentives as argued earlier (see Chapter 2).
12. This was suggested for Serbia already in 1996 by the Avramovic working group (Avramovic and Uvalic, 1996 and Chapter 4), and again in 2001 (Uvalic, 2001b).
13. An external monitoring mechanism of the insider-controlled firm could have been performed by a lead bank, which may work even if insiders are the dominant stockholders. In case of non-performance, the control rights

would shift automatically from the insider to the outsider (the lead bank of a consortium). Aoki is aware of some of the difficulties in applying this model to transitional economies: the role of banks may be limited because of their undercapitalization, low level of monitoring capacity, and the legacy of soft-budget constraints. While these problems were typical of transition economies in the mid-1990s, this is no longer the case today, not even in Serbia where the entire banking system has been bought by large multinational European banks.

14. A rather bitter comment by a well-known public figure in Serbia, Nebojsa Popov (2009), who has for many years been the editor of Belgrade's *Republika*, depicts rather well the diffused opinion of Serbian citizens regarding privatization: 'When "tycoon" privatization, based on deals among friends, is imposed as the medicine for survival, but its implementation leads to the closing down of production processes, then the medicine has the effect of poison, that dissolves up to the point of total destruction the inherited productive capacity, without any prospects as to when and how new ones will be created.'

8 Integrating Serbia into the EU

1. The Czech Republic, Estonia, Hungary, Poland, Latvia, Lithuania, Slovakia, and Slovenia became EU member states on 1 May 2004, together with Cyprus and Malta, while Bulgaria and Romania attained EU membership on 1 January 2007.
2. As indicated by the French acronym of the programme, PHARE was initially, in January 1990, launched for Poland and Hungary, but it was soon extended to other East European countries.
3. The European Community Monitor Mission was initiated in July 1991 to monitor borders, inter-ethnic relations, refugee traffic, and political and security developments in the area of former Yugoslavia. The programme was renamed as the European Union Monitoring Mission in December 2000 and today operates under the EU Common Foreign and Security Policy.
4. Total G24 assistance to the CEE and SEE transition countries, including PHARE, macro-financial assistance, debt restructuring, export credit, emergency, and food aid; see Mayhew (1998).
5. 'Obnova' is the Serbian-Croatian-Bosnian word for 'Reconstruction'.
6. ECHO is the European Commission's Humanitarian Aid department, which does not implement humanitarian projects itself but funds actions that are implemented through partner relief organizations.
7. This was done with the intention of showing to the population that responsibility for suffering caused by shortages and economic decline lay with the policy of the Milosevic regime.
8. This pilot programme focused on repairs and the supply of education-related material (such as furniture) for kindergartens, schools, and other educational institutions.
9. Some countries, like the UK, did introduce visas for Croatia as well.
10. The main partners of the Stability Pact, in addition to the beneficiaries and the neighbouring states, include the European Commission, the OSCE, the NATO, all major international financial organizations, the EU member states, the

USA, Japan, Russia, Canada, and some other European countries. On the new regional approach to SEE, see also World Bank (2000).

11. Some fishery products, baby-beef, and wine, while trade in textile products is covered by bilateral agreements.
12. After eight years of activities, the EAR was closed in December 2008, handing over management of projects to the EU delegations.
13. TAIEX stands for 'Technical Assistance Information Exchange', ISPA is the 'Instrument for Structural Policies for Pre-Accession', SAPARD is the 'Special Accession Programme for Agriculture and Rural Development', and FP6 is the Sixth Framework Programme for scientific research.
14. Since 2001, the Kosovo provisional authorities under UNSCR 1244 have prioritized the European agenda and committed to a long term European integration process. A permanent technical and political dialogue with Kosovo authorities, called the SAP tracking mechanism (STM), has been established to provide sound policy advice and guidance to Kosovo's reform efforts. Under the STM, regular meetings have been held to assess Kosovo's progress in realizing European Partnership recommendations.
15. In Serbia this issue has been used by the Radical Party to push public opinion against the EU.
16. We should recall that it took the Italian government 20 years to capture Toto Riina, one of the last-known Mafia leaders, who lived in Sicily all those years. A similar argument was made some years back in the case of Croatia concerning general Gotovina. In fact powerful groups protected him, and only when the government broke them was he arrested.
17. As mentioned earlier, in the meantime Iceland has also become a 'potential candidate', following the submission of its application for EU membership on 23 July 2009.
18. The difficult issue is how to include Kosovo, since so far it has still not been recognized by all EU member states. Kosovo unilaterally declared independence in February 2008, but more than a year later, by mid-May 2009, five EU countries had still not recognized it as an independent state – Cyprus, Greece, Romania, Slovakia, and Spain.
19. The 'Agenda 2000' was adopted by the EU in 1997, providing for fundamental reforms of the Common Agricultural Policy and other measures that were to facilitate the future EU enlargement to the CEE countries.

9 The Way to a Better Future: Remaining Challenges

1. The other elements of the new IMF policy framework include doubling of normal access limits for member countries, a new financial instrument (Flexible Credit Line) for countries with sound fundamentals, redesigning lending facilities for low-income countries, and a major simplification of existing facilities (IMF, 2009a).
2. Also in the more advanced countries in CEE these issues have not received enough attention. Enterprises operating in the Czech Republic are increasingly struggling to find qualified labour. Labour shortages seem to coexist parallel with the still high rates of regional unemployment, essentially due to educational mismatches (Svejnar and Uvalic, 2009).

3. For example, statistics on Serbia's public expenditure (in percentage of GDP) are different depending on source, whether one considers data reported by the NBS, the Ministry of Finance, the EBRD, or the World Bank. This is just one example.
4. Presently there are no official statistics on how much is spent on R&D within the corporate sector in Serbia.
5. See Republicki zavod za razvoj Srbije (2005), Ministry of Science and Environmental Protection (2007), or Ministry of Science and Technological Development (2009).
6. The Serbian government has in autumn 2009 announced the closing down of all socially owned enterprises earmarked for privatization in 2001 that are not sold out by the end of 2009.
7. As late as February 2007, an ambiguous 'blueprint for a deal' was laid out by the UN envoy for Kosovo Martti Ahtisaari without any mention of independence. The final status of Kosovo should have been decided in a new UN Security Council resolution to replace UN SC resolution 1244, but such a document has not been adopted.

References

Anastasijevic, D. (2008), 'What's Wrong with Serbia?', in *European Stability Initiative*, 31 March. Available at: www.esiweb.org. (April 2009).

Antonic, S. (1995), 'The Place and Role of Parliament', in *Challenges of Parliamentarism – The Case of Serbia in the Early Nineties*, V. Goati (ed.), Belgrade: Institute of Social Sciences, pp. 27–43.

Aoki, M. (1995), 'Controlling Insider Control: Issues of Corporate Governance in Transition Economies', in *Corporate Governance in Transitional Economies*, M. Aoki and H. K. Kim (eds), Washington DC: Economic Development Institute, World Bank, pp. 3–28.

Arandarenko, M. (2009a), 'Zaposlenost izmedju tranzicije i ekonomske krize', in *Tranzicija u Srbiji i globalna ekonomska kriza*, B. Cerovic and M. Kovacevic (eds), Beograd: Ekonomski fakultet.

Arandarenko, M. (2009b), 'Social Interests and the Global Crisis', Friedrich Ebert Stiftung conference *20 Years Towards the Market Economy*, Belgrade, 28–9 September.

Arsic, M. and V. Djokovic (2006), *Reforma infrastrukturnih delatnosti i privatizacija javnih preduzeca*, Beograd, mimeo.

Avramovic, D. (1995a), 'Reconstruction of the Monetary System and Economic Recovery of Yugoslavia, 1994: Analytic Framework, Results and Problems', *WIIW Research Report* 216, Vienna.

Avramovic, D. (1995b), 'Program II: Liberalizacija i transformacija jugoslovenske privrede', Beograd: Narodna Banka Jugoslavije.

Avramovic, D. and M. Uvalic (1996), 'Demokratizacija svojinskih odnosa na liniji privatizacije', Beograd: Narodna Banka Jugoslavije, April; also in *Ekonomika*, XXXII (6/7), pp. 313–18.

Babic, S. (2000), 'Politica economica dell'adattamento alle sanzioni in Serbia', in *Gli effetti delle sanzioni economiche: Il caso della Serbia*, M. Zucconi (ed.), Rome: Centro Militare di Studi Strategici, pp. 91–133.

Bajt, A. (1988), *Samoupravni oblik drustvene svojine*, Zagreb: Globus.

Bartlett, W. (1997), 'European Economic Assistance to the Post-socialist Balkan States', in *The Balkans and the Challenge of Economic Integration – Regional and European Perspectives*, S. Bianchini and M. Uvalic (eds), Ravenna: Longo Editore, pp. 65–84.

Bartlett, W. (1999), *From the "humanitarian" War to a Humanitarian Peace? Approaches to Post-war Reconstruction in the Balkans*, Bristol University, mimeo.

Bartlett, W. (2002), 'The EU-Croatia Stabilisation and Association Agreement – A Stepping Stone to Membership or Semi-permanent Satelisation?', 7th conference of EACES, Forlì (Italy), June 6–8.

Bartlett, W. (2003), *Croatia between Europe and the Balkans*, London and New York: Routledge.

Bartlett, W. (2008), *Europe's Troubled Region: Economic Development, Institutional Reform and Social Welfare in the Western Balkans*, London and New York: Routledge.

Bartlett, W. and M. Uvalic (1986), 'Aktuelni problemi spoljno-trgovinskih odnosa izmedju Jugoslavije i Evropske ekonomske zajednice', *Ekonomska misao*, XIX (2), pp. 69–81.
Bartlett, W. and M. Uvalic (1992), 'Economic transition, unemployment and policy response in the former Yugoslavia in the 1980s', University of Bristol, *CMS Occasional Paper* 6.
Bartlett, W. and M. Uvalic (2008), 'Innovation and Skills in the Western Balkans: A Comparative Analysis of Croatian and Serbian Policies', 10th conference of EACES, Moscow (Russia), 28–30 August.
Begovic, B. and B. Mijatovic (eds) (2001), *Corruption in Serbia*, Belgrade: Center for Liberal-Democratic Studies.
Begovic, B. and B. Mijatovic (eds) (2005), *Four Years of Transition in Serbia*, Belgrade: Center for Liberal-Democratic Studies.
Berglof, E. and J. Zettelmeyer (2009), 'European Transition at Twenty: Assessing Progress in Countries and Sectors', UNU WIDER conference *Reflections on Transition: Twenty Years after the Fall of the Berlin Wall*, Helsinki, 18–19 September.
Bianchini, S., and M. Uvalic (eds) (1997), *The Balkans and the Challenge of Economic Integration – Regional and European Perspectives*, Ravenna: Longo Editore.
Bianchini, S. (2007), 'Introduction: The Balkans, Reform of the Treaties and European Integration. The Challenges of Stabilization not yet Achieved', in *Regional Cooperation, Peace Enforcement and the Role of the Treaties in the Balkans*, S. Bianchini, J. Marko, C. Nation, and M. Uvalic (eds), Ravenna: Longo Editore, pp. 9–22.
Bojicic-Dzelilovic, V. (2001), 'International Aid Policies – A Review of the Main Issues', in *International Support Policies to South-East European Countries – Lessons (Not) Learned in B-H*, Z. Papic et al., Sarajevo: Muller, pp. 233–42.
Bolcic, S. (2003), 'Blocked Transition and Post-socialist Transformation: Serbia in the Nineties', *Review of Sociology*, 9 (2), pp. 27–49.
Bozovic, G. (1994), 'Siva ekonomija u uslovima ekonomske blokade SR Jugoslavije', in Srpska akademija nauka i umetnosti, *The Yugoslav Economy under Conditions of Blockade*, Beograd: Srpska akademija nauka i umetnosti, pp. 101–13.
Brixiova Z. and B. Egert (2009), 'Business Environment, Start-ups, and Productivity during Transition', UNU WIDER conference *Reflections on Transition: Twenty Years after the Fall of the Berlin Wall*, Helsinki, 18–19 September.
Cassese, A. and P. Gaeta (2008), *Le sfide attuali del diritto internazionale*, Bologna: Il Mulino.
Center for Liberal-Democratic Studies (2009), 'Corporate Governance in Serbia: The State of Reforms after Five Years', Washington DC: Center for International Private Enterprise, Economic Reform Feature Service.
Cerovic, B. (1997), 'Interno deonicarstvo: mitologeme i razjasnjenja', *Ekonomski anali*, XLI, 132.
Cerovic, B. (1999), 'Privatisation Methods: An Overview of Old Arguments and New Evidence', in *Recent Lessons from Transition and Privatisation – Problems of Institutions and Corporate Governance*, N. Ostojic and N. Scott (eds), Belgrade: European Centre for Peace and Development of the UN University for Peace, pp. 53–69.
Cerovic, B. (2000), 'Economy of FR Yugoslavia: Transition or Pre-transition Economy?', *Ljubljana Faculty of Economics Working Paper*.
Cerovic, B. (ed.) (2006), *Privatization in Serbia*, Belgrade: Faculty of Economics.

Cerovic, B. (2009), 'Srbija u tranziciji i krizi', in *Tranzicija u Srbiji i globalna ekonomska kriza*, B. Cerovic and M. Kovacevic (eds), Beograd: Ekonomski fakultet.
Cerovic, B. and A. Nojkovic (2008), 'Usporavanje reformi u Srbiji: trosak neiskoriscenih mogucnosti', in *Kuda ide Srbija. Ostvarenja i dometi reformi*, M. Zec and B. Cerovic (eds), Belgrade: Faculty of Economics, pp. 23–42.
Cerovic, S. (1996), 'Sam protiv familije', *Vreme*, 289, 4 May, pp. 10–11.
CES MECON (1993), 'Economic Developments in FR Yugoslavia: A Country Report Prepared for the United Nations Economic Commission for Europe', Belgrade: CES MECON.
Cohen, J. L. (2002), *Serpent in the Bosom: The Rise and Fall of Slobodan Milosevic*, revised edition, Boulder and Oxford: Westview Press.
Commission of the European Communities (1979), 'Yugoslavia and the European Community', *Europe Information* 20/79, Luxembourg: Office of the Official Publications of the European Communities.
Commission of the European Communities (1997), *Conclusions of the General Affairs Council of 29 April*, Brussels.
Commission of the European Communities (1999), *Conclusions of the General Affairs Council of 21/22 June*, Brussels.
Commission of the European Communities (2000), 'Council Regulation (EC) No. 2666/2000 of 5 December 2000 on Assistance for Albania, Bosnia and Herzegovina, Croatia, the Federal Republic of Yugoslavia and the Former Yugoslav Republic of Macedonia, Repealing Regulation (EC) no. 1628/96 and Amending Regulation (EEC) no. 3906/89 and (EEC) no. 1360/90 and Decisions 97/256/EC and 1999/311/EC', *Official Journal of the European Communities*, L 306/1, 7 December.
Commission of the European Communities (2001), 'Proposal for a Council Decision Providing Macro-financial Assistance to the Federal Republic of Yugoslavia', Brussels, 23 May, COM (2001) 277 final, 2001/0112 (CNS).
Commission of the European Communities (2002), *CARDS Assistance Programme to the Western Balkans – Regional Strategy Paper 2002–2006*, Brussels. Available at: http://ec.europa.eu/enlargement.
Commission of the European Communities (2004a), *Report from the Commission – The Stabilisation and Association Process for South East Europe – Third Annual Report*, Brussels, 30 March, COM (2004), 202/2 final.
Commission of the European Communities (2006a), *Serbia 2006 Progress Report*, COM (2006) 649 final, Brussels, November.
Commission of the European Communities (2006b), 'The Western Balkans in Transition', *European Economy Enlargement Papers*, 30, December.
Commission of the European Communities (2008), *Serbia 2008 Progress Report*, 5.11, SEC (2008) 2698 final, Brussels, 5 November.
Commission of the European Communities (2009), *Pocketbook on Candidate and Potential Candidate Countries*, Luxembourg: Office for Official Publications of the European Communities.
Cornia, A. (2009), 'Transition, Structural divergence, and Performance: EE-FSU over 2000–2007', UNU WIDER conference *Reflections on Transition: Twenty Years after the Fall of the Berlin Wall*, Helsinki, 18–19 September.
Crnobrnja, M. (1994), *The Yugoslav Drama*, Montreal & Kingston, London, Buffalo: McGill-Queen's University Press.

Curgus Kazimir, Velimir (ed.) (2001), *The Last Decade – Serbian Citizens in The Struggle for Democracy and An Open Society*, Belgrade: Media Centre.

Dallago, B. and M. Uvalic (1998), 'The Distributive Consequences of Nationalism', *Europe-Asia Studies*, 50 (1), pp. 71–90.

Daviddi, R. and M. Uvalic (2006), 'Currencies in the Western Balkans on Their Way Towards EMU', in *EMU Rules: The Political and Economic Consequences of European Monetary Integration*, F. Torres, A. Verdun, and H. Zimmermann (eds), Baden-Baden: Nomos, pp. 261–78.

Deimel, J. and A. García Schmidt (2009), 'Kosovo 2009: Uncertain Future', *Spotlight Europe no. 2009/01*, January, Bertelsmann Stiftung.

Dinkic, M. (1995), *The Economics of Destruction: Can it Happen to You?*, Belgrade: VIN.

Djelic, B. (2006), *Kada ce nam biti bolje*, Beograd: JP Sluzbeni Glasnik, B92.

Djuricin, D. (1994), *Economies in Transition: Privatization and Related Issues*, Gornji Milanovac: Decje Novine.

Dugalic, V. and V. Matic (2008), 'Analiza rada bankarskog sektora Srbije', in *Kuda ide Srbija: Ostvarenja i dometi reformi*, M. Zec and B. Cerovic (eds), Belgrade: Faculty of Economics, pp. 241–54.

Eatwell, J., M. Ellman, M. Karlsson, D. M. Nuti, and J. Shapiro (2000), *Hard Budgets, Soft States: Social Policy Choices in Central and Eastern Europe*, London: Institute for Public Policy Research.

Economics Institute (2009), *Macroeconomic Analyses and Trends and Economic Barometer*, 177/178, Belgrade, July–August.

Economist Intelligence Unit (1995), *Country Report – Yugoslavia (Serbia – Montenegro)*, 1st quarter 1995, London: EIU.

Economist Intelligence Unit (1998), *Country Report – Yugoslavia (Serbia – Montenegro), Macedonia*, 1st quarter 1998, London: EIU.

Economist Intelligence Unit (1999a), *Country Forecast – Economies in Transition – Eastern Europe and the former Soviet Union – Regional Overview*, 3rd quarter 1999, London: EIU.

Economist Intelligence Unit (1999b), *Country Report – Yugoslavia (Serbia – Montenegro)*, 3rd quarter 1999, London: EIU.

Economist Intelligence Unit (2000), *Country Report – Yugoslavia (Serbia – Montenegro)*, 1st quarter 1999, London: EUI.

Economist Intelligence Unit (2002), *Country Forecast – Economies in transition – Eastern Europe and the former Soviet Union – Regional Overview*, London: EUI, June.

Economist Intelligence Unit (2009a), *Country Report – Serbia*, London: EIU, January.

Economist Intelligence Unit (2009b), *Country Forecast – Economies in transition – Eastern Europe and the former Soviet Union – Regional Overview*, London: EUI, September.

Ekonomist, Belgrade weekly, 1999– , various issues.

Estrin, S. and M. Uvalic (2008), 'From Illyria towards Capitalism: Did Labor-management Theory Teach Us Anything about Yugoslavia and Transition in its Successor States?', *Comparative Economic Studies*, 50th Anniversary Essay, 50, pp. 663–96.

European Bank for Reconstruction and Development (EBRD) (2007), *Life in Transition*, London: EBRD.

European Bank for Reconstruction and Development (EBRD) (2009), *Transition Report 2009: Transition in Crisis*, London: EBRD and previous issues.

European Bank for Reconstruction and Development (EBRD) statistics and indicators. Available at: www.ebrd.com.

European Commission documents and statistics. Available at: http://ec.europa.eu/enlargment.

European Reconstruction Agency documents and statistics. Available at: http://ec.europa.eu/enlargement/archives/ear/home/default.htm.

Federal Ministry of Development, Science and Environment & Federal Bureau of Development and Economic Policy (1999), *SR Jugoslavija – 1998 Ekonomski Pregled*, Belgrade.

Federal Ministry of Development, Science and Environment & Federal Bureau of Development and Economic Policy (2000), *FR Yugoslavia – 1999 Economic Survey*, Belgrade.

Finnish Presidency and the European Commission (1999), 'Report to the European Council on EU Action in Support of the Stability Pact and South Eastern Europe', Helsinki, 10–11 December.

G17 (1997), *Program radikalnih ekonomskih reformi u SR Jugoslaviji (Program of Radical Economic Reforms in FR Yugoslavia)*, Beograd: Radio 92.

G17 (1999), *Final Account – Economic Consequences of NATO Bombing – Estimate of the Damage and Finances Required for the Economic Reconstruction of Yugoslavia*, M. Dinkic (ed.), Belgrade: G17.

G 17 Plus (2000a), *Bela knjiga Miloseviceve vladavine*, Beograd: G 17 Plus.

G 17 Plus (2000b), *Program Demokratske Opozicije Srbije: Za Demokratsku Srbiju*, Beograd: G 17 Plus.

Goati, V. (1995), 'Peculiarities of the Serbian Political Scene', in *Challenges of Parliamentarism – The Case of Serbia in the Early Nineties*,V. Goati (ed.), Belgrade: Institute of Social Sciences, pp. 9–25.

Goati, V. (ed.) (1995), *Challenges of Parliamentarism – The Case of Serbia in the Early Nineties*, Belgrade: Institute of Social Sciences.

Government of Serbia (2007), *Second Progress Report on the Implementation of the Poverty Reduction Strategy in Serbia*, Beograd: Government of Serbia.

Glenny, M. (1992), *The Fall of Yugoslavia: The Third Balkan War*, London: Penguin Books.

Grecic, V. (2004), 'Highly Skilled Emigration and its Implications for Serbia and Montenegro', International Conference *System Transformation Models and the Social Price of Reforms in Russia, the CIS and CEE Countries*, Moscow, 25–6 November.

Hansmann, H. (1990), 'When does Worker Ownership Work? ESOPs, Law Firms, Codetermination, and Economic Democracy', *The Yale Law Journal*, 99 (8), pp. 1749–816.

Horvat, B. (1982), *The Political Economy of Socialism* (New York: Sharpe, Oxford: Martin Robertson).

Horvat, B. (1984), *Jugoslavenska privreda. 1965–1983, prijedlozi i resenja*, vol. 1 and 2, Ljubljana, Zagreb: Cankarjeva Zalozba.

Institut ekonomskih nauka (1995), *Mesecne Analize i Prognoze (MAP)*, Beograd, April.

International Monetary Fund (2001), 'FR Yugoslavia – Request for Stand-By Arrangement', IMF, June.

International Monetary Fund (2002), 'FR Yugoslavia: Second Review under the Stand-By Arrangement and Modification of Performance Criteria', *IMF Country Report* 02/12, January.

International Monetary Fund (2009a), 'Global Economic Crisis: To Help Countries Face Crisis, IMF Revamps its Lending', *IMF Survey online*, March 24.
International Monetary Fund (2009b), 'IMF Executive Board Completes First Review Under Serbia's Stand-By Arrangement and Increases Financial Support to €2.9 Billion', *IMF Press Release* 09/169, May 15.
International Monetary Fund (2009c), 'Republic of Serbia: Stand-By Arrangement – Second Review Mission, Aide Mémoire', *IMF Press Release*, 1 September.
International Monetary Fund (2009d), 'IMF Mission to Serbia Reaches Staff-Level Agreement on Second Review of Stand-By Arrangement', *IMF Press Release* 09/387, 4 November.
Jakopin, E. and J. Bajec (2009), 'Izazovi industrijskog razvoja Srbije: makroekonomski kontekst', *Ekonomika preduzeca*, pp. 22–35.
Jakopin, E. and M. Knezevic (2009), 'Veliki privredni sistemi u kontekstu tranzicije i ekonomske krize', *Ekonomika preduzeca*, pp. 376–88.
Jelasic, R. and M. Eric-Jovic (2009), 'Current Monetary and Macroeconomic Developments – Results of Stress Testing of the Serbian Banking Sector', Belgrade, 8 October. Availbale at: www.nbs.rs., November 2009.
Jovicic, M. (ed.) (2002), *Merenje komparativnih prednosti i strategija unapredjenja spoljnotrgovinske razmene Srbije*, Beograd: Ekonomski fakultet.
Jovovic, D. (1994), 'Strategija povratka Jugoslavije u medjunarodne finansijske institucije', in *Strategija povratka Jugoslavije na svetsko trziste*, T. Popovic (ed.), Beograd: Institut ekonomskih nauka, pp. 129–36.
Kekic, L. (1996), 'Assessing and Measuring Progress in the Transition', in Economist Intelligence Unit, *Country Forecast – Economies in Transition – Eastern Europe and the former Soviet Union – Regional Overview*, 2nd quarter 1996, London: Economist Intelligence Unit, pp. 5–22.
Kekic, L. (2000), 'Yugoslavia: Revolution or Evolution?', *EIU Viewswire*, Economist Intelligence Unit, October.
Kekic, L. (2003), 'Foreign Investment in Eastern Europe: How Important is EU Membership?', in *World Investment Prospects 2003, The Future of FDI: Globalisation or Regionalisation?*, London: Economist Intelligence Unit.
Kekic, L. (2008), 'Twenty Years of Capitalism: Was it Worth it?', *Economist*, 19 November.
Kekic, L. (2009a), 'The Global Economic Crisis and FDI Flows to Emerging Markets', London, Economist Intelligence Unit, 19 October.
Kekic, L. (2009b), 'Why has Eastern Europe Performed so Badly', *EIU Viewswire*, London, Economist Intelligence Unit, 22 September.
Kedzic, Lj. (2005), 'Revalorizacija dugova i potrazivanja', Zavod za Statistiku Srbije i Crne Gore, *Metodoloske studije, rasprave i dokumentacija*, 38, Beograd.
Kolodko, G. W. (1999), 'Ten Years of Post-socialist Transition Lessons for Policy Reform', *Policy Research Working Paper* 2095, World Bank Development Research Group, April.
Kolodko, G. W. and D. M. Nuti (1997), 'The Polish Alternative – Old Myths, Hard Facts and New Strategies in the Successful Polish Economic Transformation', *UNU WIDER Research for Action Series*, 33.
Komisija Saveznih drustvenih saveta za probleme ekonomske stabilizacije (1982), *Dokumenti Komisije*, 1–4, Beograd: Centar za radnicko samoupravljanje.
Kornai, J. (1980), *The Economics of Shortage*, Amsterdam: North-Holland.

Kovac, O. (1996), 'Privatisation in Yugoslavia and its Institutional Framework', in *Privatisation in the Economies in Transition*, N. Ostojic and N. Scott (eds), Belgrade: European Centre for Peace and Development of the UN University for Peace, pp. 321–32.

Kovacevic, R. (2008), 'Strukturne promene u spoljnoj trgovini Srbije', in *Kuda ide Srbija: Ostvarenja i dometi reformi*, M. Zec and B. Cerovic (eds), Belgrade: Faculty of Economics, pp. 127–45.

Krstic, G. and P. Sanfey (2009), *'Earnings Inequality and the Informal Economy: Evidence from Serbia'*, London, mimeo.

Labus, M. (1995), 'The Yugoslav Anti-inflation Program 1994 at the Crossroads', Belgrade: University of Belgrade and Economics Institute.

Labus, M. (2003a), 'Otvorena pitanja novog Ustava', Beograd: G17 Plus.

Labus, M. (2003b), 'Transition in FR Yugoslavia a Year after Radical Political Changes', in *Post-Communist Transition to a Market Economy: Lessons and Challenges*, D. M. Nuti and M. Uvalic (eds), Ravenna: Longo Editore, pp. 285–92.

Labus, M. (2006), *Nedovrseni poslovi*, Beograd: Sluzbeni Glasnik.

Labus, M. (2009), 'Recessionary Impact of the Monetary Policy in Serbia', Belgrade Faculty of Economics International Conference *Economic Policy and Global Recession*, 25–7 September.

Labus, M. and T. Cullen (2008), *Economic Analysis of Retail Market Concentration-Primer C/C Market*, Belgrade: Belox Advisory Services.

Labus, M. and M. Dinkic (2001), 'Federal Republic of Yugoslavia: Statement of Economic Policies', Belgrade: The Federal Government.

Lampe, J. R. (2000), *Yugoslavia as History: Twice There was a Country*, Cambridge: Cambridge University Press, second edition.

Lopandic, D. (1997), *Trgovinska politika Evropske Unije i Jugoslavija*, Beograd: Institut ekonomskih nauka.

Lopandic, D. (2001), *Regional Initiatives in South Eastern Europe*, Belgrade: European Movement in Serbia.

Madzar, Lj. (1996), 'Mitologeme internog deonicarstva', *Ekonomski anali*, XLI, 130.

Mayhew, A. (1998), *Recreating Europe: The European Union's Policy towards Central and Eastern Europe*, Cambridge: Cambridge University Press.

Mencinger, J. (2003), 'Does Foreign Direct Investment Always Enhance Economic Growth?', *Kyklos*, 56 (4), pp. 493–510.

Miljkovic, M and M. A. Hoare (2005), 'Crime and the Economy under Milosevic and His Successors', in *Serbia since 1989: Politics and Society under Milosevic and After*, S. P. Ramet and V. Pavlakovic (eds), Seattle and London: University of Washington Press, pp. 192–226.

Minic, J. and M. Dereta (2007), 'Izlaz 2000: An Exit to Democracy in Serbia', in *Reclaiming Democracy: Civil Society and Electoral Change in Central and Eastern Europe*, J. Forbrig and P. Demes (eds), Washington DC: The German Marshall Fund of the United States and Erste Foundation, pp. 79–96.

Ministry of Science and Environmental Protection (2007), *Innovative Serbia: A Strategy for Action*, Beograd: Government of Serbia.

Ministry of Science and Technological Development (2009), *Strategy of Scientific and Technological Development of Serbia 2009–2014*, Beograd: Government of Serbia.

Ministarstvo Finansija Vlade Srbije (2008), *Memorandum o budzetu i ekonomskoj i fiskalnoj politici za 2009. godine, sa projekcijama za 2010 i 2011 godinu*, Beograd: Government of Serbia, December.

Ministarstvo Finansija Vlade Srbije (2009), *Memorandum o budzetu i ekonomskoj i fiskalnoj politici za 2010. godinu, sa projekcijama za 2011 i 2012 godinu*, Beograd, Government of Serbia, June.

Mladenovic, Z. and P. Petrovic (2009), 'Exchange Rate Pass-through across Different Inflation Regimes: Evidence from a Small Open Developing Economy', Belgrade Faculty of Economics International Conference *Economic Policy and Global Recession*, 25–7 September.

Narodna Banka Srbije (2009a), 'Saopstenje o rezultatima poslovanja privrednih drustava i zadruga u republici Srbiji otvarenim u 2008. godini – uporedni podaci iz finansijskih izvestaja za 2007 i 2008 godinu', Odeljenje za registre i bonitet, Belgrade, May. Available at: www.nbs.rs.

Narodna Banka Srbije (2009b), 'Saopstenje o rezultatima poslovanja preduzetnika u republici Srbiji otvarenim u 2008. godini – uporedni podaci iz finansijskih izvestaja za 2007 i 2008 godinu', Odeljenje za registre i bonitet, Belgrade, May. Available at: www.nbs.rs.

Narodna Banka Srbije, statistics available online. Available at: www.nbs.rs.

Nuti, D. M. (1995), 'Employeeism: Corporate Governance and Employee Share Ownership in Transition Economies', conference paper, in *Macroeconomic Stabilisation in Transition Economies*, M. I. Blejer and M. Skreb (eds) (1997), Cambridge: Cambridge University Press, pp. 126–54.

Nuti, D. M. (1996), 'European Community Response to the Transition: Aid, Trade Access, Enlargement', *Economics of Transition*, 4 (2), pp. 503–11.

Nuti, D. M. (1997), 'Employee Ownership in Polish Privatizations', in *Privatization Surprises in Transition Economies – Employee Ownership in Central and Eastern Europe*, M. Uvalic and D. Vaughan-Whitehead (eds), Cheltenham: Edward Elgar, pp. 165–81.

Nuti, D. M. (2004), 'I sistemi economici post-comunisti, ovvero 2001 odissea nella transizione', in *Il futuro del capitalismo*, B. Jossa (ed.), Bologna: Il Mulino, pp. 173–213.

Nuti, D. M. (2009a), 'The Impact of the Global Crisis on Transition Economies', UNU WIDER conference *Reflections on Transition: Twenty Years after the Fall of the Berlin Wall*, Helsinki, 18–19 September.

Nuti, D. M. (2009b), 'Recent Statistics (EBRD & IMF) and Some Comments', International Seminar on *Cohesive Growth in Europe after the Crisis*, Berlin, Friedrich Ebert Stiftung, 23 October.

Nuti, D. M. (2009c), 'Venti anni dopo: ragioni, processi, risultati della transizione post-socialista', in *L'Europa e la Russia a vent'anni dall'89*, R. Gualtieri e J. L. Rhi-Sausi (eds), Bologna: Il Mulino, pp. 21–47.

Nuti, D. M. and M. Uvalic (eds) (2003), *Post-Communist Transition to a Market Economy: Lessons and Challenges*, Ravenna: Longo Editore.

Olivera, J. G. H. (1967), 'Money, Prices and Fiscal Lags: A Note on the Dynamics of Inflation', *Quarterly Review*, Banca Nazionale del Lavoro, 20, pp. 258–67.

Organisation for Economic Co-operation and Development (1982), *OECD Economic Surveys: Yugoslavia*, Paris: OECD.

Organisation for Economic Co-operation and Development (1990), *OECD Economic Surveys: Yugoslavia*, Paris: OECD.

Organisation for Economic Co-operation and Development (2003), *OECD Economic Surveys 2001–2002 – Federal Republic of Yugoslavia*, Paris: OECD.

Organisation for Economic Co-operation and Development (2006), *PISA 2006: Science Competencies for Tomorrow's World*, Paris: OECD online data.

Pavlakovic, V. (2005), 'Serbia Transformed? Political Dynamics in the Milosevic Era and After', in *Serbia since 1989: Politics and Society under Milosevic and After*, P. S. Ramet and V. Pavlakovic (eds), Seattle and London: University of Washington Press, pp. 13–54.

Petrovic, P. (1996), 'Sustainability of Economic Stabilization in FR Yugoslavia and Importance of Resumption of Foreign Trade', in *The Cost of War in Former Yugoslavia*, M. Crnobrnja and Z. Papic (eds), Paris and Beograd: Evropa Press, Peace and Crisis Management Foundation, pp. 169–78.

Petrovic, P. (2003), 'Serbia: Understanding reform', WIIW Workshop on Southeast Europe, November 22, Vienna.

Petrovic, P. (2009), 'Efekat svetske finansijsk krize na Srbiju i odgovor ekonomske politike', *FREN Discussion Papers*, Beograd, April. Available at: www.fren.org.rs.

Petrovic, P., Z. Bogetic, and Z. Vujosevic (1999), 'The Yugoslav Hyperinflation of 1992–1994: Causes, Dynamics, and Money Supply Process', *Journal of Comparative Economics*, 27, pp. 335–53.

Pitic, G. et al. (1999), *Yugoslav Economy after the War*, Belgrade: Economics Institute.

Popov, N. (ed.) (2009), 'Lek kao otrov', *Republika*, XXI, pp. 456–9.

Popovic, D. (1997), 'Yugoslavia's Prospects for Sustained Growth: Controversies and Constraints', in *EU Enlargement: Yugoslavia and the Balkans*, J. Minic (ed.), Belgrade: European Movement in Serbia, Institute of Economic Sciences, Ekonomska politika, Friedrich Ebert Foundation, pp. 161–8.

Popovic, T. and S. Stamenkovic (1994), *Ekonomska drama Jugoslavije*, Beograd: Institut ekonomskih nauka.

Posarac, A. (1996), 'Social Consequences of Rejection of Transition: The Case of Serbia', in *The Cost of War in Former Yugoslavia*, M. Crnobrnja and Z. Papic (eds), Paris and Beograd: Evropa Press, Peace and Crisis Management Foundation, pp. 179–89.

Prascevic, A. (2008), 'Politicki faktori makroekonomske nestabilnosti u Srbiji', in *Kuda ide Srbija: Ostvarenja i dometi reformi*, M. Zec and B. Cerovic (eds), Belgrade: Faculty of Economics, pp. 43–67.

Prasnikar, J. and J. Svejnar (2007), 'Investment, Wages and Corporate Governance during the Transition: Evidence from Slovenian Firms', in *Transition and Beyond – Essays in Honor of Mario Nuti*, S. Estrin, G. Kolodko, and M. Uvalic (eds), Palgrave Macmillan, pp. 149–73.

Prica, I. and M. Backovic (2009), 'Financial Liberalization and Stability in the Balkans', VIIth Scientific Conference of AISSEC, University of Perugia, 25–7 June.

Prica, I. and M. Uvalic (2009), 'The Impact of the Global Economic Crisis on Central and Southeast Europe', Belgrade Faculty of Economics International Conference *Economic Policy and Global Recession*, 25–7 September.

Privatization Agency (2005), *Impact Assessment of Privatization in Serbia*, Belgrade: Privatization Agency of the Republic of Serbia, 27 October.

Privatization Agency of the Republic of Serbia. Availabe at: www.priv.yu.

Rajkovic, N. M. (2007), 'Serbia votes Westward', *The National Interest on-line*, 31 January.

Republicki zavod za razvoj Srbije (2005), *Nacionalna strategija privrednog razvoja Srbije 2006–2012*, Beograd: Serbian Development Bureau. Available at: www.razvoj.gov.rs.

Republicki zavod za razvoj Srbije (2009), *Izvestaj o razvoju Srbije u 2008*, Beograd: Serbian Development Bureau. Also available at: www.razvoj.gov.rs.

Republicki zavod za statistiku Srbije, 'Drustveni proizvod i narodni dohodak Srbije', various issues, Beograd: Serbian Statistical Office. Available at: webrzs.statserb.sr.gov.yu.

Republicki zavod za statistiku Srbije (Serbian Statistical Office), various statistics available at webrzs.statserb.sr.gov.yu. Belgrade, November 2009.

Samardzija, V. (1994), *Europska Unije i Hrvatska: Putevi povezivanja i suradnje*, Zagreb: Institut za razvoj i medjunarodne odnose.

Savezni zavod za statistiku Jugoslavije (1986), *Jugoslavija 1945–1985. Statisticki prikaz*, Beograd: Yugoslav Statistical Office.

Savezni zavod za statistiku Jugoslavije (1991), *Statistici godisnjak Jugoslavije 1991*, Beograd: Yugoslav Statistical Office.

Savezni zavod za statistiku Jugoslavije (1995), *Statisticki godisnjak Jugoslavije 1995*, Beograd: Yugoslav Statistical Office.

Savezni zavod za statistiku Jugoslavije (1998), 'Drustveni proizvod i narodni dohodak 1998', *Statisticki bilten* no. 2259, Yugoslav Statistical Office.

Savezni zavod za statistiku, Savezni zavod za drustveno planiranje (1982), *Razvoj Jugoslavije 1947–1981*, Beograd: Yugoslav Statistical Office.

Savezno izvrsno vece, Sekretarijat za informacije (1990), *Ekonomska reforma i njeni zakoni*, Beograd: Bigs.

Serbian European Integration Office (2008), 'The EU Perspective of Serbian Citizens – Trends', Results of a Public Opinion Poll, Belgrade, Government of Serbia. Available at: www.seio.sr.gov.yu.

Serbian European Integration Office (2009), 'Reports on Implementation of the National Programme for Integration of the Republic of Serbia with the European Union (NPI)', Belgrade, Government of Serbia. Available at: www.seio.sr.gov.yu.

Serbian Investment and Export Promotion Agency, Belgrade: SIEPA. Available at: www.siepa.sr.gov.yu.

Simic, P. (2000), *Put u Rambuje: Kosovska kriza 1995–2000*, Beograd, Cicero Print.

Stability Pact for Southeastern Europe, Cologne, June 1999. Available at: www. stabilitypact.org.

Stamenkovic, S. and M. Kovacevic (2004), 'Privredni razvoj – kuda dalje?', *Ekonomski anali*, January–March, pp. 39–75.

Stamenkovic, S., M. Kovacevic, and I. Nikolic (2009a), *Projekat analize investicionog oportuniteta*, Beograd: Ekonomski Institut.

Stamenkovic, S., M. Kovacevic, V. Vuckovic, and M. Busatlija (2009b), *Model ravnoteze mora da se menja*, Beograd: Ekonomski Institut.

Stiglitz, J. E. (1997), *Whither Socialism?*, Cambridge, London: The MIT Press.

Stiglitz, J. E. (2002), *Globalization and its Discontents*, London: Allen Lane, The Penguin Press.

Svejnar, J. and M. Uvalic (2009), 'The Czech Transition: The Importance of Microeconomic Fundamentals', UNU WIDER, Research Paper no. 2009/17.

Svilanovic, G. (2001), 'Results of International Activity of the FR of Yugoslavia, October 2000 – September 2001', *Yugoslav Survey* 3, pp. 3–24.

Tanzi, V. (1977), 'Inflation, Lags in Collection, and the Real Value of Tax Revenue', *IMF Staff Papers*, 24, March, pp. 154–67.

Teokarevic, J. (1998), 'Sankcije, ekonomski razvoj i demokratizacija', in *Lavirinti krize – Preduslovi demokratske transformacije SR Jugoslavije*, S. Samardzic, R. Nakarada, and Dj. Kovacevic (eds), Beograd: Institut za evropske studije, pp. 325–46.

Teokarevic, J. (2009), 'It's Time for Thessaloniki 2', Belgrade: Belgrade Centre for European Integration.

Thomas, R. (1999), *Serbia under Milosevic: Politics in the 1990s*, London: Hurst & Company.

Travaglino, R. (2009),'I Balcani: verso l'Unione europea o verso una rinnovata instabilità?', in *L'Europa e la Russia a vent'anni dall'89*, R. Gualtieri e J. L. Rhi-Sausi (eds), Bologna: Il Mulino, pp. 151–75.

Trbovich, A. S. (2008), *The Legal Geography of Yugoslavia's Disintegration*, Oxford: Oxford University Press.

United Nations Economic Commission for Europe, *Economic Survey of Europe*, various issues 1996–2004, Geneva: UNECE.

Ustav Republike Srbije 1990 (1990 Serbian Constitution), Beograd: Sluzbeni glasnik.

Ustav Republike Srbije 2006 (2006 Serbian Constitution), Beograd: Sluzbeni glasnik.

Uvalic, M. (1991), 'How Different is Yugoslavia?', *European Economy*, Special edition 2, *The Path of Reform in Central and Eastern Europe*, Brussels: Commission of the European Communities, pp. 199–213.

Uvalic, M. (1992), *Investment and Property Rights in Yugoslavia – The Long Transition to a Market Economy*, Cambridge: Cambridge University Press, Paperback Re-issue (2009).

Uvalic, M. (1993), 'The Disintegration of Yugoslavia: Its Costs and Benefits', *Communist Economies & Economic Transformation*, vol. 5, no. 3, pp. 273–93.

Uvalic, M. (1995), 'Privatization in Disintegrating East European States: The Case of Former Yugoslavia', in *Property Rights and Privatization in the Transition to a Market Economy: A Comparative Review*, R. Daviddi (ed.), Maastricht: European Institute of Public Administration, pp. 191–229.

Uvalic, M. (1996), 'Privatizacija: Obavezno, a ne dobrovoljno', *Vreme*, 289, 4 May, pp. 12–13.

Uvalic, M. (1997a) 'Privatization in the Yugoslav Successor States: Converting Self-management into Property Rights', in *Privatization Surprises in Transition, Economies – Employee Ownership in Central and Eastern Europe*, M. Uvalic and D. Vaughan-Whitehead (eds), Budapest: International Labour Office & Cheltenham, Edward Elgar, pp. 267–301.

Uvalic, M. (1997b), 'European Economic Integration – What Role for the Balkans?', in *The Balkans and the Challenge of Economic Integration – Regional and European Perspectives*, S. Bianchini and M. Uvalic (eds), Ravenna: Longo Editore, pp. 19–34.

Uvalic, M. (2001a), 'Federal Republic of Yugoslavia', *Journal of Southeast Europe & Black Sea Studies*, 1 (1), Frank Cass, pp. 183–94; also in *Balkan Reconstruction*, D. Daianu and T. Veremis (eds) (2001), London: Frank Cass, pp. 174–85.

Uvalic, M. (2001b), 'Privatizacija u Srbiji deset godina kasnije', *Ekonomski anali*, XLV, pp. 121–4.

Uvalic, M. (2001c), 'Regional Cooperation in South-Eastern Europe', *Journal of Southeast Europe & Black Sea Studies*, 1 (1), 64–84; also in Daianu and Veremis (eds), pp. 55–75.

Uvalic, M. (2001d), 'Privatisation and Corporate Governance in Serbia (FR Yugoslavia)', WIIW, Vienna. Available at: http://www.WIIW.ac.at/balkan/files/uvalic.pdf.

Uvalic, M. (2001e), 'La Serbia di Kostunica: dall'esclusione all'inclusione', *Europa Europe*, IX (6), pp. 31–5.

Uvalic, M. (2002a), 'The Yugoslav Way to Capitalism: Multiple Ingredients, Uncertain Outcome', in Economics Faculty of Sarajevo (2002) *Economic Science before the Challenges of the XXI Century*, Sarajevo, Faculty of Economics, pp. 233–46; also in Italian 'La via jugoslava al capitalismo' in B. Jossa (ed.) (2004), *Il futuro del capitalismo*, Bologna: Il Mulino, pp. 231–46.

Uvalic, M. (2002b), 'Economic Cooperation between Serbia and Montenegro: Which Way towards the European Union?', *Review of International Affairs*, vol. LIII, no. 1106, April–June, pp. 13–17.

Uvalic, M. (2003a), 'Economic Transition in Southeast Europe', *Southeast European and Black Sea Studies*, 3 (1), pp. 63–80.

Uvalic, M. (2003b), 'Southeast European Economies: From International Assistance towards Self-sustainable Growth', *Prospects and Risks Beyond EU Enlargement: Southeastern Europe. Weak States and Strong International Support*, in W. van Meurs (ed.), Bertelsmann Foundation Risk Reporting, Opladen: Leske + Budrich, pp. 99–115.

Uvalic, M. (2003c), 'Integrating Southeast European Countries into the European Union – Problems and Prospects', in *Globalisation, Democratization and Development – European and Japanese Views of Change in South East Europe*, V. Franicevic and H. Kimura (eds), Zagreb: Masmedia, pp. 93–105.

Uvalic, M. (2004), 'Privatization in Serbia: The Difficult Conversion of Self-management into Property Rights', in *Advances in the Economic Analysis of Participatory and Labor-Managed Firms*, V. Pérotin and A. Robinson (eds), 8, pp. 211–37.

Uvalic, M. (2005a) *Science, Technology, and Economic Development in Southeast Europe*, UNESCO Science Policy Series no. 1, Venice: UNESCO Regional Bureau for Science in Europe – ROSTE.

Uvalic, M. (2005b), 'Tranzicija v Srbiji in Crni Gori: Od ponavljajocih se kriz do prizadevanj za vstop v EU', in *Globalno gospodarstvo in kulturna razlicnost*, J. Prasnikar and A. Cirman (eds), Ljubljana: Casnik Finance, pp. 291–305.

Uvalic, M (2007a), 'How Different is Serbia?', in *Transition and Beyond – Essays in Honor of Mario Nuti*, S. Estrin, G. W. Kolodko, and M. Uvalic (eds), Basingstoke: Palgrave Macmillan, pp. 174–90.

Uvalic, M. (2007b), 'Transition and Economic Development in Southeast Europe', in *The Balkan Prism – A Retrospective by Policy-Makers and Analysts*, J. Deimel and W. van Meurs (eds), Munchen: Verlag Otto Sagner, pp. 233–50.

Uvalic, M. (2008), 'EU Policies towards Southeast Europe: From Stabilization towards Integration', in *Mediterranean Europe*, M. Petricioli (ed.), Brussels: PIE Peter Lang, pp. 291–303.

Uvalic, M. (2009a), 'The Impact of the Global Financial Crisis for Eastern Europe', *Eighth International Conference on Challenges of Europe*, Conference Proceedings, University of Split, Faculty of Economics, Bol, May.

Uvalic, M. (2009b), 'Regionalism in Southeast Europe', in *Globalization, Development and Integration: A European Perspective*, P. Della Posta, M. Uvalic, and A. Verdun (eds), Basingstoke: Palgrave Macmillan, pp. 176–94.

Uvalic, M. (2009c), 'Transition in Southeast Europe: Understanding Economic Development and Institutional Change', UNU WIDER conference *Reflections on Transition: Twenty Years after the Fall of the Berlin Wall*, Helsinki, 18–19 September.

Uvalic, M. and D. M. Nuti (2003), 'Twelve Years of Transition to a Market Economy', in *Post-Communist Transition to a Market Economy: Lessons and Challenges*, D. M. Nuti and M. Uvalic (eds), Ravenna: Longo Editore, pp. 9–19.

Uvalic, M. and D. Vaughan-Whitehead (eds) (1997), *Privatization Surprises in Transition Economies – Employee Ownership in Central and Eastern Europe*, Budapest: International Labour Office & Cheltenham, Edward Elgar.

Van Meurs, W. (ed.) (2003), *Prospects and Risks Beyond EU Enlargement: Southeastern Europe. Weak States and Strong International Support*, Bertelsmann Foundation Risk Reporting, Opladen: Leske + Budrich.

Vlada republike Srbije (2006), *Nacionalna strategija privrednog razvoja Srbije 2006–2012*, Beograd: Serbian Government, November. Available at: www.razvoj.gov.rs.

Vlahovic, A., M. Cvetkovic and M. Arsic (2003), 'Privatizacija preduzeca u Srbiji: dosadasnji rezultati i ocekivani efekti', *Ekonomski Anali*, vol. XLVII, April.

Vejvoda, I. (2006), 'Serbia: Current Issues and Future Direction', Testimony to the US Congress House of Representatives, Washington DC, 20 September.

Vidas-Bubanja, M. (1994), 'Jugoslavija i strana direktna ulaganja', in *Strategija povratka Jugoslavije na svetsko trziste*, T. Popovic (ed.), Beograd: Institut ekonomskih nauka, pp. 141–53.

Vujacic, I. (1996) 'Discontinued Privatisation: The Case of Serbia', in *The Cost of War in Former Yugoslavia*, M. Crnobrnja and Z. Papic (eds), Paris and Beograd: Evropa Press, Peace and Crisis Management Foundation, pp. 397–405.

Vujacic, V. (2004), 'Reexamining the Serbian Exceptionalism Thesis', *Berkeley Program in Soviet and Post-Soviet Studies Working Paper Series*, spring, pp. 1–43.

Vukovic, V. (2008), 'Sistemska neravnopravnost domacih i stranih banaka na finansijskom trzistu Srbije', in *Kuda ide Srbija. Ostvarenja i dometi reformi*, M. Zec and B. Cerovic (eds), Belgrade: Faculty of Economics, pp. 255–68.

Wagstyl, S. (2009), 'EBRD seeks big capital boost', *Financial Times*, 28 September.

Williamson, J. (1990), 'What Washington Means by Policy Reform', in *Latin American Adjustment: How Much Has Happened?*, J. Williamson (ed.), Washington DC: Institute for International Relations.

Woodward, S. L. (1995a), *Socialist Unemployment: The Political Economy of Yugoslavia 1945–1990*, Princeton: Princeton University Press.

Woodward, S. L. (1995b), *The Balkan Tragedy: Chaos and Dissolution After the Cold War*, Washington DC: The Brookings Institution.

World Bank (1996), *From Plan to Market: World Development Report 1996*, Washington DC: The World Bank.

World Bank (2000), *The Road to Stability and Prosperity in South Eastern Europe: A Regional Strategy Paper*, Washington DC: World Bank.

World Bank (2001), *Breaking with the Past: The Path to Stability and Growth*, vol. 1 and 2, Washington DC: The World Bank.

World Bank (2004), *Serbia and Montenegro – Republic of Serbia: An Agenda for Economic Growth and Employment*, Report no. 29258-YU, December, Washington DC.

World Bank (2009), *Serbia: Doing More with Less. Addressing the Fiscal Crisis by Increasing Public Sector Productivity*, Report no. 48620-YF, Washington DC, June.

World Bank, *Doing Business Indicators*, Washington DC. Available at: www.doingbusiness.org.

World Economic Forum (2008), *Global Competitiveness Report 2008—2009*. Available at: www.weforum.org.

Yugoslav Survey (ed.) (2001) 'Introduction of Sanctions against the FR of Yugoslavia and Their Lifting, 1991–2001', *Yugoslav Survey*, 25–40.

'Zakon o udruzenom radu' (1976), Beograd, *Sluzbeni list SFRJ* 53/1976.

'Zakon o sredstvima u svojini Republike Srbije', *Sluzbeni glasnik Republike Srbije* 53/1995, 3/1996, 54/1996, and 32/1977.

Zdrale, J. (2006), 'Transformation of Serbia's banking sector: ownership structure and growth of balance categories, December 2003-March 2006', *Quarterly Monitor of Economic Trends and Policies in Serbia*, no. 4, pp. 92–100.

Zec, M., B. Mijatovic, D. Djuricin and N. Savic (eds) (1994), *Privatizacija – Nuznost ili sloboda izbora (Privatization – A Necessity or Freedom of Choice)*, Beograd: Jugoslovenska knjiga i Ekonomski institut.

Zucconi, Mario (ed.) (2000), *Gli effetti delle sanzioni economiche: Il caso della Serbia*, Rome: Centro militare di Studi Strategici – CeMiSS.

Index

Page numbers in **bold** refer to figures, page numbers in *italic* refer to tables.